DESERT ISLAND DISCS

70 years of castaways
from one of BBC Radio 4's
best-loved programmes

SEAN MAGEE

Foreword by
KIRSTY YOUNG

BANTAM PRESS

LONDON · TORONTO · SYDNEY · AUCKLAND · JOHANNESBURG

CONTENTS

DESERT ISLAND DISCS

www.**transworldbooks**.co.uk

FOREWORD

by Kirsty Young

Let me ask you a question (it's a hard habit to break). What do the late Prince Chula Chakrabongse of Thailand and Ian Hislop have in common? Two men born more than half a century and half a world apart: it's tricky to imagine what could possibly unite them.

Unlike one of our best-known satirists, His Royal Highness didn't, as far as we're aware, harbour a deep-seated love of the breakfast treat Frosties. Yet when it came to choosing the eight discs they couldn't be without on a desert island, the Prince and the *Private Eye* editor were very much in tune. Though their programmes were broadcast thirty-four years apart, nestling among each man's little bundle of choices was a disc by the debonair comedy actor Jack Buchanan. Who would have thought it?

For seventy years now *Desert Island Discs* has managed that rare feat – to be both enduring and relevant. By casting away the biggest names of the day in science, business, politics, showbiz and the arts it presents a cross-sectional snapshot of the times in which we live. As the decades have passed the programme has kept pace; never frozen in time yet always, somehow, comfortingly the same.

And here we must surely tip our hat to Roy Plomley. Like most truly great ideas – the wellie boot, the sandwich, the spellcheck – the premise of *Desert Island Discs* is stunning in its simplicity. A person of significant accomplishment enters into a bargain with the Beeb: they chat about their life and we play the eight discs they've chosen. What could be more straightforward?

The humble genius of the format is that it cradles and shapes itself around each highly individual guest – like a well-tethered hammock slung between a pair of obliging palm trees.

Back in 1942 – before publicity junkets and PRs, YouTube and tweeting – one person talking to another person while other folk tuned in on the wireless must surely have seemed like a jolly bright idea. But now? In 2012? For *forty-five minutes*? Are you mad?

Well, no, you're not. Indeed, it could reasonably be argued that among the constant flow of instant verbiage that swirls, non-stop, around us these days, the opportunity to take a decent amount of time to properly appreciate and examine the life of someone significant is more welcome than ever.

But of course the chat is only part of it (twenty-nine minutes, if you're counting, and I very much hope you are). What about the other essential component – the discs? Where do castaways begin when it comes to choosing the pieces that will illustrate and illuminate who they are and how their life has been?

Naturally, no two castaways are the same and every recording takes on a character all its own. But if there is one common utterance from every single guest who sits in the studio (and there is) it goes like this: 'It was almost *impossible* to choose just eight.' The self-editing process for a guest is swingeing. If they're playing the 'game' properly it can't all be just Beethoven or Dylan. It's about pinpointing pieces that cast light on their life's most significant moments – adversities conquered, children born, lovers lost, laughter shared. As a result their little list of discs is often very surprising indeed. When the former head of MI5, the redoubtable Eliza Manningham-Buller, told me she'd decided on a track from Detroit garage rockers The White Stripes it was all I could do not to punch the air and shout 'Wowza!'

It's a formula that works, then; but the programme is hopefully never formulaic. In my mind it works best as a sort of triangulated conversation – castaway, host and listener sitting around the table engaged in a no-holds-barred dialogue about how the guest of honour got to where they are and what it's like to live the life they have lived. I say 'no-holds-barred' because that's the deal: there is no 'deal'. We never agree questions beforehand – no matter how platinum-plated the castaway. And keeping the listener engaged often means being very nosey and very persistent. Yet *Desert Island Discs* is unashamedly a celebration of achievement – the people who come on are there because they matter. From Field Marshal Montgomery to Tanni Grey Thompson, all of them have reached the heights in their chosen field. They're different from the rest of us: more talented, more ambitious, more energetic – and often more insecure.

And since we happen to be on the subject of anxiety, these days I often wonder if the only reason I'm ever asked anywhere is because people want to know the low down and dirty on *Desert Island Discs*. I am constantly filleted for information about castaways. How do we choose them? Who's been the most interesting? Who's had the worst music? Who was rudest? Who's been your favourite? Well, for fear of never being invited anywhere ever again, I hereby refuse to definitively answer any of those questions right now. But I will pull back the curtain a few inches and offer you a behind-the-scenes glimpse of what goes on 'off mic', as we say in the business.

It's well known that Roy Plomley used to take castaways to his club prior to recordings, furnishing them with what might reasonably be called 'a good lunch'. Whether it was a social nicety or a bid to loosen their tongues, it's one of the few programme traditions that's gone by the board. These days BBC budget constraints mean we run to a cup of tea or some fizzy water. There's a lot to be said for tradition . . .

So, the first chance I get to meet our castaways face to face is when they arrive for the recording. Minutes are precious then and none of them are wasted. Some turn up at the doors of Broadcasting House with an entourage. The elderly American comedian Jackie Mason was trailing three people and one of them was trailing the longest mink coat I've ever clapped eyes on. It was not a cold day. Some arrive alone. Annie Lennox (ten Grammys, four Ivor Novello Awards, eight Brits, a Golden Globe and an OBE) pitched up entirely by herself, save for a packet of shop-bought sandwiches. Then there was 73-year-old Yoko Ono in a plunging top, tiny fedora and very big, very black sunglasses. Barry Manilow was in shades too; however, unlike Yoko he did me the favour of taking them off for the recording.

For a short time we settle down in the control room – the booth with all the knobs and buttons, next door to the studio – and over tea and the occasional biscuit we listen to the castaway's choices, double-checking that for each we have exactly the right track and firming up which precise two minutes the castaway would like to be played.

Incidentally, Sir Tom Jones didn't get mere biscuits with his tea. He was accorded the privilege of home-made Welsh Cakes: not from my home but from the oven of the Welsh-born mother of the programme's producer. Mrs Buckle – I salute you. The Pride of the Valleys stuffed three in his pocket as he left.

So, with discs double-checked and entourages ensconced, it's off into the studio. But not, crucially, to the island. And that's another one of the very few differences between way back then and now. Roy Plomley would welcome listeners with the words 'on our desert island this evening'; these days (much later in the programme) I say to my guest: 'I'm about to cast you away.' Somehow that makes more sense to me. The cruelty of abandoning someone to a life of solitude and sunburn is surely bad enough; to suggest that I might actually be dumping them there myself and then swanning off seems indefensible.

And so we come to the interview, the conversation. What's its point, what's the aim? For me it's to strike up an intimacy with the guest that allows them to trust me and in turn properly reveal themselves. I want the listener to come as close as they can to meeting them without actually meeting them. The best piece of professional advice I was ever given – aged twenty-two and working at BBC Radio Scotland – was 'Listen, listen to what people say.' In the twenty-two years since, what I've also learned is: do your homework; then be ready to ditch every smarty-pants question you have on your list in pursuit of original, fresh, immediate dialogue. It's always good to be prepared, but above all else be prepared to listen to the answers and take it from there.

My predecessor Sue Lawley once described *Desert Island Discs* as 'the best job in radio'; I would find it hard to disagree.

'My castaway this week is . . .'

In June 2012 Aung San Suu Kyi, the inspirational opposition leader in Burma, finally made it to Oslo to collect the Nobel Peace Prize awarded to her more than two decades earlier. In her acceptance speech, she recalled that when she had been living in Oxford many years ago, she had listened to *Desert Island Discs* with her young son Alexander, and he had asked her whether she might ever be invited to appear on the programme. He was aware that in general only celebrities took part, and wondered for what reason she might be invited. 'I considered this for a moment and then answered: "Perhaps because I'd have won the Nobel Prize for literature," and we both laughed. The prospect seemed pleasant but hardly probable.' Yet improbable things do happen, and in summer 2012 it was announced that Aung San Suu Kyi had agreed to appear on *Desert Island Discs*.

Aung San Suu Kyi's name-checking *Desert Island Discs* at such an important moment in her struggle offers further proof that the reach of this radio programme knows no bounds. It has featured in a Tom Stoppard play (see pages 216–17) and an episode of *Absolutely Fabulous*; it has been imitated all round the world; and many among its loyal audience of around three million people need little prompting to offer their own selections of eight records – as became evident when in June 2011 some 28,000 submissions were made to the special programme *Your Desert Island Discs*, which had invited listeners to submit their personal record choices, and reasons for making them. The result (see pages 405–7) made for compelling listening.

Should you ever get the invitation to the island, this is what will usually happen.

Around three months before the proposed transmission date your name will have been raised as a potential interviewee at one of the regular meetings held to review candidates. Present at this meeting will have been the

Desert Island Discs producer, the presenter (whom for current purposes we will call Kirsty), and the researcher. The small programme team that lies behind *Desert Island Discs* nestles in Room 6045 in Broadcasting House, among the teams responsible for *In Our Time, Start the Week, Midweek* and *Loose Ends* – so the opinions of passing colleagues are also heard.

There is little science underpinning the choice of castaways, and deciding who should be invited is the subject of much – often heated – debate among the production team. So when you receive your invitation to the island, you will already have passed a test that is at the same time stringent and subjective, with a strong element of randomness. Castaways are not necessarily household names, but each one has played a highly significant role within his or her own field and lived a rich and interesting life.

Once it is confirmed that you have the right profile to be marooned, you will be approached. If the invitation plops on to your doormat in the same post as notification of your proposed knighthood or damehood, open the letter marked 'BBC' first, for whatever that other envelope might contain, being marooned on the desert island is the greater honour. (And the *Desert Island Discs* invitation is much more exclusive. Over 2,500 awards are made annually in the official Honours Lists, whereas just 42 people are cast away each year on the desert island.)

If you agree to be cast away – and it is not assumed that you will agree, since some are approached but choose not to appear – two months or so in advance of your edition being aired you will be visited by the researcher, to whom you will give your list of eight records, plus book and luxury. You will then undergo an interview about the areas of your life which the programme should cover, and in particular the details of your childhood, which might not be extensively covered in the press cuttings but which will be of considerable interest to the listener.

You will not be invited to define 'no-go areas', but sensitivities (about family matters, for example) will be discussed. In essence, the researcher will be looking for ways to express how the particular shake-up of your genetic cocktail and the circumstances of your early life have produced the person you have become.

After this interview, the researcher will draft a summary of what you have said – trying at the same time to capture the subjects that made your eyes light up, the moments when you were lost in thought and the reflections about pieces of music that captured very vivid and significant memories. The research notes – together with any books or DVDs – are sent to the presenter and producer so that they can immerse themselves in the details of your life in advance of your programme being recorded. Meanwhile, back in the office, work begins trying to meet your exacting musical demands. While most recordings are found in the BBC's Grams Library, it is not unknown for friends or family to record a track specially for the programme.

On the appointed day you will turn up at Broadcasting House in Portland Place, just north of Oxford Circus in central London. It is advisable to arrive sober, not least to avoid becoming bracketed in *Desert Island Discs* folklore with the actor who some years ago was so incoherent during the recording that he had to return the following day to do the whole programme again.

You will meet the presenter and be taken into the 'cubicle' – the control room – so that you can check that the records supplied are exactly what you have asked for, and so that the programme's producer and studio manager can confirm with you which segments of each recording are the crucial parts to be played.

This is a very important part of the process: for all the soul-searching and cathartic revelations that the *Desert Island Discs* conversation can generate, the eight records remain at the core of the programme's culture. Part of its appeal is the way it introduces even the most casual listeners to pieces of music of which they were previously unaware – and indeed have heard only imperfectly over the rustle of the Sunday papers or across the ironing board. Did sales of Puccini's *Symphonic Prelude* rocket after Kenny Everett had

Kirsty Young casts away Akram Khan, July 2012

nominated that intensely moving work to be played 'as I'm hoiked aloft in a ray of God's lovely sunbeam'? How many new fans were attracted to the idiosyncratic American musician Van Dyke Parks after Terry Gilliam had requested his infectiously upbeat song 'Opportunity for Two'? 'When I was making

Brazil,' explained the castaway, 'which was a long nine months, I played it every morning on the way to work, and it made me be happy – it made me American again – it made me optimistic.'

Once the niceties of the record extracts have been agreed, you and Kirsty will move into the studio, where you will sit across the table from her and – to put it simply – talk. The dialogue will be steered by her, but it will be a conversation which can go in any direction, so long as every now and again it pauses for the next record. Unlike the procedure during the first forty-odd years of *Desert Island Discs*, the musical choices are played into the studio rather than edited in later, and this allows the presenter to pick up on any reaction of the castaway as the music is played. (See, for example, the exchange between Kirsty Young and Betty Driver on page 486.) You can chat with Kirsty as each track is playing, or remain locked into that music with your memories. But be aware that she will be wearing headphones (though you will not), and through them, unheard by you, she will be receiving prompts and suggestions from the producer in the cubicle.

Despite the microphones, headphones and loudspeakers, the *Desert Island Discs* recording studio is a surprisingly intimate venue, and it is very easy to hear the sound of sincerely felt emotion on air. Sometimes the music acts as a time-shift, bringing an event from years ago right to the front of the castaway's memory; on other occasions, this is simply the first time that a guest has been asked to think deeply about his or her past.

Kirsty's last words to the castaway are always to thank them for letting us hear their *Desert Island Discs*. Then, as she takes off her headphones, and both she and the castaway sit back in their chairs, there is a palpable breathing-out – a sense of relief that a challenge has been met and a story properly told.

When it's all in the can to the satisfaction of producer and studio manager, you return to the cubicle to add your signature to the already glittering collection of autographs in the *Desert Island Discs* visitors' book, and then, as the producer settles down to edit the programme to the required length, you are free to go and live the rest of your life.

The aim of this book is to celebrate seventy years of *Desert Island Discs* both by tracing the programme's history and by revisiting some individual editions – from Vic Oliver in January 1942 to Sir David Attenborough in January 2012 – which reflect that history in more detail and offer a series of snapshots of the times in which they were broadcast. The primary rationale behind the selection has been an attempt to reflect the variety which lies at the very heart of the programme, in terms of both the castaway's background and achievements and the nature of the individual programmes. Thus we have the iconic (Eartha Kitt, Luciano Pavarotti), the adored (Joyce Grenfell, Sir David Attenborough), the scientifically brilliant (Stephen Hawking, Fred Hoyle), the controversial (Diana Mosley, Gordon Brown), the anarchic (Spike Milligan, Kenneth Williams, Kenny Everett), the poignant (Signalman Henry Wheeler), the inspirational (Sister Frances Dominica, Desmond Tutu), the eccentric (Margaret Powell, Alfred Wainwright), and so on and so on.

One true legend who has had to be omitted on purely practical grounds is Louis Armstrong, cast away by Roy Plomley in 1968. There is no audio of their interview, and the surviving transcript is simply too patchy to enable any part of it to be reproduced. As for the source material for the pages that follow, when there is an audio record of an individual programme, that is the source for the text, though the written word is very different from the spoken word, and in this book the language has been smoothed out to remove the inevitable instances of 'you know', 'really', 'well', 'umm' and other extraneous noises. When there is no audio, the source is the collection of transcripts housed in the BBC Written Archives Centre at Caversham, near Reading.

Beyond the records of interviews themselves and information from those involved in making the programme, the principal sources have been a small collection of *Desert Island Discs*-related books. Unless otherwise noted, all quotations from Roy Plomley are taken from the 1977 edition of his engaging and highly informative *Desert Island Discs*. Two more of his books relate to the programme: *Plomley's Pick* (published in 1982 to mark the fortieth anniversary), which contains extracts from forty-one editions; and *Desert Island Lists* (compiled with long-time producer Derek Drescher and published in 1984), which lists the choices made for the first 1,702 editions. (Of

Plomley's other non-fiction, *Days Seemed Longer* (1980) is an account of his pre-*Desert Island Discs* life, and *Roy Plomley's Desert Island Book* (1979) is an anthology of desert island literature, but not concerned specifically with his radio creation.)

Sir Michael Parkinson writes about his *Desert Island Discs* experience in his autobiography *Parky* (published in 2008), and the post-*Parky* phase is very well chronicled in Sue Lawley's *Desert Island Discussions*, published in 1990, while *Desert Island Discs: Flotsam and Jetsam* is a miscellany of facts and figures from the show compiled by Mitchell Symons and published alongside the present volume.

A word about how the choices are listed in programme entries which follow. It has been impossible in the limited space available for each featured castaway to give exhaustive information about every music choice – composer, librettist, orchestra, soloists, full description of source work, etc. The title of the piece requested appears in bold type. If the composer/writer's name is given it appears above the name of the work title; the performer's name is given below. Soloists are given only where specified by the castaway; larger works (e.g. operas, ballets, musicals) are included where necessary to identify individual items. Well-known classical composers are identified by surname only, with initials or forename if necessary for differentiation (as in J. S. Bach or Richard Strauss). In the choices panels ★ indicates the record chosen by the castaway to be saved when the tide washes away all the others; ▥ indicates the chosen book, and ♡ the desired luxury. More detailed information can be found on the *Desert Island Discs* website.

There is no more eloquent tribute to the status of *Desert Island Discs* than the list of luminaries who have appeared on it (see pages 504–18), but this is how Gwyneth Williams, the current Controller of Radio 4, sums up the appeal of the programme: '*Desert Island Discs* lies at the heart of Radio 4. The programme at its best offers up the secrets of a life, the inside track on the human condition. No one with talent and a story to tell is excluded, and the invited guests range right across our society. We are in capable and celebrated hands with Kirsty Young who, week after week, steers us through a personal journey of music and conversation with a twist at the end.'

That is the present. But we should begin at the beginning, on a cold November night in 1941 . . .

1940s

ON THE NIGHT of Monday, 3 November 1941, Roy Plomley, a 27-year-old actor and freelance broadcaster, was about to go to bed in his digs in the Hertfordshire town of Bushey when he had a bright idea. 'My coal fire had gone out,' he later recalled, 'and I was already in my pyjamas: nevertheless, I sat down at my typewriter and wrote to Leslie Perowne, who was in charge of the lighter kinds of radio programme.'

The letter which arrived in the Gramophone Department at Broadcasting House a couple of days later read as follows:

Dear Leslie

Here is another idea for a series.

<u>DESERT ISLAND DISCS</u>

'If you were wrecked on a desert island, which ten gramophone records would you like to have with you? – providing, of course, that you have a gramophone and needles as well! Today ……. will come to the microphone to answer that question.'

This is, of course, very much on the lines of the old 'I Know What I Like' series – except that the choice is limited to ten records and the artists should not be confined only to BBC staff. For example, dance-band leaders, actors, members of the Brains Trust, film-stars, writers, child prodigies, ballet dancers and all sorts of people could be included.

All best wishes,
Yours,
Roy Plomley

Plomley was at the time working for the BBC on the music programme *Swing from London*, having been involved over the previous few years with a variety of radio shows – mostly concerned with records. Earlier that year he had appeared in programmes with evocative names such as *Old Stagers*,

Some of the Good Old Ones, Radio Rhythm, Paul Whiteman's Rhythm Boys (with Bing Crosby), *When the Talkies Came to Town, Out Where the West Begins* and *Vagabond Lover: The Story of Rudy Vallee*. Some of these shows had been born from Plomley's own ideas, and Leslie Perowne was well used to being sprayed with suggestions from this ambitious young man, who made no secret of his aspirations – which he pursued with an enthusiasm undimmed by the severe practical difficulties for anyone living near London in 1941. ('Please forgive the delay in sending you these,' Plomley apologizes in one letter to a BBC executive, 'but these Blitzkrieg nights make things rather difficult.')

Many of Plomley's ideas were variations on the standard record-show format, but a particularly novel one was *I Know What I Hate*. In this, a reversal of the *I Know What I Like* idea mentioned in the letter to Perowne just quoted, prominent broadcasters would be asked to select records they particularly disliked. The proposal was swiftly turned down by Perowne, though he was not without sympathy for it:

> We have all been longing to do it for some time, but you must appreciate that it is quite impossible. The snag is that any one recording by anyone must be considered good by someone, if only the man who made it and the recording company who issued it. The BBC would, I fear, get into great trouble for sponsoring such a controversial performance.

Even shorter shrift was given in August 1941 to another Plomley idea:

> The boys and I have now digested your programme on the subject of corpulence – *This Too Too Solid Flesh*. We don't feel that this is up to the Plomley standard – indeed we picture all the fat listeners on this island writing rude letters to complain of such a broadcast.

Still, despite the ideas that never made it anywhere near the recording studio, by summer 1941 Roy Plomley was so closely woven into the BBC's output of record shows that there was internal discussion about putting him on the Corporation's full-time staff. It was decided that he should remain freelance, but even so his importance in this area of broadcasting is clear from a note sent by Perowne to the civil defence authorities in Bushey requesting that Plomley be excused compulsory enrolment 'as he is making a valuable contribution to the work of this department'.

So when this latest Roy Plomley idea landed on his desk early in November 1941, Perowne paid attention. Liking the suggestion of *Desert*

Island Discs, he promptly relayed the idea to James Langham, programme organizer for the Forces Programme. (At that point there were only two BBC radio stations: the Home Service, serving domestic listeners, and the Forces Programme, which broadcast to troops, both those encamped within the United Kingdom and some of those posted overseas.) After talking through the idea with Perowne, Langham sent him a note summing up their discussion and stressing two key issues:

> We should be glad if you would go ahead with this idea. It should make an effective series if well handled, but there were two points, if you remember, which we agreed upon:
>
> a. That in each case interesting reasons should be given for the choice of records.
> b. That additional colour would be given on occasion by what the listener might consider an unexpected choice (i.e. a comedian who prefers the little-known classic, etc.).

With such approval from above, Perowne was able to write to Roy Plomley on 19 November 1941: 'Why didn't we think of "Desert Island Discs" before? It's such an obvious and excellent idea.'

Born in 1914, Roy Plomley had lived a varied life before he came up with the programme which was to make him a household name – a life most neatly summarized by the man himself in a later radio interview:

> I did various odd jobs. I was a desperately bad estate agent for about a year, then I was a mail-order astrologer's assistant, then I thought: Well, if I'm ever going into the theatre, which is really what I want to do, I must start just about now, and I must start on the lowest rung. And I looked round for the lowest rung, and it seemed to be crowd work in movies. So I did some crowd work for a year or two.

When it became clear that his acting ambitions were unlikely to be fulfilled, Plomley gravitated towards the world of broadcasting, working as an announcer and producer. By the late 1930s he was making a name for himself at the International Broadcasting Company, where he was involved with Radio Normandy and Poste Parisien, and moving regularly between England and France.

The outbreak of war in 1939 brought all that to a halt. Plomley and his wife, the actress Diana Wong, eventually managed to get back from France to England, where he rapidly established himself in his freelance connection with the BBC – and where, clad in his pyjamas that night in 1941, he had the idea that changed his life.

What might have given rise to that idea is unclear. Plomley himself acknowledged that while he initially thought it was completely original, over the years he became aware of all sorts of precedents and parallels, some based on the interviewee taking books and some on taking records. None the less, he was the first person to apply the format to radio.

Whatever its source, the idea was a good one. When writing to give Plomley the go-ahead for the new series, Leslie Perowne asked for a list of possible castaways, and in reply was sent a list of twenty, the majority of whom are all but unknown today:

- James Agate *diarist and critic*
- Arthur Askey *comedian*
- Commander Campbell *Brains Trust/explorer*
- Frances Day *actress/singer*
- Jack Payne *bandleader*
- Christopher Stone *broadcaster*
- Pat Kirkwood *actress*
- Dr C. E. M. Joad *Brains Trust/philosopher*
- Vic Oliver *entertainer*
- Sandy MacPherson *theatre organist*
- Anna Neagle *actress*
- Noël Coward *playwright*
- J. B. Priestley *playwright*
- Leslie Perowne *Head of Popular Music Programmes, BBC*
- Roy Rich *Head of Light Entertainment, BBC*
- Chorus girl from 'Black Vanities'
- Robert Montgomery *actor/director*
- Fred Gaisberg *musician/music producer*
- Kay Cavendish *pianist*
- Harry Parry *jazz clarinettist and bandleader*

In his letter accompanying the list, Plomley acknowledged that 'a percentage of these would not play', but in fact all of them except Priestley, Perowne, Rich, Montgomery, Gaisberg and the unnamed 'Chorus girl from "Black Vanities"' were to appear on *Desert Island Discs*. Plomley also stressed that he was not proposing to put himself in the programme's front line: 'I suggest that I should make the initial contacts and give a hand with the scripts, and then hand them over to you. I feel that the programme needs a permanent Master of Ceremonies to introduce the victim and act as a feed on occasion.'

The offer to 'give a hand with the scripts' illustrates a key point about the earliest years of *Desert Island Discs*. Until the mid-1950s each programme was scripted in advance – the interviewee's words as well as the interviewer's – by Roy Plomley. And since the earliest editions of the programme were broadcast in wartime, those scripts had to be vetted in advance by the authorities, on the basis that loose talk cost lives. (No audio record has survived of any of the 1940s programmes: the extracts given in this book are taken from the scripts.)

Late 1941 was a pivotal period in the Second World War. With Germany occupying most of Europe, London was slowly and painfully recovering from the worst of the Blitz. The East End had suffered appalling devastation throughout the spring and the Houses of Parliament had been bombed out in May. Then, as letters and memos about this proposed new gramophone record programme were making their way around the BBC, the shape of the war was changed completely. On 7 December the Japanese attacked the American naval base at Pearl Harbor on the coast of Hawaii, and the previously neutral USA was catapulted into the hostilities.

On the home front, meanwhile, everyday life was becoming increasingly difficult. A wide-ranging programme of rationing severely restricted the sale of most basic foodstuffs and petrol, while the reduction in the textile ration prompted a ban on trouser turn-ups – a restriction of less direct inconvenience, perhaps, but yet another erosion of things previously taken for granted. In the circumstances, the distraction which morale-boosting entertainment could provide was of paramount importance.

The best-loved radio programme at the time was *It's That Man Again* (popularly shortened to the acronym *ITMA*), a comedy show which to modern ears tends to sound simply like a recitation of catch-phrases: 'I don't mind if I do' (Colonel Humphrey's response to being offered a drink); 'Can I do you now, sir?' (Mrs Mopp, the office charlady); 'It's being so cheerful as keeps me going' (Mona Lott, the doom-laden laundrywoman). It may have

AN 'ITMA' WISECRACK — *Illustrated by Bert Thomas*

" I'll 'ave to ask m' Dad "

'ITMA *wisecrack', postcard, c.1940*

been formulaic, but *ITMA* – and other comedy shows such as *Hi, Gang!* – had a crucial part to play in keeping spirits up.

So the nature of the BBC's radio output was a serious issue – and there was particular concern about the quality of the fare being put out for troops, with the Forces Programme ripe for an injection of new material. Throughout 1941 there had been a stream of complaints in the press. In January that year a correspondent to the *Daily Telegraph* declared:

> Many people must be amazed at the fatuity of much that is incorporated in the programmes broadcast to the Forces. Is it assumed at the BBC that the general intelligence of our fighting men is so much below that of other listeners that anything does as a stop-gap to fill up programmes, or that they are incapable of appreciating good music?

And in July 1941 Colin Dale – billed as a 'hard-hitting Australian journalist' – vented his disapproval in more robust terms in the magazine *Reveille*:

> Some people like music and some don't. It all depends on what one understands by music.
>
> Sir This and Sir That and Sir The-Other-Bloke consider the blaring of German bullies like Wagner to be music. Or they give us fugues and monotonous reiterations of scales.

As a concession they sit back biting their finger-nails in frenzy while nancy-boys cavort and jump like scalded cats in front of orchestras of the same ilk pounding out swing, and more effeminate wails about luv.

These crooners hand out meaningless dribbling noises that sound like 'boo-hoo' and 'hot-cha' and 'tickety-boo'. Or females who can't sing a note squeal and drawl like cats on the tiles.

It was in such an atmosphere that Roy Plomley and Leslie Perowne met to discuss the new series. At this point it was decided that, since each programme would have only thirty minutes of air time, the number of records selected would be reduced from Plomley's suggested ten to eight. (After their meeting, Perowne sent Plomley a note with the instruction – somewhat quaint to modern eyes – to 'Please remember to make one of the conditions the fact that no single work can spread on more than two sides of a record'. The addition of book and luxury was to come later, as was the nominating of one record above all the others.) It was also agreed that the series would consist of eight programmes – and that, despite his earlier expectation of taking a back seat, merely contacting potential castaways and helping out with the scripts, Plomley himself should be the presenter. While there is no documentary record of how that decision was made, no one would deny that putting Roy Plomley himself in the chair at the beginning gave *Desert Island Discs* the ideal anchor.

It was further agreed that the producer of the first series would be Frederic Piffard, and that the programme would need a signature tune. In *Desert Island Discs*, Plomley's book about the series that made his name, he remembered: 'My original idea for the opening and closing of each programme was to use the sounds of surf breaking on a shore and the cries of sea birds, but Leslie was concerned that there might be a lack of definition and insisted that we use music as well.' Plomley and Piffard agreed on Eric Coates's 'By the Sleepy Lagoon' as a fitting tune: it has remained the signature tune of *Desert Island Discs* ever since – and its composer was cast away to the sound of his own music in June 1951. (Many years later some listeners would point out that herring gulls – whose cries form part of the signature sequence – live in the northern hemisphere and would not have been on a tropical island. For a few months in 1964 the original flock was replaced by tropical birds, but eventually the herring gulls returned to their rightful – if inaccurate – place.)

Now all was in place to start the new series in January 1942. The original plan had been to kick off *Desert Island Discs* with C. E. M. Joad, Professor of Philosophy at Birkbeck College, University of London, and a staple participant in *The Brains Trust*, the popular panel discussion programme on which, in contrast to the standard radio fare of popular entertainment, serious issues – moral as well as practical – were debated by a panel which consisted, for the most part, of intellectuals. Even *The Brains Trust*, though, was not immune to the fashion for catch-phrases. Joad's characteristic response to an invitation to talk about X was, 'It depends what you mean by X,' while the habitual opening gambit of Commander A. B. Campbell was: 'When I was in Patagonia ... '

But Joad could not make the proposed recording date: so a change of plan brought Austrian-born comedian Vic Oliver the distinction of becoming the first ever castaway on *Desert Island Discs* – and a fee of twenty-five guineas. (Plomley received fifteen guineas per programme: ten for presenting, plus five for preparing the script.)

At the time, Vic Oliver was starring at the London Hippodrome in the musical *Get a Load of This*, and Plomley visited him in his dressing-room:

The Brains Trust, *August 1941:* (left to right) *C. E. M. Joad, Julian Huxley, Cdr A. B. Campbell*

'He gave me a list of records and his reasons for choosing them, and I went away and wrote a script' – which the castaway happily approved. The first *Desert Island Discs* programme was recorded in the bomb-damaged BBC studio at Maida Vale on Tuesday, 27 January, two days before the date of transmission.

The previous Friday, this novel series had been announced in the *Radio Times*. On the front of that edition of the weekly listings magazine was a photograph of President Roosevelt, whose sixtieth birthday on Friday, 30 January would be marked by special programmes. Inside, some of the advertisements underline that there is a war on. An ad for cooking salt includes a recipe for 'a hot dish with "points" meat . . . suitable for making the most of your corned beef ration'; Mrs Doubtful asks, 'How do I get milk for Dad's duodenal?' before being put straight about the milk supply by the Ministry of Food: 'All the shortage must be borne by us who have no priority claims.'

As well as its own listing on the day of transmission – Thursday, 29 January, when it was scheduled to be broadcast on the Forces Programme at 8 p.m. – the new series *Desert Island Discs* is plugged both on the 'highlights of the week' page ('The first choice will be made by Vic Oliver, master of the mahogany violin!') and in the 'Both Sides of the Microphone' column:

> The old question was, 'If you were cast away on a desert island with the choice of only three books, what would you choose?' Various celebrated people (one a week, starting this coming Thursday with Vic Oliver) are now to be invited, on the same supposition, to choose eight gramophone records. Probably, as with the books, the same Joad-like point will arise: 'It all depends on what you mean by a gramophone record – does a complete set of Beethoven's Fifth Symphony or *The Mikado* count as one record?' The most galling fate of all would be to be washed up on a desert island with eight records and no gramophone to play them on – or with records and gramophone but no needles.

(The hypothetical gramophone on the island was of the old wind-up variety – rather than one powered by electricity – on which the needle which ran in the disc's groove would need to be regularly replaced.)

On 29 January 1942 the Forces Programme opened at 6.30 a.m. with (in the words of the *Radio Times*) 'Greetings to the Imperial and Allied Forces

in Great Britain (recording), followed
by REVEILLE! – Cheerful gramophone
records.'

At 7 a.m. the chimes of Big Ben introduced a news summary, followed by fifteen
minutes given over to the records of Frank
Crumit. Later in the morning, that iconic
radio fixture *Music While You Work* featured Harry M. Millen at the theatre
organ. The afternoon's fare included Sandy
MacPherson at the organ; amateur boxing
('Tom Quill v. Harry Pack: commentary by
Raymond Glendenning and W. Barrington
Dalby on the six-round heavyweight contest

Radio Times *cartoon announcing the first*
Desert Island Discs, *January 1942*

from the London Fire Force Tournament'); and the Thursday edition of *Ack-
Ack, Beer-Beer*, a magazine programme 'for men and girls in Anti-Aircraft
and Balloon Barrage units'.

Following the 6 p.m. news came the weekly visit to the Plums, the
'lovable North-Country family' whose household consisted of Mr and Mrs
Plum, Uncle Ed and Ruby the maid. Then the *Orchestral Half-Hour*. Next, a
programme about forces' superstitions. At 7.30, half an hour of variety from
'a Northern theatre'.

And then, after the stroke of eight o'clock, came the sound of surf breaking on the beach, the mewing of seagulls, and the voice of the announcer
declaring:

'"Desert Island Discs". We present the first of a new series of gramo-
phone-record programmes in which, each week, a well-known broadcaster
is brought to the microphone to answer the following question: "If you were
shipwrecked on a desert island, which eight gramophone records would you
choose to have with you? – providing, of course, you also had a gramophone
and a supply of needles." The series is devised and presented by Roy Plomley
and here he is to introduce the first castaway.'

Cue Roy Plomley: 'Good evening, everyone. Our shipwreckee tonight is
a Mr Vic Oliver . . .' – and half an hour of quickfire patter interspersed with
music was under way.

The first *Desert Island Discs* – described in detail on pages 23–6 below
– was a very far cry from today's programmes. Although the structure was
essentially the same then as it is now, the requirement that both sides of the

conversation be scripted in advance excluded the spontaneity with which modern listeners are familiar, and renders impossible those swerves of the conversation into unexpected areas which give the current version so much of its appeal.

It is also striking how strongly the programme was dominated by the choice of music in those early days – more so than it is today. Partly this was a matter of the radio culture of the period; partly it was to do with simple practicality, since air time ran to only thirty minutes. The balance may have shifted, but it is important to remember that *Desert Island Discs* began life as a record programme, not as some early incarnation of *In the Psychiatrist's Chair*.

Back in 1942, immediately after that first *Desert Island Discs* the Forces Programme moved on to *Join In and Sing* – 'with some of the Royal Artillery, somewhere in England' – and the network closed down at 11.20 p.m.

To all appearances, it had been just another Thursday on wartime radio.

Next on the desert island was due to be Frances Day, the actress who, according to Plomley, 'with her generous figure, was the most glamorous girl in wartime London', but her agent could not agree a fee with the BBC. She was eventually cast away in 1955: her place in 1942 as the second *Desert Island Discs* castaway was taken by (in the words of Plomley's introduction of his so-called 'victim'), 'the eminent dramatic critic, essayist and diarist, Mr James Agate'. The programme begins with initial chaffing over how closely Agate resembles his photo in the *Radio Times* – 'My dear Plomley,' the castaway observes in the clubbable tone which pervades the early

James Agate, Roy Plomley's second castaway

programmes, 'I look like a bookmaker gone to seed,' a remark picked up by his host with: 'Well, in bookmaking parlance, what about your eight-record nap for the desert island?'

Like a greyhound from the trap, Agate is off and running: 'I should want eight very contrasting records to fit in with eight different moods and to remind me of the pleasures of the past. I would definitely start with something by Handel, the greatest Englishman ever born of foreign parents in a foreign country . . .' – and he launches into a lengthy description of the life of that composer, causing Plomley to note that, 'In addition to your choice of eight records, we're also getting a considerable amount of erudition.' Before 'Je t'aime' (no relation to the Serge Gainsbourg / Jane Birkin version, which has never been chosen as a castaway's record), Agate offers this explanation for his choice:

'This is one called "I love you", and it's in French – but that doesn't matter on this wavelength, because languages have never presented any difficulties to the forces. In the last war a soldier was asked how he managed to learn French. "Easy," he said, "it goes like this: 'Bon soir, mademoiselle.'" And love is the same in all languages.'

When Agate chooses a waltz, Plomley observes, 'I didn't know you were keen on dancing,' to which his castaway replies:

'I am not referring to the modern ballroom waltz – and you need not have looked so pointedly at my figure when you made that last remark. I mean a Strauss waltz – the most lovely waltz ever written – *Tales from the Vienna Woods*.' (The script originally read: 'I am not referring to the modern night-club mania in which people full of chicken salad revolve slowly round each other like mutes at an undertakers' ball.' Presumably this was replaced on the grounds that it was disrespectful to undertakers, or their mutes.)

Apologizing meekly when Agate asks, 'Are you doing the lecturing or am I?', Plomley casts himself as the hapless stooge, not intellectually on a par with his polymath castaway (the measure of whose self-regard can be gauged from the fact that his autobiography *Ego* stretches to nine volumes).

When Plomley asks whether Agate is taking any jazz or swing to the island, he is told, 'The only attraction that a desert island could possibly have for me would be a complete absence of horrible noises like jazz and swing,' and the final exchange of the programme underlines that here the castaway has been scripted to call the shots:

> PLOMLEY: It's about time to be rescued. Besides, it gets pretty draughty there at night. As one of your constant readers, Agate, may I also guess that the other comforts you would require on a desert island, apart from the gramophone records, would include the Hackney Stud Book, Boswell's *Life of Johnson*, and a photograph of Sarah Bernhardt?
> AGATE: Quite correct. I should also require a first-class hotel and the British Museum Library. Goodnight to you.
> PLOMLEY: Goodnight.

End of programme – but the James Agate edition is of particular interest because it formed the basis for very early audience research about *Desert Island Discs*.

The first few programmes were, for the most part, well received, though in February 1942 listener R. B. Weston of Kew took the format so seriously that he was moved to write to the *Radio Times*:

> I am deeply disappointed with the 'Desert Island Discs' programme. Its contributors appear to forget that on a desert island you want music that would bear endless repetition, especially if you are limited to eight records. Only really great music can stand this test. If I were marooned on a desert island I think I could endure the isolation if I had . . .

. . . and by the end of the sentence he had become the first, and certainly not the last, non-castaway to say what music *should* be taken to that deserted shore.

It is easy to mock Mr Weston's attitude, but his reaction is an example of how from the very beginning *Desert Island Discs* was a radio programme which drew listeners in. Then as now, they were ready to express firm views about the BBC's choice of castaway, the castaway's choice of music, the interviewer's choice of questions – what should have been asked and what should not have been asked – and just how seriously the programme should be taken.

More revealing than the single opinion of the disgruntled Mr Weston is the BBC's Listener Research Report of February 1942. This summarized the results of polling 146 military units – 88 Army, 44 Royal Air Force and 14 Royal Navy, which are stated as 'reporting on the opinions of 10,000 men' – about their reaction to the Agate programme. On a scale which stretched from C-minus for complete failure to please to A-plus for complete success, the popularity of *Desert Island Discs* was estimated at B-plus. 'Typical comments' were divided into three categories:

- Favourable: 'A most interesting series. The novel idea appeals strongly to all listeners here. This one was first class.' Or: 'A grand programme and a delightful series. The men all look forward to next week's.'
- Mixed: 'The records of this programme were hardly the type which the majority would choose, i.e. Bing Crosby, Deanna Durbin, John McCormack, Richard Tauber, Joe Loss, Nat Gonella etc. etc.' Or: 'This week's victim was more popular than the records he chose. It was quite good entertainment, but, you will admit, a bit highbrow. The "Desert Island" idea is well liked, everybody has his own views about the choice of discs.'

- Unfavourable: 'Very poor! Apparently the men who heard it did not like the records.' Or: 'Huh! Agate talks the same as he writes – his signature tune should be "I, I, I." So he doesn't care what the forces think? I suppose he thinks we care what he thinks. Switch him off, the b***** egotist.' (Presumably that remark about Agate's not caring what the forces think refers to his story about how a soldier learns French.)

The following month another report gauged the popularity of seventeen programmes among the forces, polling some large and some small groups. *Desert Island Discs* was ranked ninth by the small groups (*ITMA* was top, with *Hi, Gang!* second, *BBC Dancing Club* third and Cyril Fletcher's *Odes and Ends* fourth) and joint seventh by the large groups (who put *Hi, Gang!* top, *ITMA* second, *Big Time* third and *The Old Town Hall* fourth).

Ranked seventeenth and last – 'Very Unpopular' – in both categories was the 'Epilogue', the religious rumination which closed the day's radio output.

Commander A. B. Campbell, the third castaway, is remembered less well for himself than for his 'When I was in Patagonia . . . ' opening on *The Brains Trust*. Campbell was described in Plomley's introductory remarks as 'a man who should be an authority on desert islands; a distinguished mariner and explorer – a resident brain on *The Brains Trust* – and a brilliant comedian on the *Hi, Gang!* programme'.

'As a matter of fact,' responded Campbell, 'I have been shipwrecked several times in my career, but I've never fetched up on a desert island, and I've never been lucky enough to have a gramophone handy to while away the time until I've been rescued.'

Campbell clearly had a reputation as a practical man. 'You know, Commander,' said Plomley, 'I can imagine few people who would be likely to have less time for playing gramophone records on a desert island than you. With your naval handyman skill, I should think you'd have a six-roomed house built for yourself within a week, with hot and cold water and mains drainage . . . '

'And after that,' Campbell takes over, 'I would build a little country pub to walk to at the end of the road, even if I could only get a drink of coconut milk when I got there. But I should certainly play the gramophone while I was working.'

While much of the programme concerned the particular nature of seafaring men, one of Campbell's record choices provided the sort of love-at-first-sight moment which was to become a staple of so many editions of *Desert Island Discs*:

'Like most mariners I am very sentimental, and the next record is to remind me of a time I fell in love. ['Go on,' interjects Plomley, 'we'll keep your secret.'] I was just a boy at the time. I was ashore on leave and was having a drink at a little inn in Surrey. A girl sat down at the piano and began to sing. I don't think she was a professional artiste, but she sang a song that for sheer sentiment brought tears to my eyes. I fell in love with her at first sight – but alas, I went away to sea again and have even forgotten the colour of her eyes.'

The song the girl had been playing was 'My Little Grey Home in the West', and the Commander sighed, 'Give me that record and let me live that hour again' – a sentiment which was to recur over and over in the next three-thousand-odd editions of *Desert Island Discs*.

More castaways from the world of entertainment followed in the shape of theatrical manager C. B. Cochran, actress Pat Kirkwood and impresario Jack Hylton, followed by Captain A. E. Dingle, who wrote sea stories under the pen-name 'Sinbad' and who – highly unusually for castaways over the next seventy years – had genuine experience of being marooned: on an island in the Indian Ocean, when he was trying to find the wreck of the *Strathmore*. After their ship had broken on the rocks, Dingle and a fellow wreck-hunter were stranded on St Paul for nearly three months, sustained by penguin and goat meat.

The eighth castaway provided a change of mood, as Plomley indicated in his introduction: 'All our castaways so far have been well-known people: this evening we have someone who hopes to be well-known one day: Joan Jay, a glamour girl from London's Windmill Theatre', the Soho club which famously did not close during the war, and where – just as famously – the nude 'dancers' avoided falling foul of the law by not moving a muscle.

Plomley was clearly enchanted by his guest: 'I feel that I ought to share with you just a little of Joan's glamour by telling you that she has black hair – done in what I believe is called a page-boy bob – and big brown eyes, and she reminds me rather of Janet Gaynor. She has rushed up here from the theatre with her stage make-up on, and she's wearing a blue coat under which, she tells me, she's dressed as a Red Indian.'

Which prompts Joan Jay to correct him: 'Not a Red Indian – a Cuban dancer.'

In stark contrast to a Windmill Girl, the next castaway was both a broadcaster and a man of the cloth: the Reverend Canon W. H. Elliott, Precentor of His Majesty's Chapels Royal and vicar of St Michael's, Chester Square. Elliott appeared only on condition that he be allowed to write the script himself. Roy Plomley accepted the condition, but lived to regret it. 'What he produced', complained the presenter in his book *Desert Island Discs*, 'was a sermon. It was a good sermon, but it was out of place in a programme designed as entertainment. At the end of the broadcast he leaned back and said, "I think I've put one over on you." He had, and I didn't warm to him for it.'

Joan Jay, 1946

Plomley had much more fun with the tenth castaway, one of the great figures of *Desert Island Discs* history: comedian Arthur Askey, who until David Attenborough was washed up on the desert island on 29 January 2012 to mark the programme's seventieth birthday was the only person to have been cast away four times.

Askey has arrived at the studio laden with bags.

PLOMLEY: For Pete's sake, what is all that baggage?

ASKEY: These are my records. You asked me to bring eight records, didn't you?

PLOMLEY: But eight flat discs don't take up all that space.

ASKEY: They're not flat discs.

PLOMLEY: What are they, then?

ASKEY: Cylinders.

PLOMLEY: Phonograph cylinders?

ASKEY: Yes, I much prefer cylinders. We buy 'em wholesale – by the yard, like a roll of lino. Then we cut off a piece when we feel like it.

PLOMLEY: And what's in that basket?

ASKEY: That's my gramophone.

PLOMLEY: But the BBC has got plenty of gramophones.

ASKEY: Not like my gramophone. Swapped it with Mrs Bagwash for a plush-bottomed tea cosy and Vic Oliver's autograph.

A series which Plomley had
originally expected to last six programmes had been extended by
the BBC to eight, then further
extended to a planned fifteen.
Arthur Askey was followed by
soprano Eva Turner and jazz clarinettist Harry Parry, and on 21
April, two days before cartoonist
Tom Webster was due to become
the thirteenth castaway, Leslie
Perowne sent a memo to 'P.O.(F)'
James Langham:

Arthur Askey, in the wartime comedy Band Wagon

DESERT ISLAND DISCS

As you know, the above series is to come to an end on May 7th. It
would seem from a great amount of correspondence and from listening
figures that the series was an undoubted success. We have by no means
exhausted the number of possible shipwreckees and I'd very much like to
continue the series.

In reply, Langham asked for a list of people who had been in the first
series and another of possible castaways for a second, adding, 'On the whole
we feel it would be advisable if well-known names were used throughout.'

Two weeks later Perowne forwarded Roy Plomley's list of twenty-five
more potential interviewees; back came the response that the powers-that-
be had given the go-ahead for a new series of six programmes. The list of
potential shipwreckees had been whittled down to seven approved names:
Noël Coward, Beatrice Lillie, Emlyn Williams, Nathaniel Gubbins, Leslie
Howard, Sir Kenneth Clark and Lord Elton.

Meanwhile the first series was coming to an end, with Ivor Novello the
fourteenth castaway (see pages 27–30) and Roy Plomley himself the fif-
teenth. For that final programme on 7 May, Leslie Perowne took over the
role of interviewer:

'This week's castaway is our desert island's oldest inhabitant. For the past
fourteen weeks Roy Plomley has been putting a varied assortment of broadcasting celebrities through a severe cross-examination – but this week, the
last of the series, the tables are turned and I'm going to ask him the records

that he would take on a desert island. Well, Roy, you know the technique . . . '

The first series of *Desert Island Discs* had shaken a cocktail of entertainment – classical music, jazz and literature; castaways from the press, the Church, the military and the marine (though not yet from sport, politics and science, all of which joined the mix later) – which was to remain potent throughout the programme's life.

After a break of two months, the second series of *Desert Island Discs* kicked off with actress Beatrice Lillie, followed by actor Leslie Howard and humorist Nathaniel Gubbins. Again the series was extended, this time to ten programmes from the originally proposed six – though broadcast approximately fortnightly between July and December 1942, rather than weekly.

The programme was continuing to attract attention in the higher echelons of the BBC. In September 1942 James Langham wrote to G. P. Adams, Director of Programme Planning: 'What we would like would be (a) an occasional broadcast by people not connected in any way with the arts, i.e. politicians, business men, etc. and (b) an occasional broadcast by prominent Americans in England at the present time.' And an illustration that even in its very early days the nature of *Desert Island Discs* was already the subject of warm debate comes in a memo from Langham on Boxing Day 1942, sent in response to Plomley's most recent list of potential castaways:

> I have no recollection of approving Teyte, Helpmann or Boult. As you know, I did approve Redgrave. All this, however, was a longish time ago before we had really made up our minds about this series.
>
> Our final decision, if you remember, was that 'Desert Island Discs' would be much more attractive as [a] programme if contributed [to] by people who have no connection with the arts – or at any rate none with the musical arts . . .
>
> Let us try to keep 'Desert Island Discs' a programme which is (a) good so far as the basic idea is concerned, and (b) novel in treatment in that we bring to the microphone people whose enjoyment of music is not in any way professional.

At the end of March 1943 Langham told producer Frederic Piffard: 'As you know, we are working on the principle that this programme is well worth placing occasionally, but not again in series form or at a fixed time.'

Nevertheless, the previous week had seen the start of the third series, which included the first political castaway: Tom Driberg, one of the most flamboyant figures of post-war politics, who was combining the role of independent MP for Maldon in Essex with that of gossip columnist as 'William Hickey' in the *Daily Express*. Driberg was one of the first castaways to take a recording of the human voice: 'This one would be escapism of another sort – escape into the ivory tower of James Joyce's private language: the last few paragraphs of his "Anna Livia Plurabelle", read by the author himself in his delicate Irish voice.' That passage from *Finnegans Wake* would, says Driberg, 'soothe me very agreeably to my solitary sleep'. (He was rarely solitary for long; indeed, within weeks of appearing on *Desert Island Discs* the notoriously predatory Driberg was released without charge after an encounter with a Norwegian sailor had been observed by a policeman.)

A mark of how swiftly *Desert Island Discs* had established itself in the popular imagination came with the publication in April 1943 of a cartoon in *The Tatler* showing a barely clad man and woman sitting on a tiny desert island: he is saying to her, 'There are times, Miss Amory, when I wish you were a gramophone and eight records.' And for much of 1943 and early 1944 suggestions and counter-suggestions for potential castaways to be approached whizzed around the BBC in a sandstorm of initials – bringing in the A.D.P.P. and the D.P.P. (copy to G.D. and P.O.) and every other combination of letters imaginable.

Princess Indira of Karpurthala? No. Felix Topolski? No. David Low? Yes (but he did not appear). Ed Murrow? Yes (but a memo reported that Murrow could not be booked more than a day ahead, so the idea was not pursued). Mrs Laughton-Matthews, Mrs Jean Knox and Miss Trefusis-Forbes were considered 'not sufficiently known to the public as a whole'. Nor sufficiently well known, more surprisingly, was playwright Terence Rattigan. E. M. Forster? Yes, but the note that 'Forster is very shy of broadcasting' proved correct, and he did not make it. Clark Gable? Ooh yes – 'If you can get him.' (They couldn't.)

Ominously, a note in January 1944 from Langham to Miss Pat Osborne of the Gramophone Department agreed some names but then warned: 'I must, however, make it clear that although these names are agreed as suitable for "Desert Island Discs", opportunities to place this programme will be far less frequent in future. It would certainly not be worth while even approaching any of these people at the present time.'

There were only five transmissions of *Desert Island Discs* in 1944, and one of those caused a fuss behind the scenes. Shortly after the casting away in February of Ralph Reader, driving force behind *The Gang Show* for Boy Scouts, an internal BBC memo reported that Reader 'objected strongly to the cuts made in his script which took out the tribute to the lesser known artists who are entertaining troops abroad' – which demonstrated how seriously the leading lights of the entertainment business were taking the programme.

And throughout these early years the war was never far away. At the end of the November 1943 programme with J. B. Morton – author of the whimsical column 'Beachcomber' in the *Daily Express* – Plomley asks: 'Is it true, by the way, that Mr Goebbels has been seizing on some of your wilder satire and printing it in Germany as the latest intelligence from London?' The conflict played a central role in the interviews with such castaways as Wing Commander Guy Gibson in February 1944 (pages 31–3) and Signalman Henry Wheeler (pages 41–3) – the latter broadcast in November 1945, four months after the end of hostilities in Europe had seen the Forces Programme become the Light Programme.

There was a seventeen-month gap between the end of the third series, with Mabel Constanduros in March 1944, and the beginning of the fourth, which opened with Frederick Grisewood in August 1945 and ended six weeks after Signalman Wheeler in January 1946 following the casting away of Barbara Mullen, a young actress who was to achieve her greatest fame many years later as the housekeeper Janet in *Doctor Findlay's Casebook*.

No further programmes had been planned. Nearly two years after Barbara Mullen, in November 1947 the Acting Gramophone Director sent a note to Miss Pym in the Gramophone Department: 'It occurred to me that one of your services might care to have the Plomley series "Desert Island Discs". This was very popular when we had it on the Home Service and I don't think it ever went out on any other service.'

But nothing came of this suggestion, and no revival was scheduled. Apart from the seagulls and the piles of discarded records shrivelling in the sun, the island was empty. After sixty-seven programmes, *Desert Island Discs* was no more.

Chopin
Étude in C minor, op. 10/12, 'Revolutionary'

Haydn Wood
'Roses of Picardy'

Howard Dietz and Arthur Schwarz
'Love Is a Dancing Thing'
'One to remind me of my first West End show'

Tchaikovsky
Marche slave

Milton Ager and Jack Yellen
'Happy Days Are Here Again'
'To remind me of some of the great times I had touring in America'

Leon Jessel
Parade of the Wooden Soldiers

'I Give You My Heart'
Bebe Daniels
'Dedicated to all those people whom the war has separated from their loved ones'

Wagner
'Ride of the Valkyries'
(from *Die Walküre*)

Opposite: *Vic Oliver and Sarah Churchill*

VIC OLIVER

entertainer

29 January 1942

'I want you to know that I come from a long line of musicians'

Vic Oliver, the first *Desert Island Discs* castaway, was a hugely popular figure in the early 1940s.

An Austrian Jew, born Victor von Samek in Vienna in 1898, he had enjoyed a successful career as a musician and entertainer in the USA before moving in the 1930s to England, where he founded the Vic Oliver Concert Orchestra and soon established himself as a musician and comedian. One of his trademark comic turns was playing the violin badly (in the manner of Les Dawson on the piano in a later era): hence the mention of Oliver as 'master of the mahogany violin' in the *Radio Times*.

At the time of his *Desert Island Discs* engagement Oliver was enjoying a very high profile. He was starring in *Get a Load of This* at the London Hippodrome, and was a staple of the comic radio programme *Hi, Gang!*, which had begun in 1940 and in which he played opposite Bebe Daniels and Ben Lyon. *Hi, Gang!* the movie (with Oliver billed as 'The Nuisance with the Ideas') had come out in 1941.

But in one prominent household Vic Oliver's name was far from popular. In 1935 he had met Winston Churchill's daughter Sarah when both were performing in the C. B. Cochran revue *Follow the Sun*, and soon she was telling her father – then out of government and a vocal backbencher – that she and Oliver, sixteen years her senior, intended to marry. On 21 February 1936 Churchill wrote a letter to his wife Clementine from the chamber of the House of Commons, reporting on his encounter with his prospective son-in-law:

> The interview took place on Saturday at noon. He professed himself quite ready to give the name and address of his mother and sister. His father was a well-known cloth manufacturer at Brünn named Victor Samek. He did not impress me as being a bad man; but common as dirt: an Austrian citizen, a resident in US, and here on licence and an American passport: twice divorced [in fact he had been divorced once]: thirty-six or so he says. A horrible mouth: A foul Austro-Yankee drawl. I did not offer to shake hands: but put him through a long examination . . .
>
> You may imagine that I confronted him with the hard side of things. I told him that if there was an engagement, it would force me to make an immediate public statement in terms which would be painful to them both.

Oliver departed for the USA, where Sarah later joined him in New York – the flight from her disapproving parents causing much flurry on the society pages – and they were married on Christmas Eve 1936, subsequently returning to England. They separated in 1941 and were divorced in 1945.

A sobering measure of Vic Oliver's profile which was to emerge much later is that his name appeared on the Nazis' list of people to be arrested following the invasion of Britain by Germany. That very popularity with the thousands who would be listening to the Forces Programme on 29 January 1942 made him the perfect first *Desert Island Discs* castaway.

After the programme's opening announcement – remarkably close to the formula suggested in Plomley's original letter to Leslie Perowne, and destined to remain the *Desert Island Discs* prologue, with minor variations, for decades – come the first exchanges:

PLOMLEY: Good evening, everyone. Our shipwreckee tonight is a Mr Vic Oliver, who is, I am told, a comedian and the star of *Hi, Gang!* – which, I am given to understand, is another radio programme.

OLIVER: You might add that I am appearing with colossal success in the sensational West End stage show . . .

PLOMLEY: I'm sorry, Mr Oliver – but no advertising.

OLIVER: No advertising?

PLOMLEY: Positively no advertising. Is that your suggested list of records that you have there?

OLIVER: Yes.

PLOMLEY: May I see it? What charming notepaper!

OLIVER: I'm so glad you like it. I've just had it printed.

PLOMLEY: Crimson, purple and orange – delightful. (*Reading*) 'Vic Oliver – comedian, lightning club manipulator, violinist and comedy trick cyclist. Light work done with horse and van.' Is this a photograph of you?

OLIVER: Don't you think it's like me?

PLOMLEY: It looks quite a lot younger.

OLIVER: I must admit it was taken a few years ago.

PLOMLEY: I had no idea photography was invented as long ago as that. Shall I read out your list of records?

OLIVER: Please do.

PLOMLEY: (*Reading*) 1. Vic Oliver joins the Army. 2. The Army joins Vic Oliver. 3. Vic Oliver's Twists. 4. Vic Oliver tickles your fancy. 5. Vic Oliver tickles the ivories. 6. Vic Oliver . . . Oh, no. (*tears paper*)

OLIVER: Hey, what are you doing?

PLOMLEY: I'm sorry – no advertising.

More comic business follows – about autographs. 'My autograph is very valuable,' says Oliver. 'Yes,' replies Plomley: 'If I had waited until I had two more I might have swapped them for one of Ben Lyon's. Now seriously, Vic, what about these records?'

Chopin's Étude in C minor, op. 10/12, 'Revolutionary', achieves the distinction of becoming the first piece of music played for a *Desert Island Discs* castaway, and is followed by 'Roses of Picardy': 'It really is one of my favourite tunes,' says Oliver, 'it haunts me night and day. After all, why shouldn't it? I've been murdering it for years.'

Denied Tchaikovsky's Piano Concerto because it takes up three records – 'Couldn't I tie them together or something?' – he opts for the *Marche slave* by the same composer, followed by his own theme song 'Happy Days Are Here Again' and *Parade of the Wooden Soldiers*.

The gaps between records are short, but long enough for more banter:

OLIVER: I would like to take a record of a song that my wife and I wrote to keep the wolf from the door.

PLOMLEY: By singing it where the wolf could hear it?

OLIVER: I resent that remark. I want you to know that I come from a long line of musicians.

PLOMLEY: I know. I've seen them queueing up.

The song is 'I Give You My Heart', sung by Oliver's friend and *Hi, Gang!* co-star Bebe Daniels.

After the playing of the final record, 'The Ride of the Valkyries' ('I would like something really exciting and exhilarating – something I can use for my morning exercises and to swing through the tree-tops – like Tarzan'), the first *Desert Island Discs* ends with more comic business. There is a knock on the door and a voice sings out, 'Telegram for Mr Vic Oliver!' Oliver, fearful that the cable is bringing bad news ('My goldfish isn't at all well'), asks Plomley to open it: 'Dear Vic,' it reads, 'have just been listening to you on a desert island. Wish it were true. Bebe and Ben.'

The castaway is outraged:

OLIVER: To be insulted by a couple of third-rate stooges! It's humiliating to have to work with such riff-raff. And me! – who's been more than a father to them. It's disgusting. Goodnight, Roy.

PLOMLEY: Goodnight, Vic. You see! That's what you get for being shipwrecked on a desert island.

Roy Plomley and Vic Oliver had been engaged not in an interview but in a performance, a half-hour of patter and comic business rather than any attempt to learn much about the career or character of the castaway. The absence of any reference whatsoever to the Churchill connection might be explained by the separation from Sarah being so recent – but imagine today's generation of *Desert Island Discs* listeners putting up with such an omission. Indeed, as a mark of how *Desert Island Discs* has changed since Vic Oliver was the first castaway, just imagine how Sue Lawley or Kirsty Young would have approached interviewing him.

Vic Oliver appeared on *Desert Island Discs* for a second time in November 1955, by which time Roy Plomley had introduced the idea of taking a luxury: Oliver chose a supply of music manuscript paper. Of the eight records he had selected in 1942, 'Love Is a Dancing Thing' and 'The Ride of the Valkyries' enjoyed a reprise (though in different versions), while Tchaikovsky was again in the list, this time with *Francesca da Rimini*.

Vic Oliver – a fascinating character in his background, his life story and his turbulent association with the Churchill family – died in August 1964.

IVOR NOVELLO

entertainer

30 April 1942

'A staunch gramophile'

I vor Novello was a giant of British entertainment long before he became the penultimate castaway of the first *Desert Island Discs* series. Born David Ivor Davies in Cardiff in January 1893, as a boy he had sung at the Welsh Eisteddfod, and became solo treble in the choir of Magdalen College, Oxford. He was fifteen years old when his first song was published, and only twenty-one when in 1914 he wrote 'Keep the Home Fires Burning', which soon became the keynote anthem of the First World War.

Through the inter-war period Novello became one of the country's most popular composers and actors, writing for and performing in a succession of revues, operettas, plays, musicals and films. Among his movie appearances was the eponymous role in Alfred Hitchcock's *The Lodger* (1926), and while in Hollywood in the early 1930s he wrote the dialogue for *Tarzan the Ape Man*.

Novello's musical *The Dancing Years* had closed at the Theatre Royal, Drury Lane, on the outbreak of the Second World War and then reopened at the Adelphi – which is where he was visited by Roy Plomley to discuss his selection of eight records. Plomley, who had never met Novello before, was clearly impressed:

I heard that he was charm itself, but I wasn't prepared for anyone quite so unaffected. As I was shown into his dressing room at the Adelphi Theatre, where he was starring in a revival of his own musical play *The Dancing Years* (which was unkindly known in theatrical circles as 'The Prancing Queers') he threw his arms in the air and shouted cheerfully, 'You fool!' This was mildly disconcerting, especially as he happened to be stark naked at the time, but it appeared that he had heard a radio comedy programme of mine on the air a few evenings before, and it had made him laugh.

If ever there was a man to have been truly miserable on a desert island it would have been Ivor Novello, because he rejoiced at being in a crowd of friends, and the procession in and out of his dressing room was second only to that in Piccadilly Tube Station.

Roy Plomley's intuition about Novello's attitude towards being marooned is confirmed by the castaway early in the programme: 'I would buoy myself up with the thought that it could be only a temporary interruption to my work, and every night I would go to sleep with the firm conviction that I would be rescued in the morning.'

Novello goes on to declare himself 'a staunch gramophile' – '"Gramophile,"' Plomley cuts in, 'what a lovely word!' – with some 8,000 records. 'But I think almost as important as the actual choice of records would be to evolve a system of rationing their playing so that they would still retain part of their freshness. A gramophone session would have to be something to look forward to.'

This castaway is clearly buying into the whole *Desert Island Discs* fantasy in a thoughtful manner which none of the previous thirteen castaways have matched, a demeanour underlined by his first record, Debussy's *Prélude à l'après-midi d'un faune*. 'I have chosen it because it is most representative of Debussy,' he explains, 'and because it has a desert island quality. It might help to get me acclimatized a little . . . It conveys extreme peace and a sunny day – and I worship the sun. And the only possible compensation for life on a desert island would be the fact that there would be a lot of sunshine, no appointments and nothing matters.'

A similar sensitivity to the music attaches to each choice. John McCormack singing 'The Garden Where the Praties Grow' evokes the comment, 'I would never dare play it when I had the slightest feeling of homesickness'; Bach's 'Air on a G-String' 'seems to have all the essentials of music in it'; *On Hearing the First Cuckoo in Spring* is 'the most concentrated essence of Delius'.

And the choice of soprano Maggie Teyte singing 'De fleurs' from Debussy's *Proses Lyriques* brings a revelation:

PLOMLEY: As there is always the chance that Miss Teyte is listening, don't you think this might be an opportune moment to mention that ambition of yours that you told me about the other evening?

NOVELLO: What was that? Oh, I see what you mean. Yes, I did tell you, didn't I, that it was an ambition of mine that Maggie Teyte should record one of my songs. But of course I would never dare ask her.

PLOMLEY: Of course not – but, as I said, she may be listening.

NOVELLO: Yes, she may be listening.

PLOMLEY: Well, we've planted that seed.

(The seed fell on stony ground. Whether she was listening or not, Maggie Teyte never recorded an Ivor Novello song.)

Brahms's *Academic Festival Overture* 'makes me want to stand up and cheer. I should certainly have this record playing when my rescue ship arrived.'

Curiously, given the fact that the programme was scripted, the eighth musical choice is talked about but appears not to have been played on the programme. The record is Lionel Tertis playing the 'Londonderry Air' on the viola: 'The loveliest tune in the world,' says Novello, 'and part of its charm surely is that nobody knows who wrote it.' But Plomley declares that 'I'm afraid we have to take that as played,' and proceeds to wind up:

PLOMLEY: Thanks for letting us have your choice, Mr Novello – and the one consolation for losing you temporarily on a desert island would be that when you *were* rescued you'd have a mass of new plays and music and ideas for us.

NOVELLO: Probably written with my thumbnail on dried banana skins. Goodnight, everyone.

PLOMLEY: Goodnight.

Lionel Tertis
'Londonderry Air'

'The loveliest tune in the world'

Ivor Novello continued to work in musical theatre for the remainder of the war, though his reputation took a knock when he was gaoled for four weeks after being convicted of the misuse of petrol coupons. (The coupons in question had been appropriated by a fan, but he was culpable none the less.) His 1945 show *Perchance to Dream* – which featured another still-familiar song, 'We'll Gather Lilacs', soon to become a staple of Vera Lynn's repertoire – proved a huge success, as did *King's Rhapsody* four years later. Shortly after his show *Gay's the Word* had opened in 1951 he suffered a coronary thrombosis, and died at the age of fifty-eight. The Ivor Novello Awards, celebrating excellence in songwriting and composing, continue to be given in his memory.

GUY GIBSON
RAF pilot
19 February 1944

'This piece of music somehow seems to illustrate
the mind of every airman'

Guy Gibson VC was the epitome of the dashing RAF pilot: young (he was twenty-five when cast away), courageous, arrogant (nicknamed 'Bumptious Bastard' by ground crew), boyishly handsome, married to an actress, and already garlanded with decorations, including the Victoria Cross for his central role in the 'Dambusters' raid of May 1943.

While it was the Dambusters operation which made him one of the legends of the Second World War, he had also flown as a fighter pilot, and in all had taken part in over 170 operational flights before being transplanted to the quiet and solitude of the desert island.

Roy Plomley recalled his first meeting with this heroic figure:

> I went to see him at Adastral House, in Kingsway, where he was kicking his heels in a large, bare office. He had been taken off operational flying for a while, and was being sent round to show the flag. He had toured air stations in Canada, and travelled all over the United States, broadcasting and lecturing.
>
> On the chimney piece was a photograph of the French countryside which he had taken during a hedge-hopping sortie. The detail was amazingly

sharp; a man could be seen fishing in a stream, ignoring the low-flying plane above him. In 1944, it was hard to think of life being lived so normally in Occupied Europe; in fact it was hard to think of life being lived normally anywhere. There was something very reassuring about that French fisherman.

Where better to 'show the flag' than on *Desert Island Discs*?

Roy Plomley opens the programme with a potted history of Gibson's remarkable career:

'As soon as he left school he joined the Royal Air Force and became a bomber pilot. He made his first bombing mission over the Kiel Canal the day after war was declared. During the Battle of Britain he was transferred to a fighter squadron, where he was credited with four certainties [that is, four German bombers definitely destroyed] and two probables. He was transferred back again to bombers in January 1942. He has carried out 174 missions over enemy territory, including five trips to Berlin. In May last year he led a picked force of Lancasters in that very gallant and successful raid on the Möhne Dam. He is the most highly decorated man in the British Empire. He is Wing Commander Guy Gibson, VC, DSO and Bar, DFC and Two Bars.'

Gibson admits that he 'can't claim to know an awful lot about music at all', which has made the choice of just eight records much more straightforward than for many castaways. But while he hasn't had much difficulty in choosing the records, he hasn't known the names of several of the pieces he wanted, so had to hum them to his more musical friends or his wife in order for them to be identified.

The reasoning behind Gibson's first choice, the *Warsaw Concerto*, is poignant: 'This piece of music somehow seems to illustrate the mind of every airman. Not only that. It has a very strong sentimental appeal for me. In the days when my squadron was bombing Germany every

The dam busted, 1943

night, this was the record that, at our many parties in the Mess, we would put on the radiogram
and let it repeat itself again and again. This went
on for a long time, and a good many parties, until
there were very few left in the Mess who remembered those who had listened to it first in the days
gone by.'

Gibson's selection of the overture to *The Flying
Dutchman* by Richard Wagner has more peaceful
associations: 'I've always liked it, ever since I was
a kid. I don't believe I should ever get tired of it.
It's grand. It's probably because it reminds me of
the sea, and I love the sea.'

But as with the *Warsaw Concerto*, other
choices carry reminders of the war. 'If I Had My
Way' has to be the version sung by Bing Crosby,
as 'I've heard so many imitation Crosbys giving

out over the intercom when we're flying that it would be a treat to have the
real thing.' And the *RAF March Past* has obvious associations: 'Every time I
hear it, it never fails to send a shiver down my spine.'

Guy Gibson's eighth record is more Wagner, 'The Ride of the Valkyries':
'It's exciting, it's grandiose, it's – rather terrible. It reminds me of a bombing
raid, though I don't say it's like one.'

And then Roy Plomley concludes the programme with, 'Good luck,
happy landings, and thank you.'

The sign-off 'Happy landings' took on a terrible irony only a few months
after Guy Gibson had appeared on *Desert Island Discs*. On the night of
19 September 1944 he and a navigator took off for a bombing raid on the
Dutch–German border in a de Havilland Mosquito, an aircraft which
neither had flown before. After the attack they were returning to England
when the Mosquito crashed on farmland near Steenbergen, and both men
were killed. The cause of the crash has never been firmly established.

But Guy Gibson's reputation as a swashbuckling RAF hero lives on,
assisted by the posthumous publication of his autobiography *Enemy Coast
Ahead* in 1946, and even more by his central role – played by Richard Todd
– in the 1955 film *The Dam Busters*.

CELIA JOHNSON

actress

27 October 1945

'I'd waltz by myself'

When in October 1945 she was deposited on Roy Plomley's island shore, Celia Johnson was one of the most distinguished actresses in Britain – and less than a month later she would become even more admired with the release of *Brief Encounter*. Written by Noël Coward and directed by David Lean, that cauldron of repressed suburban sexuality gave Johnson cinema immortality in the role of Laura Jesson, the housewife whose brief encounter with doctor Alec Harvey (Leslie Howard) in a station tea-room sets in train a love story which has been boosting tissue sales for nearly seventy years. It was her third appearance in a Coward–Lean film, following pre-castaway roles in *In Which We Serve* (1942) and *This Happy Breed* (1944).

After training at RADA, Celia Johnson had embarked upon a theatrical career which would see her in many memorable productions, not only in Britain but also in the USA, which she first visited in 1931 to play Ophelia. The following year a London appearance in *The Wind and the Rain* won her critical and popular appreciation, and the early 1940s saw her in such leading roles as Elizabeth Bennet in *Pride and Prejudice* and Mrs de Winter in *Rebecca*. Through the early

part of the war she combined her acting commitments with service as an auxiliary policewoman.

Before playing the first of her eight selections, Celia Johnson declares: 'I'm afraid that most of my records would be chosen to remind me of the theatre and of home and of London. I enjoy my life much too much to want to leave it and sit all alone on a damp island.' She adds: 'I should want to take as many fragments of it as I could with me in the form of music,' which is as good a definition as you could get of the idea behind the programme – *Desert Island Discs* as mosaic.

First off is Elgar's *Cockaigne Overture* – 'Just because it's London.'

'What sort of picture does the thought of London conjure up for you?' asks Plomley the inquisitor: 'Shaftesbury Avenue and the theatres . . . ?'

The castaway cuts in: 'And the awfulness of Tottenham Court Road, and the surging crowds of shoppers in Oxford Street, and the magical effect of a wet evening when the street lights go up and shine on the wet pavements.'

Such lyricism suggests that she's about to move on to Noël Coward's paean of praise to his and her favourite city, 'London Pride', which had been written in 1941 and appeared in *This Happy Breed*. Instead she picks another Coward standard, 'I'll See You Again' from *Bitter Sweet* – which enables Plomley to make his droll observation that '*Bitter Sweet* was one of the few musical shows I've seen that had a plot which made sense.'

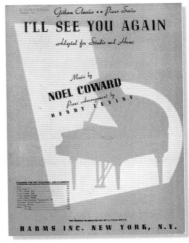

Celia Johnson's next record, a Chopin waltz, brings an allusion – but no more than that – to *Brief Encounter*: 'Just recently I've been making a film in which this music plays quite an important part – and I find it's grown on me. I find myself humming it all the time and I'd hate to be without my recording of it on that island.'

A little later she requests 'an infectiously cheerful piece of music' by Carl Maria von Weber. 'Some days,' she predicts, 'I expect, in spite of my trials and miseries, I should feel cheerful and gay and want to dance. And for those moods I should want *Invitation to the Waltz*.'

'You can have the invitation all right, but there'd be nobody to waltz with.'

'Rather like taking my harp to the party and nobody asking me to play. But never mind – I'd waltz by myself.'

Joyce Grenfell singing 'I'm Going To See You Today' ticks two boxes: 'It could give me the popular song that I wanted and, at the same time, bring to my desert island the voice of a personal friend.'

Celia Johnson closes with Beethoven's Pastoral Symphony, 'a lovely vision of fresh, green countryside – farms, villages, neat country roads. I think this record would get the most use of all.'

Celia Johnson is a member of that select band of people who have appeared on *Desert Island Discs* three times, having been cast away by Roy Plomley again in 1954 and 1975. By the time of her third appearance she had enhanced her reputation as one of the great screen actresses, not only in *Brief Encounter* (for which she was nominated for an Academy Award) but also in other classics such as *A Kid for Two Farthings* (1955) and *The Prime of Miss Jean Brodie* (1969), which brought her a BAFTA Award for Best Actress in a Supporting Role – supporting, that is, another icon of stage, screen and *Desert Island Discs*, Maggie Smith. Johnson won a British Academy of Television award as Best Actress for the eponymous role in the television play *Mrs Palfrey at the Claremont* in 1973. And she enjoyed further acclaim after being cast away for the third time for her television performances in *Staying On* (1980) and *The Potting Shed* (1981).

Created a Dame in 1981 in recognition of her singular contribution to theatre and film, Celia Johnson died in 1982.

Yvonne Printemps
'Depuis trois ans passés'

'Hers is one voice I'd like to have with me'

Opposite: Brief Encounter, *1945: Celia Johnson and Trevor Howard*

DEBORAH KERR

actress

17 November 1945

'On a desert island I should belong to no period – my existence would be completely primitive'

A beach comes instantly to mind whenever the name of Deborah Kerr is mentioned – and not the beach on which she was washed up by Roy Plomley in 1945 and again in 1977.

When Kerr and Burt Lancaster engaged in their passionate embrace on the Hawaii sand in the 1953 movie *From Here to Eternity*, they seemed preoccupied with something rather more pressing than the choice of eight gramophone records. And in that film the much-loved actress was departing from the sort of role which had earned her the description in her citation for an honorary Academy Award as 'an artist of impeccable grace and beauty, a dedicated actress whose motion picture career has always stood for perfection, discipline and elegance'.

When first cast away by Plomley she was twenty-four years old and about to be married to Squadron Leader Anthony Bartley DFC, a fact which did not go unremarked by the *Desert Island Discs* presenter . . .

The introduction is vintage Roy Plomley, summing up the career of the castaway while in a few lines expressing what made her special, and then painting in his listeners' imagination a jolly picture of a studio strewn with the booty from a shopping spree:

'Good evening, everyone. On our desert island this evening, and looking very decorative on it too, is a film star – Deborah Kerr.

'She was born in Scotland and brought up in a Sussex village. She very nearly found herself in the Civil Service but had her own ideas about that – and went on the stage. Her first job was carrying a spear and saying an odd line or two in the Shakespeare season at the Open Air Theatre in 1939. Shortly after that she was having lunch in a West End hotel one day when a film direc-

Deborah Kerr and Burt Lancaster get to know each other in From Here to Eternity, *1953*

tor came over to her table and asked her if she would make a test for a leading part in a new picture. That's the sort of thing that usually only happens in movies – but here's one case where it happened in real life. The part, which she got, was Jenny in *Major Barbara*. Other films followed: *Love on the Dole*, *Hatter's Castle*, *The Life and Death of Colonel Blimp* and, recently, *Perfect Strangers*.

'In eleven days from now she is getting married – to a Battle of Britain pilot – and most of her trousseau seems to be lying around the studio in cardboard boxes, because this broadcast comes at the end of a day's shopping.

'And now she's got to take her mind off coupons and curtain material and think about her Desert Island Discs.'

As in all of these early programmes, the necessity to move relentlessly from one record to the next rules out all but fleeting glimpses of the castaway's character. Thus with Deborah Kerr, once the introductory summary is over, finding out more about her career is simply not on the agenda. The records come thick and fast, and so do her reasons for choosing them – and if those reasons contain slivers of revelation, so much the better.

Number one on the list, Ravel's *Pavane pour une infante défunte*, offers just such a sliver. 'This is a costume piece,' says Deborah Kerr: 'There's a richness and warmth and pageantry about it. It brings to mind a picture of the beautiful colouring of the Elizabethan age – deep reds and candle-light and lace. It reminds me of a painting by Velasquez. I've got a great fascination for that period. I sometimes feel that I should have lived then instead of now. On a desert island I should belong to no period – my existence would be completely primitive – and this music would give an impression of a life that I have never known but could imagine very vividly.'

Tchaikovsky's waltz from his Serenade for Strings would set her dancing – 'I had ambitions to be a dancer at one time' – in such an outfit as could be made in the prevailing circumstances: 'Dressed in sailcloth and palm-leaves, or whatever sort of costume I could run up, I would imagine myself floating across a polished floor in a glamorous frock' – at which point Plomley, an un-romantic spoilsport for the occasion, chips in: 'Until you stubbed your toe on a rock, or skidded on a jelly-fish.'

The slow movement of Dvořák's New World Symphony has Miss Kerr coming over all lyrical again: 'Lovely peaceful music that conjures up the countryside with fields of waving corn, tall shady trees – whole vistas of scenery to imagine as a change from the sand and sea which is all, presumably, that I'd have to look at.'

Last on to the turntable is the march from *Peter and the Wolf*: 'Some rousing, stirring, barbaric music. The sort of stuff that would make me want to climb trees – and throw coconuts at the seagulls.' ('You let our seagulls alone,' retorts the interviewer.) It is, she sums up, 'music for letting off steam.'

After Plomley's sign-off – 'Very best wishes for eleven days' time and thereafter' – the continuity announcer trails the following week's programme with the intriguing words, 'Next week's broadcast will come from an actual desert island.' Who could that be . . . ?

A year after her first appearance on *Desert Island Discs*, Deborah Kerr moved to Hollywood, and before long had achieved global stardom. In addition to *From Here to Eternity* – the cast of which included, as well as Burt Lancaster, Montgomery Clift and Frank Sinatra – she starred in many classic movies, including *Quo Vadis* (1951), *The End of the Affair* (1955), *The Sundowners* (1960) and *The Innocents* (1961). Notwithstanding frolics in the surf, her best-known role of all was as the governess in the 1956 Rodgers and Hammerstein musical *The King and I*, in which she co-starred with Yul Brynner. Six times she was nominated for an Academy Award, but never won one, having to make do with the honorary award in 1994.

Of the eight records chosen in 1945, only Dvořák was still favoured in the 1977 Deborah Kerr selection. By that point in the programme's history the regular coda of book and luxury was always of special interest: Kerr chose the *Oxford English Dictionary* and a crochet hook with a supply of wool. She could have chosen Burt Lancaster, but as an animate object – and then some – he would have been disqualified, politely but firmly, by Roy Plomley.

'Danny Boy'
John McHugh

Cole Porter
'Begin the Beguine'

'If You Were the Only Girl in the World'
Anne Ziegler and Webster Booth
'A song I find myself singing when I'm thinking about my girl'

Schumann
Romance in F sharp major, op. 28/2
'Seems to dig deep down into what you are thinking'

'Beautiful Love'
Victor Young and his Orchestra

'Ah, Sweet Mystery of Life'
Nelson Eddy

Vaughan Williams
Fantasia on 'Greensleeves'

'The Holy City'
Richard Crooks

Above: Royal Navy recruits learning how to operate a signalling light, 1939

HENRY WHEELER

signalman

24 November 1945

'I'm just sitting in a hut here talking into a telephone'

The trail the week before, following Deborah Kerr as castaway, had caught the attention: 'Next week's broadcast will come from an actual desert island – from Signalman Henry Wheeler of the Royal Navy doing garrison duty on a small island off the coast of Europe.' Hostilities might have ceased, but thousands of British servicemen were still deployed overseas, and the interview with the young sailor has an especially touching quality.

Wheeler's location could not be revealed – almost all we learn is that it was cold, scarcely the palm-tree paradise imagined in most *Desert Island Discs* programmes – and the content of the programme is far from what we would now expect from an eye-witness on the front line. But the fact that a film star one week is followed by a completely unknown castaway seven days later illustrates one of the early strengths of *Desert Island Discs*: Roy Plomley's knack of thinking beyond what was obvious and easy. Then as now, variety was the essence of the programme.

The opening few minutes of the programme carry that frisson of uncertainty which then attached to any radio link to a faraway place.

IF YOU WERE THE ONLY GIRL IN
THE WORLD (3).

No one I'll ever care for, dear, but you,
No one I'll fancy, therefore love me, do;
Your eyes have set me dreaming all night long,
Your eyes have set me scheming, right or wrong,
All days we'll be together, side by side,
Always in any weather, whatever else betide.

'Good evening, everyone. Tonight our castaway is a real one – he's not in the studio with me, he's actually on an island. In just a moment we'll be going over to meet Signalman Henry Wheeler of the Royal Navy, who is doing garrison duty on a small island somewhere off the coast of Europe. I'm not allowed to tell you where it is. In fact I don't know exactly where it is. It's not strictly a desert island because there are a few other people on it too – but if "desert" isn't quite the right adjective for the island, Henry Wheeler has got a whole string of other adjectives for the place that might suit.'

Wheeler is a twenty-year-old tailor's assistant from Vernham Grove, near Bath, the eldest of a family of six children. His hobbies are athletics, carpentry and snooker. He has been in the navy for a little over two years and has completed his training on HMS *Impregnable*, having taken part in the invasion of France on 'D-Day plus one'. Now he is – where?

PLOMLEY: Calling Signalman Henry Wheeler on that island, wherever it is. Are you there?

WHEELER: Yes, here I am. Good evening, everybody.

PLOMLEY: How are things where you are, Henry?

WHEELER: Cold.

PLOMLEY: It's not so hot in London. What's happening on that island of yours tonight? Have you had some Army radio engineers over to rig up a studio on the island?

WHEELER: Yes, one or two blokes have come over – but there's no studio. I'm just sitting in a hut here talking into a telephone to British Forces Network Headquarters in Hamburg. They're picking me up from there.

PLOMLEY: I see. Well, there's a whole stack of records here for you – so we'll assume that you've sorted out the final eight that you want, and we'll go ahead and play what you ask for.

Wheeler's record choices begin with John McHugh's rendition of 'Danny Boy': 'It's a song that my father is always singing. Ever since I was a nipper I remember him singing it about the house and at family parties – Christmas and so on – and it's a song that means "Home" to me.'

His third choice is Anne Ziegler and Webster Booth (later a castaway himself) singing 'If You Were the Only Girl in the World' – 'a song I find myself singing when I'm thinking about my girl'. The girl in question is a Dutch lady named Dine, whom Wheeler met when stationed in Rotterdam:

PLOMLEY: I hope reception is good in Rotterdam tonight. Is Dine listening, do you think? Did you write and tell her about this?
WHEELER: Oh yes, she's listening all right. And this next record is for her.

But as the record ends, there's no time to indulge in thoughts about Dine, for up pops Plomley with, 'Right-oh, what's the next one?'

The next one is Schumann's Romance in F sharp major, a piano piece which clearly touches Henry: 'It's got a sort of reminiscent and far-away feeling about it. It seems to dig deep down into what you are thinking.'

Wheeler is planning to return to his job when he is demobbed – 'I hope one day to be a branch manager for the firm I was working for' – but he cannot say when demobilization might be: 'There's quite a long time to go before that happens, another eight months at least.'

Signalman Wheeler has saved to the end his favourite singer Richard Crooks's version of 'The Holy City', which he used to sing in the chapel choir at home: 'I'll always remember we were due to sing it on the Sunday after I came away. But my calling-up papers arrived, and I couldn't be there.'

The programme has an unusual sign-off:

PLOMLEY: Thank you, Henry Wheeler, for letting us hear your choice of Desert Island Discs. Usually at the end of the programme on Saturday night the castaway and I go and have a drink together, but tonight we can hardly do that – with you on that island, wherever it is. So next time you're in London come along and collect that drink I owe you.
WHEELER: I'll certainly do that. Goodnight, Roy. Goodnight, all.
PLOMLEY: Goodnight, everyone.

So different in mood from the wise-cracking bouts with Vic Oliver or Arthur Askey – what could be more poignant than this vision of Signalman Henry Wheeler, hidden away in some cold place and thinking of Dine?

Schumann
Romance in F sharp major, op. 28/2

'Seems to dig deep down into what you are thinking'

1950s

NATIONAL
REGISTRATION
IDENTITY
CARD

FIVE YEARS – almost to the very day – passed between the last *Desert Island Discs* of the 1940s and the first of the 1950s: five years which saw Britain transformed.

The direct after-effects of the Second World War were felt long beyond the cessation of hostilities in 1945. On the domestic level, two of the key symbols of wartime Britain, the National Registration Identity Card and the Ministry of Food Ration Card, lasted well into the 1950s – the former until 1952, the latter until 1954 – and both remained emblematic of a country knuckling down to rebuilding a war-damaged society. Rationing in particular was a means of promoting solidarity, as well as conserving vital provisions. Bread consumption had never been restricted during wartime, but bread rationing was introduced in May 1946 and remained in place until July 1948.

Winston Churchill (sometime father-in-law of the very first *Desert Island Discs* castaway) had been an inspirational war leader, but the popular urge to create a new order saw Clement Attlee taking over as Prime Minister in the Labour government of 1945. Sweeping welfare reform was in the air, notably with the founding of the National Health Service in 1948, and the social tectonic plates were shifting. High or low, those who previously had known their place were now not so sure.

In broadcasting, the seismic change in the late 1940s and early 1950s was the rapid growth of television. In 1947 approximately 25,000 television sets were manufactured for domestic use in the United Kingdom, as opposed to 1,981,000 radio (or 'wireless') sets. But television was rapidly catching up with radio in terms of production, and three years into the new decade it overtook the older medium. In an industry boosted significantly by the Coronation in June that year, some 1,237,000 televisions were produced in 1953, as opposed to 956,000 radios. And one of the effects of extensive television ownership was an increase in the prominence of sport in the nation's life. Royal Ascot, for example, was first televised in June 1952, and the much-loved midweek sports magazine programme *Sportsview* started in April 1954. Generally sport was exerting a much wider grip on the public imagination than it had been, and this trend was reflected in *Desert Island Discs*.

The 1950s saw a steady stream of sporting heroes following in the wake of Denis Compton and Bill Edrich (the first dual castaways, in May 1951): fellow cricketers Jim Laker (1956), cast away within weeks of his sensational nineteen wickets against Australia at Old Trafford, and legendary batsman Sir Len Hutton (1959), along with John Arlott, greatest of all cricket commentators (1953); Fred Perry, last Briton to win the men's singles at Wimbledon, who was cast away in 1952, plus another tennis player Tony Mottram (1955); athletes Chris Chataway (1955) and Chris Brasher (1957); show-jumper Pat Smythe (1955); racing driver Stirling Moss (1956: see pages 66–8); boxer Tommy Farr (1955) and boxing promoter Jack Solomons (1957); Olympic gold-medal-winning swimmer Judy Grinham (1959); yachtsman Uffa Fox (1959); and Boat Race commentator (and BBC executive) John Snagge (1959).

On the much wider stage, foreign policy was being recast as fresh alignments were established and the old imperial order dwindled. The 1950s was a decade scarred by the Korean War and the Suez fiasco, but it also brought the communal optimism enshrined in the 1951 Festival of Britain and the coronation in 1953 of the new Queen.

Radio remained at the heart of British culture. In 1952 over eleven million radio licences were sold. Radio output was a mixture of the very familiar – *Music While You Work*, a daily fixture when *Desert Island Discs* first took to the airwaves in 1942, was to continue until 1960 – and the new, with *The Goon Show* (which began life as *Crazy People* in 1951) at the vanguard of a stream of highly original programming.

Apart from *Desert Island Discs* and *Any Questions?* – the panel discussion first broadcast in 1948 – today's other notable radio survivor from this period is *The Archers*, the rural soap opera inextricably linked with one of the most memorable broadcasting landmarks of the 1950s: Grace

Archer's death in a stable fire in September 1955, widely considered a brilliant BBC spoiler for the launch of independent television broadcasting the
same evening.

When *The Archers* first went on air in May 1950, *Desert Island Discs* was
nowhere to be found in the radio schedules. It would be too much to claim
that it was conspicuous by its absence, as – apart from that brief possibility of
a revival in 1947 – it seemed to have been a programme idea which had run
its course. Certainly Roy Plomley did not seem to think otherwise, as he had
plenty of other fish to fry. He had spent the late 1940s trying to develop his
acting and playwriting career, while still working on a wide range of light-
entertainment programmes for the BBC. Among his radio assignments was
chairmanship of the popular panel discussion programme *We Beg to Differ*,
a sort of '*Brains Trust* Lite' in which the panel of celebrities – including Joyce
Grenfell, Gilbert Harding and Charmian Innes – addressed a list of not very
serious questions, such as: 'When I see the presents displayed at weddings of
friends, I am staggered by the uselessness and stupidity of many of the gifts.
Would the team suggest some really worthwhile present to give to young
couples upon their marriage?'

In early 1950 Plomley was sidelined by illness – while recuperating he
wrote to one of his BBC producers that 'I am on a regimen of light work
in the garden and light novels in the house' – but he would have found it a
great tonic that in late July the BBC management had had the idea of reviv-
ing *Desert Island Discs*. On 4 August 1950, in one of those initial-bestrewn
internal memos, P.H.S. (Clare Lawson Dick: Planning, Home Service) wrote
to H.G. (Head of the Gramophone Department):

> C.H.S. [Controller, Home Service] was interested in your plan for reviv-
> ing 'Desert Island Discs' in the evenings. The time and date we have in
> mind for it is Week 44, Wednesday November 1st, 6.30–7 p.m. However,
> before C.H.S. decides finally to accept the series he would like to have
> from you a list of the six or eight people whom you would invite to open
> the series, and a working estimate of the cost.

Cue another flurry of memos regarding the credentials of various celebrities, and the resurrection of *Desert Island Discs* was confirmed – though
in November 1950 it was decided that the new series would not commence
until the New Year. Roy Plomley, who had been paid twenty guineas per
programme at the close of the previous run in 1946, saw his fee raised to
twenty-two guineas for the new series.

It was on 3 January 1951 that *Desert Island Discs* returned to the airwaves, where – with only the occasional interval – it has remained ever since. The first castaway of the new series was actor Eric Portman, followed by novelist Monica Dickens and comic Robertson Hare, while in March 1951 eighteen-year-old singer Petula Clark became the first teenager to appear – recalling Roy Plomley's original letter to Leslie Perowne in November 1941, when 'child prodigies' are among the target groups of castaways.

Petula Clark, aged ten, performing on the radio programme It's All Yours, *1942*

Seventeenth to be cast away in the new series – in April 1951 – was actress Margaret Lockwood, whose programme is of special interest as the first for which there is a surviving audio version. Listening to the to-and-fro between the clipped tones of the castaway and the interviewer's mellifluous inflexion, it is all too obvious that this is not a natural conversation – though some castaways are better than others at reading their lines.

The world of entertainment continued to dominate the roster in 1951, with castaways whose very names seem redolent of that postwar period: Jack Buchanan, Tommy Trinder, Stanley Holloway, Phyllis Calvert – as well as even bigger stars like Joyce Grenfell (pages 57–9) and George Formby (pages 60–2). And June 1951 brought to the island microphone the diminutive form of the singer Gracie Fields, whose interview illustrates just how far *Desert Island Discs* at the time tended to reinforce the stereotype of the castaway.

Roy Plomley's script has Gracie Fields starting with, 'Hello, everyone. This is a rum do I've got mixed up in now.' On learning from Plomley that the island is 'quite deserted, nobody about, no warmth, no comfort', she quips, 'Sounds like some of the places I used to play on tour years ago.'

Actress Sally Ann Howes (later to play Truly Scrumptious in the 1968 film *Chitty Chitty Bang Bang*) was not in the same bracket as Gracie Fields in terms of celebrity, but her edition of *Desert Island Discs* on 18 September 1951 was a notable landmark, as she was the first castaway to be formally offered the chance to take a luxury. And given such a proposition, what did she choose? Garlic.

Roy Plomley subsequently explained that – as with Joyce Grenfell and her writing materials (page 59) – earlier castaways had occasionally requested some object or other without its being specifically asked of them, but it was Sally Ann Howes's garlic which put the luxury permanently on to the checklist. As with the British Constitution, while the rules of *Desert Island Discs* are not written down, many people have a general notion of what they are. Roy Plomley himself, however, had a clear idea of what constituted a luxury:

> An inanimate object which is purely for the senses; something to look at, or touch, or taste, or smell, but which is not going to help you to live. It can be something you've seen in a museum or art gallery and couldn't ordinarily hope to own, or something frivolous, like a mink coat or a bag of golf clubs.

Over the years plenty of castaways have tried their luck with bending the luxury rule, but few have asked for an item to match that requested by Harry Secombe in 1956: a collapsible concrete model of Broadcasting House, with a cast-iron commissionaire and plastic announcers, so that he could wallow in the thought of 'all the lads working their nuts off' while he was stretched out in the sun.

Three editions after Sally Ann Howes came the beginnings of another *Desert Island Discs* fixture, when actor Henry Kendall opted to take a book to the island. He wanted the latest edition of *Who's Who in the Theatre*, and for a very good reason: 'for memories of so many hundreds of plays and people – and it's always such fun looking up to see how old your friends are'.

Furthermore: 'If it were allowed, I'd take an earlier edition of the same book as well – ten, fifteen or twenty years earlier – so that I could check up and see how old they were then.'

The choice of a book as part of the castaway's baggage was not permanently installed in the *Desert Island Discs* format until later in the 1950s, and the provision of the Bible (or equivalent for non-Christian religions) and the complete works of Shakespeare on the island became established during 1960.

First in a very select line of fictitious castaways was ventriloquist's dummy Archie Andrews,

Archie Andrews and Peter Brough, 1955

marooned with his mouthpiece Peter Brough on 5 February 1952. The
following day King George VI died, and was succeeded by his daughter
Elizabeth. The date set for her coronation, early in June the following year,
provided a topical reason for one of the records chosen by the irrepressible Max Miller in March 1953. 'The Cheeky Chappie' realized that being
marooned could absent him from Britain's big day of the year: 'I'd miss the
Coronation. So I'd have my own little Coronation celebration on the island.
And the music for it would be a little song called "The Golden Coach". It's a
song I sing as well, but I won't inflict that on you. On this record it's played by
my old friend Billy Cotton's band . . .'

Roy Plomley's own profile was steadily getting higher, and it was no
surprise that occasionally he continued to branch out from the predictable life as *Desert Island Discs* presenter. In 1952 he started chairing *One
Minute, Please*, the panel game dreamed up by Ian Messiter which was to
prove the progenitor of another permanently popular radio fixture, *Just a
Minute*. And through the 1950s he continued to turn out scripts for music
programmes like *Nights of Gladness*, *West End*, *The Jerome Kern Story*
and *Myself and Music*. But *Desert Island Discs* remained at the core of his
career.

And in this decade, as throughout its history, the programme reflected
the times. Occasionally it was directly touched by real events beyond the
desert island shores – as when in spring 1955 three transmissions were
cancelled on account of a newspaper strike. Electricians and maintenance
engineers had rejected arbitration on their demand for a pay increase of £2
18s 6d per week, and for nearly a month national papers were absent from
news-stands. As some form of compensation for the resulting information
drought, the length of radio news bulletins was increased, and *Desert Island
Discs* found itself squeezed out of the schedules – as it had been earlier, and
for much longer, when off the air for nearly a year between 25 September
1953 and 17 September 1954.

By then Roy Plomley had a settled *modus operandi* for each programme.
Once he had received the list of recordings from the castaway, he passed
that on to the producer, who in turn requested the discs from the BBC
Gramophone Library. Meanwhile he would have set about mugging up on
the character and career of the shipwreckee. 'To prepare and record the programme is usually half a day's work,' he wrote. 'If my guest is someone I have
not met before, I have a preference for the latter half of the day, so that I can
invite him to lunch first and we can get to know each other over the meal.'

For male castaways, lunch tended to be at the Garrick Club or the Savile, while female castaways were taken to the Lansdowne.

After lunch, caster and castee repaired to the BBC – usually to Egton House, next to Broadcasting House – where they would go through the musical choices in a 'listening room' and work out the order in which they were to be played. Then it was into the studio to record the dialogue – but without being able to listen to the music itself as it would occur in the programme (whereas nowadays the castaway listens to the music during the recording). At the end of the recording presenter and interviewee went off for a drink in some local pub, while the producer set about splicing in the music and editing the programme to the prescribed length.

Broadly, this routine, or a version of it, applied throughout Roy Plomley's time as presenter of *Desert Island Discs* – apart from one major change in the mid-1950s. This was the switch from scripted programmes to free conversation. Plomley was later to explain:

> I believe I became quite adept at going to my typewriter after a first meeting with someone and writing a pastiche of his or her conversational style; but this was a poor sort of second-best, and it was a great improvement when, in the mid-'fifties, the BBC started the general use of recording on tape instead of acetate discs. That meant we could stop scripting and put the series properly to work to fulfil its function of revealing character.

One programme which exemplified that idea was the interview with Spike Milligan in December 1956. Milligan was a comedic genius, and this was the heyday of the masterpiece of which he was the presiding spirit: *The Goon Show*, which had brought a new lease of life to radio comedy. But it is Milligan's darker side which comes out in his session with Roy Plomley:

> I should cherish loneliness. I can't call it loneliness, I'd call it solace; loneliness is only those people who have a vacuous mind with nothing there, they must have somebody to talk to them . . . Man is self-contained in himself; when he gets together he has a fight. By himself he can't. If he's stable he stays sane; if he's not stable he goes mad and that's just as well . . .

—a notion which anticipates Milligan's own mental health problems. (For his second appearance on the programme in 1978, see pages 189–93.)

Four days after the first Milligan interview came another of Roy Plomley's diversions from the norm, when on 14 December 1956 he presented a special programme under the title *Not Quite Desert Island Discs*, in which (according to the *Radio Times* notice), 'Roy Plomley talks to some of the people on Ascension Island in the South Atlantic and plays records they wished they had with them'. Eight Ascension Islanders were interviewed, their music choices ranging from 'A Nightingale Sang in Berkeley Square' to *The Student Prince*.

Sir Thomas Beecham, 1954

The great musician and conductor Sir Thomas Beecham had long been on the *Desert Island Discs* wishlist, and late in December 1957 the chance finally came along. Beecham was taking his Royal Philharmonic Orchestra on a tour of the Continent, and their stay in Paris offered a window of opportunity. All was in place. Plomley would travel to the French capital with Anna Instone of the Gramophone Department, who on this occasion would take the place of *Desert Island Discs*' now regular producer Monica Chapman. The programme would be recorded in Beecham's suite at the Ritz.

Then Plomley fell ill, and was advised he was too unwell to travel. On hearing this, Instone suggested that they record the programme with the interviewer in London and interviewee down the line from the BBC studio in Paris.

At the appointed hour, everything was in place – except Sir Thomas himself, who was still in his Ritz suite, deaf to Anna Instone's pleas that he go with her to the studio. The great man simply would not budge: so Instone tried a new tack, suggesting that she put the pre-arranged questions to Beecham in the hotel suite and record his answers on a small tape-recorder which she had with her, then return to London and splice in Plomley's questions. With any luck, no one would hear the joins.

Roy Plomley takes up the story:

The next morning Anna returned and we assembled for a playback of the tape. She told us that she was dubious about its quality, and, sadly, her doubts were justified. Not only had her machine not been up to the job, but Sir Thomas had been his usual volatile self and, without a studio table to keep him in place, had moved about, with resultant bumps and squeaks as well as rapid changes in voice level. Lady Beecham could also be heard moving about in the room, and occasionally throwing in a remark, and there was a steady background rumble of the traffic in the Place Vendôme.

Even so, the material supplied by the castaway was so good that Plomley and Instone were determined to make a programme of it somehow.

> Despite my protests, Anna insisted that my voice should be dubbed in place of hers and, fortified by a bottle of Krug, we spent a couple of evenings in an underground dubbing channel, where I repeated the questions one by one, and a recording engineer cut them into the tape. There were sequences in which Sir Thomas's voice was virtually unintelligible, so these were replaced by bridge passages in which I changed the subject.

The finished programme certainly offers flashes of insight into the character who early in the programme describes himself as 'a man of exceeding modesty and reticence'. Reminded of the necessity to choose eight records, he says: 'I don't know many gramophone records now other than those of my own. I've always found some difficulty listening to my records, but not half as much difficulty as I've found in listening to those of other persons.' Asked whether he could look after himself on the island, he replies: 'I should find it much more difficult now than I would have done twenty-five years ago, because I've got very much used now to married life. Prior to that, I did look after myself – with the assistance, of course, of an excellent factotum.'

When signing off, Plomley can scarcely contain himself, promising Sir Thomas that he will be rescued from the island very quickly, since 'You, sir, are one of the men who give excitement and savour to the times we live in – and there are far too few, and we want you with us.'

Doubtless the soprano Elisabeth Schwarzkopf would have considered herself another who gives excitement and savour to the times, at least if her performance when marooned in July 1958 is anything to go by.

What do her first seven musical choices have in common? They were: Brahms, 'Ihr habt nun Traurigkeit' (Soloist: Elisabeth Schwarzkopf); Johann Strauss II, *Vienna Blood Waltz* (Soloist: Elisabeth Schwarzkopf); Wagner, 'Selig wie die Sonne' (Soloist: Elisabeth Schwarzkopf); Mozart, 'An Chloe' (Soloist: Elisabeth Schwarzkopf); Hugo Wolf, 'Elfenlied' (Soloist: Elisabeth Schwarzkopf); Verdi, 'Tutto nel mondo è burla' (Soloist: Elisabeth Schwarzkopf); and Engelbert Humperdinck, *Hansel and Gretel* (Soloist: Elisabeth Schwarzkopf).

From that day on, Elisabeth Schwarzkopf has loomed large in *Desert Island Discs* folklore as That Woman Who Chose All Her Own Records. Not quite all, in fact: her final record was the Prelude to Richard Strauss's *Der*

Rosenkavalier, which needs no soloist – a choice which rather undermines Schwarzkopf's later suggestion that she had misunderstood the 'rules' of the programme.

In any case, Schwarzkopf's seven – trumped in 1979, when concert pianist Moura Lympany chose eight records of herself playing – left Plomley amused rather than appalled:

The list was a piece of colossal nerve: it obviously lacked sincerity; moreover, self-advertisement was not the object of the series. However, she presented it with such aplomb and such charm – at one moment, she murmured to me, 'I'm being outrageous' – that Monica Chapman and I let her get away with it. The programme was a great *succès de scandale*, and it is very rarely that I find myself talking about *Desert Island Discs* with people in musical circles without someone mentioning it sooner or later. But it was a gimmick that could be effective only once.

Elisabeth Schwarzkopf, 1956

The very fact that Schwarzkopf's bravado should cause such a hoo-ha is a mark of the place *Desert Island Discs* had attained in the affections of its listenership. By now, the programme was more than just a very popular radio show; it was well on its way to becoming part of the national psyche. People would imagine themselves being cast away, and which eight records they would take, and book and luxury. No less a figure than Herbert Morrison, a prominent Cabinet minister in the Attlee government, was in later life said to have carried around in his wallet his list of his eight records, just in case the call came. (Sadly, he died in 1965 without that call ever being made.)

And always at the core of the programme's appeal was variety, a quality perfectly expressed in an almost surreal instruction sent in summer 1958 from producer Monica Chapman to the BBC's Head of Gramophone Programmes: 'For Monday, 18th August, please delete Elsie and Doris Waters and insert Ludwig Koch.'

Opposite: *Joyce Grenfell performing in BBC Television's* Joyce Grenfell Requests the Pleasure, *1956*

JOYCE GRENFELL

entertainer

8 August 1951

'There is no greater fun, nothing more pleasant, than making people laugh'

There was no one like Joyce Grenfell. She poked fun at English stereotypes – most famously as the infant-school teacher who is constantly having to ask George not to do that – but her satire was affectionate and uncensorious, and, unlike most of the comedy of the 1940s and 1950s, her sketches are still funny today.

Grenfell had a particular interest in radio, and for some years in the 1930s was radio critic for the *Observer*. In 1939 she met Herbert Farjeon, radio critic and author of a revue which was playing in London at the time. When Farjeon heard her hilarious description of a Women's Institute meeting she had recently attended where the main talk had been entitled 'Useful and Acceptable Gifts', he invited her to work her account up into an act for his forthcoming production, *The Little Revue*. She did so, was very well received, and never looked back.

Little George's habits made her monologues wildly popular, but she had a wide range of other characters in addition to that benevolent teacher, and her shows included song as well as satire. In the 1940s she had started acting in films, though it was not until after her first *Desert Island Discs* appearance that she established perhaps her most famous cinematic role, as the jolly-hockey-sticks gym mistress in the *St Trinian's* films.

Roy Plomley introduces Joyce Grenfell as 'distinguished authoress, satirist, revue artist, film actress, and begger to differ' – that last phrase alluding to her regular participation in the Plomley-chaired panel discussion programme *We Beg to Differ*.

Having made it clear that she would hate being cast away, Grenfell observes, 'I'd possibly be very brave and try to be a Swiss Family Robinson girl.' On the basis that if you're playing along with a fantasy you may as well make that fantasy even more unreal, she is soon away on a highly unusual *Desert Island Discs* strategy: 'I'd explore the island, and with any luck I'd find a scissors tree – and string tree and a hammer and nails tree – and a bread-and-butter pudding tree – etc. – everything I'd want, in fact . . . I don't much like the rough life. However luxurious I got the island eventually, it would never be quite as luxurious as I'd like – or think I'd like, because I've never yet experienced that amount of luxury. The main thing would be not to let go – just in case somebody else arrived. It would be a great help if I could discover a lipstick tree – and a cold-cream tree.'

She draws the line at catching fish – 'not with my bare hands, and I wouldn't like the feel of it if I did' – and hopes there will be edible berries on the island to sustain her.

Time for the records. First comes the Adagio from Johann Sebastian Bach's Toccata and Fugue. 'He is the greatest of them all, because he's a *comforting* composer . . . All his music is based on certainty, as it were, and it always resolves itself, which gives a sense of confidence. I believe he'd last longer on an island than any of the others.'

Pablo Casals playing Dvořák's Cello Concerto will 'remind me of one of my biggest and most exciting musical experiences,' watching 'my great hero' Casals rehearsing this piece with conductor Sir Adrian Boult. 'I managed to infiltrate my way through a number of obstacles until I was within thirty feet of the soloist. To watch and hear Casals play this music was really wonderful, and I think it's a poignant and appropriate choice for a desert island – because it's one of the works Dvořák wrote on his travels, and it's full of homesickness for his native land.'

Joyce Grenfell is clearly well into the spirit of *Desert Island Discs*, and follows Rachmaninov with 'my rhythm number', Judy Garland singing 'The Trolley Song'. This will be 'ideal company for me when I'm washing up the coconut shells in the creek . . . It's a song I like to sing, so Miss Garland and I would have a lot of duets.'

Later Plomley asks why she appears regularly in revue but not in stage musicals, and gets the brisk answer: 'Frankly, I have no ambitions that way at all. I don't consider myself an actress – I'm an entertainer. And revue is the ideal form of entertainment for an entertainer, don't you think?'

But how had she started in the entertainment business? 'When I left school I studied art – not very fine art; most of the time I was designing posters. I wasn't very good at it so I started to write light verse mostly and then journalism. That was better, I thought. Then I became a radio critic for a Sunday newspaper, which led rather naturally to an interest in radio. Then I met Herbert Farjeon and went into his revue and then I began to perform sketches on the radio. And now, best of all, I'm an entertainer. And believe me, there is no greater fun, nothing more pleasant, than making people laugh.'

Plomley's enquiry whether she has 'that occupational anxiety neurosis that they might not laugh' is dismissed with 'I haven't got that at all – when they don't laugh, that makes me laugh.'

Her final choice of music is 'Nymphs and Shepherds' sung by a children's choir: 'Very English and very young,' Grenfell declares, 'and the older one gets, the more one likes the young. On the hottest afternoon this would have the coolness of morning.'

And then, before the sign-off, Joyce Grenfell puts in an extra request. 'There would be one consolation: if I had paper and pencil I would at any rate have the time and the solitude to write a play, and that's what I've always wanted to do' – an idea which brings from Plomley the witty riposte, 'Better make it two pencils in case you have time to write two.'

That request for pencil and paper in addition to the eight records must have planted an idea in Plomley's head, for the following month actress Sally Ann Howes was allowed to take garlic as her luxury, and a fresh angle was opened on the castaway's character – one often more revealing than the choice of music.

Joyce Grenfell – who returned to the island in 1971 – died on 30 November 1979, one month before she was due to be appointed DBE in the 1980 New Year's Honours.

GEORGE FORMBY

entertainer

20 November 1951

'I'd last out on grass for about three weeks
– not that I like grass, mind you'

With his gormless expression, toothy grin, inane giggle and mildly risqué songs, sung in a whiny Lancashire accent and accompanied by himself on a ukulele-banjo – described by Frank Muir as 'a dreadful instrument which combined the imprecision of the ukulele with the loudness of the banjo' – George Formby cut an unlikely figure as a screen idol. But the happy-go-lucky characters he played invariably ended up getting the posh girl, while the suave villains who had tried to thwart him got only their come-uppance.

Formby enjoyed a massive following in the 1930s and 1940s, especially during the Second World War, when films such as *Let George Do It* (1940) – at the climax of which our hero punches Hitler on the nose, and which closes on Formby's catch-phrase, 'Turned out nice again' – had a magical effect on civilian morale.

George Formby, son of a music-hall performer who used the same name (his real name was James Booth), was born in Wigan in 1904 and was blind for the first few weeks of his life, until a coughing fit on the Mersey ferry dislodged the obstructive caul which had prevented his seeing. ('Every time I sneeze now', he told the *Daily Mirror* in 1939, 'I think what a miracle it was.') He trained as a jockey – though never rode a winner

– before embarking on his own music-hall career as George Hoy (Hoy was his mother's surname). In 1924 he met and married the champion clog-dancer Beryl Ingham, the redoubtable lady who henceforth ruled his career with a rod of iron.

His first two films for Ealing Studios – *No Limit* (1935), set at the TT Races on the Isle of Man, and *Keep Your Seats, Please* (1936) – were both big hits at the box-office, and for several years Formby was the highest-paid enter-tainer in Britain. Frank Muir, himself one of the comedy greats, wrote of Formby: 'In those grim, grey days of depression and imminent war he held out a reassurance that there was a special Providence which took care of simple people, if they were kind-hearted and stayed hopeful.'

At the time he was cast away on the desert island, Formby was starring in the musical *Zip Goes a Million* in the West End – which gave the interviewer his opening:

'Always an exciting event in the West End theatre,' says Roy Plomley, 'is the advent of a new star comedian. On our desert island this evening is a brand new discovery who is packing the customers into one of the largest theatres in London – but although he's new to the West End I'm quite positive that to you and me, whose horizons are larger, he's no new discovery at all. In fact he's a very old friend of ours. It's George Formby.'

What would this castaway miss most? 'The thing that would really get me down would be not being able to get a pot of tea. I'm lost without my tea, you know.'

'That's where you'd have to be ingenious,' suggests Plomley solicitously. 'You'd have to experiment with different sorts of dried leaves, and brew up in a coconut shell.'

But Formby is adamant that being cast away would be no fun at all: 'Let's face it – I can't cook, I couldn't kill anything, I don't like fruit . . . I'd last out on grass for three weeks – not that I like grass, mind you.'

The castaway's early choice of records concentrates on the vocal: Bing Crosby ('There's nobody in the world quite like him and I don't think there ever will be'); Josef Locke ('It was in a show of mine at Blackpool in 1946 that he first got noticed'); Vera Lynn ('It's a genuine pleasure to hear the clean way she hits every note, and the way she phrases the song').

By this period Roy Plomley was tending to vary the *Desert Island Discs* pace a little more than in the earliest days, by making a fresh injec-tion of autobiographical material as the programme neared its end. On this occasion he prompts his guest to reminisce about his father. 'He didn't want me to go into the profession,' says George Formby junior of George Formby senior: '"My son's going to have a proper career," he said . . . It was soon after Dad died. I went into a music hall one evening and heard a comic using the old man's gags. I said to myself, "If anyone's entitled to those jokes, I am." I went out and bought a couple of Dad's records – including the one I'm going to play now – and I learned the songs. A week later I opened at the Hippodrome, Earlestown [near St Helens].'

'As easy as that,' observes Plomley.

'It wasn't easy, I can tell you. I had to learn the whole business from the start. I was a raw amateur. But I suppose it was in my blood, and I didn't find it as difficult as I might have done. But I took the precaution of not starting under my own name. If I was going to flop, I didn't want to drag my dad's name into it.'

By now the final minute of *Desert Island Discs* brought in that newly minted question: 'If you could take one extra object to the island, apart from something useful like a knife or a kettle, what would it be?'

Formby does not hesitate: 'My uke. I'd be lost without that. But not the uke I use nowadays. I'd take the first one I ever had – the one I serenaded Beryl with when we were courting – the one I taught myself to play on first of all. It would keep my spirits up, and I might even be able to find a monkey who liked listening to it.'

In April 1952, during the West End run of *Zip Goes a Million*, George Formby suffered a heart attack. He recovered, but thereafter was unable to work at what had been his usual pace and tended to confine himself to pantomimes and summer shows along with some television work. Not long after Beryl died in 1960, he announced his engagement to a young teacher named Pat Howson. The wedding date was set, but three weeks before they were due to be married he suffered another heart attack, and died on 6 March 1961, aged fifty-six.

The film historian Jeffrey Richards summed up a very remarkable man: 'By projecting in his thirty-year career a spirit of good nature, good humour and good will, George had been able to embody simultaneously Lancashire, the working classes, the people, and the nation, and his passing was genuinely and widely mourned.'

FRED HOYLE

astrophysicist

9 December 1954

'The combination of theory and practice is the outstanding feature of modern science'

Science has long been a powerful ingredient in the *Desert Island Discs* cocktail, with castaways such as Carl Sagan in 1981 and more recently Sir Paul Nurse (pages 418–22) or Maggie Aderin-Pocock (pages 464–7) bringing to the programme a facility for explaining complex scientific or medical issues to a far-from-specialist listenership.

Fred Hoyle, the Cambridge astrophysicist who became the first pure scientist in the programme's history, was cast away in a period when science had taken on a new and deadly urgency, for the early 1950s witnessed febrile activity in the development of nuclear weapons. The war in the Far East had been ended with atomic bombs exploding on Hiroshima and Nagasaki in August 1945, and the subsequent Cold War had seen the arms race accelerate. In July 1954, only months before Fred Hoyle's shipwreck, Winston Churchill's Cabinet had authorized manufacture of a British hydrogen bomb, and questions regarding the proper use of science, given its unimaginably destructive potential, were high on the public agenda. Moreover, Hoyle – then a fellow of St John's College, Cambridge and considered a maverick popularizer by many of his scientific colleagues – was deeply involved in the heated debate over the origins of the universe, favouring the 'Steady State' model over the newly fashionable 'Big Bang' theory.

These were issues beside which the choice of eight gramophone records and one luxury seemed, for once, less than pressing.

Roy Plomley introduces Hoyle as 'a man who's shown in his books and broadcasts an uncanny gift for making the principles of even such frightening subjects as astrophysics and cosmology understandable and fascinating even to such scientific non-starters as myself' – then quickly gets down to some of the burning questions.

Is space travel possible? 'In practice I would say no,' replies Hoyle: 'It's rather like asking the question – if someone asked a hundred years ago, "Can you make an aeroplane?", well, the answer would have been it might be possible to do so, but they couldn't have done it at that time, and that's our case today.'

First choice of music? The *Trumpet Voluntary* by Jeremiah Clarke, 'because it is an example which shows that the simple and the straightforward can be extremely effective'. Hoyle goes on: 'I think in most walks of life we tend to think that only the subtle is important and counts. Well, here, I think, is a case where that is not so.'

Plomley breezily notes that according to Hoyle's calculations the world had started several thousand million years ago – 'Perhaps about four thousand million,' clarifies the castaway – which leads to the obvious question: So when will it end? Hoyle suggests that we have 'another five thousand million', prompting the assiduous presenter to observe: 'Yes, well, let's come back to a more immediate problem, and that's the next record.'

Fred Hoyle with the model of the telescope used in A for Andromeda, *the television science fiction serial that he co-wrote in 1961*

Hoyle was born in the West Riding of Yorkshire, and had been interested in science from an early age: 'My father had a chemistry set which was probably somewhat larger than the usual boy's set, and it was on that I started . . . From then on I gradually transferred over to physics. The jump was a rather painful one but I came to understand that many problems in chemistry required physical knowledge, so I had to learn physics, and in the process of learning it I became very fascinated by physics. Exactly the same thing happened again in regard to mathematics: I found that in order to understand physics I had to know some mathematics and I began to learn the mathematics and again became very interested in that. But recently I've found the tendency to drift back to physics, but so far there hasn't been any sign of completing the circle and going still further back to chemistry.'

But what about the conflicting theories of the origins of the universe? 'What one tries to do is to work out both possibilities – work out the consequences of both possibilities and then to see whether those consequences agree with the things observed. The combination of theory and practice is the outstanding feature of modern science and it is that which gives it its tremendous impetus.'

Towards the end of the programme – between Beethoven's Piano Sonata no. 29 in B flat major and Bach's 'Sheep May Safely Graze' – Plomley pops a big question: How far are scientists responsible for 'a lot of present-day anxieties'?

Hoyle chooses his words carefully in reply: 'Science does two things: it produces dangers and it produces great opportunities. Science itself will not decide between these two extremes: it is we who have to make the decision, and I think that for the next fifty years – or the next hundred years, perhaps – we are going to go through a difficult period, and that in the distant future men will look back, and if we can go through this period successfully, will look back on it as one of the really great ages, one of the times when men achieved great things in the social sense as well as in the scientific one.'

After a life spent star-gazing, Fred Hoyle chooses the unambiguously earthbound to populate his *Desert Island Discs* luxury. He asks for 'a photograph of people at a race meeting, just to see a lot of people'.

In 1958, four years after being cast away, Fred Hoyle became Plumian Professor of Astronomy at Cambridge; and it was as Sir Fred Hoyle – he was knighted in 1972 – that he returned to *Desert Island Discs* to be interviewed by Michael Parkinson in 1986. That time around, the racing crowd was replaced as his chosen luxury by a portable telescope.

A great communicator of science and a man described by Patrick Moore as 'one of the most brilliant, colourful and influential astronomers of the twentieth century', Sir Fred Hoyle died in August 2001 at the age of eighty-six.

STIRLING MOSS

racing driver

4 June 1956

'I couldn't reach the pedals'

'Who do you think you are – Stirling Moss?' Half a century after he last put on a crash helmet in earnest, the name of Britain's iconic Formula One driver of the 1950s and 1960s can still be heard on the lips of the more traditional traffic cop after pulling over a speeding motorist.

Although he never won the Formula One Drivers' Championship – he was runner-up four years in a row between 1955 and 1958 – Stirling Moss is like Lester Piggott or Muhammad Ali: an icon whose name is simply synonymous with his sport.

Moss drove competitively from 1948 to 1962 – in all sorts of classes as well as Formula One – and was in the prime of his career when flagged down by Roy Plomley and marooned on a desert island.

Having admitted that he listens to music 'because I enjoy it, but I don't know anything about it', Moss recalls how, in the Cadet Corps at school, 'I tried to play the fife, but that was mainly because it was lighter to carry a fife than it was to carry a rifle . . . I regret to say that during band practice I stood at the back so that nobody would notice I couldn't play. And then when we were on route marches I used to blow over the hole, hoping that no note would come out at the wrong time.'

But he has taken seriously the task of selecting eight records, following three criteria: (1) 'to choose some that I wouldn't get tired of too quickly'; (2) 'ones that would perhaps bring back happy memories'; and (3) 'ones that would suit the various moods which one would obviously get into under those circumstances'.

After Dave King and 'Memories Are Made of This', Moss chooses the Joe Daniels Jazz Group playing a Charleston: 'For a long time now I've

Stirling Moss wins the Mille Miglia, 1955

had many people trying to teach me, and each time I thought I'd got the hang of it, but somehow when the music starts I've never quite done it. And I thought that if I could play it over and over and over again I might be able to catch hold of the way of doing it, and also improvise my own steps.'

He relates that he started driving at the age of six: 'My father put the seat right back in the car and I sat in front of him and worked the steering wheel and twiddled around with the gear lever, but I couldn't reach the pedals.' When he was eleven he started driving a car round the family farm. 'Then when I was sixteen, when you're allowed to have a three-wheeled car for the road, that's when I bought that. And then at seventeen I started racing.'

A year before being cast away, Moss had enjoyed one of his greatest moments when winning the Mille Miglia in Italy: 'It's a race where you do just one lap, which is a thousand miles, and the main trouble is, of course, that you can't know the road – not unless you live in Italy, anyway – and the strain is very great because of the mental strain [*sic*]. You come over the brow of a hill, or round a corner, and you've no idea where it goes.'

PLOMLEY: What was your average speed?

Moss: About ninety-eight miles an hour.

PLOMLEY: Ninety-eight miles an hour, on a unknown road, for a thousand miles?

Moss: Yes – I was mad!

PLOMLEY: And the roads, of course, are closed.

Moss: Yes they are: they're sort of closed. They try to close them, but of course people do have to move round a bit . . .

The choice of a luxury for Stirling Moss poses a problem. He wants a luxury yacht – 'But I suppose you'd say I'd sail away on it.'

'I certainly would,' responds the presenter, ever the stickler for the rules. So the castaway changes tack spectacularly: 'Well, if I couldn't have a yacht I think I'd like dozens of different types and makes of hair restorer to get to work on my scalp and see what would happen. I'd most likely come back bald as a badger [*sic*] but suntanned at least.'

And while Roy Plomley has the nation's most famous driver with him, what is the Stirling Moss view of the standard of driving in Britain?

The answer: drivers should consider how what they are doing looks to other people: 'If you're going to make a right turn in a main road, then get your car into the middle of the road, not to the left and then swing across. And also, if you're coming down to join a major road from a small one, don't come screaming down and then stand on the brakes, because somebody coming along that major road may panic and do the same thing and lose control. And when there's a bus pulled up, it's pretty obvious, I think, that people are likely to go round the front just as much as round the back. So I think if you can project yourself into other people's cars or positions, that would help an awful lot.'

Eartha Kitt
'Let's Do It'

'The greatest artist I've ever seen'

In 1962 Stirling Moss lay in a coma for a month after a terrible crash in the Glover Trophy at Goodwood. He eventually recovered from his injuries, but the following year announced his retirement from Formula One – though he continued to compete in the occasional race at a lesser level, including events for historic cars. It was not until summer 2011 that, during the qualifying session for the Le Mans Legends race, he announced his complete retirement from competitive driving – at the age of eighty.

Stirling Moss was voted BBC Sports Personality of the Year in 1961, and knighted in the New Year Honours in 2000. According to the *Independent*, after receiving his knighthood from the Prince of Wales at Buckingham Palace, he was driving away when a palace guard jokingly demanded, 'Who do you think you are – Stirling Moss?', to which Moss replied, 'Sir Stirling, actually.'

EARTHA KITT

singer and actress

18 June 1956

'I took advantage of situations when they presented themselves'

It is a measure of the extra-special quality of Eartha Kitt that you simply cannot imagine her signature songs 'Just an Old-Fashioned Girl' or 'Santa Baby' being performed adequately by anyone else. When she appeared on *Desert Island Discs* in June 1956 those songs were already inextricably linked with her extraordinary purring voice, and she had a growing reputation as an actress on stage and screen.

Born in South Carolina, Kitt had been given her big break by Orson Welles in 1950, when he had cast her as Helen of Troy in his Broadway production of *Dr Faustus*. Since then she had built a career in film and television, while also returning to Broadway in 1954 in *Mrs Patterson*.

Introducing Eartha Kitt as a 'fascinating singer and fascinating person', Roy Plomley observes that she is not a stranger to the island, as 'your voice has echoed on it many times because numbers of people have chosen your records to make exile a little easier for them'. (Plomley knew whereof he spoke. Only a fortnight earlier, Stirling Moss had chosen her singing 'Let's Do It', and three other castaways in 1956 alone had asked for Kitt records: magician David Nixon, who wanted

'The Day that the Circus Left Town', actress Vanessa Lee – 'Bal, Petit Bal' – and actor John Neville – 'Lovin' Spree'.)

After opening her musical choices with a Yoruba song – 'because I think that being on an island, one automatically thinks of primitive things' – Kitt returns to more familiar ground with Ella Fitzgerald: 'I think I chose Ella because she's more or less the mother of the inventive modern musical world . . . She always makes

Eartha Kitt with members of the Katherine Dunham Company, c.1945

it seem right: whether you like that phase of the jazz world or not, it seems right on Ella Fitzgerald.'

She skips over a tough childhood – 'we were tenant farmers in the South and my parents were having a pretty rough time of it with their little farm crops' – and, declaring that 'all the important steps in my career have been mainly because I took advantage of situations when they presented them-selves,' moves on to New York City:

'I was in New York standing on the street corner, waiting to decide with a girl friend of mine whether I should take the bus home or take a train home with my dime, or whether I should walk home and buy peanuts or something – when out of nowhere came a girl who reminded me of myself when I'd first come up from the South to New York. She looked as though she was abso-lutely lost, and of course, as fate would have it her eye caught mine, and she came up to me and asked me directions to the Max Factor make-up shop. I took her there, and in the conversation she told me that she was a Katherine Dunham dancer, and I'd just read about Katherine Dunham the previous day, and so out of curiosity I said I would like to meet her, so she took me down to the school, and when we got there, there was an auditioning session going on, and as a joke someone dared me – you know how kids are with dares – and I joined the class. I knew nothing about dancing whatsoever, but as a childish prank, you know, I joined the class, and I won a full scholarship.'

That was in 1943. Five years later, having moved on from the Katherine Dunham company, she was in Paris. 'I went to a little cabaret there, and that's where Orson Welles saw me' – and before she knew it, she was Helen of Troy to Welles's Dr Faustus.

One of Eartha Kitt's more intriguing record choices is Burl Ives singing 'The Woman and the Chivalrous Shark', the tale of a shark of such refined manners that he will attack neither women nor children. 'If you suddenly decided to swim for the next shore,' she explains, 'you would like to have the feeling that no sharks would molest you.'

Just when Roy Plomley must have been thinking that it was safe to guide the programme towards its conclusion, Kitt turns out to be yet another castaway who becomes awkward over the choice of luxury. At first all seems simple enough. Miss Kitt would like a book: the writings of Emerson, 'Because I think that Emerson in his works teaches you how to find serenity in communicating with nature – and of course being on a desert island, the only thing one can do in communication is to communicate with nature.'

Plomley promises her 'the finest edition of the collected works of Ralph Waldo Emerson that we can find', and then oversteps the bounds of generosity: 'As you've chosen a book that you might possibly have under your arm when you're swimming ashore, we'll give you something else as well – another luxury.'

In that case, says the castaway, she'll have a diamond.

'A diamond?'

'Yes.'

'To wear?'

'No, not to wear, but I could use it to give SOSes, you see.'

'Miss Kitt, I think you're cheating. You shall have the works of Emerson, but I'm not at all sure about that diamond . . . '

Through the late 1950s Eartha Kitt worked mainly in films – notably *St Louis Blues* (1958) – and in the 1960s moved into television as well, while also continuing her singing career. A long-time activist, she suffered a dip in popularity in 1968 after making critical comments about the Vietnam War at a White House lunch, and she spent a good deal of the next few years away from the USA before returning to Broadway in 1978 in *Timbuktu!*. That performance won her a Tony Award as best actress – and she won another Tony for *The Wild Party* in 2000. In later years she undertook a great deal of fund-raising on behalf of gay rights.

The inimitable Eartha Kitt died on Christmas Day 2008 at the age of eighty-one.

....

📖 *Who's Who in the Theatre*

....

♡ **Typewriter, ribbons
and paper**

ROY PLOMLEY

broadcaster

12 May 1958

'If you want fresh water you cut a hole in
a dead fish and you get fresh water'

By now Roy Plomley needs absolutely no introduction. But it is interesting to assess how much,
when he is the castaway rather than the caster, the
programme tells us about the man.

The tables had been turned once before, in the very
first run of the series back in 1942, when Plomley's
inquisitor had been Leslie Perowne, the BBC executive to whom he had pitched the *Desert Island Discs*
idea. Second time round the interviewer was Eamonn
Andrews, the Irish broadcaster so famous and so familiar that he would later be affectionately lampooned as
Seamus Android in *Round the Horne*, most durable of
all 1960s radio comedy shows.

On television, Andrews had been chairing the panel
game *What's My Line?* since 1951 and presenting *This
Is Your Life* since 1955, the same year that he became
anchor of the Saturday-afternoon radio programme
Sports Report.

Plomley's first musical choice is the opening song from
a musical show: 'I don't take it because of that show,
but simply for opening choruses from the theatre in
general. On the island about half-past seven or eight
o'clock I should think of the lights up in Shaftesbury

Avenue – the actors making up, the people flocking in, and that's when I'd like to play this opening chorus from *Kiss Me Kate* – "Another Op'nin', Another Show".'

Where did his theatrical interests come from?

'I can't explain it, but as a small child I had a tremendous enthusiasm for the theatre. I used to get a thrill out of looking at a theatre poster. I used to read all the notices. I knew what was on and where, and who was in it. I never saw them, of course. I don't know where it came from. It's not in the family. My mother's family are farmers, [so theirs were] agricultural interests; my father's family have always been in some form of medicine – doctors, dentists, veterinary surgeons. My father was a chemist. But I just had this tremendous enthusiasm for the theatre. When I left school I had no idea what I wanted to be. I remember my father gave me a book called *Careers for Boys*, and I didn't even read it. I saw that the theatre wasn't mentioned, and all the other occupations – well, one was as good as another.'

Bob Hope
and Shirley Ross
'Thanks for the Memory'

'I think it's got the state of mind of the late Thirties'

As part of his dogged efforts to pursue an acting career, he tried singing in the street: 'I didn't dare do it in London. I got a cheap day return to Guildford, sang up and down the High Street. And then in the crowd I saw someone I'd been at school with, and lost my nerve.'

On his desert island, one of his record choices is of particular interest: 'There are going to be times on this island when life is going to be real and earnest. I think I should like some music to accompany my devotions and contemplations. My personal religious philosophy is a bit of a mixture. I don't belong to any established church, although I was brought up in the Church of England. I haven't chosen any Church of England music because I'm not very fond of boys' voices – I think there's a coldness about it. So I've chosen here a piece of the Mass sung by the choir of the Russian Orthodox Cathedral in Paris. It's the Eucharist Canon by Arkhangelsky, and it's a glorious and moving sound – and there are women's voices instead of boys.'

How would he, who has sent so many others to the desert island, survive on it himself? 'I've probably got more theoretical knowledge about how to manage on a desert island than anyone in this country, because I've heard a lot of the best brains in Britain tell me about it. I've picked up all sorts of tips – like, if you want fresh water you cut a hole in a dead fish and you get fresh water.'

What would he be glad to miss? 'Smoke, fumes, fog, all the noxious vapours.'

Luxury? 'When I'm working at home at my desk, I want to go out in the garden and build sheds or dig. Perhaps on the island when I'm building things and digging all day long I shall want to go and work at my desk – so can I have a typist's desk with the typewriter sunk into it, and perhaps in the drawers some paper and a spare ribbon or two?' Better than that, says Eamonn Andrews: he can have 'an endless supply of ribbons'.

And the book? *Who's Who in the Theatre*: 'Nearly two thousand pages of facts and figures, thousands of performances and hundreds of productions to think about – I think I'd get an awful lot of pleasure out of that.'

Absent from Roy Plomley's list of records is any pop music of the time. Reflecting later on the approaches of different castaways to the task of their music selection, he left little doubt as to his view regarding the suitability of pop:

> Some, with one-track enthusiasm, choose mainly the work of an especially favoured composer; others give themselves an abbreviated history of music by choosing chronologically from Palestrina to Stockhausen. There are those, too, who choose pop, although one can imagine the despair of a castaway who is isolated for years with nothing but the bashing of electric guitars and the frenzied shouting of tin-eared vocalists who, by the time he is rescued, are probably out of the music business and back on their milk rounds. Pop music as a cheerful noise is fine, but for a lifetime's listening – no!

If the phrase 'back on their milk rounds' does little to dilute the view held in some quarters that Plomley was a musical snob, his own choices on his second casting away show that he was far from an elitist.

As for Eamonn Andrews (*right*), he returned to *Desert Island Discs* as castaway a few months later in August 1958, when the natural order was restored and it was Roy Plomley again calling the shots. The Andrews list included Ella Fitzgerald, Jack Buchanan, Puccini and César Franck, and his luxury was a pair of field glasses.

*Opposite: Paul Robeson
addresses an anti-H-bomb rally
in Trafalgar Square, 1959*

PAUL ROBESON

actor and singer

1 December 1958

**'I was brought up with all these beautiful melodies,
they were part of my whole life'**

You would get little hint from reading the transcript of his *Desert Island Discs* interview (there is no audio record of this edition) that 1958 was a very significant year in the life of Paul Robeson. A world-famous actor, he also had a towering reputation as a singer, with one of the most immediately recognizable voices on the planet – described by Alexander Woollcott as 'the best musical instrument wrought by nature in our time.'

Born in New Jersey, Robeson had first acted in Britain in 1922, and the opening night of the Jerome Kern musical *Show Boat* in London in 1928 provided one of the great theatrical moments when he sang 'Ol' Man River' in that astonishing bass voice.

But the other side of the Paul Robeson story was his lifelong activism against injustice, with regard to civil rights issues and much more, which was constantly getting him into trouble with the US authorities. In 1950 his passport was confiscated by the State Department, on the basis that confining his movements to the USA – even Mexico and Canada were out of bounds – would restrict his freedom of expression to the point where he would gradually disappear from the international stage; and in 1956, having declined more than once to state whether he was or ever had been a Communist,

Robeson with Mary Ure in rehearsals for Othello, *1959*

he was summoned before the House Committee on Un-American Activities and subsequently blacklisted. No official sanction, however, could prevent his presence continuing to be felt wherever an appropriate cause was being fought for. He maintained strong British connections – he had lived in London for much of the 1930s – and recordings of his voice were often played at political gatherings in the 1950s. In 1957 he was invited by Welsh miners to be a guest at the Eisteddfod Musical Festival, but an appeal for the return of his passport was turned down by the US Supreme Court – so he sang directly to the assembled throng in Wales by means of the recently installed transatlantic telephone cable. The following year his passport was finally restored to him, and he lost little time in making for London – where, a few weeks after his arrival, the sixty-year-old Robeson was transported to that fictitious realm which requires no passport to enter.

Having welcomed 'a great artist whose public is a world-wide one', and confirmed that the castaway has a large collection of records and a wide repertoire of languages, Roy Plomley switches attention to the music choices. First up is the spiritual 'Steal Away', sung by Robeson himself, accompanied by his long-time friend and pianist Lawrence Brown: the castaway explains the choice as being 'not to hear myself so much as because I want to carry with me the memory of these years with a great musician'.

Having heard Bessie Smith singing 'After You've Gone' – 'a modern melody which Bessie makes into one of the traditional blues' – it's time for some background. Paul Robeson was born in 1898, the son of a minister in the Presbyterian Church ('He had been born a slave about 1843 – escaped'), and 'I was brought up with all these beautiful melodies, they were part of my whole life'. A noted sportsman at college, he took his first acting job to help finance his law studies – then decided that the stage was more to his liking than the legal profession. In 1925 he and Lawrence Brown gave their first concert of spirituals, which led to his being cast three years later in *Show*

Boat at the Theatre Royal, Drury Lane: 'I doubt if any artist in theatrical history has made such a success as you did with "Ol' Man River" that night,' says Plomley. In 1930 Robeson played Othello in London – 'I missed it,' declares Plomley, 'but it's still being talked about.'

And so the programme progresses amiably, the final record choice being Feodor Chaliapin – 'the greatest actor and singer I ever heard' – singing from *Boris Godunov*. This gets Robeson musing about how, looking at his eight records as a whole, 'the music and speech, the great poetic speech of people, sort of run into one another'. Different sorts and modes of music link with other types: 'The music of the Hebraic church of the synagogue and the music of the Middle East and the music of the Abyssinians and the Sudanese – this to me is one of the great links of all music and of all peoples behind all the choice of records – the music is the same, the people must be also very much the same.'

A similar passion informs Robeson's choice of luxury: 'I'm going to choose a head that I have from the Benin of Africa, one of the great African cultures, of Nigeria, which influenced the painting of Picasso and of Modigliani, many of the great sculptors and artists and painters in Europe – a head, a beautiful head of the Benin, of my African forefathers, which would always be with me as a sign of the great contributions to the culture of the world by my own folk.'

Benin Early Middle Period bronze head

In 1959 Paul Robeson played Othello at Stratford, and for many years after continued to mix political activism – he regularly appeared at peace rallies and other political events – with performing, undertaking extensive tours in Europe, the Soviet Union and Australasia. After several episodes of ill-health in the 1960s he went into semi-retirement back in the USA, and died in Philadelphia in January 1976.

A mark of just how far there was to go in combating racism and racial stereotyping in the late 1950s is that, by a quirk of *Desert Island Discs* scheduling, the castaway immediately preceding Paul Robeson on to the island was the music hall entertainer G. H. Elliott, who billed himself as 'The Chocolate-Coloured Coon'.

ALFRED HITCHCOCK

film director

19 October 1959

'I'm planning a psychological film'

A lfred Hitchcock was one of those rare artists who give their name to a particular genre of their chosen art. As with a Feydeau farce or a Henry Moore sculpture, the character and nature of a quintessential Alfred Hitchcock movie needed no explanation. It would be built around suspense – the exquisite dramatic power of suggesting what might happen, rather than showing what did.

Alfred Hitchcock was born in Leytonstone, Essex, in 1899. He made his way into film in the 1920s: among the first movies he directed was *The Lodger* (1926), in which the lead role was played by fellow castaway Ivor Novello (see page 27), and his *Blackmail* (1929) was the first British-made sound movie. Classics like *The Lady Vanishes* and *The Thirty-Nine Steps* followed in the 1930s, and Hitchcock fans who tuned in to the Home Service to listen to their hero on that October Monday in 1959 would also have seen the master director at his best in such films as *Rebecca* (1940), *Suspicion* (1941), *Saboteur* (1942) and – one of his greatest works – *Shadow of a Doubt* (1943).

The 1950s had been a golden period for Hitchcock. *Strangers on a Train* was released in 1951, to be followed in short order by a roll-call of similarly taut and engrossing films: *I Confess* (1952), *Dial M for Murder*

(1953), *Rear Window* (1955), *To Catch a Thief* (1955), *The Man Who Knew Too Much* (1956) and *Vertigo* (1958).

When cast away by Roy Plomley, Alfred Hitchcock was an undisputed master of his trade – and the best was shortly to come.

It is obvious how to introduce the desert island context: 'On our desert island this week', says Roy Plomley, 'is one of the world's top film directors. In a long career he's gained an almost legendary reputation as a master of suspense – he's chilled the blood of all of us on many occasions. Here is Alfred Hitchcock. Mr Hitchcock, you're used to putting the heroes of your pictures in very tight corners – you're now in one yourself. How do you think you'd stand up to the complete solitude and loneliness?'

The button pressed, Hitchcock – never a diffident speaker – is off: 'Not at all well. As a matter of fact, it's rather coincidental you should bring this thing up because I have actually expressed my own feelings in a picture I've just finished, called *North by Northwest*, where I place Cary Grant in a spot – that we know he's going to be shot. And where do I put him? Not at the corner of a dark alley, with the cobblestones washed by recent rains, under a street lamp, but in a cross-roads of the loneliest part of the American desert landscape – not a house, not a soul in sight for miles anywhere, and you do get then the picture of complete loneliness . . . And you know that somewhere from out of this vast space danger is coming, but you don't know from where it's coming. And maybe I'd feel that a bit myself when one is lonely. I'm not at all keen on loneliness. Period.'

As is now Roy Plomley's custom, in the wake of the second record choice comes the request for something about background and early career. Hitchcock does not disappoint:

'Apart from being a devotee of the theatre and the concert, of course, films also had an important part in one's amusements. But my interest became a little deeper – beyond, shall we say, the fan magazine stage – I think my reading at that time where films were concerned was the trade magazines, so I really got deeply interested in pictures . . .

North by Northwest: *Cary Grant pursued, 1959*

'My first job was a technical engineering job. I had studied engineering and I was in the estimating department of a cable company, and eventually I gravitated to the advertising department where, having taken a course on art in the University of London, I was able to express myself there. And through that I went into the designing of what were, in those days of silent films, the "art titles" . . .

'They are rather naïve affairs, when I look back on them. The title would say, "John was leading a very fast life", and I would draw a candle with the flame at both ends underneath.'

Hitchcock relates how he had begun to learn that 'an audience is the same the world over, and not to make films for one audience, but to make them for a world audience'.

Which, of all his films, is his favourite to date? *Shadow of a Doubt*, 'because this film combined many elements: the element of suspense, the element of the local atmosphere of a small town, and quite an amount of character'.

After his fourth record – the Siegfried horn-call – Alfred Hitchcock mentions his current project: 'I'm planning a psychological film. It's called *Psycho*, and is in the nature, shall we say, of a rather gentle horror picture.'

'Splendid!' is Roy Plomley's reaction – though plenty of alternative adjectives have been used over the years by those first encountering Alfred Hitchcock's masterpiece.

Hitchcock's chosen book is Mrs Beeton's *Household Management* ('because not only does it have all the recipes for food and how to make sausages, but how to fold napkins – all that kind of thing'); and his luxury will be the Continental railway timetable – 'which will give me all the journeys I would like to take'.

Alfred Hitchcock was an ideal castaway: interesting, articulate and fully locked into the desert island fantasy, but enough of his own man to feel comfortable delivering the occasional monologue.

North by Northwest **was released a month after Hitchcock's** *Desert Island Discs* **appearance, and** *Psycho,* **that 'rather gentle horror picture' to which he refers, came to define Alfred Hitchcock's directing career: while its popularity was rivalled by later films such as** *The Birds* **(1963),** *Marnie* **(1964),** *Torn Curtain* **(1966) and** *Frenzy* **(1972),** *Psycho* **occupies a place all its own in filmgoers' affections.**

Alfred Hitchcock – one of the all-time greats of the cinema – died in 1980.

JOAN SUTHERLAND

soprano

23 November 1959

'I can make a fire and boil a billy,
and I think I'd survive'

Joan Sutherland was at the height of her considerable powers when cast away on the desert island. Just turned thirty-three and acclaimed the world over as possessing one of the greatest voices in opera history, she was still basking in the triumph of her performance in *Lucia di Lammermoor* earlier that year: directed by Franco Zeffirelli at the Royal Opera House, Covent Garden, her riveting rendition of the title role had taken her already high reputation to a fresh level. In 1960, the year after she was marooned, she would earn from the audience at La Fenice in Venice the soubriquet 'La Stupenda', which would remain attached to her for the rest of her life.

Born in 1926 in a Sydney suburb, she had made her concert debut at the age of twenty before moving to London to study at the Royal College of Music, first singing at Covent Garden in October 1952 – since when a succession of outstanding performances in the world's great opera houses had steadily enhanced her stature.

Roy Plomley starts by lobbing his castaway an easy one: 'Miss Sutherland, you're an Australian, aren't you?' Indeed she is, which leads the presenter to wonder why

Joan Sutherland on stage, January 1960

Australia, with its small population, should produce so many fine singers. Is it the climate?

'I should say that climate has a great deal to do with it,' says the castaway. 'I come from the eastern part of Australia where the climate's very like that of Italy, and I guess that that is some of the reason for the singing – and I also feel that there's a great deal more opportunity given to young artists in Australia than perhaps here.'

What was her early experience of music?

'The first music I heard would be the singing of my mother. She was a mezzo-soprano, and although she never made a career in Australia at all, never really sang professionally to any extent, she nevertheless had a very fine voice – and I think would have been one of the great singers of her day, had she pursued her career to the extent that I have . . . She used to practise around the house, and I used to imitate her.'

Sutherland's 'first engagement of any real merit' was a concert performance of Purcell's *Dido and Aeneas* in Sydney, given while she still had a day job as a secretary: 'Very shortly it came to the point where I had to choose between one or the other, and I decided that I might as well try the singing first. I could always go back to secretarial work if necessary.'

In London, an early Covent Garden opportunity was as Clotilde in Bellini's *Norma* in 1952, with Maria Callas and Ebe Stignani in the leading roles: 'I was a terrified beginner, standing backstage listening to the wonderful ovation that they received, and I was wondering whether that could happen to me ever. I didn't really think it could.'

Plomley mentions Joan Sutherland's seven years of Covent Garden performances and asks, 'Is there any one person that you feel inspired you or helped you in your work more than anyone else?'

'Yes, I do,' replies Sutherland, 'my husband', the conductor and pianist Richard Bonynge. 'We always work together on my roles, and he has this great love of the early nineteenth-century operas and convinced me that they were the roles I should sing.'

After playing a record of herself singing the 'mad scene' from *Lucia di Lammermoor* – 'I expect that I must have one recording of my own' – she is asked to address the matter of what sort of castaway she will make. 'I'm not terribly fond of camping,' comes the pessimistic reply: 'When I go on holiday I like to be looked after. I don't like to have to do things for myself, but being Australian, I can make a fire and boil a billy, and I think I'd survive.'

Pausing only to observe that 'like almost all Australians, you'd obviously be a very efficient castaway', Plomley establishes that her record of records would be Rosa Ponselle and Marion Telva singing the duet from *Norma* ('then at least I'd have two voices'); that her luxury would be a bed ('on the desert island there'd be no telephones, and I'd be able to indulge in lying in bed in the morning, which I can't do very often now'); and that her book would be the memoirs of 'the Swedish Nightingale', Jenny Lind.

Bellini

'Mira, O Norma'

Soloists: Rosa Ponselle and Marion Telva

'I think Ponselle has the most beautiful voice that I have ever heard'

Joan Sutherland made her US debut at the Dallas Opera in 1960 and first performed at the Metropolitan Opera in New York the following year. She remained one of the world's great sopranos until her voice started to decline in the late 1970s. Her last public appearance was in a gala performance of *Die Fledermaus* at Covent Garden on New Year's Eve 1990, where she was joined by Luciano Pavarotti (see pages 174–7) and Marilyn Horne.

Awarded the DBE in 1979, Dame Joan Sutherland died in October 2010 at the age of eighty-three.

1960s

SOCIAL REFORM, BEHAVIOUR, class, culture, science, politics, sport – wherever you looked, the 1960s was a decade of comprehensive upheaval.

In its very first year Mervyn Griffith-Jones QC could ask the jury at the *Lady Chatterley's Lover* trial whether D. H. Lawrence's novel was 'a book that you would even wish your wife or your servants to read'. But shortly afterwards there began a succession of sweeping social reforms in the United Kingdom which would consign such lofty attitudes to the dustbin of anachronisms: the end of capital punishment; reform of the laws on abortion and divorce; contraceptive advice and the Pill on the National Health Service; and the decriminalization of homosexual acts between consenting adults.

In 1961 John F. Kennedy became the youngest ever US President – succeeding the then oldest, Dwight D. Eisenhower – underlining the new prominence of youth. In fashion, with designers like Mary Quant, models like Twiggy, the Carnaby Street culture and that emblem of the decade, the mini-skirt, and in politics – most graphically in the events of 1968 in Paris and the anti-war demonstrations at the US embassy in London – young people were making their voices heard.

Nowhere was the sense of clearing out the old and bringing in the new sharper than in popular music. As the decade opened Michael Holliday and Anthony Newley topped the charts, with just a hint of what was to come in the early career of Cliff Richard; but the floodgates opened when in January 1963 the single 'Please Please Me' by a hitherto little-known Liverpool quartet named The Beatles was released. It was soon climbing the charts, to be followed in April by 'From Me to You' and in August by 'She Loves You', and the group's second album *With The Beatles* was released in November. Further albums through the 1960s, culminating in *Sergeant Pepper's Lonely Hearts Club Band* in 1967, made the Beatles a phenomenon of pop music. Just one of the Fab Four was to be cast away on the island – Paul McCartney in 1982 (see pages 239–43) – but the group's manager Brian Epstein was marooned in 1964 and producer George Martin in 1982 and 1995.

In the wake of John, Paul, George and Ringo came a surge of other musicians who defined the 1960s: the Rolling Stones (who finally made the castaways' list when Charlie Watts was interviewed by Sue Lawley in 2001: he revealed that he had eighteen dogs, plus various items of clothing which had belonged to the late Duke of Windsor); Bob Dylan, whose songs more than anyone else's painted the portrait of the decade, and who drew a crowd of 150,000 to the Isle of Wight festival in August 1969; Tom Jones and Joe Cocker; the Animals, Kinks, Hollies, Bee Gees, etc. etc. (The Beverley Sisters, marooned in January 1961, were the first triple castaways.)

The insatiable appetite for pop music, at a time when television broadcasting was coming into its own, led to the start of programmes like *Ready, Steady, Go!* in 1963 and *Top of the Pops* in 1964. That rapid increase in television ownership had a major effect on sport, too. Take horseracing. In the mid-1960s the great Irish steeplechaser Arkle became the first equine superstar of the television age, his doting public able to watch him in action in all his big races. The Grand National was first televised in 1960, with Peter O'Sullevan (see pages 393–7) the principal commentator – a television personality rarely seen on screen but instantly recognizable by his voice. Sports commentators Dan Maskell, Kenneth Wolstenholme and Cliff Morgan were all cast away in the 1960s. The decade also produced human superstars of sport, whose demeanour on the field and off

DJ Jimmy Savile presenting the first edition of Top of the Pops, *January 1964*

mirrored the loosening of the stays in wider society – notably the mercurial footballer George Best, who seemed to bring the spirit of the 1960s with him on to the pitch. His domination of the game when Manchester United won their first European Cup in 1968 epitomized a new sporting mood.

And the greatest domestic sporting occasion of the 1960s found its place on the desert island. In the very last programme of the decade, Tommy Steele took as his record of records the commentators' summing up after the England football team (one of whom, Jackie Charlton, was cast away in 1972) had beaten West Germany to win the 1966 World Cup.

England, captained by Bobby Moore, wins the World Cup, 1966

As broadcasting changed, so did audience habits. No longer would the whole family gather round the wireless set: instead, they would settle in front of the 'goggle box' to be enthralled by the doings of Ena Sharples or Len Fairclough. Listening to the radio was becoming much more of a solitary activity – especially as the number of cars with built-in radio was steadily increasing. And sometimes audience change ran ahead of the broadcasters: BBC resistance to widening its demographic in the early 1960s led in 1964 to the beginnings of 'pirate radio', which broadcast non-stop pop music from ships anchored off the English coast. The BBC responded by starting its own dedicated pop station in September 1967, naming it Radio 1. At the same time, the Light Programme became Radio 2, the Third Programme was renamed Radio 3, and the Home Service was henceforth Radio 4.

While scientific advances were driving change in television and radio – for example, the advent of transistors, which meant that it was no longer necessary to wait while valves in the radio set warmed up – breakthroughs on a much larger scale were grabbing public attention, above all, the advent of space travel. In 1961 Yuri Gagarin returned safely to Earth, but the race to land a man on the moon was won by the USA when Neil Armstrong took his one small step in 1969. (On

Walking on the moon, 1969

his co-moonwalker Buzz Aldrin, see pages 300–1.) In medicine, the wide availability of the contraceptive pill brought its own revolution, and the first heart transplant was performed in 1967 by Dr Christiaan Barnard (cast away in 1976 – see pages 178–81).

Looming in the background throughout the 1960s was the menace of the Cold War. Just imagine what it must have been like listening to the one o'clock news on the Home Service, and then the *Desert Island Discs* programme which followed immediately afterwards, on Monday, 22 October 1962.

The news bulletin led with coverage of the latest blood-chilling developments in the rapidly deepening Cuban Missile Crisis, informing listeners that the previous day President Kennedy had been discussing with his top advisers the USA's two main options: make an air strike against the Soviet missile bases on Cuba, and risk nuclear retaliation; or put in place a naval blockade to prevent weapons-making materials being delivered to the island, and again risk nuclear retaliation. With the world teetering on the brink of nuclear war – closer to the edge than at any time before or since – finding out which eight gramophone records Norman Tucker, director of opera at Sadler's Wells, would take to the desert island was of somewhat limited interest. Never mind getting to the repeat of the programme later in the week – that Monday afternoon it was more a matter of whether listeners would make it as far as the eighth record before the four-minute warning sounded.

Desert Island Discs itself trembled occasionally as the times changed. As the 46-year-old Roy Plomley talks to the 20-year-old Cliff Richard in October

1960, the mutual incomprehension across the 'generation gap' (itself a new concept) is palpable: 'When you sing, Cliff, you perform these rather frenzied movements . . .' (see page 107).

But the format of the programme changed very little in the 1960s. The programme was broadcast every week – usually at Monday lunchtime – with the occasional extra edition slipped in, and repeated most weeks: in all, 529 new editions were broadcast in the 1960s, and the interview with Viscount Montgomery in December 1969 (see pages 141–5) celebrated the one-thousandth in the programme's history.

By the early 1960s *Desert Island Discs* was a part of Britain's national culture, and plenty of people went a step further than simply indulging in the fantasy of which records they would take: they wrote to the BBC offering themselves as castaways. Thus in May 1962 producer Monica Chapman received a letter from a gentleman in Lincoln: 'I listen regularly to *Desert Island Discs*, and although I feel fairly sure you would not think me sufficiently illustrious to appear on your programme, I am sending you a rough autobiography just in case the idea might be thought worth while.'

The correspondent, who assured Chapman that 'I have a very wide knowledge of classical music', is a surgeon; not only that, he has travelled in eighty countries: 'I have lived among the Aboriginals of Australia, with the Lapps in the Arctic and with the Arab camel men of Southern Tunisia.' Summarizing his case, the doctor acknowledged the great stumbling block: 'By and large I think therefore that my knowledge and appreciation of music and a fairly interesting life might qualify me for this programme, except that of course I am quite unknown, and I realize you prefer celebrities.' There's the rub. But he received a charming reply from Monica Chapman, who promised him, 'I have added your name to our long list of possible castaways.'

The blunt truth was that *Desert Island Discs* had no need of someone 'quite unknown', for through the 1960s the queue of castaways was becoming ever more stellar,

Marty Wilde and friends, 1960

and continued to reflect the preoccupations of the age. The likes of Marty Wilde, Cliff Richard (see pages 104–8) and Adam Faith were probably not Roy Plomley's ideal castaways, but it was important for the programme to cover its audience's current interests. Professor A. C. B. Lovell, the nation's top star-gazer by dint of his work at Jodrell Bank, represented the wondrous scientific advances which were driving the ambition to get to the moon. Footballer Danny Blanchflower was cast away at the start of the 1960–1 season which would famously end with his Tottenham Hotspur team pulling off the then very rare achievement of winning the First Division and FA Cup, while in 1963 the Australian legend Scobie Breasley was the first jockey to be cast away. In 1969 Lillian Board, runner-up in the women's 400 metres at the previous year's Olympics, arrived at the island. 'She glowed with life,' wrote Roy Plomley, 'and was the friendliest and most natural of people – and scarcely six months later she had succumbed to cancer.' International stars of stage and screen, including significantly more from the USA, were regularly washed ashore Among them were Julie Andrews, Marlene Dietrich (pages 120–3), Charlton Heston, Hermione Gingold and Bob Hope, who told Roy Plomley that he could look after himself on the island, as 'Bing claims I can do spear fishing with my nose.' One 1960s castaway who certainly would not cope well was the legendary Tallulah Bankhead. When in December 1964 Roy Plomley asked her his standard question about survival, the then 61-year-old actress admitted: 'I can't even put a key in the door, darling. I can't do a thing for myself.'

Plomley had direct experience of Bankhead's incapacity. 'She was a very frail and ailing old lady,' he recalled of the day of their interview,

> and I was shocked to see how old and ill she looked as I helped her out of a taxi. She had come from her hotel wearing a mink coat slung over a pair of lounging pyjamas, and she leaned heavily on my arm as I supported her to the lift. Her eyes were still fine, and there was still beauty in the bone structure of her face beneath the wrinkles and ravages of hard living. Her hands shook, and when she wished to go to the loo she had to ask Monica Chapman to accompany her to help her with her clothing.

(Assisting a screen legend in such a way must have been one of the more unusual tasks undertaken by Monica Chapman in her sixteen years as producer – 'during which time,' said Roy Plomley, 'we never exchanged a cross word'.)

Ginger Rogers, cast away in May 1969, related one of the great encounters of show-business history. She was in New York, rehearsing for the Gershwin musical *Girl Crazy*, when *New Yorker* editor Harold Ross took her to another show – and, as she told Roy Plomley,

> afterwards he said, 'Would you like to go backstage and see Fred? – he's a friend of mine – and Adele, his sister?' I said I'd love to meet them, so backstage we went, and I was introduced to both the Astaires, and later Fred called me and asked me if I'd go to dinner with him, and dancing at the Central Park Casino. And so we had a couple of dates together and a lovely time dancing, but I never had the least suspicion that there would be a time when we would be dancing professionally.

In early March 1963 Monica Chapman sent round a routine memo headed 'Desert Island Discs: Home Service: Weeks 14–16', to confirm the identity of two upcoming castaways: Sir Harry Whitlow (described in the memo as 'Man of affairs, musician, mountaineer, and mystic') for Monday, 1 April and Ted Willis ('Playwright, and author of film and television scripts') for 8 April.

Roy Plomley with producer Monica Chapman (left) and Margot Fonteyn, April 1965

Sir Harry Whitlow was scarcely a household name, but one of the joys of listening to *Desert Island Discs* has always been discovering interesting people of whom one has never previously heard, and there was no reason to think that Sir Harry would not have a gripping story to tell.

Strangely, he had become Sir Harry Whitlohn by the time the listing of his programme was printed in the *Radio Times*, but no matter – he turned out to be a fascinating castaway, whose final record choice was a montage of the street sounds of Lichtenstein, and whose luxury was a mountain.

The story of how Sir Harry came to be cast away on Roy Plomley's desert island began with a letter to the *Desert Island Discs* presenter from a parson in Leicestershire, asking: 'Have you noticed that April 1st falls on a Monday this year?' Plomley discussed the wheeze of a non-existent castaway with Anna Instone, head of the Gramophone Department, and she in turn referred the idea to her superior, who gave the go-ahead.

The next step was to find someone to play Sir Harry. According to Plomley, 'I went to see the bulky, ebullient Henry Sherek, one of our most distinguished theatrical impresarios, who had an impish sense of humour, was of Central European parentage and, while being very British, could sound faintly foreign, if pushed.' (He had been cast away in June 1959.)

Sherek agreed to play the part, and Plomley went off to write the script – but not before the joke had been underpinned by a contract for the programme being issued in the name of Sir Harry Whitlohn.

Sir Harry turned out to be every bit as fascinating as the most exacting listener could have hoped. When explaining why his first record choice was part of Brahms' Symphony no. 3, he revealed that as a child he had been taken by his Viennese mother to meet the great composer, and was struck by his habit of chewing cloves. Young Harry had told Brahms that he had written music himself. 'He put a pile of manuscripts on the piano stool,' remembered Whitlohn, 'and sat me on top of it, and I played a little melody I'd written. He appeared enchanted with it. He lifted me off the stool and played it through himself, in several different ways, muttering to himself and spitting out little bits of clove. The upshot of it was that he took my little theme and used it as the cello melody in the third movement of his Third Symphony.'

Sir Harry's final record is of the street sounds of Lichtenstein, as heard from outside a café in the capital, Vaduz. 'Our very progressive Chamber of Overseas Industrial Development made a record of typical sounds of Lichtenstein,' explains Sir Harry, 'and they sent this record at Christmastime to friends overseas.'

*Sir Harry Whitlohn
aka Henry Sherek*

Roy Plomley remembered: 'Apart from such obvious sounds as trams, mule carts and cash registers, we also heard the siren of the *Queen Elizabeth* and a Cockney voice shouting, "*Evening News – Standard*".'

As for that luxury of a mountain, Sir Harry insists that 'even one a hundred feet high will do, providing it's climbable' – and his preferred book is a telephone directory for any city in the world.

Plomley was well aware that tampering with what was already a national radio institution could bring the wrath of loyal listeners down upon his head, 'and in that case the top brass of the Corporation would be bound to take action and heads would roll – mine in particular'. In the event there was little adverse comment – just three complaints from forty calls to the Duty Officer. But just as, much more recently, a proportion of Radio 4 listeners to *Down the Line* with award-winning phone-in host Gary Bellamy were outraged by such a programme demeaning the airwaves, so in 1963 there were plenty who simply did not get the joke. Plomley reported that about a quarter of the letters he received were from listeners who had taken the programme seriously, to the extent of asking him to pass on letters of appreciation to Sir Harry himself.

At the time Sir Harry Whitlohn was enjoying his thirty minutes of fame there was some internal discussion at the BBC regarding whether after twenty-one years *Desert Island Discs* was due a rest, and in June 1963 Roy Plomley and Anna Instone proposed a spin-off programme called *At Home*. Their memo to the programme controllers outlined the idea:

> One of the chief reasons for the success of *Desert Island Discs* is that it satisfies listeners' curiosity about the ways of the famous. Any substitute whilst this long series is rested must therefore be able to sustain this element of curiosity and the following variation on the 'choice' theme might well prove to be the solution.
>
> The object of the programme, called tentatively *At Home*, would be to select a well-known person and then for an interviewer to talk to him/her *at home*, giving listeners an impression of his past, present and future in relation to his background and surroundings. Records and music would

be mentioned in the course of the conversation, though the number of discs to be played would not be rigidly specified so that the programme would have the maximum flexibility.

Possible subjects were then suggested – including pioneer castaway Vic Oliver, violinist Yehudi Menuhin and cricketer Ted Dexter – and a different interviewer for each celebrity: Roy Plomley would do one, as would other notable radio presenters on the roster, such as Jack de Manio and Robert Robinson.

Two months later the future of *Desert Island Discs* was still far from certain. When the Drama Booking Manager contacted the Gramophone Department about Roy Plomley's fee, there was discussion about whether it was a good time to increase this as it was possible that the programme would be coming off the air from the first quarter of 1964.

In the event, nothing came of the suggestion for a new programme – nor of the suggestion that the old one be axed. The established *Desert Island Discs* formula was clearly considered the best, and the programme continued with little change to its basic structure.

The ride was not, however, always a smooth one for Plomley; for example, it was during the 1960s that he fell foul of an enduring BBC concern: the necessity for political balance in the Corporation's output.

On 14 August 1967 the castaway was Jeremy Thorpe, who had recently become leader of the Liberal Party – very much the third party of UK politics at a time when Harold Wilson was Prime Minister in the Labour government and Edward Heath leader of the opposition. The early part of the interview was uncontentious to the point of blandness, but then Plomley asked Thorpe whether the Liberal Party 'favours going into Europe' – that is, joining the infant European Common Market – to which Thorpe replies that had the UK joined at the beginning, 'We could have helped draw up the rules, and we could have probably been leading Europe today.' There followed an exchange about the Liberal position on nationalization, and then Roy Plomley asked, 'If the party came to power next month, what would be the first thing to tackle?' and is told that Thorpe's priority would be to 'break the arrogance of the power of the executive, and give power back to the people', keep a check on public expenditure, set up select committees to cross-examine ministers, and give Scotland and Wales their own parliaments: 'Once you've got the machinery of government effective, then Parliament will be able to get down to doing the real job.'

Desert Island Discs *turns 25: Roy Plomley outside Broadcasting House, London, January 1967*

Two listeners were moved to telephone the BBC and complain that the programme had been politically biased in allowing Thorpe a platform for his Liberal views, and senior management responded by issuing a decree to the effect that *Desert Island Discs* should avoid having politicians as castaways. And if they were ever invited on to the programme, they should be kept well clear of current controversy. This rebuke was passed all the way down to Roy Plomley, who seemed to have taken the chastisement – 'a very large rocket that came down the line from a very great height indeed' – in his stride, claiming that he had asked a political question of Jeremy Thorpe 'just because I wanted to know'.

If senior BBC management were anxious that the other party leaders would want to follow Thorpe on to the desert island, they had good cause. Sure enough, September brought a letter from John Lindsey of Conservative Central Office: 'Having heard Jeremy Thorpe choosing his *Desert Island Discs* a few weeks ago I have been wondering whether you would care to invite Mr Heath to appear on your programme. You will, I am sure, be aware of his deep interest in music . . ?'

But that gently dispensed political pressure was resisted, and Edward Heath did not appear on the programme until 1988. Harold Wilson did not appear at all, but the interview in 1969 with his wife Mary – whose poetry was highly popular at the time – caused a mild ripple. John Lindsey of CCO wondered whether having the then Prime Minister's wife on the island was not further political favouritism, and was told by J. A. Camacho, Head of Talks and Current Affairs (Radio):

Yes, Mrs Wilson is doing a Desert Island Discs programme. But I wonder

Mary and Harold Wilson

whether this is an area where we should have mathematical balance. There just isn't another Mrs Wilson! There is some public interest in her taste, her poetry, etc. but I don't think this is of a political nature and I would think it unlikely to be an electoral advantage.

Compared with the row which followed Sue Lawley's interview with Gordon Brown in 1996 (see pages 374–80) or the news stories spun from Kirsty Young's programmes with Nick Clegg (who came out as a smoker) in 2010, and in 2012 with John Prescott (who, it was claimed in some quarters, had been significantly hesitant when asked who the next Labour prime minister would be), the flurry of internal memos caused by Jeremy Thorpe's comments seems disproportionate. But then, as now, the BBC was sensitive to such issues.

SHIRLEY BASSEY

singer

9 May 1960

'I got tired and fed up with the smell of fish and chips'

In May 1960 Shirley Bassey was a 23-year-old singer whose uncannily powerful voice had already started to make an impact on the pop charts. Her first single, 'Burn My Candle', had been released in February 1956 and promptly banned by the BBC on account of its suggestive lyrics, and it was a year later that she first entered the charts with her rendition of 'The Banana Boat Song'. The following year brought more success before 'Kiss Me, Honey Honey, Kiss Me' (whose lyric about blowing my top presumably managed to creep under the BBC radar) reached the Top Ten in December 1958. Bassey had her first No. 1 with 'As I Love You' in January 1959 – she was reputedly the first Welsh artist to make the top spot – but in spring 1960 her song 'With These Hands' had barely caused a ripple in the charts.

Bassey's was a proper rags-to-riches story. Daughter of a Nigerian father and a British mother, she was born in 1937 in the boondocks of Tiger Bay in Cardiff. While in her teens at Splott Secondary Modern School she started to perform in local pubs and clubs; and on leaving school (and finding herself pregnant at the age of sixteen) she took a job in a local factory while continuing to perform whenever opportunity arose.

Having been introduced by Roy Plomley as 'a young singing star with an international reputation in cabaret and revue', and having confessed that what she would be happiest to get away from is 'agents and managers ringing me up', Shirley Bassey reveals that worrying about which records to take to the island had kept her awake for half the night – eliciting from Plomley the well-mannered response: 'Oh, I apologize for that, for giving you a sleepless night – that's awful.'

He then turns to her childhood. Where did her interest in music come from?

'When I was quite young I used to go to tap-dancing classes, where they played records to tap dance to ... When I was about fourteen I used to sing in working men's clubs, and I wasn't supposed to: I was smuggled in and out ... I was much too young. And when I was sixteen and a half a producer approached me after I sang in one of these clubs, and said, would I like to go into one of his shows, which was called *Memories of Jolson*.'

These recollections are interrupted in order to play a record by the Chipmunks. (Cyril Fletcher the previous year is the only other castaway to have taken a record by that novelty group.) Why the Chipmunks? 'I feel that there would be some monkeys on this island,' the castaway explains: 'I hope there would be, anyway, and I'd play this record and they would all come round and I'd pretend that I was giving a little party – and on top of that, it's quite funny. I feel that somewhere along the line I would have to laugh. I'd need something to cheer me up.'

After *Memories of Jolson* had finished its tour she moved to a show called *Hot from Harlem*. 'Then I decided I should retire. I'd had enough of show business. I'd saved quite a bit of money and I thought I could live on this, and I went home. And then suddenly I'd run out of money, and I had to find something to do. So I took a job as a waitress, and after two months I got tired and fed up with the smell of fish and chips on my clothes. And just in time I received a telegram to ring a certain number in London, which I did, and it was a friend of mine who said would I like to go to Jersey for two weeks with him – do him a favour because he couldn't get a singer any-where. And I did, and while I was appearing there a certain agent heard me and signed me up to tour the music halls as a solo artiste, which I did for six months – and then Jack Hylton discovered me.'

Jack Hylton was one of the big impresarios of the time – eminent enough to have been the sixth castaway back in 1942 – and he took his new protégée to sing in the show *Such Is Life* in the West End. From there the

Shirley Bassey career blossomed – Las Vegas, Hollywood, Australia . . .

So it comes as a bit of a let-down when, in response to Plomley's question regarding her current plans, she replies: 'I have six weeks in Coventry in a revue called *Spring of 1960*, then I go to Bournemouth for the summer season for six weeks.' But after that, she hopes, it's back to the USA.

One of Bassey's more eye-catching record choices is Debussy's *Clair de lune*, played by her friend Liberace (right), himself cast away two weeks later – 'a wonderful entertainer and also a very fine pianist'– followed by Judy Garland singing 'Life is Just a Bowl of Cherries' – 'because that's how I feel it'.

How would she do as a castaway? 'I don't think I'd make out very well at all. I'd probably starve to death' – which gloomy view she quickly amends to: 'I suppose that if I was really hungry I would find some way of whipping myself up a nice meal.' And she is a good swimmer: 'When I was a young girl in school I won three certificates for swimming and diving.'

As her final record, she chooses herself singing George Gershwin's ' A Foggy Day in London Town' – 'because after listening to all these wonderful entertainers I would like to be reminded that I also was once an entertainer'.

Half a century on, Shirley Bassey's worldwide following needs no such reminder. A steady stream of unforgettable tracks have made her one of the most popular female vocalists of the postwar years, among them her second No. 1, the double-A-side 'Reach for the Stars' and 'Climb Ev'ry Mountain' in 1961; 'As Long As He Needs Me', which spent thirty weeks in the charts in 1960 and 1961; her two signature songs, 'I Who Have Nothing' and 'Hey, Big Spender'; and the theme songs for three James Bond movies: *Goldfinger* (1964), *Diamonds Are Forever* (1971) and *Moonraker* (1979).

In recognition of a stellar career, she became Dame Shirley Bassey in the 2000 New Year Honours. But for her taking exception to the smell of fish and chips on her clothes, we might have been denied one of the all-time great singing careers.

CLIFF RICHARD

singer

31 October 1960

'My main hobby is buying records
and my second hobby is playing them'

Ironically for a performer whose show-business career has been marked by an astounding longevity – well over half a century and still going strong – Cliff Richard's sole appearance as a *Desert Island Discs* castaway came less than three weeks after his twentieth birthday. On stage he pouted and gyrated in the manner of an early Elvis Presley imitator, but in the studio he proved himself a very well-behaved and thoughtful young man.

In the previous two years he had seen nine of his records reach the Top Ten, beginning in 1958 with his first single 'Move It', which reached No. 2 – and in which he was backed, as on so many of his best-known songs, by the Shadows. Three of those nine Top Tenners made it to No. 1: 'Living Doll', which made the pinnacle in July 1959; 'Travellin' Light', in October the same year – after Craig Douglas ('Only Sixteen'), Jerry Keller ('Here Comes Summer') and Bobby Darin ('Mack the Knife') had kept the seat warm for Cliff, who in turn was then ousted by Adam Faith with 'What Do You Want?' and 'Please Don't Tease', which held the summit for two weeks in August 1960. The same year had also seen the release of *Expresso Bongo* – his second film, and the movie which established Cliff Richard as spokesman for the coffee-bar generation.

In the light of Roy Plomley's observation on page 75 about pop singers and their milk rounds, and given that according to the transcript of the programme (there is no surviving audio) he twice addresses his castaway as 'Cliff Richards', it is reasonable to speculate whether this was an edition of *Desert Island Discs* which saw the presenter at his most engaged.

The issue of the castaway's age is addressed head-on. 'You still aren't twenty-one,' says Plomley, 'is that right?'

'That's right,' replies Cliff. 'I've just turned twenty, actually, just a few weeks back. I've just left my teens, and I don't like it. I don't feel any older, though.'

'You don't look any older. Now you, more than most of us, live in the middle of crowds of people – crowds that in your case sometimes appear to be trying to tear you limb from limb. How do you react to the complete opposite to all that? How would you stand up to isolation and loneliness?'

Not, in the long term, too well: 'I think like any normal person, being on your own can be very maddening, and I think I'd go a bit mad.' On the other hand, 'I think taking records is a simply marvellous idea.'

Plomley's enquiry, 'You play the gramophone a lot?' is answered strongly in the affirmative: 'My main hobby is buying records and my second hobby is playing them.'

First on the turntable is Pearl Bailey singing 'Beat Out Dat Rhythm on a Drum' from *Carmen Jones*. So far so good, but the second choice comes with baggage. Debbie Reynolds singing 'Tammy' unlocks a memory. 'This I think was my first film star crush. I walked about for weeks in a terrible daze.'

'Does the crush still last?'

'I still like Debbie Reynolds, but the crush has gone.'

Cliff was born in India, where his father was working: the family did not return to England until he was seven. 'When I was in India I used to be in a choir – the school choir – and I started taking an interest in pop music at the age of about eleven or twelve. But the real feeling that I wanted to be a singer or anything came when rock'n'roll first came out.'

He joined a skiffle band, and fell under the influence of Elvis Presley: 'I used to try and look very much like him – playing guitars and things.' Then he got an audition with the famous impresario Norrie Paramor, and recorded 'Move It': 'I was very lucky with the record. I turned professional just a month before it was released. And after my first TV show it got into the charts, and it climbed slowly up to No. 2.'

Cliff Richard mobbed by fans, 1959

Pause for Elvis singing 'Heartbreak Hotel', and then it's down to the nitty-gritty: the name.

'Cliff Richard isn't your real name?'

'No, it's not. My real name is Harry Webb.'

'Why did you change it?'

'Well, when I had this group, it was called the Drifters, and we were working in a coffee bar in the West End. And we were offered a job in Derby for the weekend, playing in a dance hall, and the gentleman who booked us wanted to have a name: you know, "Something and the Drifters" – "Harry Webb and the Drifters" – and I said, "Oh no, it sounds too square." So we all sat around wondering how to decide it. And names cropped up, and one of the last few names that cropped up was Russ Clifford, and I said it sounds rather like ballad singing, and so we changed it round to Cliff Russard. So I said, "Well, I like Cliff, but I definitely don't like Russard." So someone came up with the ingenious idea of calling me Cliff Richards. But that "S" on the end – we decided that knocking the "S" off and making it two Christian names, would make it more easy to remember.'

Plomley brings up another delicate issue:

'When you sing, Cliff, you perform these rather frenzied movements. Do you rehearse these with each song, or is it a sort of spontaneous expression of how you feel?'

'No, it's all spontaneous, because I don't think you can do this kind of thing by practising it. It's literally just letting yourself go, and letting whatever comes just happen.'

Plomley asks about Cliff's fan base:

'Most of your fans are very young people, aren't they?'

'I think you can say five to fifteen, but overall five to twenty, I think.'

'And nearly all girls?'

'Nearly all girls, yes.'

Poor Cliff can hardly walk along the street without being mobbed – it's worse in the provinces, he says, than in big towns – but Plomley wants to know more:

'That means you can lose the buttons off your clothes?'

'Oh, you can quite easily. They don't mean to do any harm.'

'Do you carry special insurance against that sort of thing?'

'Well, I am insured personally, and of course all the clothes I buy are insured, and the guitars which I bought are insured, and the amplifiers . . .'

What's going on here? The castaway is a brooding, hip, edgy pop singer barely out of his teens and notorious for his 'rather frenzied movements' on stage, and they're talking about insurance? Better play another record quick . . .

Cliff's penultimate choice is 'Rock Around the Clock' by Bill Haley and the Comets: 'I'm sure that everybody knows that rock 'n' roll has meant more than just a sort of hobby to me. It meant my career, and it made the opening to do something I really wanted to do – and if I'm going to go away for the rest of my life, I'd definitely like to take a memory of something that's meant more to me than anything else.'

Debbie Reynolds
'Tammy'

'This I think was my first film star crush. I walked about for weeks in a terrible daze'

Unlike plenty of other castaways over the years, Cliff is not tempted to take any of his own discs – 'I think I've had enough of those' – and he's in no doubt that the Bill Haley is his record of records: 'Whenever I play Bill Haley music it always brings to mind thousands of people and I think of jostling crowds and people jiving about, and I think if I'm alone I'd like to think of lots and lots of people.'

Casting away Cliff Richard when he was so young offers an interesting angle on his career, but the programme carries little hint of what was to make him one of the most enduring figures in British showbiz.

The early 1960s brought his two best-loved films, *The Young Ones* (1961) and *Summer Holiday* (1963), both of which had memorable theme tunes, as well as a stream of hit records. Somehow managing to remain a chart presence in the era of the Beatles, Rolling Stones and other more fashionable performers, he had no fewer than seven No. 1s in the 1960s, including 'Congratulations', which was narrowly beaten in the 1968 Eurovision Song Contest (a competition taken more seriously in those days than in recent years). He continued having chart-toppers until well into the 1990s.

Knighted in 1995 in recognition of his charitable work, Cliff Richard continues to defy musical trends and remain a popular performer. A measure of his appeal was the announcement in December 2011 that *Cliff Richard 2012* was the third most popular celebrity calendar of the year, out-sold only by the *X-Factor* contestants and JLS. And in June 2012 he gave yet more evidence of his mind-boggling musical longevity when belting out a medley of some of his main songs – including, appropriately enough, 'Congratulations' – at the Buckingham Palace concert which formed part of Her Majesty the Queen's Diamond Jubilee celebrations. (Other musical castaways to perform at that concert were Sir Paul McCartney, Dame Shirley Bassey, Sir Tom Jones, Sir Elton John, Annie Lennox, and Suggs (of Madness) – while castaways Rolf Harris, Lenny Henry and Rob Brydon kept things ticking along between acts.)

PETER SCOTT

naturalist

3 April 1961

'There hasn't been a time when I can't remember animals being very exciting'

Peter Scott, whose lasting legacy is the Wildfowl and Wetlands Trust he founded in 1946 as the Severn Wildfowl Trust at Slimbridge in Gloucestershire, was a prominent naturalist and broadcaster in the 1950s and 1960s, and one of the founding fathers of the BBC Natural History Unit in Bristol.

Scott's father was the Antarctic explorer Robert Falcon Scott, who when their son was very young advised his wife to 'make the boy interested in natural history if you can; it is better than games'. As it turned out, the younger Scott did both: in addition to his highly influential work on nature and conservation, he won a bronze medal for sailing in the 1936 Olympic Games, and a class in the British Gliding Championships in 1963. And as if excelling in two separate worlds was not enough, he was also a highly acclaimed painter of natural subjects.

'From your studies of birds in desolate parts of the world,' Roy Plomley suggests to his castaway, 'you must have experienced solitude many times, and therefore solitude must to some extent have lost its terrors for you.'

Scott thinks he'll manage: 'I've had to fend for myself once or twice; perhaps I could on a desert island.'

Painting and natural history: which had come first in Peter Scott's life?

'They almost came together. I suppose natural history came first, because I thought I was going to be a naturalist. I thought I was going to be a biologist before I ever thought I was going to be an artist. But there hasn't been a time when I can't remember thinking that animals were very exciting, and there hasn't been a time when I can't remember wanting to draw them.'

Scott's first major expedition to observe bird migration had been to the Black Sea in the 1930s: 'I started by going to Hungary and to Romania, and then finally I went on to the Caspian Sea, all in the pursuit of these curious little birds called red-breasted geese' (pictured opposite, painted by Scott).

In recent years Scott has been filming for television in exotic places. 'I suppose the Galapagos Islands was the most exciting [expedition] from the animal point of view,' and the most beautiful place to which he has been is Fiji – 'but I can't go to Madagascar for a bit, because my old chum David Attenborough went there recently, and he rather knocked the bottom out of the market.'

After such a wealth of experience, what is Peter Scott's view on that intriguing question of how birds navigate? 'I think there is still a mystery,' he declares; 'I don't think we know the whole story yet. But we do know that they do it possibly with their eyes – that is the sense they principally use – and that the Sun plays a very important part. In the case of night migrants, the pattern of the stars plays a very important part, and quite recently we think we've discovered that the Moon can also be used by them – although its action is very much more complicated, of course, than the movement of the stars and the Sun.'

Scott describes the thinking behind setting up the Wildfowl Trust: 'We were worried about some of the species of wildfowl in the world disappearing altogether: they were becoming so rare that they were [almost] exterminated. We felt that we must do something about this, and the first thing to do was to learn a great deal more about the birds than was then known. Practically no scientific work had been done on their conservation at all. So our first thing was to set up a research station, and at the same time to tackle the educational side and try and teach people that it really would be rather sad if these things disappeared for ever.'

How many species of wildfowl does the Trust accommodate? 'We keep a collection of tame ones there, from all over the world. There are a hundred and forty-seven species in the world, and we have a hundred and twenty-one of them there at the moment.' Among them is the Hawaiian goose, the rarest goose in the world. 'There were only fifty, ten years ago. And at that time they sent us three. And from the three we've reared a hundred and twenty-six – no, it's more than that now, because there were five hatched last week. So it's a hundred and thirty-one.'

Scott's music selection includes a private recording made by himself: 'I would like to go back to Fiji, and bask in the nostalgia of the place. There's a most lovely little traditional farewell song that they sing to you on the lovely warm evenings underneath the palm trees, and it's called "Isa Lei".'

But the record with the most unusual back-story is his final choice, from *Der Rosenkavalier* by Richard Strauss. 'I once heard Richard Strauss himself conduct it in Munich, in the State Opera there, and I was afterwards invited to go round with a young music student to meet Strauss. He was staying with Hans Knappertsbusch, who was the resident conductor there, and when we got there we found that they were playing poker – Strauss was very keen on card games . . . I'd previously been asked whether I knew the rules, and I did and I was roped in, and played poker with Strauss that evening.'

Who won?

'I believe I was about five marks richer when I walked out than I had been when I went in, but I'm not sure whether Strauss lost.'

In the 1950s Peter Scott had started working with the International Union for the Conservation of Nature (IUCN), and just a few weeks after being cast away on the desert island became involved with setting up, initially in partnership with the IUCN, the World Wildlife Fund. Along with Gerald Watterson, Secretary-General of the IUCN, Scott devised the famous WWF panda logo. He continued to work on all manner of conservation initiatives – on coral fish as well as other non-avian species – and in 1973 was knighted in recognition of his work.

Sir Peter Scott died in 1989, a few days short of his ninetieth birthday.

FANNY AND JOHNNIE CRADOCK

cooking double act

15 October 1962

'Cooking is a clean and creative art, not a grubby chore, and I'd be ashamed to wear an apron'

The story of Fanny and Johnnie Cradock is one you could not make up. Fanny had been born Phyllis Nan Sortain Pechey in 1909. She would peddle the story that her father was a gambler who during Fanny's childhood spent the winters in Nice with his much younger wife. While father was at the casino (so the story went), mother would entertain in their hotel room, and Fanny, bribed to absent herself, would go down to the hotel kitchen and watch the cooks going about their business. (An alternative version of her early years was that she had been abandoned by her mother and raised by her grandparents, and that in her teens she had been expelled from boarding school for engaging in spiritualism.)

Her first husband was an RAF pilot who was killed soon after their wedding. 'I married on Wednesday,' she claimed, 'settled his debts on Friday, and he died on Sunday' – though a more reliable account dates his death four months after their marriage. They had a son, who was adopted by her husband's parents and did not see his mother until he was twenty-one. She also had a son with her second husband, but left both of them when the boy was still a small baby. She was apparently committing bigamy at her wedding to her third husband, and not long after marrying him met a Royal Artillery officer named Major John Cradock. He was married with four children but fell under her spell – and thus began one of the strangest of double acts. From 1950 to 1955 Fanny and Johnnie wrote together as 'Bon Viveur' for the *Daily Telegraph*, providing a column which concentrated on cookery and restaurant reviews. This served as a springboard – first to the stage, where they presented cookery demonstrations in theatres which had been turned into restaurants for the occasion, and then to television.

Their fabled cookery programmes – she clad in a ballgown and several layers of make-up, he the hapless skivvy handing her the utensils while constantly being exhorted to keep up – started in 1955, and they were at the height of their small-screen fame when cast away by Roy Plomley.

Johnnie has scarcely started to expand on how often they play the gramophone before his redoubtable partner butts in: 'Not only do we play it a lot, but we have a number of them, because John can't resist anything mechanical, and so each design is superseded by yet another and another, and we have one which pipes out music on to the terrace where we eat in the summer, and one in our vast kitchen, and portable ones we carry into the bath. We're drenched in music, aren't we?'

Are they musicians? Johnny used to sing 'when I was younger, and didn't smoke so much'. As for Fanny: 'I studied violin and piano and ballet from the time I was five, and very seriously indeed – but I changed course later on.'

The pair toss a coin for first record. Johnnie wins, and asks for Chopin's *Les Sylphides*, for an unexpected reason: 'Because I will then have the opportunity to practise my ballet. I am a frustrated ballet dancer. I'm quite convinced that in a previous incarnation I was a female ballet dancer. In this incarnation, unfortunately, my shape and figure is wrong for it' – he was not far off sixty – 'but I still have the inclination.'

'Well, darling,' chimes in Fanny, 'you must admit you still do rise to your pretty toes, in spite of your six feet and bald pate, round the domestic house.'

How did they meet?

'I picked her up on the Hackney Marshes,' says Johnnie, 'on a foggy night, in the blackout at the beginning of the war.'

'This is outrageous!' fires back Fanny. 'In point of fact, I went down at the invitation of your Colonel – and well you know it – to hear a troop concert. And during the session afterwards – everybody was drinking, an enormous crowd – a hand came over the crowd with a glass, and I recognized what was in it. It was what I liked, so I took it – and Cradock was on the other end of the glass.'

Later in the programme Roy Plomley turns to the couple's time as 'Bon Viveur' which, he says, 'started with a roving commission to find out what was good and what was bad in British hotels and restaurants.'

Fanny recalls how diffident they had been at their first hotel. 'We dodged about in alleyways, until the manageress beckoned us in. And then when we offered the card of this famous newspaper after the bill was paid on that first meal, and in John's pocket, and when we'd discussed it over the coffee and decided that we'd write it up, we handed in this newspaper card – and it was returned to us with the statement that the manager was too busy. And this discourtesy so infuriated the pair of us that we were never ever frightened again.'

They have a special memory of a Scottish hotel, where the chatelaine 'wore pince-nez', according to Fanny. 'She had two bright blue spots on her hair, and looked like a whipped-cream walnut. Her dining room, which was very tatty mahogany, had a dirty notice which said: "No smoking in this dining room. Other people respect their food, even if you don't". Well! We looked at each other and we said: "If the cooking is really first-class, this will be wonderful."'

It was not. 'I met the old girl in the corridor,' continues Fanny, 'and I said, "Madam, we have just had the dubious pleasure of eating the most disgusting meal we have ever eaten in our lives," and she coloured up and said to us both, "Get out of my hotel! Never in thirty years has anybody dared to complain before!"'

On to their stage career. What was their biggest audience? 'Six and a half thousand,' says Fanny, 'in the Royal Albert Hall.'

Then to television. Recently the pair have achieved what Plomley called 'the incredible feat' of cooking a three-course meal from scratch in less than a quarter

Fanny Cradock resplendent in ballgown at London's Café Royal, 1956

of an hour. 'And we're planning to do four courses – with complementary wines, service, lay the table and do the flowers – together in under fifteen minutes next time.'

But what about cooking in a ballgown? Fanny has a ready answer. 'When a great chef comes into the restaurant from cooking a dish because you want to compliment him, his whites are always spotless, aren't they? Well, what difference is it, me having a ball-dress or a cotton frock for it? Mother never wore an apron, my grandmother never wore an apron, and they were both magnificent cooks. I say cooking is a clean and creative art, not a grubby chore, and I'd be ashamed to wear an apron.'

For the perfect meal, Johnnie would have roast pheasant, accompanied by 'the best Burgundy I could get, probably Champs de Terre '29.' And Fanny? 'That's a very nice meal. I accept his Burgundy, but I shall start with oysters, I shall have a grouse, I shall have some Stilton cheese and celery, old brandy and a cigar.'

'Prepared in fourteen and a half minutes?', Plomley asks Fanny.

'Eaten in about two hours.'

Through the late 1960s and into the 1970s, the appeal of the eccentric Cradock brand steadily wilted. The bizarre sight of a ballgowned curmudgeon bossing around her down-trodden consort in order to produce increasingly anachronistic meals predictably palled as a fresh generation of television chefs such as Delia Smith started to appear.

After Johnnie had faded from view in the early 1970s following a heart attack, Fanny soldiered on with a series of assistants. But in 1976 her television career was derailed in the wake of her overbearing treatment of a Devon housewife who had won a nationwide cookery competition, the prize for which was the chance to prepare a banquet for various VIPs (including former prime minister Edward Heath). The programme was televised on the Esther Rantzen series *The Big Time*, and Cradock's *de haut en bas* performance showed that her career had passed its sell-by date.

The following year Fanny and Johnnie did what it was widely assumed they had done decades earlier: they got married.

Johnnie died in 1987 and Fanny in 1994. Together they had formed one of television's oddest couples.

Rachmaninov
Piano Concerto no. 2 in C minor
Soloist: Sergei Rachmaninov

'All the Way'
Frank Sinatra

Noël Coward
Love scene from *Private Lives*
Noël Coward and Gertrude Lawrence

Vincenzo Bellini
'Casta diva' (from *Norma*)
Soloist: Maria Callas

William Shakespeare
'Shall I compare thee to a summer's day?' (Sonnet 18)
Spoken by Edith Evans
'I would certainly be quite happy with this on a desert island for the rest of my life'

'The Critics'
Peter Sellers and Irene Handl

⭐ **'Hole in the Ground'**
Bernard Cribbins

Verdi
'Dies irae' (from the Requiem Mass)

📖 ***The Human Situation* by MacNeill Dixon**
'This is to me a classic'

💙 **Painting materials**

Opposite: *Noël Coward and Gertrude Lawrence in* Private Lives, *1930*

NOËL COWARD
playwright
28 January 1963

'Thank you for a remarkably painless experience'

On New Year's Eve 1962, Noël Coward took leave of the old year in his diary: 'I look with dismay at the jangling world around me, at the close of this clamorous year. How much longer can all this lack of control, non-discipline, self-indulgence and wild futility last? The books I like to read, the music I like to hear, the paintings I like to see all belong to the past. This is really old age, I suppose. And yet there is a margin for doubt. I never liked formlessness, bad manners, obscurantism and vulgarity even when I was young! Hail 1963!'

What he omits to say is that despite all that gloom, he has at least one reason to be cheerful: the day after tomorrow he has a date to record *Desert Island Discs* with Roy Plomley.

When ushered into studio B4 at Broadcasting House, 'The Master' – most suave, refined and sophisticated of British theatrical icons – had recently turned sixty-three. Behind him lay a life of stellar success: in the theatre with enduring works such as *The Vortex* (1924), *Hay Fever* (1925), *Bitter Sweet* (1929), *Private Lives* (1930 – in the original version of which he played opposite his lifetime friend Gertrude Lawrence), *Present Laughter* (1939) and *Blithe Spirit* (1942); on the big screen with *In Which We Serve* (1942), *This Happy Breed* (1943) and *Brief Encounter* (1945); and as a singer of his own songs, some

of which are comic classics – 'Mad Dogs and Englishmen', 'Don't Put Your Daughter on the Stage, Mrs Worthington' or 'The Stately Homes of England' – while others are among the finest romantic songs of the twentieth century: 'Sail Away', 'I'll See You Again', 'A Room with a View', 'London Pride'.

Roy Plomley welcomes listeners to 'rather a special occasion' – the twenty-first birthday of *Desert Island Discs* – and pronounces himself 'delighted to tell you that to celebrate this occasion the island is being visited by that brilliant man of the theatre, The Master himself, Noël Coward.'

Does he have the temperament to be marooned by himself? 'I don't think that anybody would like it indefinitely, but I think that I would qualify for it more than quite a lot of people I know, because I don't mind being alone. I rather like it.'

First choice of music is Rachmaninov's Piano Concerto no. 2 in C minor – which to millions of moviegoers is better known as the main music in Coward's best-loved film, *Brief Encounter*. Coward points out that it was 'also, curiously enough, in the first movie I was in, called *The Scoundrel*. We used it, so it's sort of in my brain, and I love it, and I know every note of it, and I very often play it.'

In the now customary biographical core of the programme, Coward recalls his early theatrical experience. 'I used to be taken to the theatre on my birthday by my Mama, either in the gallery or the pit, ever since I was five. And I used to be taken to most of the musical comedies, and I suppose I got the theatre bug then.'

One record choice is himself and Gertrude Lawrence, who had died in 1952, performing a scene from *Private Lives*: 'As I was deeply fond of her and we worked together so much in our lives and I shall miss her always, I thought I'd like on my desert island to be able to hear her voice again occasionally.'

What, wonders Plomley, does Coward think of 'the new movement of young playwrights, the so-called Kitchen Sink school'?

'I think that Harold Pinter is a very extraordinary and original writer, with immense talent. I think that Wesker is too. I think that Wesker's *Chips with Everything* is a very very fine piece of work. I think that when he treats the officer class he is a little self-conscious, and not quite accurate. I think that there's a sort of class hatred going on which is rather a bore.'

John Osborne? *Epitaph for George Dillon* 'had some very good stuff in it' and *Look Back in Anger* had 'a little too much invective – highly pardonable because it was a very dramatic presentation'. But as for the rest, 'His other plays I've not cared for so much.'

Coward himself has been taking flak from the critics in London. Does he think, asks Plomley, that the critics 'have been doing a disservice to the theatre lately, by going for – shall we say? – the far-out plays?' Up to a point, answers the Master: 'I think they've got a bee in their bonnet about the far-out plays, and I think that is rather a disservice, but of course as nobody pays very much attention I don't think it matters.'

Is there any risk of the critics in London becoming 'the vital factor' in a play's success, as is the case in New York?

'Oh, no, no, no – because the English public think for themselves. The American public do not.'

Coward and Lawrence, Private Lives, *1930*

After a somewhat surprising penultimate record choice – 'Hole in the Ground', the Bernard Cribbins novelty song sensation of 1962 – Coward completes his eight with the 'Dies Irae' from Verdi's Requiem Mass – ' so tremendously dramatic . . . and I think that when I was really falling to pieces at the end of my long and misspent life on the island, this really would wake me up for a few extra moments of pleasure'.

The choice of one record above all the others takes us from the sublime to the ridiculous: 'Oh, what a ghastly question! Very cruel. I think the only one that I would never get sick of is "Hole in the Ground", because I could translate it into French as I walked up and down the beach.'

'Thank you, Noël Coward,' signs off Roy Plomley, 'for letting us hear your choice of Desert Island Discs and for being here to celebrate with us this programme's twenty-first birthday.'

'Thank you for a remarkably painless experience.'

Noël Coward had been the essence of affability in the *Desert Island Discs* interview, but eight days after the recording he was in a grump again, writing in his diary: 'I am becoming almighty sick of the Welfare State; sick of ugly voices, sick of bad manners and teenagers and debased values.'

Coward hated the way Britain was changing, and spent an increasing amount of his time at Firefly, the house in Jamaica where he lived with his long-time partner Graham Payn. It was there that he died in March 1973.

MARLENE DIETRICH

actress and singer

4 January 1965

'Oh no, no, no, I'm frightened of nothing'

The interview with screen legend Marlene Dietrich was conducted not in the BBC studio but in the star's dressing room at the Queen's Theatre in the West End, where she was performing her one-woman show.

Not that Plomley was complaining about the inconvenience. He later wrote that in the confined space of the dressing room he and the German-born siren conducted the interview 'with our heads together over a portable recorder, and my eyes were not more than ten inches from that sensational face. Does it bear close inspection? It certainly does, and not only her face and figure but her movements and gestures too are those of a young woman.'

Dietrich was far from a young woman in January 1965 – she was sixty-three – but agelessness was her trademark. Her many films had included *The Blue Angel* (1930), when she made 'Falling in Love Again' her signature song; *Morocco* (1930), for which she received her only Oscar nomination; *Shanghai Express* (1932); *Destry Rides Again* (1939), in which she gave a memorable rendition of the song 'The Boys in the Back Room'; and Alfred Hitchcock's *Stage Fright* (1950).

By the late 1930s she was living in the USA, firmly rejecting attempts from the Nazi party to persuade her to return to Germany. She took US citizenship in 1939, and spent much of the war performing for Allied troops in Europe and Africa. In recognition of her wartime efforts she was awarded the *Légion d'honneur* by the French government in 1947.

In the 1950s and 1960s the main thrust of her career switched to cabaret and stage performance, which gave her the opportunity to exploit the success of her well-known songs such as 'Lili Marleen' (in its original incarnation a wartime favourite of troops) and later 'Where Have all the Flowers Gone?'

The early exchanges suggest that Roy Plomley is dealing with one of his more uncooperative castaways.

Would she find it frightening to be on the desert island? 'Oh no, no, no, I'm frightened of nothing.'

What would she be happiest to get away from? 'Nothing, no.'

How has she chosen her records? 'It's rather difficult for me because at the moment I'm not at home, because when I'm at home it's easier to recollect and look at things that I have and that I like.'

But the pace picks up when she introduces her opening record. 'The first thing that came to my mind was naturally Stravinsky, who is one of the great idols of my life – *Sacre du Printemps*, which I have always had with me. I never travel without it. When I met him I told him that, and I told him I loved most the part where the girl runs away from the man in the woods. He looked at me and he said, "I've never written any such thing." So I said, "Well, that's how the music sounds." And he said, "Well, if it sounds like that to you, that's fine, but that's not at all what I meant." But I still think that when I hear the music.'

A question about her childhood ambition gets short shrift – 'I don't think I had any ambition even then, and I don't have any now . . . My ambition . . . was to be a useful human being, and that's what I've tried to be.'

She had studied as a violinist until injuring a finger. 'In those days they put you in a cast, and when I came out of the cast they told me that I could never last a concert, and I gave up the violin – much to the distress of my mother because she had thought that I would be a violinist. But even then I hated doing things in halves, and so I said that if I could never play a concert, I'll give it up now.'

Dietrich tells Plomley that, after drama academy, 'My first professional appearance was as the widow in the fifth act of *The Taming of the Shrew*.'

'That's a very tiny part, isn't it?'

'Yes.'

'Then plays and musical comedies and revues. You were in a play by Bernard Shaw in Berlin, I believe.'

'Yes – *La Séance*.'

'And you made a number of films playing leading parts. In fact your career was getting along very well, and then there was one engagement that gave you international success, *The Blue Angel*.'

'No, that's not true. My career was not going well at all. *The Blue Angel* was the very first film I made.'

'Mmmm . . . and you made this film in three versions.'

'No, in two.'

Plomley has done his homework and knows that she is rewriting history – indeed, he has his notes in his pocket to prove it. But, ever smooth, he lets things move on.

They talk of her going to Hollywood.

'Did you go there with the intention of staying a long time?'

'No.'

'Out of all those Hollywood films – *Morocco*, *The Scarlet Empress*, *Desire*, *Destry Rides Again*, there are so many – which ones do you look back on with the most affection?'

'I cannot say that I look at any one with affection . . . I don't like challenges at all. I was thrown into this business and I try to do my best, and it was hard work all along the line.'

Plomley changes tack. The war must have been a heartbreaking time for her, 'with your natural affection for your own people in the back of your mind'.

'No, it was not; it was not a heartbreaking time. I did what I thought was right and I did the best I could.'

After playing his castaway another Bacharach song in the shape of 'A Message to Martha' (the Adam Faith version, no less), Plomley returns to her cabaret career. It must have been an emotional moment when the curtain went up in Berlin on her first appearance in her native country for so many years? 'No, that wasn't a particularly emotional moment, no.'

As for the future, she has said that she has never had ambition. But, asks Plomley, 'Isn't there anything that you want, anywhere you want to play – do

Burt Bacharach

'Always Something There to Remind Me'

'A great friend of mine and he's also an absolutely wonderful man'

you want to direct, do you want to create in any way?'

'No.'

Doesn't she want to take one of her own records onto the desert island? 'Oh no, no, no. I never listen to my own records. I don't think anybody who has ever done anything or created anything likes to look at it. I've never seen a painter who likes to look at his own painting. I think it's for the other people to listen to if they like it.'

Despite his castaway having been somewhat less than forthcoming, Roy Plomley is generous when it comes to Marlene Dietrich's luxury, allowing her to take a box into which she could put: a bunch of white heather 'that the people of Scotland brought me'; a pair of ballet shoes given to her by the

Marlene Dietrich in Destry Rides Again, *1939*

children from the Bolshoi Ballet School; and a collection of records by the pianist Sviatoslav Richter, whose playing of the Beethoven 'Appassionata' piano sonata as one of her eight records was not enough to satisfy her.

In his book *Desert Island Discs*, Roy Plomley revisited the moment when he realized that Marlene Dietrich was giving a less than accurate account of her early film career:

> There was a twinkle in those large, expressive eyes, and a tiny, challenging smile at the corners of her mouth as she watched for my reaction. She knew that I knew she was lying, and she was enjoying the moment. I hope my decision not to challenge her was instinctive. It is a beautiful woman's privilege to juggle with time, especially when, as in Marlene's case, she has defeated it, and if she wished to delete a few years from the chronology of her career, then her wish should be respected.

One more detail of Dietrich at the Queen's Theatre. According to Plomley, her dressing room was sparsely furnished, with no furniture or pictures of her own. Except, that is, for a framed photograph of Ernest Hemingway, inscribed by him 'To my favourite Kraut'.

After many years of ill health, Marlene Dietrich died in May 1992 at the age of ninety.

SIR BASIL SPENCE

architect

1 February 1965

'Can I have a hundredweight of spaghetti?'

Not many architects have been marooned on the desert island, but there was no disputing Sir Basil Spence's castaway qualifications, nor any dispute about which building made him a household name in the mid-1960s: Coventry Cathedral.

Predictably, there had been a massive public debate about the ultra-modern building, erected partly on the ruins of the old cathedral, all but destroyed by German bombers in 1940 – a discussion heightened by the appearance of the new church, including as it did the work of contemporary artists such as Jacob Epstein, Henry Moore and, most controversially, Graham Sutherland, whose massive tapestry was placed behind the altar and dominated the whole interior.

Born in India of Scottish parents (his father was a chemist in the Indian Civil Service) in 1907, Basil Spence had studied at Edinburgh College of Art; moved to London to work with Sir Edwin Lutyens; returned to Edinburgh to complete his architectural training; and joined an Edinburgh practice in 1931. He spent much of the 1930s designing large country houses for wealthy clients who liked his blending of the traditional and the modern. His career interrupted by the outbreak of war, he joined the Royal Artillery and became a major in the camouflage unit, later working in intelligence. While in Normandy he saw the bombed-out ruins of many churches, which sharpened his determination, were he to survive, to design a church. After the war he worked on several structures for the 1951 Festival of Britain in London, and that August learned that he had won the competition to build the new Coventry Cathedral.

He was knighted in 1960.

On the desert island, what would Sir Basil be happiest to get away from? 'The rat race.'

Has music played an important part in his life? 'Yes it has, but I must say that I listen to it rather like a savage, which may be appropriate on a desert island. I don't know a great deal about music but it is food and drink to me, and on occasion I've found it very soothing. I get great solace from it.'

One of his wartime achievements, he recounts, was designing a dummy beach as a decoy to attract enemy fire during the D-Day landings and afterwards. 'When I think back on this it makes me shiver: how fantastically stupid it was that I had actually suggested that it would be a good thing for Spence to make a target of himself taking in dummy ducks, making a dummy beach between ourselves and the Germans and attracting all the shells and mortar bombs which came down. I must say it was quite successful, and there was I jumping about being mortared to blazes for forty days. But that required certain architectural knowledge. It may have been of a warped nature, but it was certainly required.'

Working on the Festival of Britain was 'a wonderful adventure' for him, but Coventry Cathedral was a project on a vastly different scale. Had he, asks Roy Plomley, ever dreamed of designing a cathedral? 'Yes. It was a childish ambition, I suppose, but I've always wanted to build a cathedral, partly because I used to lecture on history, and the whole history of architecture can be traced through temples, through all the ages.'

The contest for the commission to design the cathedral was an open competition throughout the Commonwealth, and had attracted 219 contenders who had stayed the course. Spence had gone to look at the site, and 'I knew exactly what I had to do, and for better or for worse I was convinced from the first five minutes, and it hasn't altered.' But he had considered his chances of winning the competition 'absolutely nil'; so the discovery that he had in fact won 'was a great spiritual experience, apart from anything else'.

Picking up that comment, Plomley asks: 'You did feel that designing this building was an act of worship?' He had indeed felt that, to the point of telling his wife that he proposed not to submit his plan, as it would be looking to make financial gain from that spiritual experience. 'She advised me very strongly to hand it in,' he continues, 'she thought I'd be very foolish not to.'

At this point he asks for Bach's Brandenburg Concerto no. 3, 'one of the records that I played again and again and again when I was designing the building. Incidentally, hearing these records now, they sort of drive my wife crazy. She can't stand them now, but I did play the six Brandenburgs over and over again.'

Is it true that the inspiration for the solution to one technical difficulty came in a dream at the dentist's? 'That is true. It so happened that the design was going very badly at the time. I got an abscess and I went to my dentist in Edinburgh, and he said that he had to pull out a tooth. He gave me a local anaesthetic and I passed out unfortunately – but I had a vivid dream. I dreamed I was walking through the cathedral in some bright colours. The sun slanting in looked marvellous, the organ was playing, the choir was singing. It was absolutely terrific – far better than the finished product, I assure you. But when I got to the altar I couldn't see any stained glass, and so I turned around and there, the whole building was opened up, with the stained glass shining towards the altar. I was determined to try it out.'

Another inspiration came from a photograph in a natural history magazine that his son had been reading: 'I saw an enlarged section of a fly's eye, and this gave me the idea for the vault.'

Plomley widens the scope. 'Do you agree, Sir Basil, that in the main this is an ugly period in the history of architecture, with great slab-shaped monstrosities that are put up as offices or blocks of flats?'

'I think it's a displaced period. I mean, some work can look awfully good in some parts of the world that doesn't look well here. For instance, these American skyscrapers look absolutely marvellous in New York, but in London they seem to shake their fist at the sky. London's a beautiful city with a rich silhouette, and I think that sometimes they're graceless and they deny our heritage – which I believe we have – of sensitivity and scale and quality: these three things that we have, and we can prove in our old architecture.'

His sixth record choice is Benjamin Britten's *War Requiem*, which had first been performed in the new cathedral: 'I know he wrote it for the cathedral, and it seemed to fit awfully well . . . The whole thing is wonderful. I think he's a very great man, and this is one of the most beautiful pieces of music I know.'

Unusually for a *Desert Island Discs* castaway, Sir Basil knows how to build a boat, and is confident that he could find a means to navigate away from the island: 'One knows when the sun rises and sets, and knows something about the stars.'

Now, 'one luxury'.

'I'd like to take my wife.'

'That, I'm afraid, is not allowed.'

'Not allowed? Oh. Well, can I have a hundredweight of spaghetti?'

Plomley, ever the generous spirit, says he can have two hundredweight.

His profile raised spectacularly by a building which remains an emblem of the architecture of the 1960s, Basil Spence went on to leave his mark on many other places: in more churches; in the new universities, especially Sussex, and extensions to the older foundations; in city-centre redevelopment; and in the Knightsbridge Barracks for the Household Cavalry which overlook Hyde Park in central London.

But Coventry Cathedral (*below*) remains his most familiar work – a lasting monument to a man who brought real flair to contemporary buildings and helped change the look of the British townscape in the 1960s.

Sir Basil died in 1976.

Ravel
'Daybreak' (from
Daphnis and Chloe)

Mozart
Sinfonia Concertante
in E flat major
Soloists: Yehudi Menuhin
(violin) and Rudolf Barshai
(viola)

★ J. S. Bach
Passacaglia and Fugue
in C Minor
'One could sit there imagin-
ing one was in a very beautiful
cathedral'

'Mañanita de San Juan'
Teresa Berganza and Felix
Lavilla
'Something for my Latin blood'

Berlioz
'Dies irae' (from
Requiem Mass)

Chopin
Étude no. 3 in E major,
op. 10
Soloist: Sviatoslav Richter

'Honeysuckle Rose'
Lena Horne

Puccini
'Perchè tarda la luna?'
(from _Turandot_)

📖 _Hadrian's Memoirs_ by
Marguerite Yourcenar

♡ **Skin-diver's mask**

DAME MARGOT FONTEYN

prima ballerina

12 April 1965

'What I've looked forward to most of my life would
be an old age on a desert island'

Roy Plomley liked to have an especially eminent
castaway for landmark editions of _Desert Island
Discs_, and the 750th programme was marked by the
appearance of the incomparably elegant form of Dame
Margot Fonteyn.

Born in 1919, she had spent much of her childhood
overseas – her father's work took the family to the USA
and China for substantial periods – and it was on a visit
home in 1931 that she was inspired by seeing Alicia
Markova (cast away 1958 and 2002) in _Les Sylphides_.
She undertook serious study of the ballet, and was soon
showing herself an exceptional performer, working
with legends such as Frederick Ashton (cast away 1959
and 1981): by the time she was twenty she had danced
the lead in _Giselle_, _Swan Lake_ and _The Sleeping Beauty_
for the Sadler's Wells Ballet.

After the war the company moved to Covent Garden,
and a triumphant appearance in New York in 1949
established her firmly as a performer of international
repute – such repute that in 1956 she became Dame
Margot Fonteyn.

At the time of her casting away, Dame Margot's principal partner was Rudolf Nureyev, who had defected

from the Bolshoi Ballet to the West in 1961. Ninette de
Valois (cast away in 1966 and 1991) invited Nureyev
to dance with her company – now the Royal Ballet
– and for his debut asked Fonteyn to perform with
him in *Giselle*. She was forty-two at the time and he
twenty-three.

This castaway enters into the spirit of *Desert Island Discs*
straight away. 'I'm very tempted by the surroundings that
I'm going to live in. In fact, I'm quite looking forward to
this desert island. I can already imagine it quite clearly,
and I can see the sunshine blazing all day long.'

*Margot Fonteyn and Rudolf Nureyev
rehearsing* Paradise Lost, *Royal
Opera House, Covent Garden, 1967*

As a child, she took her dancing 'terribly seriously'. She had been 'always very
anxious to do exactly what I'd been told, to the extent that in my concentration
I would almost always stick my tongue out at the side of my mouth, trying so
hard to get everything right – and I remember my mother would be somewhere
in the wings, or my dancing teacher would be there saying, "Smile! Smile!"'

She recalls that first sight of Markova, and performances at Sadler's Wells: 'I
think that from that moment I knew what ballet was and then knew that I would
like to try to do it, although I never thought I had any possibility of succeeding.'

At fourteen she went to the Sadler's Wells School, run by Ninette de
Valois, then started to dance with the company: 'It was very small in those
days, so one could have one foot in the school and one foot in the company,
which I did for quite a while. I was still a student when I was already dancing
small solos in *Les Sylphides*.'

When Alicia Markova left the Sadler's Wells Company there arose the
question of who would replace her as prima ballerina. 'There was such an
enormous gap between Markova and the rest of us, and I was then two years
younger than some of the other soloists in the company. Roughly what
would happen is that Ninette de Valois divided Markova's place between five
of us: Mary Honer, Elizabeth Miller, Pamela May, June Brae and myself. She
kind of pushed us all into the gap to try to fill it. We didn't quite fill it, but
between us we made an attempt.'

'And it was indeed on repertory lines?', asks Roy Plomley: 'You danced
Giselle one evening and would be back in the *corps de ballet* the next?'

'Yes. In the same evening we would be in two or three ballets. We would
be in every ballet and in one of them we would perhaps be the principal, and
in the others we'd be in the *corps de ballet*.'

Pause for J. S. Bach's Passacaglia in C minor, which sets Fonteyn off on a flight of fancy: 'I can imagine those very tall palm trees making an almost arched cathedral effect, and one could sit there imagining that one was in a very beautiful cathedral and listen to this most perfect and beautiful of all music.'

A far less pleasant scene is suggested when Dame Margot describes a narrow escape for the company during an overseas tour as war was breaking out: 'Costumes, scenery and music were left behind in Holland when the Germans invaded that country, and we left rather hurriedly in an improvised manner in what we were wearing, and what we could wear on top of our ordinary clothes.'

The company was so close to the invasion that 'I saw them landing by parachute.' Later in the war the company returned to continental Europe, but 'in khaki uniforms this time – we went as an ENSA unit'.

Further evidence of Dame Margot's playing along with the whole desert island fantasy comes with her penultimate record choice: 'I've been thinking of various aspects of my life on this desert island, planning it quite carefully. I'm fairly industrious by fits and starts, and terribly lazy in between. I thought that at some stage or other I would probably discover how to ferment coconuts and make coconut wine, and at that point I would want some kind of night club atmosphere, something very sentimental. And after a lot of thought I chose Lena Horne, as one of the most beautiful nightclub artists, and a tune that dates me very much, that a lot of people of my generation will be very happy to hear. I've chosen "Honeysuckle Rose".'

And her final choice? The 'Invocation to the Moon' from the first act of Puccini's *Turandot* – 'the most perfect music for finishing a beautiful lazy day on a beautiful desert island'.

In 1955 Margot Fonteyn had married Roberto de Arias, son of a former president of Panama, and in 1964 – the year before her *Desert Island Discs* appearance – he had been shot and paralysed, leaving him wheelchair-bound for the rest of his life. (According to the *Oxford Dictionary of National Biography*, his assailant was 'a colleague whom he was alleged to have cuckolded.') Fonteyn's career carried on for many years, but she and her husband spent more and more time in a remote Panamanian village where they had a farm.

Her final appearance on stage was at the age of sixty-seven, as the queen in *Sleeping Beauty* in Miami in February 1986. Five years later, in Panama City in February 1991, she died.

Opposite: *Fonteyn and Nureyev in* Marguerite and Armond, *London Coliseum, 1977*

HAROLD PINTER

playwright

14 June 1965

'I do not consider that I am making any distinct stylistic contribution to the world of drama'

Since there is no audio record of Harold Pinter's interview with Roy Plomley in June 1965, we have no way of knowing how long the castaway paused before answering each of the presenter's questions. The Pinter Pause may be a cliché now; but in the mid-1960s that brief, freighted silence was the hallmark of the dramatist's work.

Several of the early plays which had established Pinter as a remarkable and highly unsettling new dramatist had already been staged – notably *The Birthday Party* (1957), *The Caretaker* (1960) and *The Homecoming*, which had opened at the Aldwych Theatre, then the home of the Royal Shakespeare Company, earlier in 1965. Like John Osborne (first cast away in January 1959), Pinter was a new voice in the theatre – but, unlike Osborne's, his was a voice which was expressing itself in a freshly minted dramatic language. Pinter's biographer Michael Billington wrote of his output at this period:

> What linked all Pinter's work was his distinctive use of language. He was clearly alert to the banalities of everyday speech. He also showed how such language could become poetic through its echoes,

symmetries, and repetitions. Above all he seemed highly conscious of the way words could be used as either strategic weapons of domination or a tactical means of evasion.

The Homecoming, *RSC, 1965: Vivien Merchant with Michael Bryant* (left) *and Paul Rogers*

Early on in the interview, Pinter declares that 'there would be great relief in being quite alone with the elements', while 'the only thing that bothers me is the intense cold'. Does he have a religious faith that would help him survive? 'No, I don't. I would have to fall back entirely on my own resources.'

What would he be happy to have got away from? 'Noise, I think, and the racket that we live in. Of course, there wouldn't be complete silence on the desert island – there would be the sea and the wind and the leaves, and I would be very very happy to sit and listen to something which did not consist of engines turning over, and disc brakes and so on.'

First record choice is J. S. Bach. So is the second ('I think I could have devoted the whole programme to Bach'), which occasions a brief exchange between interviewer and interviewed which is almost Pinteresque in its minimalism:

'Why do you choose this?'

'I like it.'

Pinter had an unusual theatrical apprenticeship. 'I went over to Ireland and worked with a Shakespearian manager called Andy McMaster, who was an actor too. We played a most extraordinary rep of plays each week, travelling over southern Ireland in all sorts of towns and villages and stops. The rep consisted of, say, *Hamlet* on the opening night, then *The Merchant of Venice, Othello, King Lear, Oedipus Rex, The Importance of Being Earnest . . .* Then I came back and was out of work for a good deal of the time, and then I played with [Donald] Wolfit a bit and then went all over the country in reps – Agatha Christies and every conceivable sort of play.'

How did he fill in between jobs? 'All sorts of things. I was a postman every Christmas, of course, and sold books in Oxford Street, and the best job I ever had – and the most interesting – was as chucker-out at a ballroom in

Charing Cross Road, which I do not think I was fitted for. But I did not have any trouble, and I did enjoy it.'

He started writing around the age of thirteen – 'poems mostly, and short prose pieces' – but did not write his first play, a one-act drama, until 1957. 'It was called *The Room*. It was done by a friend of mine at Bristol University. I saw it, and was rather astonished by the feeling of seeing one's own play on the stage.'

His next play, *The Birthday Party*, was well received on its pre-London tour but when it came to the Lyric Theatre in Hammersmith, says Plomley, it 'was savaged and massacred by the critics – it only lasted a week.' Was he very discouraged by that?

'Yes, I was. It was a great shock, and I thought of giving the whole thing up. My wife [actress Vivien Merchant] spoke very sensibly to me and I didn't. And I carried on writing.'

The Caretaker was well received, but following that he did not write a play for five years, concentrating instead on television and film scripts – 'both very fascinating mediums, but of course the stage I still regard as the most important of all, the most difficult and the most challenging, the most naked.' Now *The Homecoming* was playing at the Aldwych Theatre, which is 'a great relief' to Pinter.

Roy Plomley comes to the crunch: 'Now, Harold, your first full-length play *The Birthday Party* was shouted down by the critics, we assume because you were off on a tack of your own and they were not with you. In particular, you had evolved this new and very effective stylized rendering of everyday speech. Had you spent a long time evolving this?'

'No. I was not at all conscious of it, in fact I am still not conscious of it. I wrote quite naturally. I had no idea that anything I did was in any way singular, and still have not, really.'

Plomley persists. 'But this thing about your dialogue, that four lines of Pinter does not sound like four lines of any other playwright, which does put this very individual stamp on your plays, and this rendering of the normal incoherent speech. In fact, if I can quote your own words at you: "The more acute the experience, the less articulate the expression."'

'Did I say that?'

'Yes.'

J. S. Bach
Brandenburg Concerto no. 4 in G major

'I find his precision, his exactitude, his serenity quite beguiling'

'Well, I think that has got a bit of sense in it. I think it is just a little too categorical. But I find people do tend to speak to each other in broken sentences – as I am doing now, really – and I do not consider that I am making any distinct stylistic contribution to the world of drama. It is just writing what the characters say to each other. That is all.'

Are his plays allegorical, asks Plomley – does he mean to say more than he sets down?

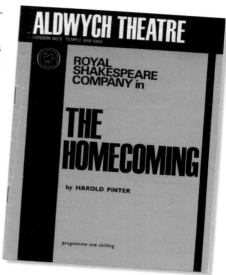

'I think any given person, when he speaks there is always a lot that he does not say and is not prepared to say and cannot say, and so there are bound to be undertones. Human beings are complex people, and of course there are going to be undertones and overtones. But I would say quite definitely that I never intended any kind of allegorical significance. I would not know a symbol if I saw one, and I cannot write like that.'

How does he write a play?

'It is very difficult to describe. It is a matter really of the first page, and a given stage, which is usually a room, and someone is there, and someone comes in, and if something sparks between them then I carry on to the second page, and hopefully to the third page and the fourth page, and then they are moving on their own, working on their own, and I have just to control them.'

Harold Pinter continued to 'control them' for decades, his reputation further enhanced by plays like *Old Times* (1971), *No Man's Land* (1975) and *Betrayal* (1978), and scripts for films such as *The Go-Between* (1970) and *The French Lieutenant's Woman* (1981).

In 1980, he and Vivien Merchant were divorced and he married historian and biographer Lady Antonia Fraser, herself cast away in 1969 and again in 2008.

Harold Pinter was awarded the Nobel Prize for Literature in 2005, and died in December 2008.

ALAN BENNETT

writer and playwright

28 August 1967

'I'd like an unending supply of afternoon teas'

When cast away on the desert island in August 1967 at the age of thirty-three, Alan Bennett was in a sort of professional no-man's-land between his early satirical period and the beginning of the play-writing career which would see him attract public affection of a depth unmatched by any contemporary British writer.

Satire had been at the heart of *Beyond the Fringe*, the mould-breaking revue of the early 1960s in which he performed with his Oxford contemporary Dudley Moore and two young men who had come through the Cambridge Footlights route: Jonathan Miller and Peter Cook. In his influential *Observer* review of the show, Kenneth Tynan wrote: 'Mr Bennett, in manner the mildest of the quartet, is perhaps the most pungent in effect. One will not readily forget the oleaginous blandness with which [he] delivers a sermon on the text: "My brother Esau is an hairy man, but I am a smooth man."'

A little over a year after his *Desert Island Discs* appearance, October 1968 would see the first pro-duction of Bennett's play *Forty Years On* (with John Gielgud as the Headmaster and Bennett himself as Tempest). That was followed in the 1970s by *Getting On*, *Habeas Corpus* and *The Old Country*: plays which would establish him as a serious dramatist whose work is characterized by an irresistible combination of humour, wistfulness and humanity.

Bennett's part in his interview with Roy Plomley is shot through with the diffident demeanour which was to characterize so much of his work over the ensuing half-century. Having established that he would be happy to have left behind noise, and specifically noise from cars ('Do you drive yourself?' – 'Yes I do, but rather with a guilty conscience'), his first choice of music is informed by that trademark summoning of a childhood memory. The piece is William Walton's Symphony no. 1: 'When I first got to like music was in Leeds when I was a boy. I used to go on Saturday nights to concerts given by the Yorkshire Symphony Orchestra – which was Leeds' own orchestra, I suppose, and which was later disbanded – and we used to pay sixpence and go and sit behind the double basses at the back of the orchestra, and this was one of the things that they played.'

What, wonders Roy Plomley, had his ambition been when a boy?

'I didn't really have any ambitions to be anything. I remember my mother used to say, "You ought to be a gentleman farmer, and then you could earn £10 a week," which seemed princely to her at that time.'

Had he been fascinated by entertainment? 'Not really. There was a time when I used to go every Saturday to matinees in the theatre and to concerts at night. This was between fourteen and seventeen, and then for a long time I didn't go at all.'

After leaving school he did his National Service, which in his case meant spending over a year on a course, learning Russian.

'Have you used Russian since?'

'No. But it was a delightful period because it wasn't like being in the army at all. We didn't wear uniforms. We used to live in a country house just outside Cambridge. It was one of the happiest periods of my life.'

Then to Oxford, to read history. He stayed on after graduating, as 'I had an opportunity to do research and I wasn't really sure what I wanted to do.' His research topic was Richard II in the period 1388 to 1389 – 'It seems very small to most people but there was a great deal going on' – and he combined research with teaching: 'I enjoyed teaching very much more than I did research. I miss it now, really.'

It was at Oxford that he began performing. 'I started quite late on in my university career doing things at odd smoking concerts [informal revues] which we used to have in college. And it was there that I first did a sermon,

Alan Bennett and some of the cast of The History Boys, *October 2006 – with future castaway James Corden on extreme right*

which stood me in good stead later on.' (Indeed it did, for not only was a later version of it to take Kenneth Tynan's fancy, but the sketch 'Take a Pew' – 'Life is like a tin of sardines', etc. – was to become a staple ingredient of *Beyond the Fringe*.)

It is at this point of the programme that Bennett asks for 'not music – I'd like the sounds of an English summer's day on a quiet country railway station, if that can be arranged'. With *Desert Island Discs* anything can be arranged, and the listeners are treated to fifty-five seconds of rural tranquillity, complete with cows mooing, a rooster crowing, chickens, and the fading whistle of a train.

'Alan,' asks Roy Plomley, 'at Oxford, did you know a Mr Miller or a Mr Moore or a Mr Cook?'

'I'd seen Jonathan Miller and Peter Cook in various Footlights revues which had come to Oxford. Dudley I came across because he wrote to me saying, would I audition for him in a cabaret evening which he was organizing, and I wrote back very high-handedly and said no, I wouldn't audition, but I would perform.'

'Bravo!'

'I went along to do two pieces, and I did one of them and then Dudley found the evening was going on rather longer than he'd imagined, and tried to stop it without my having done the second piece, which was the sermon, and I bustled forward and insisted on doing it.'

In 1959 he went with an Oxford revue to the Edinburgh Festival Fringe, where he was spotted by John Bassett (assistant to the Festival director Robert Ponsonby). It was Bassett who had the idea of putting him together with Cook, Moore and Miller, and the result was that the quartet returned to Edinburgh in 1960 as *Beyond the Fringe*. 'It was a runaway success,' says Bennett: 'we were praised for all sorts of virtues that we didn't know we possessed at the time. I mean, we were told that we'd done away with all those trappings of revue, all that scenery and so on. In fact this was simply because we'd have had to pay for any scenery or any costumes that we used out of our own salary, and we didn't do it – too mean!'

**West of Exeter
(railway sounds)**

'I'd like the sounds of an English summer's day on a quiet country railway station'

Beyond the Fringe arrived in the West End in May 1961, and the following year the original four performers took the show to the USA (leaving a substitute cast to carry on the show in London). Had they changed the script for the American version? 'No. We felt that since it was an English import – like tweeds, or whisky, or other prestige things – its very nature was English and so it ought to remain so, and this worked. The Americans laughed at the jokes, and if they didn't understand them, then they pretended that they understood.'

Bennett has recently had his own television show *On the Margin*, which Plomley describes as 'a very funny half hour on two levels – it's got music-hall jokes and intellectual jibes all mixed up'.

'Well, I like a belly laugh and I like broad humour, but I also like very esoteric private jokes, and I think the two mix well very well and appeal to people on different levels, in the same way as *Beyond the Fringe* did.'

He is currently working on a programme about the nineteenth-century diarist, the Reverend Francis Kilvert.

'You've been in trouble with the Kilvert Society?'

'Yes – mistakenly, really. They imagine that it is going to be a savage and stinging satire on nineteenth-century clergy, and of course this is very much mistaken. It will, I hope, be a very affectionate portrait.'

'This raises a point,' says Plomley. 'To me the most joyous part of *Beyond the Fringe* was your sermon, "Take a Pew", and parsons have turned up in

On the Margin. You have something of a reputation for clergy-baiting.'

'Yes – an ill-deserved reputation, in a way. I think that generally speaking one only makes fun of the things for which one feels an affection, and this is very true of my attitude towards the clergy, and towards dons and eccentric people. It does spring out of affection . . . I'm very conscious when I go into a church that people might think I was there to make notes.'

Which leads to another of the eight records, a congregation at St Paul's Cathedral singing the hymn 'Now Thank We All Our God'. The castaway explains: 'This would remind me of the Anglican church services, of which I'm very fond, and also of my father playing his violin to the hymns on the wireless on Sunday night.'

How would he survive on the island?

'I cook for myself, but whether I could do it there I don't know. I've only once ever caught a fish, and then was terrified by the wrigglings on the end of the line.'

His book is a complete run of the literary magazine *Horizon*, edited by Cyril Connolly – 'I've read most of it, but it's something I'm always going back to' – and his luxury is a quintessentially Alan Bennett choice:

'I'd like an unending supply of afternoon teas.'

Surprisingly, in view of his later achievements, Alan Bennett has never made a return journey to the desert island – a distinction which plenty of lesser talents have managed. He once wrote of the 'tiresome conventions' of the programme, which may indicate that he did not altogether enjoy the experience in 1967 and perhaps had no appetite for repeating it.

The four and a half decades since his casting away have seen an outpouring of memorable work: more plays, such as *A Question of Attribution, The Madness of George III* and *The History Boys*; films such as *A Private Function*, plus several screen versions of his plays; audio and television masterpieces like *A Woman of No Importance, An Englishman Abroad* and *Talking Heads*; and many books, including *The Lady in the Van, Writing Home, Untold Stories* and *The Uncommon Reader*.

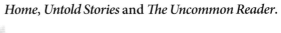

'Battle Hymn of the Republic'
Mormon Tabernacle Choir

'My Love is Like a Red, Red Rose'
Kenneth McKellar

Lehár
'You Are My Heart's Delight' (from *The Land of Smiles*)
Soloist: Richard Tauber

Carl Maria von Weber
Invitation to the Waltz, op. 65

★ **Carl Zeller**
'Sei nicht Bös' (from *Der Obersteiger*)
Soloist: Elisabeth Schwarzkopf

'All Through the Night'
The Treorchy Male Voice Choir

'Cockles and Mussels' ('Molly Malone')
William Clauson

Mendelssohn
'O, for the Wings of a Dove'

📖 *The History of Warfare* by **Viscount Montgomery of Alamein**

♡ **Piano**

VISCOUNT MONTGOMERY OF ALAMEIN

soldier

20 December 1969

'When things are bad in the battle you go out in front'

The 1,000th edition of *Desert Island Discs* was a very noteworthy landmark in the programme's history – and attracted a very noteworthy castaway.

Bernard Montgomery, eighty-one years old when setting foot on the desert island, was arguably the outstanding British soldier of the twentieth century. Having commanded the Eighth Army in North Africa to beat Rommel in the second battle of El Alamein in 1942, he was commander of British troops in northern Europe in 1944, playing a major role in the D-Day landings. And it was at Montgomery's headquarters on Lüneberg Heath that the Allied leaders took the German surrender in May 1945.

The *Desert Island Discs* team agreed to record the programme at the Field Marshal's home in the country and Roy Plomley remembered how he and his then producer Ronald Cook drove down to Hampshire: 'A housekeeper showed us upstairs to the sitting-room, where Monty was waiting for us. A smaller figure than I had expected, he was dressed in slacks and blue sweater and was deeply suntanned. "My doctor says if I look after myself and don't go out at night, I'll see my century."'

In his clipped but assured tones, Monty explains the principles behind his choice of records: 'I chose first of all "The Battle Hymn of the Republic" because I'm a soldier, and the last one, "O, for the Wings of a Dove", because I thought I might be able to fly away from this island. And then in between I filled in numbers two to seven with songs and tunes I'm very fond of indeed and like to listen to. And that's how I did it.'

The son of a clergyman who became Anglican bishop of Tasmania when Bernard was two years old, Montgomery had had a spartan childhood. 'My father was a saint – if any saints do walk upon this earth – and I worshipped him. My mother was a disciplinarian. She was married when she was sixteen and she had her seventeenth birthday on her honeymoon and, of course, children began to appear and she was the wife of a very busy London vicar, and shortly afterwards the wife of a bishop. And there was no time to attend to the children – well, she didn't know how to do it because she was so young.'

He concedes that in his early years in Tasmania he could be something of a handful. 'I was very rebellious, and when my mother demanded discipline from me, I refused to give in. I said, "No", and took my beating.'

A particular incident is recalled: 'I was caught one day in the garden, smoking. I didn't want to smoke, but I just thought I would. I was smoking a cigarette behind a bush or something and I was caught and taken into the house, and my father heard about this and he took me into our little chapel which we had in the house, and we knelt down and he prayed to the Almighty that I might be forgiven this dreadful sin. And then there was a little silence, and I thought that the matter was settled: the Almighty had accepted my sorrow. Not at all. When we opened the door and went out, there was my mother with a cane. She thought more earthly correction was needed as well, and I got beaten. I took it. But the point is really that when people say to me, "What makes you tick?", I think what makes me tick was that I absolutely refused to give in when I thought there was no need to. For instance, my mother said to me once, "Bernard, you will sign the Pledge." I said: "Never will I sign the Pledge. I don't want to drink – I don't drink – but I am not going to sign the Pledge." That was the sort of thing which moulded my character. I like to think it did – and it was good for me.'

Mendelssohn
'O, for the Wings of a Dove'

'I thought I might be able to fly away from this island'

Monty in action in the Western Desert, 1942

He can remember wanting to be a soldier from the age of five or six: 'I saw soldiers going off to the Boer War – in their red coats in those days – and I said, "That's the stuff for me." Now that was very unpopular indeed with my family, who wanted me for the Church. It was always assumed that because I was like my father in face, I must be a clergyman. And then when I got to St Paul's School in London and they said, "What are you going to be?", I said, "A soldier."'

So it was thence to Sandhurst and India, and by August 1914 he was a young subaltern. 'I was very badly wounded in the first battle of Ypres, and I was taken back to an advanced dressing station, and they thought I was dead. There was an officer there who was dead, and they dug two graves, because I was just about to die. Well, I defeated them: I didn't die, you see.'

The outbreak of the Second World War saw Monty with the British Expeditionary Force in France. In 1940 he returned to Britain with the evacuation of Dunkirk, and—'The rest of your war story,' says Roy Plomley, 'is history. The Western Desert, Tunis, Sicily, Italy, the Normandy landings. You were in your fifties and you suddenly became a national figure, and you became a character, an instantly recognizable character – the unmistakable Monty with the beret with the badges on it, and the flying jacket. Now, this was a morale-building project and a public relations job in which you had a considerable hand, wasn't it?'

'It was, really. I thought in those days that the staff and the generals were remote from the soldiers. Now, I've learned in my career that that doesn't pay – that the soldiers are really the people who in the end win the battle, and you've got to be with them all the time. And they must know you.' So when he was given a beret with a Tank Corps badge in it, 'I stuck my general's badge in and had two badges, and for the rest of the war I wore it. The Army Council didn't like it and I got ticked off, but I stuck to it. I said, "It's worth a couple of divisions" – because when things are bad in the battle you go out in front, and if you just wear a red hat they don't know who it is. But once they saw the beret with the two badges they said, "Ah, there's the old boy – must be all right."'

His relationship with Winston Churchill had not always been smooth, because Churchill had himself been a soldier in a different age and did not fully appreciate how warfare had changed. 'I don't mind telling you that when I was fighting the battle of Alamein, he wanted me to attack Rommel in September. I refused because of the moon. I had to have a moon for purposes of handling the mines and things. And I won't be ready, I said, by the September moon. He wanted September to synchronize with Stalingrad: he'd fixed it up with Stalin, you see . . . You are bound to have tussles with your political master. You can't help it. But Winston was very good, once he saw that it was no good going on with it. And when he came to stay with me in the field, which he did several times, I used to make it quite clear to him. I said: "Sir, you are here in the zone of the armies. You must do what I tell you, because we can't afford you to take risks. I shall get into awful trouble if you got bumped off by a shell or something."'

Montgomery would be unlikely to try to escape from the island – perfectly understandable at the age of eighty-one – but 'I should keep a jolly good look out for passing vessels – smoke and things like that.'

Record number 7 is the Irish air 'Molly Malone', requested by its popular name of 'Cockles and Mussels'. 'I want that, of course, because I really am part Irish. The Irish are a great people, you know. They like fighting. And if they can't find anyone to fight, then they generally fight each other.'

Luxury? A piano, so that he could teach himself how to play it.

And a book? 'Well, it may horrify you for me to say so, but I would like a book which I wrote myself about war: *The History of Warfare*, in which I make it quite clear that the generals, besides fighting wars, have got to play their part in preventing them. This book at the end goes into the question of how to stop fighting, and I would have lots of time, and I would ponder over how we could stop people fighting – so that when I came back, which I hope to do, one might be able to do something about it.'

Roy Plomley's later recollection of the visit to Monty describes him as 'surely one of the most complicated men I have ever interviewed', and in particular mentions

> a constant tendency to namedrop . . . Almost every sentence brought in a reference to a political leader or a royal personage, with a parenthetic comment such as 'I know him well,' or 'He's a great friend of mine.' This is a common habit among men of humble origin, who have never lost their awe of mingling with the mighty, but Monty was the son of a bishop and a man whose training was aimed at taking men only for what they were worth.

To be fair to Montgomery, this does not come across from the broadcast programme. Certainly the Field Marshal is no shrinking violet, but he displays an engaging candour and certitude; and for that special occasion of the thousandth trip to the island, he was great value.

Viscount Montgomery did not live to 'see my century'. He died in March 1976 at the age of eighty-eight.

1970s

IF THE VISUAL emblems of the 1960s are mini-skirts and kaftans, and Bobby Moore being chaired round the Wembley pitch with the Jules Rimet Trophy, and four mop-haired Liverpudlians in collarless suits, those of the 1970s are of a different nature altogether: glam rock and platform boots, the Sex Pistols and safety pins; factories closed and lights dimmed during the three-day week; piles of rat-infested rubbish on the streets; and Margaret Thatcher reciting St Francis of Assisi on the steps of No. 10.

Politically it was a topsy-turvy decade. Edward Heath unexpectedly defeated Harold Wilson in the 1970 general election and was then defeated by Wilson in 1974. In 1973, the UK joined the European Economic Community; in 1975, a referendum was held on whether it should stay there. (Twice as many people voted to stay in as to come out.) In March 1976 came Wilson's shock resignation, leaving James Callaghan to soldier on as Prime Minister through the 1978–9 'Winter of Discontent' until May 1979, when he was succeeded by the United Kingdom's first woman premier – and the first premier of either sex to have previously been cast away on Roy Plomley's desert island.

The roots of the social reforms planted in the 1960s became more deeply embedded, with the Gay Liberation Front founded in 1970 and the feminist magazine *Spare Rib* in 1972; meanwhile the economy slid into chaos, with inflation reaching an eye-watering 26.9 per cent in 1975 and the International Monetary Fund coming to Britain's rescue the following year. At least North Sea oil seemed to be offering a significant new income stream for the country. In Northern Ireland 'the Troubles' became ever worse, especially in the wake of 'Bloody Sunday' in January 1972, when fourteen unarmed civilians were shot dead by British troops.

In popular music, while the 1960s had been characterized by exuberance, freshness and invention, the 1970s were defined first by the superficial glitz of glam rock – David Bowie in Ziggy Stardust mode, Gary Glitter, Marc Bolan (right) et al. – and the self-consciously serious 'progressive' rock of such bands as Pink Floyd and Yes, and then later in the decade by the singular British cultural phenomenon of punk rock.

Throughout the 1970s *Desert Island Discs* remained secure in its status of national institution. No longer was any BBC executive foolhardy enough to speculate whether it was a programme that had run its course. Indeed, there was plenty of evidence to the contrary – principally the roll-call of castaways, which was becoming ever more varied and ever more elevated, if not ever more voluble: screen legend James Stewart caused a problem on his appearance in May 1974 by nodding, rather than voicing, his assent to Roy Plomley's summary of his wartime experience, so that after the initial session he had to record variations on the word 'Yes', which were then spliced into the interview. Still, such hiccups notwithstanding, the great and the good from all spheres were still queuing up to be asked whether they could fish or build a shelter.

From the world of classical music came Yehudi Menuhin (see pages 185–8), Luciano Pavarotti (pages 174–7), Alfred Brendel (luxury: a Bavarian rococo church), Isaac Stern, Victoria de los Angeles, Tito Gobbi, John Lill, Vladimir Ashkenazy, Josephine Barstow, Jacqueline du Pré, Moura Lympany (who, as previously noted, chose eight records of herself playing, and whose luxury was wine from her own vineyard) and Elisabeth Söderström.

From stage and screen – in addition to James Stewart – came international luminaries such as Lauren Bacall (pages 198–201), Bing Crosby, David Niven, Alec Guinness, Richard Chamberlain, Judi Dench (who wanted Basil Brush films – and a projector – as her luxury), Ian McKellen, Omar Sharif, Derek Jacobi and Ralph Richardson.

There were artists – David Hockney (pages 165–8) and Elisabeth Frink and Edward Ardizzone and Peter Blake and Ruskin Spear – and more musicians: Ravi Shankar and Peggy Lee and Burl Ives and Alan Jay Lerner and Tony Bennett and Charles Aznavour.

There was explorer Wilfred Thesiger (whose luxury was a supply of acid drops); authors as diverse as Shirley Conran, Daphne du Maurier and Arthur C. Clarke; Gwen Berryman, who played Doris in *The Archers*; and Joan Bakewell (luxury: a yellow Lamborghini) – who would return to the island in 2009 (when her luxury was paper and pencils). And there was Marcel Marceau, who mercifully did not mime his answers to Plomley's questions.

In football, England's hold on the World Cup had lasted only up to the quarter-finals of the next contest in 1970, when they were knocked out by West Germany. But the new decade had its own generation of sporting heroes, several of whom became castaways – among them rugby players Gareth Edwards and Barry John, swimmer David Wilkie, athlete Alan Pascoe, boxer John Conteh, Formula One driver Graham Hill, snooker player Ray Reardon, and that quintessential 1970s sporting icon, motorcyclist Barry Sheene. Cricket remained the best-represented sport on the island, with the 1970s marooning Tony Greig, Derek Randall, Mike Brearley and Fred Trueman, as well as commentators John Arlott and Brian Johnston.

In among all these were the more unusual interviewees, such as Quentin Poole, Head Chorister of King's College, Cambridge, marooned on Boxing Day 1970 at the age of thirteen – the youngest castaway in the programme's history; or Group Captain Peter Townsend, best known for his ill-fated romance with Princess Margaret in the 1950s (which is not mentioned in the interview); or Margaret Powell (pages 156–60), the former domestic servant whose first volume of autobiography, *Below Stairs*, had made her a publishing sensation.

French mime artist Marcel Marceau

No one in their right mind would have expected to find on the desert island some of the decade's wilder emblematic figures, such as Sid Vicious or Derek 'Red Robbo' Robinson, but none the less, one factor dividing the programme from the new generation was the widening gap in age between the presenter and the average castaway. Between the marooning of conductor Bernard Haitink on 19 January 1974 and John Brooke-Little, Richmond Herald of Arms, a week later, Roy Plomley turned sixty. Since 1942 he had presented over 1,200 editions of *Desert Island Discs*, and some castaways' recollections of being on the programme in the 1970s suggest that by this stage in its life, and his own, Plomley's engagement with his interviewees was less than it might have been.

In October 1979 Michael Palin went to the Garrick Club for the pre-recording lunch with the presenter, and afterwards wrote in his diary: 'Considering he does fifty-two programmes a year . . . it's not surprising, though a little disappointing, that once on air Plomley clicks into a routine. He doesn't listen all the time and, having confessed that he has seen only two Python shows and no *Ripping Yarns*, there is little chance of a similarity of interests. So it's a touch formal, but he seems very happy.'

Another castaway in the 1970s who did not relish the experience of being shipwrecked by Roy Plomley confessed as much to Kirsty Young in the *Archive on 4* seventieth anniversary programme in January 2012: 'He took me to the Garrick Club for lunch. We then came back to a broom cupboard at the BBC – it seemed to me – and had this desultory conversation about my musical choices. And then the worst thing of all was that I'd anticipated the music flowing into the programme, but not a bit of it. I'd say, "Well, I'd like Stan Kenton" – silence, and then the interview started again. I thought this was silly, because it defeats the purpose of the exercise. The genius of the programme – or part of it – is that while you're listening to the music, things might occur to you.'

That castaway was Michael Parkinson.

But plenty of castaways enjoyed the experience wholeheartedly. After the presenter had thanked her for appearing, in July 1970, Barbara Cartland could scarcely contain herself: 'Thank you so much for having me. I've loved being here, I've loved meeting you all, and all the people in the studio. It's been very, very exciting.' And it is worth noting Barbara Cartland's reason for her final record choice:

'My last record I'd want to have about myself. I'd like to have something to show what I'd do if I got the chance of being – not being really the prime minister of England, I don't think women will be very good at that – but I'd like to have a chance for women to influence the men more than they are at the moment. I think women have failed in their job, because the world has always been ruled from the pillow, and by women – the petticoat government behind the government – and I think women today have ceased to be feminine. They're so busy trying to be pseudo-men and trying to have equality – which is ridiculous, when you can always rule things far better

Barbara Cartland, queen of romantic fiction

by being a superior and very, very elusive and attractive sex, and so I'd like this because I think women bring happiness. I think women are the flowers in life and that's what they should aim at, to leave the world a lovelier place because they've been in it. And therefore for my last record I'd like "If I Ruled the World".'

Politics of a more conventional kind occasionally reared its head. In July 1971, some months after Mrs Margaret Thatcher, Secretary of State for Education, had done away with free school milk for pupils over seven – hence the rhyme 'Maggie Thatcher / Milk Snatcher' – John Cleese chose as his luxury a life-size *papier mâché* model of Margaret Thatcher and a baseball bat. (When Cleese was marooned again in 1997, his luxury was his former *Monty Python* colleague Michael Palin – stuffed.)

Milestones in the 1970s include increases in transmission time – from thirty to thirty-five minutes in 1977, and to forty minutes in 1979, providing the opportunity to add more meat to the interviews; the first foursome cast away, the Amadeus String Quartet in February 1978; and the first (but not last) time an inflatable woman was chosen as a luxury – by Oliver Reed in November 1974.

Another luxury that caused a bit of a stir came in one of the very last programmes of the 1970s. On 15 December 1979 the castaway was American writer Norman Mailer. All had gone smoothly with the record choices, which included Elgar, Gershwin, Kern, Miles Davis and Beethoven. One of the biggest and most carnivorous beasts of the literary world was proving perfectly amenable. Only the closing formalities to go. And then . . .

'. . . one luxury you're allowed to take,' prompts Roy Plomley.

'I would take a stick of the very best marijuana I could find,' says Mailer, 'and I would save it for years and hope it didn't get too stale, because I know that I would have one opportunity to smoke it and only one – and so I'd wait for that perfect day on the desert island when all the conditions were right.'

'This is illegal talk, Mr Mailer!'

'Well, here we are – in trouble again.'

Trouble enough to send the *Desert Island Discs* team – led by Derek Drescher, who had been the main producer since the middle of the decade – to the Radio 4 executives for clearance to transmit the offending section. They got it; and although after the broadcast there was predictable outrage,

the affair soon blew over. Normal service was resumed when, in the interview immediately following Mailer's, Sir Osbert Lancaster – cartoonist and writer – took as his luxury a live sturgeon, from which he could enjoy a constant supply of caviar.

'In trouble again' – Norman Mailer

For many years Roy Plomley had been keen to cast away Alistair MacLean, the author of blockbuster thrillers including *The Guns of Navarone*, which in 1961 was made into an acclaimed film starring Gregory Peck (cast away in 1980). MacLean was reluctant to give interviews – even on such a relaxed and informal stage as *Desert Island Discs* – so when Plomley heard that the BBC had at last received his agreement to do the programme, he was understandably elated. Possibly that elation proved a distraction, for when Plomley phoned MacLean to invite him to the Savile Club for a pre-recording lunch, he did not pause to wonder why the author's office was in Ontario House, headquarters of that Canadian state's operation in London. MacLean accepted the lunch offer graciously, Plomley dug out the cuttings and a copy of his castaway's latest novel, and all seemed set fair.

Plomley himself takes up the story: 'When I rose to greet him as he was shown into the Morning Room at the club, I was surprised to see that, although he was the lithe and slender middle-aged Scot I was expecting, he had slightly more hair than I remembered noticing on the television screen.'

They went for a pre-prandial drink in the club bar, where Plomley enjoyed his guest's amiability and 'pawky Scots humour that presaged a first-rate broadcast'. Strange, as 'on the screen, he had shown a quality of shyness which was no longer present'.

Having ordered a second drink, Plomley turned to the question of how the highly prolific MacLean wrote his books:

'Which part of the year do you put aside to do your writing?'

'Writing?'

'Yes, your books.'

'I'm not Alistair MacLean the writer.'

'No?'

'No. I'm in charge of the European tourist bureau of the Government of Ontario.'

Oops. Confining his alarm to one lifted eyebrow, Roy Plomley let the conversation move on – and to his even greater credit, took the line that since this kindly man had been invited to be interviewed for *Desert Island Discs*,

The Savile Club

that agreement should be honoured. 'We went upstairs to the dining room,' Plomley recalled. 'There is a strict rule in the club that no papers shall be produced in that room, thus keeping out all thoughts of toil or commerce. I confess I broke the rule: I slipped a piece of paper beside my plate and made surreptitious notes as we ate. After all, I had researched one Alistair MacLean and, in an hour or two, I was to interview another one, of whose background I knew nothing.'

After lunch they returned to the BBC to work on getting his records together, then – with the producer Ronald Cook looking on baffled as presenter and castaway talked a good deal about Ontario but nothing about writing books – recorded the programme.

Naturally enough, Alistair MacLean (the Ontario one) wanted to be told when his edition of *Desert Island Discs* would be broadcast, as his children would be keen to hear it. Ronald Cook assured him that they would let him know, but that didn't solve the sticky issue of what to do with the programme. Roy Plomley described the final episode in one of *Desert Island Discs*' strangest stories:

The top brass called a meeting. They spend a lot of their time at meetings. They listened to the recording and were unanimously agreed that Alistair MacLean, of Ontario, is an exceptionally gifted broadcaster but that the subject of tourism in Ontario is not of sufficient general interest for a *Desert Island Discs* programme. Mr MacLean would receive his fee, of course, but also a polite letter of apology for the fact that, due to a misunderstanding, his programme would not be broadcast.

It was a pity. One thing I know: Ontario tourism in Europe is in exceptionally capable hands.

As for the other Alistair MacLean, he never did appear on *Desert Island Discs*.

MARGARET POWELL

Below Stairs author

14 November 1970

'Wah-hah-hah-hah-hah!'

There was never a laugh like Margaret Powell's. *Wah-hah-hah-hah-hah!*, it went, like the screech of some exotic bird in the Amazonian rainforest, and it endeared the former kitchen maid to all who heard it.

Well – nearly all. On 1 December 1970, a fortnight after Mrs Powell had been welcomed on to the desert shore, John Lade, Chief Assistant in the BBC Gramophone Department, sent a memo to H.P.Ops.R., copy to H.P.S.G.R. and various others:

'In reply to your memo of 26 November to H.G.D., I have listened very carefully to Tape No. TLN45/GF1963 and find it perfectly acceptable. I do agree that Margaret Powell's laughter could be considered a little irritating, though personally I found it rather infectious, as did Roy Plomley.'

Leaving aside disappointment that among the *Desert Island Discs* audience there breathed anyone so small-minded that they were moved to write and complain about her laugh, Margaret Powell had a captivating story to tell.

Born Margaret Langley in 1907 in Hove, Sussex, she had to abandon her dream of becoming a teacher as her parents could not afford to finance her training. Instead she went into service as a kitchen maid, rising to become a cook. 'Eventually', she wrote, 'I took the only escape route open to a servant: I got married. I left domestic service with an enormous sense of inferiority and the ability to cook a seven-course dinner.'

It was only after her three sons had grown up that she was able to get the education she had craved for so long. Her reminiscences at an evening class of life downstairs were recorded by a local BBC community unit; in turn they caught the ear of publisher Peter Davies, which led to publication in 1968 of her best-selling book *Below Stairs*. 'Domestic service does give an insight and perhaps an inspiration for a better kind of life,' she wrote: 'You do think about the way they lived and maybe unbeknown to yourself you try to emulate it. The social graces may not mean very much but they do help you to ease your way through life.'

In late 1970, with *The Margaret Powell Cookery Book* just published, Mrs Powell was at last easing her way through life very nicely – all the way to the desert island.

Margaret Powell could endure loneliness, she tells Roy Plomley – 'especially as people say to me that one of my chief failings is that I never wait for answers when I talk. It would be fine on a desert island, wouldn't it, because there wouldn't be anyone to answer.'

Music does not loom large in her life, but her first record choice – Amelita Galli-Curci singing 'Sempre libera' from *La Traviata* – takes her back in graphic detail to her early years below stairs:

'I heard this years ago when I was fifteen and in my first place as a kitchen maid. On one particular night when we had a huge dinner party, I was struggling up the stairs at twelve o'clock at night feeling absolutely begrimed, greasy with the washing up because we only had a horrible great cement sink that smelled and great big iron saucepans, and I'd been working like a slave all the evening and then sitting at the supper listening to vulgarity from the older servants which at fifteen I knew nothing about. And as I went up the stairs feeling immersed in dirt and grime – our back stairs were sort of parallel with their front stairs until you got up above – as I got to the first floor of our stairs, through the door that led to their part, although the door was shut, came this glorious voice. I was absolutely spellbound. At that time of night, and feeling dirty and tired, I sat on the stairs and listened to it. And it was like a kind of mountain stream. It made you feel clean – inwardly anyway, if not outwardly.'

Her mother and grandmother were in domestic service – 'they both started as kitchen maids and worked up to be cooks' – and her father was a painter and decorator, which made her early life precarious, as people did not want their houses decorated in the winter. 'And what you have to remember in those days is that when a man was out of work there was no money at all coming in, because there wasn't any dole.'

Thwarted by the family's lack of money in her ambition to be a teacher, Margaret took her first job at the age of thirteen. This was 'to push a very aristocratic old dear around in a bath chair. She once had lots of money – a big house, lots of servants – but all she'd got left was a crabby old retainer. And I used to get there at ten o'clock in the morning and help to dress her – put a lot of capes round her and wind one of those long feather boas round her neck. I used to wish it was a boa constrictor' – and *Wah-hah-hah-hah-hah!,* the first laugh crackles through the air.

'One day she got me to push her all the way to the West Pier – quite a long way from Hove when you're only thirteen – and when I'd got her there, nothing was right for this old dear. First the sun was in her eyes – turn the chair round. Too windy – turn the chair round again. "I can't see anything" – so I just left her there and walked back home. *Wah-hah-hah-hah-hah!* My mother was very taken aback but my father just laughed, and after a week he said, "I wonder if that old girl is still at the West Pier." *Wah-hah-hah-hah-hah!* Nothing more was heard. I reckon she just got out and pushed it back herself.'

Within two years she had left home for her first full-time job in domestic service. 'What were your duties?' asks Roy Plomley.

'First of all, you had to keep all the kitchen – the scullery, the passage, the front door and everything – clean. Do all the boots and shoes, knives, forks, cutlery, copper saucepans. Wait on all the servants, lay out their meals and wait on them. And in my first place as a kitchen maid I wasn't even allowed to eat with the servants. I had to take mine out in the kitchen and eat it by myself.'

Verdi
'Sempre libera'
from *La Traviata*

'It was like a kind of mountain stream ... it made you feel clean somehow inwardly'

How early did she start? 'Rise at five-thirty – six o'clock on Sundays – and then a long list of things that you had to do before eight o'clock in the morning.'

One record choice is *Invitation to the Waltz*, for good reason. 'I've always been smitten with the culture bug, and I thought that I should appreciate this what I call high-falutin' music. So I went to a concert one night. Albert, my husband, wouldn't come, because he said one in the family was enough. I sat next to a lady and they played all this stuff, I couldn't understand a word of it. And in the interval she turned to me and she said, "Oh, absolutely fantastic, wasn't it? What execution! What profundity! There's no comparison, is there?" I didn't even know what she was comparing it with, so I just nodded and smiled. And then after the interval the first tune they played was this *Invitation to the Waltz*, which I thought was marvellous, and I could understand it. So I turned to her to speak, and I saw she had a terribly pained expression. I said, "Oh, wasn't that marvellous?", and she said, "Dreadful – like Turkish Delight."' *Wah-hah-hah-hah-hah!*

'I'm very fond of Turkish Delight,' says Roy Plomley indignantly.

'Me too,' agrees his castaway: 'I like Turkish Delight – especially the pink bits.' *Wah-hah-hah-hah-hah!*

At eighteen she moved on, and became a cook. 'One of the first things I came a terrible cropper over was this question of cooking a turkey, you see. I'd only been there three months and it was Christmas, and I had to cook in a kitchen range. I never was much good – either had them boiling hot, or not hot enough. I'm not exaggerating. I'm sure that up to half an hour before that turkey should have been ready it was lovely, but when I got it out just prior to serving, it was as black as your hat. I was horrified. I scraped it all off with a nutmeg grater – *Wah-hah-hah-hah-hah!* – and I liberally sprinkled it with golden breadcrumbs, and I thought: well, it doesn't look too bad. When the parlour maid came down from serving it I said, "Did they say anything up there?" She said, "Well, Sir Walter muttered something about good cooks being a dying race."'

As for the man who became her husband, he was the milkman who called at the big house where she was a cook, and who was renowned locally for having once lost his horse and cart. 'He said it was an absolute dense fog, and the horse was such a sagacious animal that couldn't really get his bearings, and it was the horse trying to find out where it was. *Wah-hah-hah-hah-hah!*

Albert used to look lovely, driving his horse. He looked just like Ben Hur. *Wah-hah-hah-hah-hah!'*

Now Margaret Powell has a wholly new life. She has written three volumes of autobiography, appears regularly on radio and television, and goes on lecture tours. 'I used to get nightmares, thinking it was all over. But now I've bought two four-foot wardrobes to contain all my clothes, and they're right opposite my bed, so if I wake up in the night with a nightmare, I look at them and think: "Still going on – good!"' *Wah-hah-hah-hah-hah!*

Her desert island luxury? 'What I would like, as I've got the record player there, is to have records of one foreign language, preferably one that goes with desert islands. Perhaps Tahiti.'

And her book? 'We have in our front room at home an enormous great volume, which seems to weigh at least ten pounds. I bought it second-hand, years ago. It's Gibbon's *Decline and Fall of the Roman Empire*, and there it sits, a living reproach to me, because I feel I ought to be reading it. And I open it – it's about five thousand pages at least, if not more – and I think, "No, I can't, this isn't the day – put it back." So I put it back. But if it was the only book I had there, I would simply have to read it.'

'We'll try and get you a better edition,' says Roy Plomley.

'Oh, thank you – very kind of you.'

Margaret Powell was an unlikely celebrity, but she continued to appear on radio and television long after the novelty of *Below Stairs* had waned, and in 1972 even recorded a single, 'I Laugh and Laugh and Laugh', which was released by RCA Victor but failed to trouble the upper reaches of the charts. And she branched out into writing novels, the last of which, gloriously entitled *The Butler's Revenge*, was published in April 1984 – the month that she died at the age of seventy-six.

That BBC memo deliberating over the irritant qualities of Margaret Powell's laugh at least ends on a properly positive note: 'I think it is worth pointing out that the number of letters and telephone calls have proved this edition of *Desert Island Discs* to have been one of the most popular – if not *the* most popular – of the whole series.'

Wah-hah-hah-hah-hah!

IVY BENSON

bandleader

16 October 1971

'I've got them in hot pants at the moment'

They don't make 'em like Ivy Benson any more. She played piano on the BBC at the age of nine; at ten, she won a talent contest at the Leeds Empire, singing 'Yes, We Have No Bananas'; she worked in a factory in order to pay the instalments on her first clarinet; and through sheer determination she established a female presence in the very male world of the dance bands, remaining at the top of her tree for decades.

Born in Leeds in 1913, she inherited musical talent from her trombonist father. Hearing a Benny Goodman record inspired her to take up the clarinet (to which she later added the alto sax and tenor sax), and at the age of sixteen she joined Edna Crowdson's Rhythm Girls. After playing with other northern outfits, she moved to London in the late 1930s and started to form her own bands. Ivy Benson and her Ladies' Dance Orchestra became the BBC's resident swing band in 1943, broadcasting to overseas troops at all hours of the day and night. They remained popular after the war until change in public taste saw the dance bands go into gradual decline as guitar-based groups took over in the 1960s.

'Ivy,' says Roy Plomley by way of welcome, 'for a good many years now you've been in more or less perpetual motion, touring around with anything from a dozen to twenty girl musicians. How does the idea of complete isolation strike you?'

'Absolutely wonderful, Roy!'

After her first record (Count Basie, 'my favourite band'), Ivy Benson reveals that her father had been a brilliant musician – 'He worked in the Leeds Empire in the pit' – and that he had started teaching her piano when she was five: 'I did my first pianoforte recital on the BBC in *Children's Hour* when I was nine.'

Her aspirations to become a professional musician were hampered by lack of money, but even while working in a clothing factory 'I was able to pay my weekly instalments for my first clarinet – that was my first instrument.'

'When did you start playing professionally?' asks Roy Plomley: 'While you were still working in the factory?'

'Yes. When I was seventeen I used to do dances in the evening, but working in the factory from eight until six and then rushing and playing eight till two and three in the morning. I had a nervous breakdown and I had to give up the factory.'

There was plenty of musical work about, but at that time girl musicians were very poorly paid and, she says, 'looked on as something rather freakish and something odd that had invaded a masculine field'.

Fired by the idea that she would make her fortune in London, at twenty-three she moved south. 'I starved. I couldn't get a job. I finished up with a trio – not mine, it belonged to somebody else – in a very sleazy nightclub in Piccadilly.'

Initially she was more concerned about making a name for herself than about forming a girls' band, 'but then I was rather appalled at the terrible jobs girl musicians were getting and the appalling pay they were getting, and I decided to do something about it'.

Her first girls' band consisted of 'five dreadful musicians, all years and years older than myself'. But 'I tried to – what do they say? – make a silk purse out of a sow's ear,' and the band started touring. More musicians were recruited for bookings in Glasgow, 'and then I augmented [the band] again to go to Covent Garden during the war years', when the Royal Opera House was used as a dance hall. By this time the Ivy Benson Band was eighteen strong and ready to move into broadcasting – and made its first recordings in 1943.

'You did some really valiant work entertaining the troops,' recalls Roy Plomley – 'It was part of my life I wouldn't have missed at all,' responds his castaway – adding that the band went to Berlin for the Allied victory

celebrations: 'There is a nice story about you and the girls doing a little smuggling, I believe.'

Indeed. Nearing the border from Austria into Italy, the band came across three Italian children – two brothers and their sister – who had been brought into Austria and now found the border closed. 'They just couldn't get home,' remembers Ivy Benson: 'The two brothers were going to make a dash for it across the border and leave their little sister. I was crossing into Italy, so the wardrobe mistress, the driver and myself decided we'd just put them all in amongst the luggage – so we did, and they went on ahead. When we got to the Italian border I was horrified to see the luggage standing there, and it only had a cover over it, with the Italian guards walking round it. So I just collected all the bottles out of the bus and invited the guards to have a drink – and they got so drunk that they just passed us through!'

Roy Plomley wonders whether there is still prejudice against women musicians. 'Not as much as there used to be,' says Ivy Benson: 'I think I've crushed that a little bit.'

And, says Plomley, the members of her band 'always look terrific: they're much more decorative than male musicians, aren't they?'

'Oh yes. I've got them in hot pants at the moment.'

But all that touring around brings its own problems. Instruments get stolen – and sometimes even people could vanish, as Roy Plomey discovers when he asks:

'You've lost the instruments, you've lost the costumes. Ever lost any girls?'

'Oh yes. I had a very fine pianist from Manchester College of Music. Her boyfriend came into the hall in Germany where I was working, and she left the stage. That was two years ago, and I haven't seen her since.'

Among Ivy Benson's record choices is the Beatles singing 'Can't Buy Me Love': 'This is nostalgic. During my work in Hamburg I was in a ballroom and underneath in a little cellar called the Kaiserkeller were the Beatles – four determined young men, smashing fellows, not very much money. I had a great admiration for them.'

To the island practicalities. Roy Plomley asks, 'Could you get enough to eat, cultivate, fish?'

'Sure I could.'

'Would you try to escape?'

'No – I've been looking for a desert island all my life!'

Ivy Benson continued to lead her all-women band until 1982, when it was wound up with a final performance at the Savoy Hotel – though it re-formed in 1983 for an appearance on Russell Harty's television show to mark Ivy's seventieth birthday. She retired to Clacton-on-Sea, where she entertained holidaymakers in local hotels on the electric organ, and where she died in May 1993.

DAVID HOCKNEY

artist

5 February 1972

'I've always thought of myself as a rather ordinary artist'

There could be no more graphic illustration of the standing of David Hockney in the public appreciation of art than the long queues for his exhibition *The Bigger Picture* at the Royal Academy in London in early 2012. A total attendance in excess of half a million people provided a demonstration of the affection and regard which this most accessible of artists still attracts.

He was in his thirties when cast away on the desert island, but already admired for works such as *A Bigger Splash* (1967).

Hockney declares candidly, 'I don't know anything about music, I just play records,' and his choice of eight has been straightforward: 'I think maybe there's one or two of them that were prompted by events or memories of a place, or a thing, or a person, but most of them are simply just bits of music that I thought I'd like to hear.' And he certainly has an unorthodox reaction to his first choice, the Liszt arrangement of Beethoven's Fifth Symphony: 'When I first heard it, which isn't too long ago, I kept laughing – which isn't usual for Beethoven – but I did enjoy it.'

He was born in Bradford, and was about ten when he decided that he wanted to be an artist, though he kept changing his mind: 'Maybe I'd be an engine driver.' In 1953 he left Bradford Grammar School and enrolled at the Bradford College of Art, where he was asked whether he had a private income: 'I said I didn't know what that was, and they said, "Well, if you've not got one you can't be an artist, because you'll never make a living at it." I thought it was really bad to start discouraging innocent sixteen-year-olds, so I took no notice.'

Had his parents discouraged him from what appeared likely to be a very precarious existence? 'They didn't. They just thought, "Well, maybe it's a good idea to be an artist" and never gave it a second thought.'

He won a scholarship to the Royal College of Art, but first had to do his National Service, working in hospitals in Bradford and Hastings: 'I thought it was a bit of a waste of time, but then on the other hand, when I went back to art school I used the time perhaps more eagerly, and worked perhaps a bit harder.' At the RCA he won the Gold Medal, and to receive it wore a gold lamé coat: 'Well, it's not really gold, but their medal wasn't gold either.'

He had already started selling his pictures, and was featured in the exhibition *Young Contemporaries*, which was heralded as the arrival of Pop Art. 'This hardly seems accurate,' says Plomley: 'you weren't painting soup cans, or doing collages of advertisements, and that sort of thing.'

'I did some paintings of a packet of tea,' responds Hockney, 'which probably caused that. I've always thought of myself as a rather ordinary artist.'

In 1971, the year before his *Desert Island Discs* appearance, there had been a retrospective exhibition of his work. 'I'd not seen it when they were hanging it up, because I'd been in France until the day it opened. I must admit I'd been rather apprehensive about it, thinking the early pictures just wouldn't stand up – they'd be a bit thin – and I must admit even I was slightly impressed with it, only because I saw there was a continuity in the work ... I don't keep photographs. I keep a few slides – though I never get them out – I don't keep press cuttings or anything. So that was my first chance to look at it all.'

Later, Plomley suggests: 'You move in a male world, and that's the world that you like to paint. Women rarely feature in your work.'

'Very rarely. I did a painting of a girl and her husband – Ossie Clark and his wife' – the painting entitled *Mr and Mrs Clark and Percy*, depicting Clark, his wife Celia Birtwell and their cat. 'I've drawn his wife quite a lot, actually. I must have done two dozen drawings of her. She's very beautiful.'

His fifth track, Jeanette MacDonald singing 'San Francisco' from the film of the same name, is there for a special reason: 'Only because it's about

David Hockney in front of Mr and Mrs Clark and Percy

California. I think this is a very pretty song, and I like it because it used to be sung by a marvellous drag queen in a bar – which isn't there any more – in San Francisco, and he actually looked like her in the film, and sat on a swing, and swung out into the bar. It was really terrific.'

Time to talk survival. Could he build a shelter? 'I suppose so. Yes, I could.'
Live off the land? 'I'd manage.'
Can he fish? 'No, I've never fished.'
Would he try to escape? 'Oh, immediately, yes.'
Does he know anything about navigation? 'No, but I think I'd try, rather than stay on the island.'

Luxury? 'Some paper and pencils and a battery-operated pencil sharpener.'

Book? 'I decided the only kind of book you'd really want to read, and re-read a lot, would be a pornographic book – otherwise you might fantasize too much on the island. So I've chosen *Route 69* by Floyd Carter, which I think is out of print now. I think it was written by a little man in an office on 42nd Street, and it's full of bad grammar and spelling mistakes, but quite touching in a way. It covers a great deal of interesting things.'

At the Third Paris Biennale of Young Artists, 1963: left to right, *Peter Phillips, Peter Blake, Derek Boshier, Allen Jones, David Hockney*

What is striking about Roy Plomley's interview with David Hockney is that it contains almost no discussion of the art itself – which is curious in the light of his most popular painting, *Mr and Mrs Clark and Percy*, having been completed only the year before the programme. Still, it is understandable that Plomley may not have wanted to discuss some of Hockney's earlier work, like *Peter Getting out of Nick's Pool* (1967), lest the conversation go off-piste.

'If we are to change our world view,' Hockney tells Paul Joyce in the book *Hockney on Photography*, 'images have to change. The artist now has a very important job to do. He's not a little peripheral figure entertaining rich people, he's really needed.'

THOR HEYERDAHL

anthropologist

13 April 1974

'We could see the stars through the wall, as it was just a wicker-work cabin'

Despite being fifty-nine years old when cast away, Thor Heyerdahl was better qualified than most to endure the privations of desert island life. Leader of the Kon-Tiki expedition in 1947 and of many other remarkable endeavours, he combined an extraordinary imagination with the courage and persistence to try his ideas out in the most practical way, by the simple but arduous – and in many cases highly dangerous – means of replicating what he thought had happened.

Heyerdahl was born in 1914 in the Norwegian coastal town of Larvik. His combination of curiosity and practicality, and his interest in zoology, soon became apparent in his building a small museum at home – with a viper as the star attraction. His studies in geology and zoology at the University of Oslo sparked a fascination with the history and culture of Polynesia – a fascination which led to his first expedition, to Fatu Hiva.

Kicking off a *Desert Island Discs* interview with Thor Heyerdahl is an open goal for Roy Plomley: 'Dr Heyerdahl, in all your sojourns in lonely places, you've always been accompanied by your wife or by a colleague. Do you think you could put up with complete and absolute loneliness?'

The man who led the Kon-Tiki expedition has few fears on that front. 'As a young student in Norway I used to go up into the mountains, sometimes for a week or more at a time, or in a tent, all alone with my dog' – and like so many other castaways would be glad to get away from the city streets, 'with all the automobiles and all the exhaust coming out of them'.

As for the records, 'I know nothing about it, but I am absolutely crazy about listening to good music.'

Heyerdahl was originally a biologist, and in that role went to the Pacific island named Fatu Hiva, southernmost of the Marquesa Islands in French Polynesia, 'to study how the animal life had arrived at an island that had originally been born out of the bottom of the sea by a volcanic eruption – because in the beginning there could be no animals there. But when I was living on this island for one year, I became more and more puzzled about another problem, and that is: how had man come to the island before the Europeans? Because when the Europeans came there, Polynesians were living with Stone Age culture. I gradually started interesting myself more and more in so-called primitive culture – and particularly Polynesian culture – more than the animals.'

While living on the island and thinking such thoughts, Heyerdahl noticed something. 'The whole year, day and night, wind and current will come in from one direction, and that direction happens to be the opposite of the theories about Polynesian movements at the time. The wind always blew from South America to these islands, and the ocean current ran like a big river from South America to the islands, bringing all sorts of driftwood – and brought in the original primitive animal life with it. So I concluded that perhaps the first people to discover this island came as accidental drift voyagers from South America, rather than from Asia . . . When I came back home I accumulated from museum collections and libraries all the evidence that indicated this theory was correct. And then I decided to prove that it could happen, because science said at the time it could not have been so.'

Then the war intervened. Heyerdahl fought with the Free Norwegian forces, and at the end of hostilities started to look for backing for an expedition to test his theory. It was an uphill struggle against the prevailing scientific scepticism. 'They said that no American Indian could have travelled into the ocean before Columbus, because the American Indians only had rafts – a certain type of raft made of balsa, and according to the experts

Kon-Tiki

balsa wood would absorb water and sink after two weeks. Even all the maritime experts said that you can't cross four thousand miles of open ocean on a raft. Nobody believed in the possibility of the voyage, so the main difficulty before I started was really to get the expedition organized, and to show that such a raft was possible.'

Eventually the money was raised and the balsa-wood raft *Kon-Tiki* – about 35 feet long and 18 feet wide – was built, to carry a crew of six (five Norwegians and one Swede).

'We couldn't steer it too much,' Heyerdahl continues. 'First of all, none of us had ever travelled on the raft before, and as for the steering wheel, if we turned it too much over we found that the square sail would just turn round and we would drift in the same direction, only backwards. So actually the steering was rather limited. It was a drift voyage, but it still led to Polynesia' – and the point was proved.

Before moving on from *Kon-Tiki*, Roy Plomley asks about the waterproof qualities of the bamboo cabin on board. 'It certainly wasn't weatherproof,' says Heyerdahl, 'because we could see the stars through the wall, as it was just a wicker-work cabin. But that saved our life in the landing, because it was so flexible – like a basket – that just by pulling the strings after it had fallen down it came up again, and as nice as ever.'

In 1969 Heyerdahl undertook the Ra expedition, designed to dis-prove the accepted theory that the papyrus boat of ancient Egypt and Mesopotamia could only be used on a river. 'I was convinced that this boat, which was so important to all the early civilizations in the Mediterranean, and in the Middle East and nearby islands, and all the way to the Atlantic coast of Morocco, wouldn't have been this widespread and have survived for thousands of years – it is still being used in some areas – unless it was a seaworthy boat. And I found that this same type of vessel, built with another kind of reed very similar to papyrus, was the main vessel used by the big marine Inca civiliza-tions in America when Columbus came. So I suspected that perhaps people had come across before Columbus in this type of vessel.'

Johannes Hanssen
The Valdres March

'It brings me back to the snow in the high mountains in Norway'

The crew had no modern equipment: 'We just had what ancient people could, and we carried it like them. I had a hundred and sixty ceramic jars made exactly as the Egyptian jars in the museum in Cairo, and we had water like ancient people in ceramic jars and in goat-skin bags.'

Roy Plomley – who has done his homework – mentions that the sort of papyrus used for boat-building in ancient times no longer grows in Egypt. 'No,' says the castaway, 'it is an extinct plant in Egypt, so today, to get the reed that was common on the Nile in former times I had to go to the source of the Nile, at Lake Tana in Ethiopia, and ship the reeds from the lake over the mountains down to the Red Sea.'

The Ra expedition went down the Moroccan coast before striking out into the Atlantic, past the Canary Islands and then due west. 'We came as far as one week short of Barbados in the West Indies when the ropes burst, and we started to lose papyrus in all directions . . . That was after fifty-seven days, and we might have been able to reach land, but I was responsible for all of the men on board, so I decided to interrupt the trip and start all over again.'

Seven of the eight-man crew – from eight different countries – returned for Ra II; the eighth was from Lake Titicaca, where the people were used to very stormy weather and were able to tie the papyrus together 'in such a fab-ulous way that it was just like a ball, and it went all the way over to the West Indies'. QED.

Then there was the expedition to Easter Island – 'the loneliest island in the world', according to Roy Plomley – to examine the history of those extraordinary gigantic stone heads. 'By digging,' says Heyerdahl, 'we found statues of a completely different type that were much older and which were strikingly similar to those found in the Andes of South America, in type and dimensions. And also we discovered by living for half a year among the islanders of Easter Island that they still had oral traditions as to how this work had gone on in the past. They actually had twelve of the natives re-erect one of the big fallen statues in eighteen days, working just by the means of two big logs and a lot of stones . . . We used radio-carbon dating and we found that they were at least one thousand years older than what science had assumed so far.'

Heyerdahl's luxury is a wood-carving kit: 'I would imagine that the island would be full of driftwood – they usually are – and one of my hobbies is wood carving.'

'Splendid!' laughs Roy Plomley: 'And one day in hundreds of years' time, an expedition would try to decide who had carved all that wood on this island.'

Thor Heyerdahl, whose adventures gripped a worldwide audience to such an extent that his book *The Kon-Tiki Expedition* has to date sold over 20 million copies in sixty-seven languages, died at the age of eighty-seven in April 2002 – and, as a mark of his standing in his native land, the Norwegian government gave him a state funeral in Oslo Cathedral.

LUCIANO PAVAROTTI

tenor

14 February 1976

'I am a man of company'

Luciano Pavarotti was born in 1935 in northern Italy, the son of a baker (and amateur tenor) and a worker in a cigar factory. At the age of nine or so, he recalled, he started singing with his father in the church choir; later in his youth he would watch Mario Lanza films at the cinema, then go home and try to copy him in the mirror.

He began his professional career as a tenor in 1961. By the time of his *Desert Island Discs* appearance he was one of the most instantly recognizable figures in world music – though even greater fame was to come later.

In response to Roy Plomley's asking whether he had ever imagined himself as a Robinson Crusoe, Luciano Pavarotti demurs, 'because I am a man of company, and even if my imagination is very large I cannot imagine myself alone for more than one day.'

The criteria for the early musical choices of one of the world's greatest singers are straightforward enough:

First, the 40th Symphony of Mozart – 'my preferred composer', with whose works he can surround himself 'from the morning till the end of the night'.

Second, Enrico Caruso – 'my preferred tenor'.

Pavarotti comes from Modena, near Bologna, where the opera house is a little less important than it once was, 'but still a theatre of tradition', and as a child he heard much opera, not least because his father was himself a tenor.

Roy Plomley asks, 'Did you have the idea as a boy that you were going to be a professional singer?'

'No doubt. Everybody in my city had this idea. I was not the only one, but I am the only one who did become a singer. My barber, my baker, everybody wanted to become a tenor . . . I remember we sang serenades: "La donna e mobile", for example, or "Di quella pira" – not so romantic – just to let the girl hear which kind of tenor voice we have.'

He had been a teacher, but at twenty embarked on six years of serious study of music. In 1955 he went with the Modena City Chorus to Llangollen in Wales for a choral competition: 'We won first prize, and it was like a bomb explosion of fifty-five people in black coats, and to be reminded of that now is still very, very, very exciting.'

Pavarotti first sang in London in 1963, in *La Bohème* at Covent Garden, and this led to his finding a nationwide audience when he was called upon to stand in for Giuseppe di Stefano in *Sunday Night at the London Palladium*, then the must-watch television programme on the eve of the working week. That Sunday afternoon he was in Sussex having his first experience of horse-riding, when he was called and asked whether he could substitute for di Stefano. Of course, he could, but when? Now! – 'and they put me on a train with a steak in a piece of bread in one hand and a Coca-Cola in the other hand and somebody was waiting at Charing Cross station'. On introducing him in the show, Pavarotti recalls, Bruce Forsyth had told the audience that the artist they were about to hear had been on a horse all day, so 'don't judge how he is going to walk but judge him how he is going to sing'. He sang, of course, unbelievably – and soon afterwards was performing at Glyndebourne and singing with Joan Sutherland.

One of his record choices is *La Fille du régiment* by Donizetti, and thereby hangs a tale, as its selection reminds the castaway of a bet he had with conductor Richard Bonynge:

'Before I performed it, the aria of Tonio was never sung in the original key. Everybody transposed the key down a tone, so that instead of singing C natural at the end you sing B flat – which is much more easy, I can tell you, but less exciting. Ricky said I could do this and I said no. At the dress rehearsal I sang in full voice [that is, he sang the C] and the orchestra was standing to applaud, which encouraged me very much and I sang a beautiful

Luciano Pavarotti in L'elisir d'amore, *Royal Opera House, Covent Garden, 1990*

performance, and after me a lot of other tenors took courage and sang in the right key.'

Recently, says Plomley, Pavarotti has started giving more recitals. 'How big a part of your work is that going to be?'

'Let's say now fifty per cent of my career.' At recitals, with just himself and his white handkerchief and the piano, 'you have to put out all your personality with music, with feeling, with contact with the public.'

It is not always easy. Does he enjoy recording?

'Unfortunately I was born on the twelfth of October, then I am a Libra. Like Libras, I am never satisfied by anything. I would like to try to see the perfection where the perfection does not of course exist, because we are human, and I would like to hear all beautiful things. But when I hear a record of myself, the good things don't come to me. Just if it is one little mistake, it disturbs me for all the recording.'

On the island, could he build a house? 'Yes. Who doesn't try to do a private house when you are a kid? You take mud, you take stones, and go to find a big plant to cover and you try to do a house. Of course I would be able to do this.'

Grow vegetables? 'Sure, sure.' Fish? 'Suppose I am not a good fisherman, I would become a good fisherman very soon.' Escape? 'Like I told you before,

I am not a man of solitude. Then I try to escape just if I am sure to arrive somewhere.'

Pavarotti's final record has figured on many castaways' lists over the decades, but his explanation for the choice is striking:

'I hear this record for the first time when I was in Australia. My wife was with me and she left – she went home to our child – and I drove her to the airport. And when I came back I had the very, very stupid idea to put this record on. And after five minutes I was crying and thinking about all the crashed planes and all the things, but still it gave to me an incredible feeling – and from that moment on is one of my preferred pieces of music.'

Pavarotti's luxury is a bicycle.

Already feted as one of the world's greatest tenors, Luciano Pavarotti saw his career gain a new lease of life in 1990 through football – an unlikely medium but an appropriate one, since one of his boyhood dreams had been to play professional football as a goalkeeper. His rendition of 'Nessun dorma' from Puccini's *Turandot* was the BBC's theme music for its coverage of that year's FIFA World Cup in Italy, and on the night before the final he joined Placido Domingo and José Carreras in a memorable performance as 'The Three Tenors' at the Baths of Caracalla in Rome. This *coup de théâtre* vastly increased the public appetite for opera – an appetite which Pavarotti and his fellow tenors set about satisfying as best they could. He appeared in many outdoor concerts, entertaining among others audiences of 150,000 in London's Hyde Park, 500,000 in Central Park in New York and 300,000 in Paris.

His final performance in opera was at the Met in New York in March 2004, and his final on-stage appearance at the 2006 Winter Olympics in Turin. Luciano Pavarotti died in September 2007.

CHRISTIAAN BARNARD

heart surgeon

17 April 1976

'I think the time will come when we will prevent
rejection completely'

The interview with Dr Christiaan Barnard, who had performed the first heart transplant operation in October 1967, was one of those editions of *Desert Island Discs* in the course of which listeners effortlessly learn a good deal about a subject of which they previously knew little or nothing.

The South African cardiac surgeon, by then a household name, was born in 1922 and had early experience of the grim power of heart disease: one of his three brothers died of a heart condition at the age of five. In 1956 Barnard undertook postgraduate training in cardiothoracic surgery at the University of Minnesota, where he got to know Norman Shumway, who had performed much pioneering work on the possibility of heart transplantation. Barnard himself undertook further research over several years, and on 3 December 1967, assisted by his brother Marius, performed the surgery which gave a 54-year-old grocer named Louis Washkansky a new heart. Washkansky died (of pneumonia) only eighteen days after the operation, but the breakthrough had been made.

Roy Plomley asks Christiaan Barnard whether he has ever experienced loneliness. 'Oh yes, often. Even loneliness with people around me I've experienced. For example, after my first transplant patient died I remember very clearly – it was early in the morning as the sun was coming up in the eastern sky – he died and I had people around me, but I've never been so lonely in my life.'

What would he be happiest to get away from? 'The telephone is my biggest enemy because every time it rings, especially at night, it usually means there are problems.'

And why, asks Plomley, had he become interested in medicine?

'I really became influenced by my brother' – son of a Dutch Reformed Church minister, he had three brothers – 'my eldest brother who was at university and was studying engineering. He had friends who were in medical school, and him talking about the medical students made me interested in medicine.'

Roy Plomley has read that when Dr Barnard witnessed his first surgical operation, he fainted. Is that a common reaction?

'It often happens to young students when they have the drama of the operating room – and especially in those days the smell of the anaesthetics, which of course we don't have any more – the smell of ether.'

Plomley notes how his castaway's early medical experience had concentrated on gynaecology and then general practice, 'dealing not only with coughs and sneezes but things like the results of an attack by a leopard'.

'Yes, that's right. It was a woman. The leopard was coming down across the farmyard and she got in the way of the leopard and got very badly mauled, and I treated her. She needed many stitches because she was torn up quite a lot by the leopard.'

As a young doctor in the medical school at Cape Town he was offered the chance to work in the USA: 'I went there to do general surgery. I didn't know that open heart surgery was being developed there, and it just so happened that I went to the centre where modern open heart surgery was started, so I got in at the ground level.'

Funding himself and his young family in the USA with all sorts of jobs – 'I had to wash cars and mow lawns and things like that' – he continued his medical studies, writing a thesis on congenital malformation of the bowel.

When he returned to South Africa, American funding allowed him to start a heart surgery unit. By now, open heart surgery had progressed to the point where certain congenital malformations could be corrected. 'In those days we weren't able yet to replace heart valves by means of artificial valves, and the more complex congenital heart diseases were not within our reach, so it was very much in the early phases of open heart surgery that I went back to Cape Town.'

In 1967 he had been the first man to attempt a heart transplant. How many similar operations has he done since then?

'We have to qualify the type that we're referring to. There's the heart transplant where the patient's heart is removed, called the orthotopic heart transplant. I've done nine of those. And then there's the new technique that we use where we don't remove the patient's own heart: we put a second heart in his body just to assist his own heart – the heterotopic transplant. I've done five of those.'

Is that technique a marked improvement on the earlier procedure?

Ray Charles
'I Can't Stop Loving You'

'One of the greatest recordings ever made'

'It's too early really to be dogmatic about it. I'm very impressed with the early results of this new technique. It appears that patients do much better initially than they used to do with the transplant where the patient's own heart is removed. Of the five patients that I've operated on with the heterotopic transplantation, four are alive and three of them are already out of hospital. One is fourteen months after transplantation and I'm really very impressed with the very rapid return to normal life with this operation.'

Will such operations soon be commonplace? 'I think so. I think the only stumbling block still is rejection, which is the body's ability to recognize the transplanted heart as foreign, and it therefore then sets up a reaction to the foreign-ness, and that will eventually kill the transplanted heart unless you do something about it. We are not able yet to prevent rejection, but I think the time will come when we will prevent rejection completely.'

Roy Plomley asks Christiaan Barnard for suggestions about how heart disease can be avoided.

'That is a difficult question. The only way in which one can avoid heart disease is when you know the cause of the disease. We know the cause of smallpox and therefore we can make a vaccine to stop people from getting smallpox. Unfortunately the cause of the heart disease that we're now discussing, which is coronary heart disease, is unknown. There are many factors which they believe contribute towards the formation of this disease, but no single factor can be pinpointed that caused the disease.'

'There's no dietary solution?'

'This is a part of the game, but it's not the full story. It's been said that people who have a diet high in animal fat are more prone to get the disease than others, but you will find that there are many people that eat high animal fat content all their lives and they never get the disease.'

None the less, you can't help wondering how many listeners to the first transmission on Saturday evening might have decided to have a smaller helping of roast Sunday lunch and go for a brisk walk round the park afterwards . . .

At the time of his *Desert Island Discs* appearance Christiaan Barnard – who chose as his luxury Michelangelo's *David* – was the most famous doctor in the world, appearing as regularly in the gossip columns and society pages as in the medical columns – and he seemed to relish the fame. And whereas the social gossip faded, the medical legacy endured: heart transplantation was soon to become a routine medical practice, as was the double-transplant technique which he pioneered.

Barnard carried on as head of the Department of Cardiothoracic Surgery at the University of Cape Town until 1983, when developing rheumatoid arthritis in his hands rendered impossible the continuation of a surgical career. He died in September 2001 at the age of seventy-eight.

PHILIP LARKIN

poet

17 July 1976

'The previous librarian used to scrub the floors as well, but I said I didn't want to do that'

On 26 May 1976 Philip Larkin – then fifty-three – wrote to a friend, the historian Robert Conquest. The letter briefly describes Larkin's recent visit to Hamburg, where he was awarded the Shakespeare-Preis, before continuing: 'This has all been wiped out by doing a Desert Island Discs yesterday, was it, yes, Christ, only yesterday. I must never undertake unscripted stuff again: I just get old-fashioned mike fright and freeze. Everything I remember saying makes me curl up like apple peelings.'

The publication two years earlier of Larkin's most recent volume of verse, *High Windows*, had solidified his reputation as one of the twentieth century's most accessible and popular poets – not least through its inclusion of his best-known poem 'This Be the Verse', which opens with the unforgettable lines, 'They fuck you up, your mum and dad, / They may not mean to, but they do . . .' This was later described by Larkin with characteristic acerbity as a piece which 'will clearly be my "Lake Isle of Innisfree". I fully expect to hear it recited by a thousand Girl Guides before I die.'

As for curling up like apple peelings at the recall of his interview, Larkin is too hard on himself, as the conversation delivers much illuminating material.

'I never think of myself as a gregarious man,' says Larkin in response to Plomley's standard first question, 'but having thought about your island for a few weeks I've come to the conclusion that I probably am. I should be very happy there for about twenty-four hours, and fairly happy for another forty-eight hours, but after that I suspect that I should miss people and society in general.'

Larkin is well known as a jazz fan – he reviewed jazz records in the *Daily Telegraph* for many years – and his first choice is Satchmo: 'I suppose any jazz lover has to decide which Louis Armstrong record he is taking, because there are so many, and Louis is such a combined Chaucer and Shakespeare of jazz.'

Had he been brought up in a house with many books? 'I suppose I was. My father was not a literary man but he was a great collector of books, and when I went up to Oxford I found that I had in fact been brought up with many more books than my contemporaries.' But he had no clear view of what might follow Oxford: 'This was the war – 1940 – and I don't think one really had a view to anything in those days. One thought one would be called up after about four terms, and after that it was all in the lap of the gods.'

But he was not called up, and started writing, aiming initially at fiction – 'but after a couple of novels, the third one never got finished, and I had to fall back on poems.'

After Oxford, his first job was at a public library in Shropshire: 'It was an ordinary public library where one lent books to old-age pensioners and children and performed the various simple tasks like putting newspapers in the newsroom. I was the librarian, and the only librarian. I stoked the boiler and opened the doors in the morning and closed them at night. I can really claim to have started at the bottom. The previous librarian used to scrub the floors as well, but I said I didn't want to do that.'

His first book of poems was published in 1945, and then the novels *Jill* and *A Girl in Winter* – 'and then a profound silence descended.'

From Shropshire he moved to the library of University College, Leicester, then to Queen's University, Belfast, and then in 1955 to the University of Hull, 'where I have been ever since.'

Roy Plomley suggests that Larkin's output has been remarkably small – 'A slim volume, really, every ten years' – but the poet points out: 'I suppose it depends whom you are comparing me with. I don't think it's too small compared with Housman, for instance. This has not been intentional. I write as much as I can and publish as much as I can.'

Does he write for himself, or to communicate a feeling to others? 'I certainly write to be read. There would be very little point in writing something that nobody was going to read, but it is not quite communicating in the sense of writing a letter to *The Times*, for instance. You try to create something in words that will reproduce in somebody else who has never met you and perhaps isn't even living in the same cultural society as yourself, that somebody else will read and so get the experience that you had, and that forced you to write the poem. It's a kind of preservation by re-creation, if I can put it that way . . . I think that a poem should be understood at first reading, line by line, but I don't think it should be exhausted at first reading. I hope that what I write gives the reader something when they read it first, enough in fact to make them read it again, and so on *ad infinitum*.'

'If just one of your poems were to survive,' asks Roy Plomley, 'which one would you like it to be?'

'That really is a most difficult question because one doesn't really think of one's poems as favourites, or better or anything like that. I suppose I should choose "The Whitsun Weddings" as being a full expression of one particular theme that I wanted to deal with.'

On the island, would he fish? 'The only time I saw a fish caught I was so horrified that I could never try to do it myself.'

Would he try to escape? 'I should certainly consider the situation. It would depend how far off the mainland was, and how many sharks there were in between.'

Philip Larkin

Larkin continued to discharge his professional duties as Librarian at the University of Hull despite an ever-growing status as a writer. His last major poem was 'Aubade', first published in the *Times Literary Supplement* in 1977; thereafter he felt that his poetic gifts were spent, and he declined Margaret Thatcher's offer of the post of Poet Laureate on the death of John Betjeman in 1984. The previous year, 1983, he had published *Required Writing*, a very well-received volume of miscellaneous memoirs, reviews and criticism, and in 1985 he was given the lofty decoration of Companion of Honour. In December that year, at the age of sixty-three, he died.

YEHUDI MENUHIN

violinist and conductor

16 April 1977

'Maybe I could smuggle in another one or two records'

Yehudi Menuhin, widely acknowledged as the finest violinist of the twentieth century, first appeared on *Desert Island Discs* in July 1955 (when he chose a violin as his luxury, and an indefinite supply of strings). Constantly searching for fresh musical avenues to explore, in 1966 Menuhin had begun a long association with the sitar player Ravi Shankar; and just a year before his second arrival on the desert island in April 1977 he had taken his art to a new audience through his collaboration with the great jazz violinist Stéphane Grappelli.

Only eight records? asks Yehudi Menuhin – 'Very cruel, very cruel you are.'

Menuhin was born in New York in 1916, the son of Russian parents who had met in Palestine.

Little Yehudi wanted a violin 'as soon as I heard one', and was given a toy one: 'I was disgusted with the violin and with myself, and it took a little while until I could even crank up a vibrato. I had a lot of trouble getting the vibrato, which of course I was very anxious to get, because my dream of a violin sound is – and was – the human voice. In fact, I notice on this choice that I have perhaps subconsciously not included any solo violin on it at all, but a number of vocalists.'

When he was ten he moved – along with the whole family – to Europe to pursue his study of the violin, and first performed in London at the age of thirteen in 1929. He made his first recordings at the age of twelve, and in 1932 rehearsed the Elgar violin concerto with the composer himself present – at least for a time:

'I was in the room with Ivor Newton at the piano, waiting to play the concerto for Elgar. I'd just prepared it within the previous month, and was rather nervous about it. Elgar came in – this fine grandfatherly figure, very benign, the first living composer I'd met. Here was a gentleman, and I'd never thought of gentlemen as composers. But of course I've changed my mind since then. And we started playing, and after a very few minutes he interrupted and said he had no doubts about the recording. Everything would go beautifully. He had full confidence. It was a beautiful sunny afternoon, and he was off to the races. That was where he wanted to go – leaving me, of course, somewhat disconcerted, again realizing that I hadn't quite sufficiently anticipated the gentleman instead of the composer. But he turned out to be not only both, but a wonderful friend – almost a grandfather in feeling, and a wonderful conductor.

'And two days later we were in the Abbey Road studios, where I still record, and for two days I was in utter bliss, playing this great work to the sound of an orchestration I'd never played to before – certainly the richest orchestration of any great classical concerto.'

By the time Menuhin was twenty, says Roy Plomley, 'you had mastered all the main concertos and sonatas in the repertoire, and you'd worked with most of the great conductors. It was an age of giants – Bruno Walter, Toscanini, Beecham; as a youngster, did you find any of these conductors overpowering?'

'No, curiously enough I didn't. In fact, Bruno Walter was perhaps, along with Barbirolli, the most wonderful accompanist that I've ever known. And of course there was Enesco, because even though he was my great master for the violin, I did most of my orchestral recordings at the same time with him. I didn't find them overpowering; even Toscanini, who came the closest to being – who might have been – overpowering. I held my own there, and didn't quite capitulate.'

What makes for a great violin? 'It's the craftsmanship, certainly. It's the fact that it was great art, that one cannot imitate an art. There are a few very fine violin maker–artist creators today, although I've yet to see a modern

Opposite: The ten-year-old Yehudi Menuhin, 1926

violin which can equal in beauty of varnish, let alone beauty of sound, the greatest of the old instruments.'

Purcell

'When I am laid in earth' (from *Dido and Aeneas*)

'The most heartrending piece I know'

To practical matters. Has he ever fished? 'Yes, I nearly caught a salmon once.'

Would he try to get away?

'It depends how comfortable you make me. Naturally I'm not holding you responsible for it, but it's at your invitation that I'm going there. And if it really is pleasant, and my wife is along above all, and maybe I could smuggle in another one or two records, and some scores to study—'

'Well,' cuts in Plomley, 'you'd have to smuggle in your wife for a start, because we keep watch on that sort of thing.'

'—oh well then, I'll have a second thought about this whole business in that case.'

Yehudi Menuhin continued to perform and conduct for much of the remaining two decades of his life. He became a British citizen in 1985 – and thus able to style himself Sir Yehudi, having been awarded an honorary KBE twenty years earlier – and in 1993 was given a life peerage, in recognition of both his musical genius and his tireless educational and charitable work away from the concert hall.

Yehudi Menuhin gave his final public performance in Gstaad in 1996, and died in March 1999. As the critic Michael Kennedy wrote, Menuhin 'regarded music as a healing art and himself as a power for good'.

SPIKE MILLIGAN

comedian, actor, writer

4 February 1978

'I am a jobbing clown: that's what I am'

When Spike Milligan first appeared on *Desert Island Discs* in October 1956 he proved as anarchic a castaway as the programme had yet had. *The Goon Show* – the classic radio comedy which he wrote, and in which he co-starred with Harry Secombe and Peter Sellers (and, for a while, Michael Bentine) – was already gathering a cult following, and his trademark quickfire humour was soon bouncing off the studio walls. By that time Roy Plomley had stopped scripting both sides of the interview, which made steering the Milligan programme particularly hazardous. Although that 1956 interview had its darker side (see page 52), the comic Milligan was never far away:

'What are you going to choose now, Spike?'

'It's another record, Roy – you crazy predictionist, you . . .'

Or:

'Was there any precedent of show business in your family?'

'No, we never had a President in our family – ha ha ha!'

Or:

'How long were you at the factory?'

'About five foot six, I would imagine.'

Over twenty years later, Milligan was no more controllable.

Spike Milligan was born in India, where his first school was in a tent in the desert. 'We had to sit on the tent pegs, and when the wind blew up we each had a tent peg to sit on to hold it down.'

When he was about fourteen his family returned to England. What did he want to be?

'I wanted to be a fighter pilot, and we came to England with that reason in mind. I sat the exam at Kingsway, and I failed because I was hopeless at mathematics. But strangely enough, when the war came on and they were getting shot down left, right and centre, I suddenly received a communiqué from the RAF saying, "We are re-thinking about you joining the Air Force, and we think you would make a splendid rear gunner."'

'And what did you reply?'

'I wrote back and said, "No, I don't want to be a rear gunner. I want to see what's coming at the front."'

His first job was in an engineering works in Deptford 'for thirteen shillings a week, getting my hands trapped in the Miller 6 machine, making little round plugs for some water pumps'.

Plomley states, 'You were also playing trumpet in a dance band,' and Milligan replies: 'Yes. That's a good terse answer, isn't it? Yes, yes, that's the end of it.'

He becomes Gunner Milligan in the Royal Artillery, billeted at Bexhill Girls' School – 'We unfortunately got there just after they left' – where he carried on playing jazz with fellow soldiers.

His first record has been Respighi; his second? 'Jesse Owens doing the 100 yards at . . .' no, the Chieftains singing 'Women of Ireland': 'I have latent Celtic roots; you may see them hanging out sometimes.'

Milligan takes the opportunity to tell a joke: 'An Irish woman got into bed with her husband and said, "I've set the alarm for six," and he said, "Why? – there's only the two of us."'

'It's getting worse,' mutters the presenter wearily, before moving the Milligan life story on. 'Well then, in 1943, North Africa, life got real and earnest and very dangerous – you were wounded.'

'I wasn't wounded in North Africa, no.'

'You were blown up, weren't you?'

'What – you mean like a balloon, or what? No, I was blown up in Italy.'

'You were blown up in Italy – that was after Africa?'

'Yes, yes, yes, but I came down again.'

And as Plomley tries to steer the castaway back to what he was planning

to do after the war, off goes Milligan on another joke:

'There's a man teaching a chap the law of gravity at school, and he couldn't get it, this idiot. "Well, I will tell you what the law of gravity is," the teacher said: "Stand over there and jump up and down." So the chap jumped up and down, and the teacher said, "Did you see what happened? You have jumped up in the air but you had to come down to earth again. Now why?" "Well, because I live there."'

Moving hastily on, Plomley establishes that Milligan travelled round Europe with a band – 'We formed a Hot Club de France sort of trio and we did comedy on the stage, and we were a big hit with the troops at the end of the war . . . Bit by bit, I drifted into writing.'

'What did you write for a start?'

'Cheques – well, I wrote bits and pieces for Peter Sellers and Alfred Marks and Harry Secombe.'

From there came *Crazy People*, which became *The Goon Show* – a landmark comedy series which played from 1951 to 1960. When the Goons came to an end, suggests Roy Plomley, 'You had done all the work but Peter and Harry soared up to international stardom, leaving you a bit behind. Did that worry you at the time?'

'Yes, it did. When it all finished I was sort of an unemployed scriptwriter, and Peter of course had done well in the film world and Harry had done well on stage, and I had no confidence at all. I still have a very great lack of confidence . . . I thought that I'm a good clown and I'm going to push myself, so we did this play called *Oblomov*, which is terrible, so I ad-libbed the whole thing, and it became a great hit in London . . . I am a jobbing clown: that's what I am.'

After choosing Paul McCartney ('one of the most beguiling commercial singers') performing 'Yesterday', Milligan briefly switches into old man voice to sing his own version: 'Yesterday, someone came and took the cat away'

– to which Plomley responds, 'Don't go and wreck it, it's a good song.'

Milligan's work since the Goons has included the play *The Bed-Sitting Room*, written with John Antrobus; his hugely successful trilogy of war memoirs; the novel *Puckoon*; and several books for children. And then there is the art:

'I remember the first painting of yours I saw,' says Roy Plomley. 'It was at an exhibition at the Leicester Square Cinema, in the foyer, and this one was called *Painting Done with Knife and Fork*. I thought it was very, very good indeed.'

'I wanted to see if you could paint with a knife and fork, so I dipped them in and painted.'

'Did you sell it?'

'No, I couldn't sell that.'

The Beatles
'Yesterday'

'Paul McCartney I find one of the most beguiling commercial singers'

He has been writing television shows with Neil Shand: 'What we try to do is write original ideas, to infuse new ideas to television. It's easy to write sort of stand-up comic joke ones, just straight-forward sketches. We try to put on ideas like, for instance: two chaps walking saying, "This looks like a good place for a sketch." And they knock on an invisible door, and a chap comes up and these chaps at the door have got stocking masks over their faces, and they are wearing clerical clothes – vicars' collars – and he says, "Who are you?", and they say, "We are Jehovah's Burglars, and we are being persecuted for our beliefs." The man says, "What do you believe?", and they say, "We believe you have got a lot of money in here" – mad things like that.'

Milligan has a particular concern about world population: 'The Earth is a lifeboat. There is enough room for so many people in a lifeboat, and nobody is piloting this lifeboat in any sensible form at the moment. They are just taking passengers on board all the time. It will sink.'

Spike Milligan's island luxury is a Barclaycard – 'I mean, while I have a Barclaycard there I'm saving money' – and his book is *Future Shock* by Alvin Toffler.

'What's it about?', asks Roy Plomley.

'It's about three hundred pages, I think . . . Bye bye, Roy, and keep taking those tablets, won't you?'

Even those who consider Spike Milligan a comic deity must have had some sympathy for Roy Plomley. The presenter always tried to be calm, measured and helpful towards the castaway, steering him or her in just the right direction and at just the right speed – and here was the unpredictable Milligan, slippery as an eel. This castaway might have been manageable had he stuck to the wisecracks – at least then the presenter could have sat back and joined in the fun – but Milligan would switch in an instant from a silly joke to an apparently poignant mood. You simply did not know what he might do next.

The two Spike Milligan programmes are remarkably similar in tone, with Plomley in both cases making some attempt to get answers to the required questions, while perfectly aware that anything might happen. Milligan's capricious demeanour was by no means confined to his *Desert Island Discs* appearances: many other presenters had a similar experience. Sir Michael Parkinson, for example, who interviewed him on television and radio, admitted that he 'could be difficult, not to say impossible. He could also be generous and warm and wonderfully funny.'

Milligan made a brief appearance in the film *Monty Python's Life of Brian* in 1979, and through the 1980s and 1990s continued to write and sometimes perform (in, for example, later episodes of the eccentric television series *Q*). But increasingly he was turning his attention to various contentious causes – campaigning against, for example, smoking, domestic violence, vivisection, factory farming and noise pollution.

Spike Milligan, a tortured genius if ever there was one, died in February 2002.

MARGARET THATCHER

Leader of the Opposition

18 February 1978

'I knew it was absolutely the right thing to do'

When Margaret Thatcher was cast away in February 1978, she had been leader of the opposition for three years – almost to the day – and with the Labour government led by James Callaghan struggling in the opinion polls, she seemed to be well on course to become the United Kingdom's first woman premier. And she had already attracted the epithet 'The Iron Lady' – bestowed by a Soviet Defence Ministry newspaper following her January 1976 speech regarding the perceived Russian threat.

In his book *Plomley's Pick*, published in 1982, the presenter declared:

> I was very impressed by Mrs Thatcher. Come to that, I still am. At the time we recorded *Desert Island Discs*, she was about as busy as any woman could be, but she found time to invite me to her home, so that we could get to know each other before we worked together, and she took a tremendous amount of trouble in choosing her records. Our recording came at the end of a long day, and she had a heavy cold, but she could not have been more co-operative or forthcoming.

The Iron Lady indeed.

Music is important to Margaret Thatcher. 'It's what I go to when I want to take refuge in something completely different, when I really want to get away from worries and go from the very logical life that I've lived, and that I've always been trained to live, to a different depth of experience.'

Her upbringing had been strict – 'We went to church twice on Sundays and to Sunday School twice' – but 'my father taught me very firmly indeed: "You do not follow the crowd because you are afraid of being different; you decide what to do yourself. If necessary you lead the crowd, but you never just follow." It was very hard indeed, but my goodness me, it stood me in good stead.'

During school holidays she would help out in the shop. 'This is where one learned to see and talk to so many people, and talk easily.'

Her father had an active life in local politics, and the 1935 general election brought young Margaret Roberts her first political experience. 'I was only ten but I do remember it very vividly. We used to go to the Committee Room . . . and the polling station to get the lists of the numbers of people who had voted, and go and check them off. It seems so strange to me now, but it was quite a thrill for those of us working in the Committee Room when the candidate Victor Warrender – then the Member of Parliament – came round and talked to us. It never occurred to me that I'd be in the same position.'

'You felt the excitement even then?'

'I felt excitement, yes.'

But her first job was in the development section of a plastics factory: 'Sometimes I tease some of my Labour MP friends and say, "You know, I've had more experience of working in a factory than you have!"'

In 1949 she was adopted Conservative candidate for Dartford in Kent – 'an absolutely hopeless seat,' observes Roy Plomley – and after the selection meeting was so busy working the room that she missed the last train back to London. Help was at hand in the shape of one Dennis Thatcher, managing director of a paint company, who drove her home. They were married two years later, and their twins were born in 1953. 'I had the children in August, on the day we won the Ashes,' she recalls. The twins had taken a long time to arrive, and Dennis 'had sort of mooched off somewhere'.

After fighting Dartford unsuccessfully in 1951 and 1955, she entered Parliament in 1959 as MP for Finchley, and rose rapidly through the ranks. In 1967 she was promoted by Edward Heath to the Shadow Cabinet – the Conservatives had lost to Labour under Harold Wilson in 1964 – with the fuel and power portfolio. She recalls her first debate from the opposition front bench: 'They were all wondering how this woman would tackle fuel and power. I had worked like a Trojan, and I had worked at all the facts and figures. Someone got up and cited a whole list of figures as illustrating a certain point, and I was able to say, because I knew the moment he spoke exactly which figures they were: "Yes, those figures would have proved that point had he quoted the right year, but he has quoted the wrong year!"'

Then to her taking over the Tory leadership from Edward Heath. 'It all really happened rather suddenly. It was quite clear that there was going to be an election for the leadership. After all, Ted had been there for ten years, and it's a very distinguished thing to have been leader of a party for ten years. And then it looked as if no one would put up for the leadership. I remember very vividly saying, "Well, if no one else will do it, I will." And the moment I said it I never had a moment's hesitation about it. I knew it was absolutely the right thing to do.'

Her luxury: a photograph album of her children.

And her book: 'Well, I think if I had the Bible and Shakespeare I'd be having enough intellectual and philosophical exercise, so I should turn to something practical, and I've found a book. It's called *The Survival*

Margaret Thatcher's first day at No. 10, May 1979

Handbook: Self-sufficiency for Everyone.
It even tells you how to make a boat. It
tells you how to weave, it tells you how
to cook all sorts of things, and about
making longbows and arrows. Don't
you think that would just be right?'

Four days after transmission, the
programme was discussed at the BBC's
Radio Weekly Programme Review
Board, a gathering of senior radio
personnel which met every Wednesday
to discuss the previous week's output.
The meeting noted that Roy Plomley had

extracted from Mrs Thatcher information not revealed before, though one
less enthusiastic member was minuted as saying that Conservative Central
Office must have been delighted at the image of a very nice woman projected
by the programme. It was stated Mrs Thatcher's principal political opponent,
premier James Callaghan, had been invited to appear on *Desert Island Discs*,
since the aim was to keep a rough balance between the parties. The minutes
also recorded that Mrs Thatcher had asked to appear on the programme, but
so did many other people, and the discussion concluded that Mrs Thatcher's
appearance, accepting that this was an entertainment programme, had been
very well handled by all concerned.

   As for the lady herself, in May 1979, fifteen months after being cast away,
she came ashore as Prime Minister, a position she held through two more
general elections – in 1983 and 1987 – before standing down in November
1990. She left the Commons at the 1992 general election and took a life
peerage, becoming Baroness Thatcher of Kesteven. Her husband Dennis
Thatcher died in June 2003.

   Love her or hate her, political life was never dull when Margaret Thatcher
was in No. 10. Her period of office included the Falklands War in 1982,
the miners' strike of 1984–5 and her own dramatic toppling in 1990, and a
measure of her influence is that, unlike most prime ministers, she gave rise
to a true 'ism'.

LAUREN BACALL

actress

3 March 1979

'I was just determined that I was going to be noticed'

In his book *Plomley's Pick*, the presenter recommends Lauren Bacall's autobiography *By Myself* as 'very honest, very emotional and, at times, unbearably sad'. He goes on: 'Through it all, as through my interview with her, is that laconic wit which is typical of the New York Jewish people, and, while reading or listening, one pictures that challenging, quizzical, beautiful look with which she faces the world.' He then adds, helpfully: 'She had the deepest voice of any woman I know.'

'As long as I can remember, I guess I wanted to be something that I wasn't,' says Lauren Bacall when Roy Plomley asks how she became stage-struck. Her first ambition was to be a ballet dancer – but never mind that, Plomley wants to know who were her heroes and heroines in the movies.

As a child in New York City, where she was born in 1924, did she go to the theatre as well as the movies? 'I went to the theatre once or twice, but the theatre was a little beyond me, because it was too expensive. The first play I ever saw was John Gielgud in *Hamlet*.' ('Not a bad introduction,' says Plomley.) Watching that play 'absolutely did me in. I was so moved by it – even though I was really very, very young – that

I remember bumping into people as I was leaving the theatre. I was really dazed.'

But she still wanted to be a ballerina – until she realized that 'I really didn't have the feet for it – I was just in constant pain when on point – no Margot Fonteyn, I.'

She enrolled at the American Academy of Dramatic Art – as Betty Joan Perske, her real name – but money ran out after a year, and she was thrown upon her own devices. She undertook some modelling, and then, while working at a clothing store, or 'garment centre', had the bright idea of selling theatre papers outside the theatrical restaurant Sardi's so that her face would become familiar – in however unlikely a context – to producers.

'That shows that I was crazy from the very beginning, doesn't it? I was just determined that I was going to be noticed, as I was going in and out of those producers' offices, pounding pavements, looking for work, and I decided that I was not just going to be one of the actresses who got, "Oh yes, come back tomorrow, or come back next week, or whatever." I said, "They're going to remember me somehow – differently." And I prevailed upon the man that published *Actor's Cue*, the actor's magazine giving tips as to what was being cast, and I sold it outside Sardi's during my lunch hour. I would come up from the garment centre, rush into Waldgreen's, get the *Actor's Cues*, stand in front of Sardi's and buttonhole anyone that I recognized at all, hoping they would never forget me.'

As part of the same effort to keep her face in the subconscious of theatrical New York, she worked as a theatre usher, and thus attracted the attention of the influential critic George G. Nathan – not least because at the interval she would deliver the 'No smoking, please' request 'playing all kinds of I-don't-know-what dramas'. Nathan, says Bacall, 'was very sweet. Once a year he wrote the Bests and Worsts of the Year, and I was in the Best column, fortunately, as the prettiest usher at the St James Theatre.'

All this effort to attract attention eventually paid off, and she first trod a professional stage in a play called *Johnny Two-by-Four*. 'I had what I called an outstanding walk-on. To anyone else a walk-on is a walk-on, but to me, if you walked on the stage in three acts – which I did, in each of the three acts – to me that was outstanding, because I was given extra stuff to do.'

And another small step: 'The first line I spoke was in a play called *Franklyn Street*, which was directed by George S. Kaufman and produced by Max Gordon – one of the men I'd buttonholed outside Sardi's.'

Lauren Bacall with Humphrey Bogart in To Have and Have Not, *1944*

From New York, the play went to Washington, 'and down the drain after that', but Bacall – her mother had changed her surname – was on her way. Up to a point, at least, as theatre work was by its nature irregular, and she returned to modelling. Film producer Howard Hawks was told about this model who had appeared as a blood donor on the front cover of *Harper's Bazaar*, liked what he saw, and brought Bacall out to Hollywood. She was still only seventeen.

'When I went for my test – for my contract of course – I was taken to Perc Westmore at Warner Brothers, and Perc Westmore sat me down in front of a mirror and looked at me and said, "Well now, if we tweeze your eyebrows and make a thin line like Dietrich's and then we straighten teeth, then we do something with your hairline" – I was panic-stricken. I rushed to the phone and called Hawks, and said, "Oh, they're going to change everything – please, please come down – help, help!" – and he came down and he said, "No, Perc, leave her just as she is – I want the crooked eyebrows, I want the crooked teeth, the crooked hair, the crooked everything" – and that's what he got.'

Her first movie role was in *To Have and Have Not* in 1944, opposite Humphrey Bogart at the height of his post-*Casablanca* fame. 'Were you a fan of his?' asks Roy Plomley: 'Was he one of your favourites?'

'No, no. I knew he was a good actor, but he was not my type, I didn't think.'

She was wrong. She appeared with Bogart in three more films, including *The Big Sleep* in 1946 and *Dark Passage* the following year; and before *The Big Sleep*, in May 1945, they married.

How, wonders Roy Plomley, did that particular Lauren Bacall pose – 'looking sexily from under your eyelids' – come about?

'Because I was a nervous wreck and because I used to shake all the time – now I only shake some of the time – in order to keep my head still I discovered that if I held my chin down I was able to keep my head a bit steadier, and then I looked up at Bogart and that became "The Look".'

As for her later films, she declares that 'I loved *Murder on the Orient Express*', before suggesting: 'I haven't been in that many films, you know – I've not been in that many good ones, certainly.'

But she has a new film coming up – *Health*, directed by Robert Altman: 'I play, so Robert Altman tells me, an eighty-three-year-old virgin, which I think is wonderful.'

With regard to being cast away, is she practical? 'Well, I always thought I was practical, but I don't know . . . I love the outdoors, but on a desert island that's it. You'd better love the outdoors. Where else do you go?'

Shakespeare
'My mistress' eyes are nothing like the sun'
(Sonnet 130)

'I could go from youth to middle age to old age and I could let my imagination run wild'

Lauren Bacall told Roy Plomley that she had not been in many films, but since the *Desert Island Discs* interview in 1979 she has been in a fair few more – notably *The Mirror Has Two Faces* in 1996, for which she won various awards and was nominated for the Oscar for Best Actress in a Supporting Role.

Opposite: Edmund Hillary and Sherpa Tenzing Norgay on the approach to the summit of Everest, May 1953

SIR EDMUND HILLARY

mountaineer

14 April 1979

'It's really a sort of pyramid of effort'

Sir Edmund Hillary achieved world renown when on 29 May 1953 he became the first man to climb Mount Everest, then officially measured at 29,028 feet (8,848 metres). Along with his companion Sherpa Tenzing Norgay, the 33-year-old New Zealander stood on the summit at 11 a.m. local time, remained there for a quarter of an hour, and then started the descent to lasting fame and recognition. News of the achievement reached Britain on 2 June, the day Queen Elizabeth II was crowned.

There is nothing sophisticated about Sir Edmund Hillary's method of choosing his eight records. 'I have a redoubtable ability to whistle songs – the same one for about three hours – which has irritated my family for many years . . . I had great doubts about just precisely what songs I should choose because I have a terrible memory for names, so I telephoned my daughter in New Zealand and said, "Sarah, what are my eight favourite songs?" – whereupon very accurately she remembered the names of them, and they were the songs that I would have chosen.'

Sir Edmund is a New Zealander of Yorkshire stock – 'three of my grandparents came from Yorkshire, and one from Ireland' – and his father combined editorship of the local newspaper with keeping bees, plus a few cows: 'He was a great reader and he used to find milking cows a rather boring procedure, so by hanging a book on a rack over the back of a cow, he got through quite a lot of literature.'

At what stage had young Edmund's interest in climbing begun? 'The first time I ever went to the mountains as such – where there was snow and ice – was my last year at high school. I went skiing and I found it tremendously exciting, and for a few years I did a little bit of skiing and a lot of walking about in the forest and in the mountains. It wasn't really until I was about nineteen or twenty that I became interested in mountaineering as such.'

A family trip to Europe brought his first experience of the Alps – 'we tackled pretty much the routine type of routes on the mountains and we had a very exciting time' – and the next step was the Himalayas, where he first went with three fellow New Zealanders. 'We climbed a number of peaks of over twenty thousand feet, and this brought us to the notice of the famous mountaineer Eric Shipton, who had just had permission to take an expedition to reconnoitre the south side of Everest, and he invited two of us to go along. So that's how I got involved in the Everest story.'

Carson Robison
and his Pioneers
'There's a Bridle Hangin'
on the Wall'

'If I'm properly prompted, I can even do a rendition myself'

'I can understand the exhilaration of climbing,' says Roy Plomley, 'but I've been reading your autobiography *Nothing Venture, Nothing Win*, and the dangers really seem daunting. It's a long catalogue of avalanches, fishing chaps out of crevasses, casualties through frostbite. Does one get inured to all this?'

'Well, I think perhaps that one has to remember that during the period you spend on an expedition, there's only about five per cent of the time you are involved in tooth-and-nail activities. The other ninety-five per cent is really good fun . . . And the five minutes of excitement – and of fear, perhaps – is a stimulating factor during the course of the trip.'

And so to Everest. Was it the availability of oxygen which made that expedition possible? 'I think oxygen played quite a big part, although now of course the mountain has been climbed without oxygen. But in 1953 we still had these grave doubts as to whether it was physically possible to climb the mountain even with oxygen, and that sort of problem had to be overcome – that psychological barrier really had to be broken before people could attempt Everest without oxygen.'

How big was the expedition, asks Plomley – 'How many chaps?' Ten climbing members, including expedition leader John Hunt; three others involved with filming and reporting; and some thirty Sherpa porters. 'It's really a sort of pyramid of effort: you carry vast quantities of stuff to your first camp, and then a little less to the next one, and so on and so on up the mountain.'

They established a camp on the South Col at 26,000 feet, then withdrew a short way down the mountain to rest and organize themselves for the last stage. It was not until this point that John Hunt decided that Edmund Hillary and Sherpa Tenzing Norgay should be the ones to make the final assault. Off they went, and it was when they reached the south summit, where they established Camp 9 at 28,000 feet, that Hillary became confident they would indeed reach the very top. 'Up until then it had all been very debatable: I really didn't know whether or not we were going to be successful. There was a step in the ridge which we knew might be a problem, and we did have a little problem getting up to it. But once we got up that, then for the first time I was quite confident that we were going to get to the top.'

'Your summing up when you came down from the peak,' says Roy Plomley, 'has now passed into the history books. Will you repeat those immortal words yourself?'

'I should explain that these weren't really meant for the listening public of the world. I was talking on the South Col and came down and met George Lowe, my fellow climbing New Zealander, and I said, "Well, George, we knocked the bastard off."'

Climbing Everest made it easier to get funding for other expeditions. Hillary crossed Antarctica with Vivian Fuchs, and later returned to the Himalayas in search of the 'Abominable Snowman', the Yeti:

'I'm afraid that we went into things fairly thoroughly and investigated a lot of the evidence, and we came to the conclusion unfortunately that the Yeti is essentially a mythological creature. I would dearly love to be proved wrong about this, because I think we'd all like there to be a Yeti, and for it to exist, and I know there are many people – including Lord [John] Hunt actually – who still like to feel that the Yeti does tramp around the Himalayas on odd occasions. But my feeling on this expedition essentially was that the creature is mythological.'

'All those bones and skins and so on that are preserved in various monasteries?'

'They all had a logical and practical explanation, which didn't require the existence of the Yeti.'

'That's very disappointing.'

The first children to attend the school founded by Edmund Hillary at Khumjung, Nepal

Then there was the expedition up the Ganges in jet boats – 'almost a cultural pilgrimage through the centre of India by travelling up Mother Ganga, which is of course the holy river of India, and as it happened this aspect of it became increasingly important. We were really taken into the hearts of the Indians as we travelled along, and I think for the period at least we all became Hindus . . . We of course started at sea level, and we finished up with the boats almost fifteen hundred miles up, at about four thousand feet. But from then on we walked on foot up to the very sacred shrine of Badrinath at ten thousand feet, and ultimately we climbed this mountain of over nineteen thousand feet.'

Sir Edmund has been involved in setting up an assistance programme for the Sherpa people who live on the south side of Mount Everest: 'Over the years I've built up quite an affection for these people, and have been aware of the fact that they may lack a lot of the things that we take for granted. So for quite a number of years I've been involved in the establishing of schools for their children, building a couple of hospitals, and various bridges and airfields and things of this nature.'

As Roy Plomley states between the final two records, 'Sir Edmund, you are one person I do not have to ask the usual questions about your capabilities to cope on a desert island.'

While it was scaling Everest which made Hillary a household name – and earned him a knighthood in the Coronation honours list – he subsequently engaged in many other remarkable ventures, notably in Antarctica and India, and spent much of his later life involved in charitable work for the Sherpa people.

Sir Edmund Hillary died at the age of eighty-eight in January 2008.

ROALD DAHL

writer

27 October 1979

'It is impossible, after listening to great music,
to write absolute rubbish'

'He is a giggler,' writes Roy Plomley of Roald Dahl in his book *Plomley's Pick*: 'he sees the funny side in everything, which is probably why he writes so successfully for children as well as for adults.' By the time he was cast away, Dahl – born in Wales to Norwegian parents in 1916 and educated in England – had been enhancing the reading lives of young and old alike over several decades since *The Gremlins* was published in 1943.

Many of his children's books have long been classics, notably *James and the Giant Peach* (1961), *Charlie and the Chocolate Factory* (1964), *The BFG* (1982) and *Matilda* (1988), while his collections of verse, such as *Revolting Rhymes* (1982) and *Rhyme Stew* (1989), are perennial favourites. In addition to his literary output, he wrote screenplays for several well-known films, among them *You Only Live Twice* (1967 – the last James Bond film with Sean Connery), *Chitty Chitty Bang Bang* (1968) and – of course – *Willy Wonka and the Chocolate Factory* (1971).

Having declared his attitude to being alone on the desert island – 'I hate to say it, but I would love it' –

'My little hut in the orchard'

Dahl turns to the place of music in his life, and offers invaluable advice to all writers: 'In the old days, before I was married, I never used to start writing in the morning before putting on some very great music, like a Beethoven quartet, and sitting and listening to it in the hope that some of this greatness would rub off on me, and that I would write better. As a matter of fact, it helped quite a lot, because it is impossible, after listening to great music, to write absolute rubbish.'

But does he play music while writing? 'Oh, goodness me, no. A little hut, curtains drawn so that I don't see the squirrels up in the apple trees in the orchard, the light on, right away from the house, no vacuum cleaners, nothing.'

As a child he was an avid reader, including Dickens, Thackeray, 'and there was an American fellow who, when I read him, I couldn't turn the light off at night – a short story writer called Ambrose Bierce, who had a wonderful title to his collection, which was *Can Such Things Be?*' (We learn later that he was also very keen on the swashbuckling novels of C. S. Forester.)

Not wishing to go to university, he took his mother's advice to try to find a job which would take him to distant lands, and went for an interview with Shell. 'I remember my housemaster saying, "I don't know what you're wasting your time with this for. There'll be people like the Head Boys of Eton and Harrow and God knows what there." But this imposing board of directors interviewing sixty boys for five places – they all brightened up when I said I'd won the heavyweight boxing at school, and that got me one of the places.'

He went to places like Dar es Salaam in Tanganyika (now part of Tanzania): 'It was rather marvellous for a chap that age. You learned Swahili. You drove round and visited the sisal plantations and the diamond mines, and things like that. See that the chaps had the right kind of lubricating oil for their machinery . . . It was so adventurous.'

Then war broke out. Dahl joined the RAF and ended up in the Middle East, where he was invalided out of active flying following a crash. He was moved to the USA, where he became Assistant Air Attaché at the British

Embassy: 'I didn't last very long, because I'm a tactless sort of fellow, and that's the one thing a diplomat mustn't be.' He left the embassy, but before long was back – in the intelligence section, 'which was much more fun'.

While in Washington, Dahl had an encounter which was to change his life: 'America was hardly in the war then and we were trying to do as much propaganda as we could to get help from America. I was sitting in my room in the embassy, and a door opened and a little round face poked in with thick glasses and said, "May I come in?" And I really did think that this little man was going to ask for a job of some sort – not that I could have given it to him. And he said, "My name is C. S. Forester." And I said, "Oh, go on." And he said, "No, honestly." And being an avid reader – one of my gods was walking into the room. And he said, "Look, will you come out to lunch with me and tell me your most exciting adventure in the war, and I'll write it and it'll be in the *Saturday Evening Post*, and it'll be good for Britain." And I said, "Yes, I jolly well will."'

As lunch progressed, Dahl was offering Forester plenty of material: 'We were eating duck, and he was trying to make notes and shovel this stuff into his mouth. There was a mess and I was trying to talk, and I said, "Look, if I scribble this down this evening and send it you, you can put it in proper shape. Would that help?"'

It would. 'A little story seemed to emerge from it,' which Dahl sent Forester, 'and a week later I got a lovely letter from him and a cheque for a thousand dollars, saying he hadn't touched it and he'd sold it to the *Saturday Evening Post* for me, and they wanted more.'

By the end of the war Dahl was writing more and more, and Plomley raises the subject of his short stories – 'Sometimes rather gruesome, often very funny.'

'I've probably got a warped sense of humour,' says Dahl, 'but I think it's terribly funny if somebody gets killed by being hit on the head with a frozen leg of lamb, or something like that. You really can't call that tragic, can you?'

His children's books have enjoyed huge sales – in particular, *Charlie and the Chocolate Factory*.

'And it's been made into a film?' prompts Plomley – referring to the 1971 musical *Willy Wonka and the Chocolate Factory*.

'It was made into rather a crummy film. I wasn't pleased with it at all . . . I originally wrote the screenplay, but made the mistake of letting Hollywood have a free hand, and I shall never do that again . . . I'm not in love with cinema directors, let's just put it that way, except for the James Bond one.'

The presenter finds safer ground in Dahl's relationship with the American actress Patricia Neal, to whom the castaway was married at the time of the interview. Neal had had more than one stroke, and Dahl had become deeply involved in her care, and in setting up treatment centres: 'It was simply my original small idea of how to treat a stroke patient, and give her very intensive therapy as soon as possible after the stroke.'

Is he a disciplined writer? Does he work set hours? 'Yes, I am a disciplined writer. I don't think any writer writes particularly long hours, because he can't. You become inefficient. I work from ten to twelve, and from four to six. And then it's time for a drink. It's time for a drink after twelve, and it's time for a drink after six. So I hot-foot it down from my little hut in the orchard and have a drink.'

(The transcript of the programme records how towards the end of the conversation Dahl breaks off from talking about his novel *My Uncle Oswald* and turns the spotlight back onto his interrogator: 'I must say something about you, Roy, because I've listened to – I don't know what – one, two hundred of these programmes, on and off. We've just had a hilarious lunch. You come across as quite a serious chap here, and then you were the jokiest man in the room. I'm not sure that they' – the listeners – 'know this.' Plomley replies drily, 'Well, it depends if I'm with a jokey companion' – and moves on.)

Is Dahl a gambler? 'Yes, I've been a gambler all my life. I'll gamble on anything: horses, dogs. I once bred racing greyhounds, just after the war. I had twenty or thirty of them.'

'Successfully?'

'Not particularly, no. But you see a gambler doesn't care whether he's successful or not, as long as he can gamble. It was enormous fun, breeding them and running them in little flapping tracks in the country. But you see all this gambling, whatever it's on, has allowed me to write three or four or five stories to do with gambling.'

Back to the island. Would he try to escape? 'No, no – I'd love it. I'd absolutely adore it. I wouldn't escape. I'd stay there and hope that no smoke or funnel hove into the distance.'

The luxury? 'This causes great problems for a sybarite like me. The two things that I wouldn't want to do without are smoking and drinking. I toyed with the idea of a still, because then I could distil my liquor. There'd be coconuts or something . . . or a packet of tobacco seeds so I could grow the tobacco. Or even a bunch of cuttings from a great vineyard like Romany Conti in Burgundy – and try to plant them, and then in time you would have the grapes for ever.'

'That would take a few years, wouldn't it?'

'Yes, I'd be without drink until then. I'd like to have the still and the cuttings and the tobacco seeds. But I can't have them all—'

'We'll pack them all up in a box, yes. They're all yours.'

Roald Dahl died in November 1990 at the age of seventy-four. According to his granddaughter, the writer and model Sophie Dahl, he was given 'a sort of Viking burial' – with snooker cues, a decent bottle of Burgundy, chocolates, HB pencils, and a power saw.

1980s

AT THE BEGINNING of the 1980s *Desert Island Discs* was sailing happily along, with Roy Plomley's hand resting gently on the tiller and the programme continuing to recruit castaways from every sphere of life – and even death, with the medium Doris Stokes being marooned in 1985.

Throughout the decade, the programme offered its own special perspective on some of the significant events of the time. Castaways in 1988 included both Michael Heseltine, who had resigned from the cabinet in 1986 over the Westland helicopters affair, and Arthur Scargill (pages 266–9), who led the miners through the bitter dispute of 1984–5, while Ian Botham, hero of the scarcely believable 1981 Headingley test match against Australia, was marooned on the desert island in 1989.

Securing the royal presence in January 1981 of HRH Princess Margaret (pages 234–8) was a major coup, and the Queen's sister was followed on to the desert island by two other princesses: Princess Grace of Monaco (1981) and HRH Princess Michael of Kent (1984). And in January 1982 the fortieth anniversary of the first programme brought pop music royalty to the *Desert Island Discs* studio in the form of Paul McCartney (pages 239–43).

Special mention must be made of Arthur Askey, whose appearance on 20 December 1980 made him the first person to be cast away four times, and of Dame Edna Everage, who in July 1988 joined that very exclusive club confined to fictitious castaways: before Dame Edna, the only members were ventriloquist's dummy Archie Andrews (who had appeared with his handler Peter Brough in 1952), and Sir Harry Whitlohn, castaway of the April Fool edition of 1963 (see pages 94–6).

Roy Plomley himself broke new ground in 1984 with a television spin-off from *Desert Island Discs*, a programme called *Favourite Things* which involved his visiting celebrities at home and talking to them about objects close to their hearts.

But the decade was barely a month old before the calm of the sleepy lagoon was disturbed. Otto Preminger, the Austrian-born film director, was the castaway, and had already shown signs of prickliness before Plomley suggested: 'There are actors who've worked for you who say that you're very tough on the set, in fact that you're rather a frightening man to actors, and something of an ogre.'

'Who told you that?' growled the apparently annoyed castaway: 'Which actor told you that? You are incredible – you read things and you believe everything bad about me.'

Plomley insisted that he had raised the matter only in order for Preminger to deny it, and after the castaway had declared that the two things he disliked in actors were unpunctuality and failure to learn lines, the conversation continued. The damage had been done, however, and Preminger's irritation soon surfaced again when it was time to discuss the island formalities.

'Mr Preminger, you're an independent and self-reliant man. Could you look after yourself on a desert island?'

Celebrating the fortieth anniversary in January 1982: Roy Plomley and castaways

'Could I look after myself on a desert island?'

'Yes. Could you build a hut? Are you any good at carpentry?'

'Build a hut?'

'Yes.'

'You must be out of your mind. I can't even build a box, or anything. Can *you* build a hut?'

'No.'

'Then why do you expect me to build a hut?'

'I don't *expect* you – I just wanted to know, with an enquiring mind, if you thought you could build a hut …'

And a moment later:

'If you could only have one of the discs, and not the eight, what would it be?'

'I won't tell you. Which one would *you* like best? Ah, you see, you can't answer. You ask all these questions. If I ask you one question, you just get red in your face – and your head, particularly – and you can't answer.'

Otto Preminger, 1975

'I could answer it but I'm not going to. I won't tell you.'

'Fine, then I won't answer it either.'

The geniality with which Roy Plomley fails to rise to his castaway's baiting – in particular the gratuitous remark about the presenter's bald head – was admirable, but Derek Drescher, who produced that edition, recalls that Preminger's performance was 'very tongue-in-cheek. He had a twinkle in his eye – he knew he was being wicked.' (To add to his wickedness, all this castaway's music choices were soundtracks from his own films, and his chosen book was 'a beautiful autobiography – by Otto Preminger.') Plomley wrote in his book *Plomley's Pick* that Preminger's 'heavy-handed mock aggression' had been aimed at getting publicity: 'He certainly succeeded in getting column-inches in the newspapers, although the comments were not all flattering, and one headline read, "'Orrible Otto". It was an abrasive encounter, but I enjoyed it.'

The 1980s brought a very high-profile indication of the place *Desert Island Discs* had found in the national psyche.

On 16 November 1982 Tom Stoppard's play *The Real Thing* opened for its West End run at the Strand Theatre, with a cast that featured Felicity Kendal and Roger Rees. In the second scene, playwright Henry is up early and scrabbling through his records when his wife Charlotte comes into the room.

Henry will shortly appear on *Desert Island Discs*, and is having trouble reaching his quota of records. What, he asks Charlotte, was that open-air dance band playing outside their window in Bournemouth or Deauville (it was Zermatt, she says) while he was writing his play about Sartre? He is due to give the *Desert Island Discs* team his choices the next day, but so far he only has *Finnegans Wake* and five records – and he is supposed to be giving them eight pieces of music which reflect turning-points in his life.

Charlotte reminds him that she herself represents a turning-point in his life, and when they were in Zermatt his favourite record had been the Ronettes singing 'Da Doo Ron Ron' – the *Crystals*, he corrects her – and she advises him to keep it simple: just choose his eight all-time greats and remember what he was doing at the time. What could be wrong with that?

Henry's reply gets to the heart of the castaway's dilemma: 'I'm supposed to be one of your intellectual playwrights. I'm going to look a total prick, aren't I, announcing that while I was telling Jean-Paul Sartre and the post-war French existentialists where they had got it wrong I was spending the whole time listening to the Crystals singing "Da Doo Ron Ron".'

Henry later confesses that he considers 'the Righteous Brothers recording of "You've Lost that Lovin' Feelin'" on the London label was possibly the most haunting, the most deeply moving noise ever produced by the human spirit.' That track ends up as one of his eight records, and is playing on *Desert Island Discs* at one of the pivotal moments of *The Real Thing* – indeed, a moment so pivotal that the radio gets kicked across the stage.

Tom Stoppard himself was cast away in January 1985, when his homage to *Desert Island Discs* was duly acknowledged by Roy Plomley.

On 28 May 1985 Roy Plomley died suddenly of a heart attack at the age of seventy-one. For some time he had been aware that he had lung cancer, but he had kept the news to himself. 'Although Roy knew his illness was fatal,' his widow Diana was quoted as saying in the *Daily Mail*, 'he never spoke of it to me, but I think he guessed I was aware. He was undemanding, too concerned with life ever to plan what would happen after his death ... When Roy suffered the fatal heart attack, his doctor called it a blessing in disguise. It was quick and merciful.'

Colleagues as well as close family were stunned by the news. 'I don't think any of us realized that he was that unwell,' recalled producer Derek Drescher when he spoke to the BBC for the special seventieth anniversary programme in 2012. 'He'd had shingles, which knocked him back a bit, but when the end came it was a terrible shock. I certainly wasn't expecting it. It was a terrible blow.'

Between Vic Oliver on 29 January 1942 and actress Sheila Steafel on 11 May 1985 (already scheduled as the last programme in that series), Roy Plomley had been involved in 1,786 editions of *Desert Island Discs* – including two as castaway (see pages 18–19, 73–5) – over more than forty-three years.

Roy Plomley with his wife Diana, July 1984

Newspaper obituaries were generous in their praise. 'The longevity of *Desert Island Discs*', read the obituary in *The Times*, 'was based on the brilliant simplicity of the idea – which was Plomley's own – and the unfailing courtesy of his chairmanship.' And later Richard Ingrams gave a good summing-up of Roy Plomley's special nature: 'Plomley was one of those unobtrusive little men whose gifts are only appreciated after they are dead. To the casual listener he sounded bland and obsequious. But the secret of good interviewing is not what the interviewer may say or sound like, it is in what he manages to extract from the interviewee. Above all, the art lies in putting him at his ease. At this Plomley excelled.'

Radio 4 broadcast a tribute programme on 29 June 1985, with a memorial service taking place the following month at All Souls, Langham Place, the church next to Broadcasting House. Newsreader and television presenter Richard Baker told the congregation: 'It's wonderful to see you all here. As Roy might have said in his acting days, "It's a splendid house for a matinee."' And humorist Denis Norden said that Roy Plomley 'was a consummate broadcaster and a man who will be difficult to replace'.

Difficult to replace: there was the rub. Could *Desert Island Discs* continue without its moving spirit over all those years? Simply carrying on with someone else in the presenter's chair was not a straightforward option for the BBC, as the rights lay with Roy Plomley.

Some three weeks after Plomley's death the London *Evening Standard* ran a story reporting that the BBC had already received 'at least a dozen' applications to be the new presenter, and that Diana Plomley's own inclination, were the programme to continue, would be to appoint her husband's old friend John Mortimer QC, barrister and author.

Two days later the BBC Board of Management noted the *Evening Standard* story, and declared: 'The death of Roy Plomley had marked the end of a particular tradition of broadcasting and, despite the speculation about other presenters, he would be difficult to replace. Programmatically, *Desert Island Discs* was a valuable property; if the BBC were to discontinue the series, others might take it up. Radio [i.e. the department] would be considering the prospects for the future in consultation with Roy Plomley's family; a decision would be reached in due course.'

In this case, 'due course' meant a little more than four months. On 5 November 1985, under the headline 'Music Flows Again from Desert Island', the *Evening Standard* reported that the programme would return to the airwaves the following January. The paper quoted Radio 4 Controller David Hatch: 'We wondered whether *Desert Island Discs* should continue after Roy's death, but hundreds of devotees of the programme wrote asking us to bring it back, and Mrs Plomley is happy as Roy's name will be perpetuated.' (His name is enshrined to this day in the words 'Created by Roy Plomley', part of the on-air credits given by the Radio 4 continuity announcer after each edition.)

The next few days saw much speculation about the identity of the new presenter. On 10 November, Richard Brooks in the *Sunday Times* wrote that finding a replacement for Roy Plomley 'has been a bit like naming a new Pope. A puff of white smoke is expected above Broadcasting House this week when the new presenter of radio's longest-running programme is announced. The college of cardinals – David Hatch, Radio 4 controller, Derek Drescher, the programme's producer, and Mrs Plomley, the former actress Diana Wong – will by then have deliberated enough to determine the successor.'

Brooks offered a brief form guide. Peter Ustinov, he wrote, was Mrs Plomley's ideal, but also in the reckoning was Richard Baker, who told Brooks, 'I'm not denying or confirming anything.' Other possibilities, according to the *Sunday Times*, included Robert Robinson, a fixture in so many game shows; musician and panel-game regular Steve Race; Radio 1 disc jockey Simon Bates; and John Timpson, presenter on the *Today* programme and chairman of *Any Questions?*. There had been talk of making a wholesale change by installing a female presenter, reported Brooks, but that idea had been dropped.

On 11 November the keenly awaited skein of white smoke duly puffed out of the roof of Broadcasting House. The new presenter of *Desert Island Discs* would be . . . Michael Parkinson, king of the television chat show.

The choice occasioned a good deal of comment, both inside and outside the BBC, but there was no denying Parkinson's great experience and ability – the principal example of which was his late-Saturday-night BBC television chat show, first broadcast in 1971 and for over a decade a part of the traditional weekend routine. The television popularity of Parkinson – who initially described his new role as 'one of the plum jobs in radio' – was no guarantee that he would please the millions of loyal *Desert Island Discs* listeners, and for Parky the bar was set higher by the programme's undeniable status as a crown jewel of British broadcasting. During the run-up to the new series, the debate about whether he was a suitable replacement for

A new face on the island – Michael Parkinson, January 1986

Roy Plomley continued unabated in lounge bars the length and breadth of the country.

Eventually the waiting was over, and on 5 January 1986 a new phase in the life of *Desert Island Discs* began with the casting away of film director Alan Parker. At one point in the programme Parker criticized the British film industry, allowing the *Daily Express* to report that 'Michael Parkinson hosted *Desert Island Discs* for the first time yesterday – and brought a note of controversy to the long-running Radio 4 show.'

Despite Diana Plomley being quoted in the *Sun* as saying that Parkinson was 'a good interviewer, but I don't like his voice', and telling the *Express* that he was 'very different from Roy', the new era seemed to be off to a reasonably placid start. The *Times* radio critic reported: 'Well, after all the brouhaha, it was more like Plomleyson than Parkinson, wasn't it? Maybe there is some rapier work to come – the wretched victim raining drops of sweat onto his choice of discs as he dodges his tormentor's blade – but the first edition of the new-style *Desert Island Discs* was near enough in the tradition of the old . . . Perhaps we should not absolutely count on Michael Parkinson as the Torquemada of the palm-fringed shore.'

And following the second programme – with violinist Nigel Kennedy – *The Listener* took a similar line, stating that '*DID* is not much different under Parky – just less compulsive'.

But by the time that fashion designer Bruce Oldfield was cast away in early February, the press was distinctly warming to the new regime – the critic of *The Times* going so far as to suggest that *Desert Island Discs* would never be the same again. The Oldfield edition was considered to have been a more adversarial encounter than Roy Plomley would ever have produced – 'Can you imagine the late Roy asking anybody whether his occupation could be called a real job?', asked *The Thunderer* – but none the worse for that, and the Parkinson approach was widely praised for happily merging a sharper edge with the essential character of the programme.

Inside the BBC the programme continued to provoke a fair bit of discussion. In mid-February the Programme Review Board minutes recorded that 'in general, Michael Parkinson was proving more adept at drawing out his guests than Roy Plomley', but the following week a Board of Management minute read: 'Referring to suspicions that *Desert Island Discs* had been taken over by a "Yorkshire mafia" . . . all the guests who had so far appeared on the programme under Michael Parkinson's chairmanship had indeed been born in Yorkshire . . . The general view of the Radio Programme Review Board

[was] that Parkinson was getting more out of his subjects than Roy Plomley had done.'

An entry in the minutes cannot easily demonstrate whether a remark is made tongue in cheek, but in any case the suggestion that all Parkinson's castaways had been born in Yorkshire was demonstrably untrue – and in his autobiography Parky pointed out that of his first six castaways only Maureen Lipman was Yorkshire-born.

But Parkinson was clearly never very comfortable as *Desert Island Discs* presenter, and it came as no huge surprise when in October 1987 he announced that he would be returning to the mainland the following spring – that is, after just over two years with the programme. 'Two years of *Desert Island Discs* is about right,' he told Richard Brooks, by then with the *Observer*: 'It was never going to be a pensionable occupation.'

Nevertheless, Parkinson's *Desert Island Discs* experience clearly rankled – and, having long kept his own counsel in the face of public criticism from Mrs Plomley and the press, he allowed his discontent to surface in his autobiography: 'I knew there would be resistance to my appointment and planned to see that die down, make a point and then move on. I certainly didn't want to spend the rest of my life hosting a parlour game, which is what, in fact, it is.'

With the presenter's seat about to be vacant again so soon, some seventy hopefuls reportedly offered their services to the BBC – and again there was plenty of speculation in the press. John Dunn? Bob Holness? Frank Bough? Noel Edmonds? Andy Kershaw?

The answer, announced in December 1987, was again not someone whose chance had been much discussed. It was Sue Lawley – widely admired as a newsreader, presenter, journalist and one-time mainstay of the early-evening television news magazine *Nationwide*.

Sue clearly relished the opportunity to make her mark on the programme. 'I think the talks with guests should be about trying to gain a little bit of wisdom from them through the lives they have led,' she told the *Daily Telegraph*: 'The programme gives you the opportunity to uncover things about people they might not reveal in other interview situations. They know they've got to talk about their warts and all.'

The announcement that Sue Lawley was to be the new presenter came, coincidentally (or perhaps not coincidentally), a month after she herself had been cast away by Michael Parkinson. Her record choices included the Beatles' 'Hey Jude', Puccini, Purcell, Dory Previn, Ella Fitzgerald, the choir

Presenter number three – Sue Lawley, March 1988

of King's College, Cambridge, singing the Holst setting of 'In the Bleak Midwinter', and Sir John Gielgud reading from T. S. Eliot's *Four Quartets*, and her record of records was Rachmaninov's *Rhapsody on a Theme of Paganini*. Her chosen book was *French Provincial Cooking* by Elizabeth David, and as for her luxury: 'I would like to have an endless supply of freshly laundered white linen sheets – clean sheets every day.' She even offered to launder the sheets herself, and, if allowed an iron and an ironing board, to iron them as well: 'I find ironing extremely therapeutic.'

In her book *Desert Island Discussions*, Sue Lawley recalled her reaction to her new assignment: 'If I had felt honoured at being chosen as a castaway, I felt ennobled now. I knew that *Desert Island Discs* was one of the most prestigious programmes on BBC Radio and I was sure that if I handled it well my reputation would not suffer. I was attracted to it for those reasons – but they were not the only ones. My experience in television had taught me that people enjoy listening to good talk. They like to hear about the famous and the distinguished in a way which is simple, pleasing and revealing, without being prying or intrusive. *Desert Island Discs* struck me as the perfect setting for that kind of broadcasting. Because it is such a good programme for its guests, it is a good programme for the interviewer as well.'

Big news on the global stage at this time was the summit meeting between US President Ronald Reagan and Soviet Union leader Mikhail Gorbachev, and in his *Daily Mirror* column, Michael Parkinson could not resist indulging in a little playful fantasy at the expense of his former programme:

> There can be few more historic weeks than the one that saw Mr Reagan meet Mr Gorbachev and Miss Sue Lawley become the next *Desert Island Discs* presenter . . .
>
> Commenting on Miss Lawley's intention to 'raise the profile of the show', the [BBC] spokesman said this was in response to criticism of Mr Parkinson's 'lowbrow' taste.
>
> Future programmes would include the world's leading player of the Peruvian Nose Flute, every winner of the Booker Prize and President of the Albanian Yodelling Contest . . .
>
> The news caused a revival on the Stock Exchange. There are hints at a further cut in the Bank Rate.
>
> Moscow Radio played solemn music.

In March 1988, Parkinson's final castaway was the former athlete Brendan Foster, and two weeks later Sue Lawley's first was Quintin Hogg, Lord Hailsham – one of the great characters of postwar politics and Lord

David Essex

Chancellor in two Conservative administrations, who endeared himself to the new presenter by tiddly - om-pom-pomming along to his first record choice, 'I Do Like To Be Beside the Seaside'.

Sue Lawley's debut attracted rave reviews. In the first programme, according to the *Daily Telegraph*, 'she put paid to the notion that the format has had its day by making it a programme so lively, structured and thoughtful, it seemed brand new'. And after two programmes *The Listener* diary wrote: 'So far she has handled things beautifully, restoring the silly but essential fantasy elements to the programme.'

The Lawley style was soon in evidence, with her first twenty castaways including several from the political arena:

in addition to Quintin Hogg came Arthur Scargill, Neil Kinnock, Douglas Hurd, David Owen, Lord Armstrong and the Reverend Ian Paisley. But that first twenty also included such diverse figures as Jane Asher, Michael Gambon, Rowan Atkinson, Rabbi Lionel Blue and David Essex.

Shortly after the David Essex interview, the *Listener* diary had some advice: 'I most politely suggest that the *Desert Island Discs* studio is in future equipped with a bucket of cold water. It would have come in very handy when Sue Lawley had David Owen as her guest, and still more so when David Essex was in what can only be described these days as the hot seat. The flirting was quite outrageous. I think she is going to have to choose less inflammatory male guests if she wants to remain Queen of the Desert Island. Remember, Sue, they're only men.'

Sue Lawley's interviewee after David Essex presented a different sort of challenge, the lady in question being Dame Edna Everage. No worries about how she would cope on the island: 'I think I've got a few little enzymes

'I was born on a desert island'
– Dame Edna Everage

in me, not to say hormones, which would enable me to carve out a pretty rough existence for myself on a desert island. And remember – I was *born* on a desert island. Australia!'

Her eight records included one by herself and four by other Dames (Nellie Melba, Joan Sutherland, Kiri te Kanawa and Vera Lynn), but she stressed that she remained a suburban housewife at heart: 'I am still metaphorically up to my wrists in washing-up water; I still wear spiritual Marigolds.'

As her book, Dame Edna chose her Filofax ('crammed with all the gorgeous things that I do and the names of my friends, and the ex-directory telephone numbers of famous people'). What about her luxury? Her oldest friend came to mind:

'I think Madge Allsop would be my luxury.'

'You can't take a human being – it has to be an inanimate object.'

'I can assure you, Madge is an inanimate object.'

'You promise?'

'Well, when I saw her last she was pretty well comatose.'

EARL HINES

musician

24 May 1980

'Al Capone came in . . .'

Plenty of iconic jazz musicians have been on *Desert Island Discs* – Louis Armstrong, Dizzy Gillespie, Lionel Hampton and Dave Brubeck, among others – but none has been quite as entertaining as Earl 'Fatha' Hines.

This magical pianist, born in Pittsburgh in 1903, had first been cast away by Roy Plomley back in 1957, and for his second appearance twenty-three years later – 'I didn't think I was that old!' – he chose a fresh octet of records. He was then seventy-six, and a mark of his place in jazz aristocracy is that over the few years before his return to the desert shore he had played twice at the White House and once for the Pope.

A good summary of the spirit of Hines playing piano comes from the jazz writer Whitney Balliett: 'Hines' sudden changes in dynamics, tempo, and texture are dramatic but not melodramatic . . . He gives the impression that he has shut himself up completely within his instrument, that he is issuing chords and runs and glisses not merely through its keyboard and hammers and strings but directly from its soul.'

And for those who like to mix their musical genres, Hines' wonderful improvised duet with guitarist Ry Cooder on the Cooder album *Paradise and Lunch* (1974) is an uplifting taster of his extraordinary technique.

'You haven't put on a pound in twenty-three years,' observes Roy Plomley. What keeps him so trim? 'I usually exercise quite a bit . . . I carry my own implements with me: stretching exercises and the hand-clips that I use for playing the piano and all that, and the regular leg-stretching and arm-stretching and what-have-you. I wish it was television – I could show you!'

Roy Plomley's asking whether Hines can remember the first record he himself made triggers a fascinating image of recording technology in the early twentieth century:

'The first record I made was with Lois Deppe, and that was in Richmond, Indiana, on the Gennett label. Each instrument had its own horn, and it was a room that was full of steam – they steamed that room for tone, in order to get sound. We'd stay in there about fifteen, twenty minutes, you had to take your coat and your shirt off, and then they had wax for records. We had to wait for the wax to be set up, and it took about fifte, twenty minutes before the wax was hot enough for them to record. The trouble was, it's not like tape now. You had to be very careful of every little sound you made, because if it was ruined we had to wait another twenty-five or thirty minutes before the other wax was hot. So everybody was very careful, waiting especially for that drummer on the end: "Don't drop a cymbal!" Everybody stood quiet, and you'd sit there like a mouse.'

Hines tells Roy Plomley that as a child he was surrounded by music: 'My father played cornet and my mother played organ, my uncle played all of the brass instruments, and my auntie was in light opera.' His mother gave young Earl his first piano lessons, and he played the organ in church for three dollars a month. Then came the cornet, but he gave that up – 'It used to hurt me behind my ears' – in favour of the piano,

Earl Hines at the piano, with Count Basie (right), 1944

and took to performing in public with small bands: 'We were playing in a lot of halls where we didn't have amplification and they had upright pianos, and they'd give me a solo, and I was still trying to play a little fingering like

I used to do on my classical tunes, and I couldn't be heard. So I thought of the trumpet style; I thought of what my father was playing to lead the band with. I used trumpet style, playing octaves on the piano, and I cut through the band. That's why all the pianists began to do the same thing.'

At sixteen he started working in a club, then moved with the club band to Chicago, where he met Louis Armstrong. They became great friends, and Roy Plomley asks whether it is true that 'you and Louis Armstrong used to fill in bad patches by playing in a cinema for silent movies'. Hines confirms this: 'We were working in the Sunset Café at night, and we'd leave there about four o'clock in the morning and we'd have to open at a theatre around eleven in the morning, and it was terrible . . .

Al Capone (right), *Chicago in the 1920s*

We were playing for silent pictures . . . We were trying to watch the director and trying to look at the movies too, and Louis and I had never experienced looking at the movie in a theatre like that, and when they got a good picture in there, instead of us watching the director we were looking at the movies . . . and he said he had to let both of us go.'

In his early twenties he formed his own band at the Grand Terrace Café in Chicago – where he encountered a local figure of some influence: 'Al Capone came in after we had been open about two years, and he said, "We're going to take 25 per cent." Just like that – and the gentleman who owned the club was a guy who couldn't talk very good English. And he says, "What do you mean, take 25 per cent?" "We're going to take 25 per cent – we're going to give you protection." The owner said: "I don't need no protection. For two years I've been making money, I don't need no protection now. For one year I had to suffer. I just now begin to realize that I'm making a living for my family and I." Capone said: "You've got two children – you like them, don't you?" The owner said: "You wouldn't do that." Capone said: "No I wouldn't, but unless we get 25 per cent . . ." So we give him 25 per cent, and every night there would be a man come in the back door, two of them on the floor and one in the front door, and one was at the cash register. So that's all they took: 25 per cent. And he called a meeting one day – not him, but his lieutenant, whose name was Fosco – he called a meeting and said: "I want to meet everybody that's in the organization – the show people, the band musicians and the waiters," and he said, "I want all of you to be like the three monkeys: you hear nothing, you see nothing and you say nothing!" And that's what we did, and that's why we got along.'

Hines goes on to describe Al Capone as 'a very congenial fellow', and recalls his acts of kindness. He also remembers how close he himself had been to the garage where on 14 February 1929 the so-called massacre took place: 'The Valentine Day, I was about a block away from that. Al Capone said, "They blamed me for that – I was nowhere around."'

'Apart from music,' asks Roy Plomley, 'what are your relaxations? You used to be crazy about baseball: you still follow the team?'

'I like all sports. I came up in the sports world. My father opened a boys' club when I was a youngster . . . I learned boxing, because my father wanted me to know how to protect myself . . . I used to travel with a black team called the "Homestead Greys" in baseball, and then I loved football in college. I was a sprinter. I ran and they couldn't catch me – if they gave me the ball, I was gone. There was one team put two two-hundred-pound boys on that side to wait for me, so my father said, "That's the end of it – no more football."'

Even though he is in his mid-seventies, this is a castaway completely confident in his ability to look after himself on the desert island: 'I'm going to carry all of my exercise implements and I'm going to do a little walking around the island and I'm also going to do running around the island if it's possible.'

Would he try to escape? 'No – not as long as I had this type of recordings.'

Despite his years, Earl Hines continued astonishing audiences with his bravura technique right up to his final days – three years after his second *Desert Island Discs* appearance. He gave his last performance in San Francisco shortly before he died in nearby Oakland on 23 April 1983, and his tombstone bears the inscription: 'Piano Man – He enriched the world with his music.'

TOM LEHRER

singer and satirist

12 July 1980

'I don't cook very much – I thaw'

Tom Lehrer famously pronounced in 1973 that political satire became obsolete when Henry Kissinger was awarded the Nobel Peace Prize, but by then he had all but given up offering his own individual perspective on the world.

At the heart of a classic Tom Lehrer song is the incongruity of celebrating a gruesome theme (nuclear annihilation, masochism, dismemberment) to the accompaniment of a jolly melody, and there is no better example than his best-known creation 'Poisoning Pigeons in the Park', which – in pounding waltz time – lauds the traditional Sunday-afternoon activity of slaughtering local wildlife for the sheer fun of it.

The incongruity was heightened by Lehrer's mild manner on stage. His act was simply a man at a piano, and what is more, a man who looked less the professional performer and more the bespectacled Harvard professor – which is exactly what Tom Lehrer was.

His enduring popularity is based on a very small body of work, the foundation stones of which are just three albums: *Songs by Tom Lehrer* (1953), *An Evening Wasted with Tom Lehrer* (1959) and *That Was The Year That Was* (1965). On these are favourites such as 'The Masochism Tango' (which the sheet music requires be played 'painstakingly'), 'The Vatican Rag' and 'The

Elements', in which the Periodic Table is sung to the tune of Gilbert and Sullivan's 'I am the very model of a modern Major General'. Later compilations have expanded the *oeuvre* a little, to include such gems as the merriest song ever written about sexually transmitted disease, 'I Got It from Agnes'.

Throughout his musical career, Lehrer continued to practise as a mathematics professor – at MIT and Wellesley as well as Harvard – and when he joined Roy Plomley to discuss being cast away he was spending half the year teaching at the University of California at Santa Cruz.

Tomfoolery, a show of his songs, had opened in the West End earlier in 1980.

Roy Plomley welcomes his castaway, 'the American composer and singer of cynical songs'. What would he most like to have got away from? 'I hate to say dogs because then everybody will write in . . . No, just noise – and that's the point that I would most like, the silence.'

Lehrer concedes that his musical taste is 'not that wide – I think most of my interests are in the field of musical theatre of one type or another, ranging from music hall to opera, rather than orchestral music.'

He was born in Manhattan, but has lived for most of his life in Cambridge, Massachusetts, home town of Harvard University. He took to the piano spontaneously as a small child. 'I used to sit there and pick out little tunes, I guess, and then my parents gave me piano lessons and classical regular serious music – Chopin and all that stuff – and then I would dutifully do the minimum practising that I needed for that, and then in my "off" hours I would go and pick out popular tunes. They finally realized that was where my interests lay, and so they found me a popular music teacher, which was very rare in those days.'

Tom Lehrer backstage at London's Palace Theatre, May 1959

Having entered Harvard at the precocious age of fifteen, he studied mathematics and statistics, and once engaged in postgraduate work started entertaining his fellow students. One of his early compositions was 'Fight Fiercely, Harvard', a parody of the traditional macho college songs.

'Were you kicking against the sporting establishment?', asks Roy Plomley.

'I never did understand sports,' says the castaway. 'I don't participate, and I prefer to lie down whenever possible. But I never understood that fervour for, or the concept of, what's called in American "rooting" – that is where you have some team, and just because you happen to go to the same school that the members of the team go to, therefore you prefer that they win the game. I've never understood that.'

After graduating he stayed on at Harvard to teach, and found his songs becoming so popular that he decided to make a disc. 'About 1953 I realized that everybody that was interested in these songs around Harvard, which was the only place I had ever performed, was pretty sick of them. So I decided that I would make a record . . . I recorded and paid for myself a few hundred copies to sell around Harvard, but I did take the precaution of putting my address on the back of the jacket, so that mail orders began coming in.'

Then people started coming to his college rooms to buy the disc. 'It was a small queue of bizarre people, but what really happened is that people began taking them home – students took them home for vacation – and summer went past and I began getting mail orders from various places.'

Record companies became interested – until they received the material, that is: 'They listened to it and said, "Oh no, this isn't the sort of thing we want on our label."' So Lehrer continued to handle orders himself, and then made an arrangement with the production company to look after distribution.

In time, his records started making a stir in England. 'Originally they were smuggled over, brought over by various unsavoury characters, and it took me a long time to get a British company interested in releasing them.' Eventually he was taken on by Decca, and the songs were played regularly on the radio – 'even *Desert Island Discs* occasionally' – at which point Roy Plomley points out that 'there are still a few of your songs that the BBC are a bit toffee-nosed about'.

In recent years Lehrer has written and performed very little. Why? asks Plomley. 'Nine years in California, Roy, can do terrible things to a man's brain. I hate to use the word "maturity", because that is something I've always tried to slip through unobtrusively, and go right from adolescence to senility. But I think that one of the things that maturity does, it gives you a little perspective and you begin seeing both sides, and then you can't really attack anybody any more.'

Of particular interest among Tom Lehrer's selection of eight records is one by Randy Newman. 'Very few of the current singer-songwriters can I ever understand, and one of the few that I do – and sympathize with – is Randy Newman. He's written many, many marvellous songs, and I think he shares a certain cynical attitude that I have . . . He tries to do some of the sort of thing I like to do, which is to take some sardonic or biting subject or attitude, and set it to very pleasant music, thus disguising the thorns in there.'

The show *Tomfoolery*, produced by Cameron Mackintosh – 'a producer of exquisite taste' – is based on twenty-seven of Lehrer's songs: 'We weeded out the ones that would be totally incomprehensible to a British audience.' Plomley wonders: had he been tempted to perform in it himself? No: 'I can't tell you what a relief it is to be in the audience.'

To the practicalities. Could he look after himself on the desert island? 'I would probably be able to manage if the fruit fell from the trees without my having to climb them and if I could get some water somewhere, but it would be pretty boring.'

Can he cook? 'I don't cook very much – I thaw.'

Would he try to escape? After all, suggests Plomley, he's a mathematician, so should know about navigation. 'No, you're thinking of engineers, I believe. Mathematicians don't know anything about anything. We don't even deal with things like *1, 2* and *3*. We deal with *x, y* and *z*, and that's quite a different concept. So I could probably imagine the theoretical procedure for escaping from a desert island, but as far as putting it into practice, I'm afraid I would be hopeless.'

Luxury? As with so many other castaways, a piano: 'I'm sure it would go out of tune in an instant but, on the other hand, that's the way I sing.'

Since appearing on *Desert Island Discs*, Tom Lehrer has continued to give his worldwide following a precious few more shards of his inimitable wit. He retired from academic life, and his final lecture at Santa Cruz in 2001 was on the subject of infinity.

Sousa
'King Cotton'
The Band of Her Majesty's
Royal Marines

'Scotland the Brave'
The Pipes and Drums,
1st Battalion Royal Highland
Fusiliers

'Sixteen Tons'
Tennessee Ernie Ford

Brahms
**Symphony no. 2
in D major**
Conductor:
Arturo Toscanini

'Rule, Britannia'
Soloist: Elizabeth Bainbridge

★ Tchaikovsky
**Waltz from Act II,
Swan Lake**

Carl Ravazza
'Rock, Rock, Rock'
Sidney Phillips and his Band
*'When I was a young thing and
quite enjoying life'*

'Cwm Rhondda'
Pendyrus Male Choir

. . . .

📖 *War and Peace* by
Leo Tolstoy

♡ **Piano**

Opposite: *Princess Margaret
with her sister, father and mother
at Y Bwthyn Bach, 'The Little
House', a gift from the Welsh
people to Princess Elizabeth.*

HRH PRINCESS MARGARET

the Queen's sister

17 January 1981

'I think one was brought up to be able
to talk to anybody'

To have a senior member of the Royal Family agreeing to be cast away was a tremendous achievement for *Desert Island Discs*. Admittedly, there had been attempts by the Palace to peel away some of the mystique of royalty during the 1970s, but even so, for the Queen's sister to appear as the guest on a radio programme represented startlingly new territory.

Princess Margaret Rose was born in Glamis Castle in August 1930, over four years after the birth of her sister Elizabeth. Her father was then the Duke of York, whose brother Edward, Prince of Wales, was first in line to succeed George V as monarch. She spent her early years at the family's home at 145 Piccadilly, but her position in public life changed dramatically when her uncle Edward, who had acceded to the throne in January 1936, abdicated in order to marry the divorced Mrs Wallis Simpson. This made Margaret's father King George VI, and her sister heir to the throne – with herself second in the line of succession.

Princess Margaret was to spend her adult life in her sister's shadow, and the headlines she did attract tended

to be the opposite of happy and glorious. After the war she struck up a romance with one of her father's equerries, Group Captain Peter Townsend (see page 150). But the Group Captain was a divorcé, the Church of England refused to sanction the marriage, and eventually, at the end of October 1955, Princess Margaret announced that, 'mindful of the Church's teachings that Christian marriage is indissoluble, and conscious of my duty to the Commonwealth, I have resolved to put these considerations before others'.

In 1960 she married the photographer Antony Armstrong-Jones, later Lord Snowdon. They had two children before divorcing in 1978; their son David Linley was cast away in 2002.

Princess Margaret with her husband, Antony Armstrong-Jones, later Lord Snowdon

By the time she was cast away at the age of fifty, Princess Margaret had long been staple fodder for the society pages and gossip-mongers. As her sister continued to fulfil her role as sovereign with exemplary devotion to duty, Margaret pursued what was euphemistically called 'a colourful life', fuelling the conversation of pub bores across the country.

But she would have little to fear from her interview with Roy Plomley.

'I'm delighted that our castaway this week is Her Royal Highness Princess Margaret, Countess of Snowdon. Ma'am, could you endure isolation for a long time?'

'No, not for very long,' answers the Princess.

Would she feel fear? 'Yes, I think I should invent in my mind a great deal of fearsome things. Especially the dark. I'm very frightened of the dark.'

After that interesting early revelation, Plomley moves his illustrious castaway on to the subject of music, and we learn that she keeps her old 78s in the attic; that she started taking piano lessons when she was about five years old; that nowadays she still plays the piano sometimes, 'just for singing'; and that she has composed 'one or two things, but very slight'.

Record number one? 'I suppose I thought back to my childhood, and then I thought of practically the first record that my sister and I used to play

– mostly in Scotland – and it was a march by Sousa, and we used to march up and down the drive at Birkhall to it with a few cousins.'

'Singing at the top of your voices?'

'Absolutely the tops of our voices.'

Education came not at school but with a governess. 'Did you feel,' asks Roy Plomley, 'that you were being left out of a great deal of companionship?'

'Well, no, because my sister and I were very close, although she's nearly five years older than me. We never did lessons together, we always did lessons separately – but then of course we had quite a lot of children who came to the Guides, for instance. We had a choir we used to sing in, and there were pantomimes we used to do, and dancing class. You know, one saw quite a lot of one's age group . . . I think one was brought up to be able to talk to anybody.'

That ability to talk to anybody proved highly useful on the famous occasion in May 1945 when the two princesses went out from Buckingham Palace to celebrate with the teeming throng the end of the war in Europe: 'It was most exciting. We went out with a party of friends, and of course they were all in uniform then, including my sister, who was in the ATS. We went everywhere. We rushed down the street. We had an uncle with us – my mother's brother – who was very jolly and gay and encouraged us to behave very badly as usual.'

Now the presenter must tread with particular care. 'Few people have suffered more than you from wild and inaccurate and irresponsible press stories, especially in foreign papers. Can you laugh at them, or do you find them aggravating?'

Brahms
Symphony no. 2 in D major
Conductor: Arturo Toscanini

'The most beautiful tune in the world'

'I find them extremely aggravating. Of course, if they're absolutely invented, like sometimes they are, one can laugh at them with one's friends. But I think that since the age of seventeen I've been misreported and misrepresented.'

No ambiguity about Plomley's position. 'A lot of it is beneath contempt, and of course you can't keep on issuing denials.'

'Well, they're not worth denying, really, because they're usually inaccurate.'

A few *Desert Island Discs* formalities to tie up. What sort of shelter would she make? 'Palm fronds would do very well.' Could she fish? 'Not bad – if I had something to fish with.' Would she plan to escape? 'Oh yes – I like life too much to live on a desert island.' Could she navigate? 'No, I've never done that – although I was in the Sea Rangers, I'm ashamed to tell you.'

One record? 'I would take *Swan Lake* – I could imagine the scene.' And she could dance to it. 'With no one else to look, I'd probably be beautiful.'

Luxury: a piano. Book: *War and Peace* – 'a good long read, and rather needs reading several times, so that would keep me going for a long time'.

'I should think it would. And thank you, Your Royal Highness, for letting us hear your Desert Island Discs.'

'Thank you, too.'

Her *Desert Island Discs* appearance was not to be Princess Margaret's only foray into mainstream Radio 4 territory. In 1983, two years after being cast away, she appeared in *The Archers* as part of a fund-raising campaign for the National Society for the Prevention of Cruelty to Children.

Princess Margaret died in February 2002 at the age of seventy-one.

Princess Margaret at the Desert Island Discs *fiftieth birthday party at the Reform Club, 1992*

PAUL McCARTNEY

musician

30 January 1982

'I'd probably wave hankies at the passing boats'

For the fortieth anniversary edition of *Desert Island Discs*, Roy Plomley's guest was the only Beatle to appear on the programme: Paul McCartney, who was just five months younger than *Desert Island Discs* itself.

By early 1982 it was well over a decade since the Beatles had split, a matter of months since Wings, the new band which McCartney had founded following that break-up, had itself come to an end – and not much more than a year since his fellow Beatle and co-songwriter John Lennon had been murdered in New York in December 1980.

'Paul, how well could you endure loneliness, perhaps for a long time?'

'Good question. I give in. Next question.'

'Right—'

'No, no, seriously, folks. How well could I endure loneliness? I don't really know. When I was a kid I never used to mind it too much. Since then I haven't actually been very lonely, so I haven't kind of tested it lately. I used to quite like getting away on my own.'

What would he be most pleased to get away from? 'People snatching photographs when I don't want to be photographed.'

The Beatles, 1963

His first record choice is Elvis Presley singing 'Heartbreak Hotel', which 'takes me back to when I was first buying records. Up until that point it had been sort of Billy Cotton and swing and bebop and stuff, but suddenly rock-and-roll burst on the scene, and Elvis was one of the first people that really made me take an interest. I remember being at school when this record came out.'

McCartney's mother was a nurse (she died when he was in his early teens); his father was a cotton salesman and – of much greater genetic import – a keen amateur musician who had a group named Jim Mac's Band.

Was his father trained, asks Plomley, or did he play by ear? 'He played by ear.'

Jim McCartney was very influential in his son's musical education: 'He used to tell me the old thing that if you go to a party it's handy to be able to play a piano because you get all the drinks bought for you, and you're the life and soul of the party.'

But he was unimpressed by the sort of music his father was playing: 'I was more interested in rock-and-roll . . . The first record I actually bought was "Be-Bop-a-Lula" by Gene Vincent. At the time those were the things that just made tingles up my spine. To me it seemed like a whole new direction of music. Pretty respectable people had been singing up until then, but then there were all these people in kind of crazy clothes, and guitars and stuff, and slicked-back hair. Lonny Donegan was the other big influence – that's what made all the kids buy guitars at the time.'

Paul's first guitar was a Zenith. 'I took it home, and I couldn't play it at all – couldn't even begin to play it. And then I worked out it was because I was left-handed and the guitar wasn't. So I strung it the other way round and then I was able to.'

He joined a local group called Cass and the Casanovas, who appeared on the talent show *Carroll Levis Discoveries*: 'We failed miserably. Got beaten by a woman who played the spoons.'

Through a friend he met John Lennon, who went to Quarry Bank School and had a group called the Quarrymen: 'I think I must have been about fourteen and he was sixteen.' He sat in with the Quarrymen, impressing them by knowing all the words to Eddie Cochrane's 'Twenty Flight Rock', and shortly afterwards they invited him to join the band.

The Quarrymen became Johnny and the Moondogs. Why? McCartney explains that his father 'used to keep changing the name of his group because no one wanted them back, so the only way to get a return booking was to change the name'. The Quarrymen were applying the same principle, and when auditioning to back a singer named Johnny Gentle they changed again, becoming the Silver Beetles. They got the engagement, and while on tour with Johnny Gentle, McCartney changed his own name – to Paul Ramon. ('Oh, that's nice,' says Plomley.)

Fast forward to playing in various clubs in Hamburg, by which time they have become the Beatles, and then to the Cavern in Liverpool.

'I've never visited it,' Plomley confesses, 'but from what I hear it seems to have been something of a claustrophobic hell.'

'Well, yeah,' replies McCartney: 'I mean it depends who you are. It was a claustrophobic hell, but it was a great one.'

The songwriting partnership with John Lennon started while McCartney was still at school. Paul would play truant – 'sagging off, as we used to call it' – and they would go back to the McCartney house: 'My Dad never left any tobacco around – he left empty pipes – so we used to smoke Ty-Phoo tea. And we used to sit around being very artsy and think of ourselves as Dylan Thomas or someone, and we started writing together then.'

How did they work together? 'Every possible permutation, really. We never got a formula. We used to just sit down with two guitars, and if neither of us had an idea we'd just start to look for one – with guitars, just sort of strumming – and wait till one came out. Or quite often one of us would have thought of a first line or a second line or a chorus or something, and he'd start on that, or I'd start on it.'

Enter Brian Epstein. The Beatles' future manager ran a local record store, and one day was asked whether he stocked a record made in Hamburg – of Tony Sheridan singing 'My Bonnie', backed by a band called The Beat Boys. (As for the name, McCartney explains that for the German market they'd 'changed it to something a bit more obvious'.) Epstein did not stock that record, but having learned that the group in question was playing down the road at the Cavern, he decided to check them out. 'So he came in one day,' McCartney tells Roy Plomley, 'looked at us, and apparently thought there was something there – because we were all leather and sweat at that time. He sort of cleaned up the act a little bit and said, "Well, you know, we've got to try for London and stuff, so you're going to have to get suits" – which no one was very keen to do, but we went that way.' Epstein became their manager, and arranged auditions with record companies in London, but: 'Everyone turned us down.'

'Yes,' says Plomley, 'and they've been eating their hearts out ever since.'

Then came the audition for the Parlophone label, which took them on and entrusted them to producer George Martin. 'It turned out that they tended to throw him stuff nobody else really wanted. He got all the comedy, and he was a little bit at the light end of the record label he was on. So we'd been steered his way because no one else would have us. He thought there was something quite interesting there, but he didn't really like our early songs. He was right, too.'

George Martin tried hard to get his new protégés to record a song called 'How Do You Do It?' He had told them that it was going to be a hit, so it was just a question of whether they wanted to do it or not – and they did not: they insisted on recording their own material. So that song duly became a huge hit for Gerry and the Pacemakers.

McCartney has not put any Beatles tracks on his list of eight, but 'to sort of sum up the whole thing' he has chosen 'Beautiful Boy' from John Lennon's album *Double Fantasy* – 'which I think is a beautiful song, and it's very moving to me'.

Starting Wings – in which his wife Linda sang – involved, in McCartney's opinion, returning to Square One. 'We took a van and went out and did concerts at universities and stuff. We took the kids, the dogs, everything in this van. And we used to charge fifty pence at the door – very good value for money ... We'd just turn up at the university and say, "Do you want us to play here tomorrow?", which threw them into a blind panic. The Student Union feller would race around and then say, "Yes, OK, you can have the dining hall" – or whatever it was. So we used to do that.'

Wings: Paul and Linda McCartney with Denny Laine

As regards the practicalities of the desert island, this castaway has the distinct advantage of having been a Boy Scout – and, even better, of having got his Bivouac Badge: he can make a fire and cook over it. On the other hand, he is a 'hopeless' sailor: 'I'd probably wave hankies at the passing boats.'

Paul's final song returns the focus to his father. McCartney senior had written one song, and while on a visit to Nashville his son had recorded 'Walking in the Park with Eloise' with some friends: 'The friends were Chet Atkins, whom I happened to be working with, and Chet brought along Floyd Kramer, and I had the drummer from my group at the time, Geoff Britton, and we got together and we made a little recording of this, specially to play to my Dad.'

No surprise with Paul McCartney's luxury – a guitar – nor with his book: *Linda's Pictures*, 'because that's got pictures of my kids in it and it's got a lot of stuff of Linda's'.

Linda McCartney died of breast cancer in 1998.

In the thirty years since being cast away on the desert island, Paul McCartney has continued to perform, and to show unflagging energy and musical inventiveness – even well into his sixties – which have made him one of the all-time greats of popular music. A few statistics map out his pre-eminence: *Guinness World Records* rate him 'the most successful musician and composer in popular music history', with sales of over 100 million singles in the United Kingdom alone; his song 'Yesterday' has reputedly been covered by over 2,000 other artists, and has been played more than seven million times on US television and radio; and in the *Sunday Times* 'Rich List' published in April 2012, he and his third wife Nancy Shevell are listed as being worth £665 million.

But never mind the money. At the core of the McCartney magic is live action: in 2011 he performed twenty-four gigs, starting in Peru and ending in Liverpool, while twin highlights of 2012 were McCartney topping the bill at the Queen's Diamond Jubilee concert outside Buckingham Palace, and a few weeks later performing at the opening ceremony of the Olympic Games.

You do wonder, though, what happened to the woman who played the spoons . . .

SHIRLEY WILLIAMS

politician

23 March 1986

'I had a passionate desire to be an opera singer, rather than a politician'

A few weeks after his first interview as the new presenter of *Desert Island Discs*, Michael Parkinson welcomed ashore Shirley Williams, President of the Social Democratic Party.

Born in 1930, daughter of the political scientist Sir George Catlin and the feminist and pacifist writer Vera Brittain (best known for her autobiographical *Testament of Youth*), Shirley Williams was educated at Oxford and entered the Commons as Labour MP for Hitchin in 1964. Rising rapidly through the ranks, she served in the Cabinet under both Harold Wilson and James Callaghan. In 1981 she resigned from the Labour Party as one of the 'Gang of Four' who founded the Social Democrats, returning to the House of Commons later that year as the new party's first MP. At the time of her casting away, however, she was out of the Commons, having lost her seat at the 1983 general election, and was thirsting to return at the earliest opportunity.

The celebrant may be different, but the order of service remains the same. Does Shirley Williams, asks Michael Parkinson, have a musical background? She does. Her grandmother produced recitals in the Midlands. 'And my mother knew a lot about music because her brother, who was killed in the First World War, was in fact intending to be a professional violinist, so she could play very well as an accompanist to a violinist, and that side of my family was really richly musical.' Her father was less musical – 'He was entirely a literary man' – which tended to overshadow her mother's love of music. 'But in her quieter moments she often used to take up the piano, and she often used to sing to the piano as well.'

Did Shirley have any musical ambitions herself? 'I had a passionate desire to be an opera singer, rather than a politician, when I was a small girl. I imagined myself standing there singing the great arias, and completely and absolutely bewitching the audience.'

Her first record choice is Elgar's *Introduction and Allegro for Strings* – 'partly because it shows I think some of the extraordinarily stormy temperament that Elgar had, and also because for me it's associated with my family and with their strange mixture of great patriotism and great criticism of their own country'.

Shirley Williams recalls some of the world statesmen who visited her family when she was a small child: Pandit Nehru, 'a rather remote figure'; Chief Lethuli of the African National Congress; George Lansbury, leader of the Labour Party; and 'Major Attlee, a little-known figure who was not expected to become Prime Minister . . .

'A pretty fair river of both European and international political leaders flowed through our home, partly because both my parents in different ways were very much connected with international movements. And my mother, of course, whose books were burned at Nuremberg, was particularly associated with the attempt to try to bring Jewish refugees to Britain. And so quite a lot of the refugees that she managed to get away from Nazi Germany stayed in our house on their way to being settled with other more lasting houses and homes of various kinds.'

Beethoven
Piano Concerto no. 4 in G major

Soloist: John Lill
'I think he interprets it beautifully'

Late in 1940 she and her brother were evacuated to St Paul, Minnesota – 'And ever since then, I suppose, I fell in love with the United States. It was a country where everything was possible, and where everything was exciting.'

It was during that period in Minnesota that Shirley Williams was screen-tested for the part of Velvet Brown in the film *National Velvet*. 'I don't really think I was cut out to be a film actress. I doubt if my looks would have lasted, and maybe they weren't appropriate anyway, but what happened was this. They were looking for the lead part in *National Velvet*, which was a film essentially about the Grand National, and the heroine was a lovely blonde English girl who could ride like a dream, and all the rest of it – this was the screen requirement, and somebody had a brilliant idea of asking all the American film critics to put forward a candidate.'

Critics in the Midwest nominated young Shirley Catlin, while the name of 'an unknown character called probably at that time Betty Taylor' was put forward by critics of the West Coast. 'Both of us had screen tests . . . And Betty Taylor, by some strange fluke, actually won, and of course set off on the great film career that today is represented by Elizabeth Taylor.'

Shirley returned to the USA on a Fulbright scholarship in the 1950s, and then it was time to find a job. 'Once I'd got over my early ambition to be an opera singer, the other thing I thought I wanted to be was a journalist, and so when I finally completed my various kinds of education I started work on the *Daily Mirror*.' But she did not enjoy being 'a human interest reporter', and moved to the *Financial Times*.

Then came politics. 'My father, who'd stood twice as a parliamentary candidate and not been successful, between the wars, in a way wanted very much for one of his children to go into politics, and of course we had been brought up in the Labour Party from the very beginning. So into politics I duly went.' After being defeated twice, she was elected to the House of Commons at the 1964 general election.

Michael Parkinson comes to the formation of the SDP. 'You were Minister for Prices and Minister of Education in the Labour government; you were tipped as a leader of the Labour Party; you were tipped as a future Prime Minister of this country. What was it that made you dissatisfied, that made you want to break away from the Labour Party and form another party?'

'I couldn't identify with the Conservatives, whom I'd fought all my life, but I couldn't really increasingly identify with the Labour Party. And I think that one of the early seeds of the SDP, one which has been very little noticed in the press, was the strong support

The '*Gang of Four*': left to right, *David Owen, Bill Rodgers, Roy Jenkins, Shirley Williams, 1981*

that those of us who later formed the SDP had for the European Community. We shared Mr Heath's ambition.'

In 1971 she had defied a three-line whip in order to support her European ideals, and in 1975 had become leader of the Labour Committee for Europe at the time of the referendum on the UK remaining in the Community. 'So I think that part of the genesis of the SDP was discovering that we had a distinct position in politics which was not shared by the official leadership of the Labour Party because it was so pro-European.'

Is she optimistic about the state of the nation? On the one hand, there is decline all around, 'and I think the economic situation could be dire . . . On the other side, I myself believe that the coming of the information society could be very good for Britain. It's a creative, inventive country . . . We could see a re-creation of Britain, a kind of new dawn almost, providing that we make some decisions right. And there's one of those that to me is quite central. I think we will have to give a much higher priority to education and training. We cannot have a country in which seventy per cent of people end their education, or virtually end it, at the age of sixteen. It won't do.'

As for the desert island practicalities, 'I think I'd be good. I'm quite an outdoor toughie . . . I could climb trees for the coconuts, I could go fishing. I could build myself a camp fire, and I think I could build myself some kind of shack'; plus, 'I'm quite a good swimmer.'

Her book is the collected poems of W. B. Yeats – 'he has that astonishing mixture of imagination and passion and sometimes madness that constitutes Ireland' – and her luxury the BBC computer (that is, the so-called 'BBC Micro' which had first been produced for the BBC Computer Literacy Project in 1981): 'I insist on having it linked up across these thousands of miles back to Britain, and then of course I would have a window on the world.'

Shirley Williams stood for Parliament again at the 1987 general election – this time as SDP candidate in Cambridge – but was defeated, and her days as an MP were over. In 1988 she supported the merging of the SDP and the Liberals to form the Liberal Democrats, and after being created a life peer in 1993 served as leader of the Liberal Democrats in the House of Lords between 2001 and 2004.

She returned to the desert island in 2006, to be interviewed by Sue Lawley. Second time round, her luxury echoed her 1986 choice: she asked for a PC with internet connection.

ELTON JOHN

singer–songwriter

1 June 1986

'I used to go up to Baker Street and sit on the Circle Line for three hours, and then come home'

Elton John – born Reginald Dwight in 1947 – was one of the most successful and popular entertainers in the world when marooned on the desert island by his friend Michael Parkinson in June 1986. His nineteen albums to date had included classics such as *Tumbleweed Connection* (1970), *Goodbye Yellow Brick Road* (1973), and *Too Low for Zero* (1983), and he had co-written with Bernie Taupin a stream of iconic singles – like 'Your Song', 'Rocket Man', 'Crocodile Rock', 'Candle in the Wind' and so many more, while 'Don't Go Breaking my Heart' proved a huge hit in the version he recorded with Kiki Dee.

He had appeared in The Who's film version of *Tommy* – playing the song 'Pin Ball Wizard' – and the year before being cast away had performed at the Live Aid concert in Wembley Stadium.

Michael Parkinson introduces Elton John as 'one of the legendary figures of rock 'n' roll', and 'the only chairman of Watford Football Club to have sold eighty million records'. When, asks the presenter, did he start taking piano lessons?

Probably when he was about six or seven – 'But I originally started playing piano by ear, because I grew up being looked after by my grandmother and mother because my father was in the air force. I was born in my grandmother's house in Pinner Green in Middlesex, and we always had a piano in the house because my auntie used to play.'

Piano lessons gave him a solid grounding, 'but I was never that much interested in becoming a classical musician because ever since I can remember I've always wanted to do something in music, but popular music. Winifred Atwell was my first influence . . . I could rattle off all her stuff. And then Russ Conway – I can still play "Side Saddle" to this day.'

While at Pinner County Grammar School he won a scholarship to the Royal Academy of Music, 'which meant that you went to school Monday to Friday and you went to the Academy Saturday and you did your homework Sunday. So I was very very much anti the Royal Academy – the fact that I had no leisure time, I couldn't play football or anything like that. So I went there and I used to enjoy the choir, but mostly at the end of it I used to play truant. I used to go up to Baker Street and sit on the Circle Line for three hours, and then come home.'

He started playing in a band, then through his uncle Roy Dwight – the Nottingham Forest footballer – got a lowly job with Mills Music Publishing, as 'a tea boy and sort of general run-around . . . I think I was there for about a year and I really loved it.'

His 'little band' was called Bluesology, and they made two records for the Philips label: 'I wrote the songs but they were awful.' Then Bluesology started backing 'Long John' Baldry, newly famous from his big hit 'Let the Heartaches Begin', but that led to cabaret, which Elton hated: 'It's such a nightmare for someone to play music while people are not really interested.' Through an advert in *NME* he got a job with Liberty Records, and met Bernie Taupin. 'Initially we had to write two or three songs a week for other people like Cilla Black or Tom Jones, and they were so bad nobody ever recorded them, except that when Lulu did the Eurovision Song Contest [in 1969] we got one into the last six of the British heat, and it came sixth.' But

Bernie Taupin and Elton John, 1971

success eventually arrived: 'The first record that really got me noticed was called "Lady Samantha" – and when I say noticed, it got a lot of airplay on the BBC.'

Parkinson suggests that he's not a natural extrovert. 'No, but I became an extrovert, because in my teenage years I found that I was more or less overweight quite a bit . . . My success happened in my twenties, and I lived my teenage years through my twenties. I could do exactly what I wanted to do for the first time in my life, and consequently if I wanted to wear an outrageous piece of clothing, I did.'

But the performing life has not been easy. 'In six years I made – God knows, about seventeen albums and I made separate singles as well and I did tours. And those six years I worked and worked away because I couldn't believe initially it was happening to me . . . After six years I'd burned myself out musically, and indeed I hadn't had much time to myself in my private life. And so for two years I said, "I've got to stop, I've got to stop." . . . I love performing but if you go on stage and you perform and you suddenly start thinking, "Well, what time's the plane tomorrow? What am I going to wear?" And you're halfway through a song and then you panic and you think, "Oh, what's the next word?" – then it's time for you to stop, because you can't cheat on a live performance . . . But the ego is such that you think, "Well, someone's going to take over my crown." In fact my crown had already slipped. You can only have the crown for two years tops, probably, and then you know there are always bridges to cross and as a musician I think there are always other fields to conquer. But you just have to refresh yourself, you have to stop and build up your passion again.'

As far as the castaway's book is concerned, Elton is unimpressed by the presence of the Bible and the works of Shakespeare – 'I probably wouldn't have taken those either, but I don't want to stir up a hornet's nest' – so Artur Rubinstein's autobiography is just pipped by *Interview with a Vampire* by Anne Rice.

His record of records is Elgar's *Enigma Variations* – 'because of England and because it's just a most wonderful piece of music' – and his luxury is a telephone. (Imagine Roy Plomley agreeing to that.) 'Because I'd still be the lost chairman of Watford Football Club,' explains the castaway, 'I'd have

Opposite: *Elton John in Ken Russell's* Tommy, *1975*

to take a telephone and phone up for the scores, but I wouldn't know the matches, and I don't know whether they'll be playing away or at home, and I wouldn't know the time difference, but I'm sure I could work that out eventually . . . I could phone up and say, "Well, you don't know where I am – I'm

still alive – but who's doing what to whom, and what's happening? Because everybody likes a good gossip.'

Then follows a request which few castaways have received. 'Would you play us out?', asks Michael Parkinson, and Elton John picks out the first couple of bars of 'By the Sleepy Lagoon' on the piano before the orchestra takes over.

Elton John might have declared in 1986 that a performer has 'two years tops' with the crown, but his later career as a global musical phenomenon shows that there is an exception to every rule. His memorable performances are numerous, and his many awards include an Oscar (shared with Tim Rice) for the song 'Can You Feel the Love Tonight?' from the Disney movie *Lion King* in 1994. In 1997 he performed 'Goodbye England's Rose' – a reworking of 'Candle in the Wind', his song about Marilyn Monroe – at the funeral of his friend Princess Diana in Westminster Abbey. This became the fastest- and biggest-selling single of any released to date, with over 33 million copies sold.

Elton John's charitable work, in particular through the Elton John Aids Foundation, which he set up in 1992 and which to date has raised over $200 million, has been tireless. In recognition of these endeavours he was knighted in 1998.

ROBERT MAXWELL

businessman

5 July 1987

'I will have left the world a slightly better place by having lived in it'

Had we known then what we know now, the bulky figure cast away by Michael Parkinson in early July 1987 might have been billed as one of the most notorious fraudsters of the twentieth century.

On 5 November 1991, less than five years after his *Desert Island Discs* appearance, Robert Maxwell's body was found in the Atlantic Ocean off the Canary Islands, near where his yacht had been anchored. What had happened to him has never been conclusively established. Did he fall from the yacht while having a heart attack? Was foul play involved? Aware of how close his business empire was to meltdown – it had debts of around £2.7 billion – had he thrown himself overboard?

The cause of Robert Maxwell's death remains a mystery, but the scale of his fraud was soon clear for all to see. From start to finish, he was a man with an extraordinary story.

In his opening remarks, Michael Parkinson observes: 'If our castaway needed the money – which he doesn't – he could sell his life story to Hollywood for a blockbusting mini-series. It supports the theory that often truth is more exotic than fiction. He was born in Czechoslovakia, the son of a peasant farmer, and was commissioned in the British Army and decorated for bravery. He became a Member of Parliament – possibly the only chairman of the House of Commons Catering Sub-Committee to speak nine languages. Today he's recognized as one of our most formidable businessmen. It's been said of him in business terms that he's a big league player with the resources and the bravado to walk where angels fear to tread.'

Robert Maxwell has indeed been asked to write his life story, but he has no time to do so just yet: 'All I've got time for is to deal with the issues of the day and plan forward a little to get things done.'

As for his eight records, 'they have moved me when I first heard them and I'm happy to take them along as loving companions on to the desert island with me,' a standard castaway line to which he makes an interesting addition: 'I consider people who write music to be the greatest geniuses of all – not those who make money or play football. I think that people who can think out a tune, write it down, orchestrate it and get it played – that's marvellous human creativity.'

Robert Maxwell, born Jan Ludwig Hoch, comes from a very poor family – 'All I remember was being hungry most of the time' – and had only three years' primary education, but possessed a remarkable facility for learning new languages. 'I discovered that I had a gift quite early on in life. I could learn a language very quickly.' He had arrived in England aged seventeen, 'and when I landed I didn't speak a word of English – yet within about six to eight weeks I spoke it as well as I do now'.

At that time, in September 1940, Maxwell was a young soldier: 'I was a member of the Czech Army serving in France, and I escaped into unoccupied France and eventually made my way via Gibraltar to Liverpool.' He joined the British Army, was commissioned in the field in Normandy, and in January 1945 received the Military Cross from Field Marshal Montgomery.

Michael Parkinson suggests that the war had been a personal crusade to Maxwell. 'It was because my family were wiped out with millions of others in Auschwitz, and I had a determination to kill Germans which equalled the horrors that they were inflicting on a lot of innocent people . . . The sorrows of those losses are ever before me.'

George Gershwin
'Summertime'

'made an indelible impression on me'

His business career was kicked off by a £25,000 overdraft from the banker Sir Charles Hambro, on the strength of which he set up his first publishing business, and in 1964 he entered the House of Commons as Labour MP for Buckingham: 'I did the Clean Air Act, which I'm very proud of.'

For Maxwell, business has long been booming. Is there a trick to making money?

'No, there is no trick other than hard work, creativity, care and recognizing that duty is more important than love . . . Whatever you do, you must give it total concentration and commitment, and if you are out selling, for instance, and it's five o'clock and you have a date with your girl,

Daily Mirror *pensioners demonstrate, June 1992*

but if you stayed on and walked a further mile you may talk to a customer and fulfil their requirements, then you'd better do that rather than going on your date . . .

'That's what I've done all my life, and that's also what I'm trying to teach my children or anybody who asks me for advice . . . It separates the achiever from the talker. Lots of people will talk to you about what they want to do but never really do it. If you want to do it you must get on with it and be single-minded . . .

'I regret not having gone to university, which I could have done after the war, and I have not seen as much of my family as I really should have done. But all life is a choice, and if you want to succeed then you have got to commit yourself to getting things done.'

According to Robert Maxwell, the achievement of his life is simple: 'I will have left the world a slightly better place by having lived in it.'

Although there is no reference anywhere in his *Desert Island Discs* appearance to any murkier side of Robert Maxwell's business operations, he had been stalked by controversy for years. In 1971 an inquiry by the

Department of Trade and Industry into the dealings of his Pergamon Press declared: 'We regret having to conclude that, notwithstanding Mr Maxwell's acknowledged abilities and energy, he is not in our opinion a person who can be relied on to exercise proper stewardship of a publicly quoted company.' Maxwell lost control of Pergamon in the UK, but subsequently regained it, eventually selling the company in 1991.

Following his death it emerged that he had used vast sums from his companies' pension funds in the attempt to prevent the collapse of his business empire. His companies filed for bankruptcy in 1992 and many employees were left without their pensions – lending a terrible irony to that *Desert Island Discs* declaration that 'I will have left the world a slightly better place by having lived in it'.

KENNETH WILLIAMS

entertainer

26 July 1987

'I had this terrible desire to show off'

From mimicry of his father in the family's hairdressing shop near King's Cross to an extraordinary impression of Dame Edith Evans doing *her* impression of Sir John Gielgud as she bastes the Sunday joint, Kenneth Williams' 1987 interview with Michael Parkinson is one of the great *tours de force* of *Desert Island Discs* history.

Not only did Michael Parkinson allow this castaway plenty of scope for set pieces, the programme seemed to capture the peculiar personality of Kenneth Williams – that dizzying mixture of high culture and low comedy, introspective rumination and outrageous showing off.

Williams had already been marooned by Roy Plomley back in May 1961. At the time of that first appearance he was a staple of the *Carry On* films and Tony Hancock sitcoms, and a star of the great radio show *Round the Horne*, where his personae as the ultra-camp Sandy ('this is my friend Julian'), Rambling Sid Rumpo, and the lewd Gruntfuttock had carved him a special place in the affection of listeners. (And from 1968 he was to become a regular on another radio classic, *Just A Minute*.)

With Roy Plomley in 1961, Williams seemed relaxed about his performance as castaway. After hearing the broadcast version he was, according to his diary, reasonably well satisfied, though he thought that his voice had sounded a little 'common and pouffy'. The first public indication that he had not altogether enjoyed the experience came with publication of his autobiography *Just Williams* in autumn 1985. Roy Plomley had died earlier that year, enabling Williams to give vent to his waspish side. He related how in early May 1961 he had had a very good meeting with Noël Coward, and had gone home feeling elated. But, he wrote, this confidence left him the next day when he went to the BBC for *Desert Island Discs* with Roy Plomley, who filled him with 'inhibition' and caused 'the whole thing to become turgid and phlegmatic'.

By contrast, after the 1987 interview he had told Michael Parkinson that he found his second appearance on *Desert Island Discs* much more to his taste, because this presenter was direct and honest and allowed him to be uninhibited.

Just how uninhibited is clear early in the programme. After introducing his castaway as 'one of the great institutions of British entertainment' and asking how well he will cope on the desert island – 'I'm very practical,' says Kenneth Williams – Michael Parkinson asks about his castaway's attitude towards music. 'It's always been a great solace to me, and my tastes have

Carrying on – with Charles Hawtrey in Carry On Again, Doctor, *1969*

always been towards the funereal, the dirge-like in music. I love things like requiem masses. I love the requiem of Fauré – and so Fauré sets the turntable spinning, not with the Requiem Mass but with the Barcarolle no. 1 in A minor.

Williams, notes Parky, lives 'not a stone's throw' from the place he was born. Is this a conscious effort to stay close to his background?

'Yes, you're right, you've hit on something there, because I like to be where the roots are, and I think where your roots are, you're reminded all the time of what you are – which is a very, very good thing because it stops any sort of illusion . . . I've always had the one room, kitchen and bathroom, and I shove the 'Arpic down the loo and I do it all myself.'

Roger Quilter
'Now Sleeps the Crimson Petal'

Kathleen Ferrier
'I adore her personality'

And lest he start getting any pretensions, his mother Lou lives in the next-door flat, and would soon bring him down with a bang. 'So would my old man. My father was a great one for saying, "Don't talk with a plum in your mouth, mate . . . You don't remember where you came from. I was a van boy on the LMS [railway] – and that's what it was, an 'ell-of-a-mess."'

As a hairdresser, Charlie Williams lacked one skill. 'He had no diplomacy,' recalls his son: 'I actually saw a woman say, "I would like, Mr Williams, to have a henna dye." He said: "You wanna look like a tart? Henna dye on your 'ead. Have you looked at your face? . . . Leave it as nature intended, missus."'

It was his mother's acting out little scenes from her daily routine which first made the very young Kenneth interested in acting: 'She would come back from shopping expeditions or from the pub, and say, "And that woman came in – pushed right in and said, 'Oh excuse me, could I have half a penn'th of ale.'" I was giving these sorts of impressions myself, and I got that all from my mother.' His father had his own patter. 'They were always turning round: "I turned round to him and I said if you don't like it you can get out, and he turned round and he said to me, 'Look here, mister' – and I turned round and said, 'Look here'" – I grew up in a world where all these incidents were dramatized.'

The idea of Kenneth going on the stage got short shrift from his father. 'He didn't like anything to do with the acting profession. He said to me, "All the women are trollops and the blokes are all pansies. I've 'ad 'em in 'ere with their, "Oh, give us a blow wave" – 'I said, "I'll blow you right off the bloody premises – get aht."'

Had his father lived long enough to be proud of him?, asks Michael Parkinson. 'He did come and say, "Well, I thought I'd see your name up one day," sort of grudgingly.' But true to character, when his parents went to see him at the Apollo Theatre in the West End, Charlie Williams refused to join his wife and son in taking a taxi: 'Get aht of it, I'm not paying their prices – one and sixpence all the way to Piccadilly – I can get a bus for tuppence.'

Williams started taking on cameo roles in *Hancock's Half Hour*, but the way he milked the audience for laughs began to irritate Tony Hancock himself. 'It upset him terribly, because, he said: "I don't want you coming on here halfway through the show, getting enormous rounds of applause and destroying the pattern of the show, which should proceed like a real narrative every week – not like a variety show which is stopped in the middle by some character coming on and taking all the applause."' He is not unsympathetic to Hancock's thinking: 'You would reasonably resent somebody who seems effortlessly to be walking on and getting away with murder, as I did.'

Dame Edith Evans makes her stately way into this edition of *Desert Island Discs* through the medium of Williams' way-over-the-top imitation of her famous gushing tones. At the theatre where they are playing together, she envies Williams the ability to chat with other members of the cast, to which he explains that he is an ordinary performer while she is a very big figure. 'Well, I'd like them to pop in,' says the *grande dame* of British theatre. 'I'm very ordinary' – and off Williams goes in a flight of mischievous mimicry of Dame Edith declaiming, 'I sit at home on a three-legged wooden stool, basting my joint. I like to baste my joint and make my Yorkshire pudding, and Johnny G. – Johnny Gielgud – comes down and says, "Oh, Dame Edith – it's delicious Yorkshire pudding!"'

Then a change of mood. So far Michael Parkinson has scarcely been able to get a word in edgeways, but manages to ask whether Kenneth Williams has ever had a close relationship with anybody. The castaway switches to contemplative mode: 'Well, I suppose I've had some good friendships, but that's about all. I don't think it's given to us all. I remember a recent announcement by the Pope, talking about this test-tube baby business. There was this marvellous sentence where he said, "For some, it is natural they don't have any children, and they'll just have to accept it." I thought, how wonderfully simple and honest. That's the truth for hundreds of bachelors, I suppose: they are not meant to share in that way.'

Then he brightens up: 'So they share it in some other way, and I've always had the advantage of an audience, and this is an enormous advantage because a whole wave of affection can go through an auditorium if your work turns out right.'

Williams has been keeping a diary since he was fourteen – initially recording his apprenticeship in technical drawing and then

With Barbara Windsor and Hattie Jacques on the set of Carry On Camping, *1969*

his time in the army. 'I started putting in bits of conversation, almost a bit of entertainment for myself. If I heard something funny I put it all down, and so it became a terribly useful compendium on which I could draw.'

But revisiting points of his life while writing his autobiography can be uncomfortable. 'I realized from much that I wrote in the early period what an arrogant little nasty person I was. I had this terrible desire to show off, and at somebody else's expense, and I think I've lost that now.'

Just before the end of the programme, the mood takes a steeper downturn. 'I quite look forward to death . . . I just hope it's not painful. I don't want a kick up the backside with a bus or something like that. I want it to be nice.'

In the event it was not a bus that killed Kenneth Williams, but an overdose of barbiturates at his London flat in April 1988 – less than a year after his second *Desert Island Discs* appearance; soon after he had started increasing his medication for a stomach ulcer; and shortly after he had written the final sentence in his diary: 'Oh – what's the bloody point?'

He was sixty-two, and the inquest recorded an open verdict.

MAYA ANGELOU

writer

2 August 1987

'I hope to become a better human being'

Michael Parkinson's castaway, he tells *Desert Island Discs* listeners, 'has been a writer, stripper, political activist, waitress, editor, singer, actress and a dancer, and a few more things beside'.

But Maya Angelou is probably best known for her series of autobiographical books which began with *I Know Why the Caged Bird Sings*, published in 1969.

She was born Marguerite Ann Johnson in St Louis, Missouri, in April 1928 and raised in Arkansas. ('Maya' came from her brother's habit of calling her 'my-a-sister', while she became 'Angelou' much later, working as a dancer in the Purple Onion Club in San Francisco.) As the interview illustrates, her upbringing in the Deep South gave her plenty of direct experience of racism, and later in life she became an active civil rights campaigner alongside, among others, Malcolm X and Martin Luther King.

Michael Parkinson assumes that, as Maya Angelou grew up in the Deep South, music has played a significant part in her life. How young was she when she first felt its influence?

'Probably about four or five. My grandmother had a wonderful voice, and she sang in church and she'd sing around the house – unless she was asked to sing. If

I'd ask her, "Mama, would you please sing," she'd say, "Now go on, girl, you know Mama can't sing." But if you'd leave her alone, she'd open this magnificent voice out and put it out in the air like hot gold – like melting gold, it seemed to me. And the only voice similar to hers that I can remember – I mean as I remember her voice – is Mahalia Jackson's.'

And so the first record is Mahalia Jackson . . .

Maya Angelou was brought up by her grandmother – her parents had parted when she was three – in Arkansas. 'I remember my grandmother owned a store. It was the only black-owned store in the town, so we had goods on the shelves. Mama, however, was a typical West African market woman. I never knew that until I moved to West Africa, but she sold things, so the people who had no money, the poorer people, would go down and get the handouts – powdered eggs, powdered milk, lard, margarine (which was white, just like lard, but with yellow stuff you could mix it with to make it butter-coloured). And they would bring that stuff back to the store and swap with my grandmother. She would give them tins – so many tins of

mackerel in exchange for so many buckets of powdered eggs. It turned out my brother and I were the only kids in school who were eating powdered eggs! If we wanted peanut butter we'd have to go round to somebody's back door, because Mama would have traded our peanut butter for some powdered milk, which was horrible.'

When did she first encounter racial prejudice? 'I guess I was about eight . . .

'We went to the movies, my brother and I, and there was a white girl behind the box office who would take all the dimes off the white kids – take them by hand – but when my brother put our dimes up she had a cigar box, and she would tell him, "Rake

Maya Angelou, 1970

them into the cigar box." Mind you, she was from a family so poor they lived on my grandmother's land. And I couldn't believe this meanness. And then all the white kids would go right in through the front door, and the black kids would have to go up a very rickety outside staircase – it was very dangerous, I thought, it was so shaky – and then almost crawl into a roof which hadn't been swept I guess since the place had been built, so there were peanut shells and paper and all that stuff on the floor. And it was pitched at such a rake, such an angle – this balcony which they called the Buzzards' Roost – that you had the feeling you might topple down on top of all those white folks.'

When she was seven, she was raped by her mother's boyfriend in St Louis (where she had gone to live with her mother). The rapist was later murdered – and it was this that so traumatized Maya that she did not speak for five years: 'I decided that my voice had killed him – that because I told who did it, that my voice was the culprit, and so I decided that I'd better not talk, because anybody whose name I called or who heard me, might die. So I stopped.'

Mahalia Jackson
'How Great Thou Art'

'Mama, would you please sing?'

She was rescued from that state by a friend of her grandmother's named Bertha Flowers, who encouraged her to read poetry aloud: 'You'll never like it until you speak it,' her mentor had said: 'Until you feel it come across your tongue, through your teeth, over your lips, you will never love poetry.'

Angelou has just published her fifth volume of autobiography, *All God's Children Need Travelling Shoes*. Is she interested in writing a novel? 'I don't really do fiction very well. I've written short stories, just because they are so challenging.'

A little later, Parkinson puts one of the more unusual *Desert Island Discs* questions – 'it might sound silly but it's serious, actually': 'Have you ever wished you were six foot, white and male?'

'No – God, no. I wouldn't want all that. Oh my God, all those unfortunate unachievable expectations. My expectations are just beyond my reach, and they have to do with me, not with the world. I hope to become a better human being – a kinder, wiser, funnier, more courageous human being for *me*. I think a number of white males have the expectation of making other people conform for *them* . . .

Maya Angelou at the inauguration of President Bill Clinton, January 1993

'No – no thank you. My fantasy is to be a six-foot-tall black female American, a writer – successful – who laughs a lot and drinks just enough Dewar's White Label Scotch and a little white wine, and goes to church on Sunday, and really means it . . . and loves her mother.'

Maya Angelou has been garlanded with honours, and in January 1993 recited her poem 'On the Pulse of Morning' at the inauguration of President Bill Clinton – the first poet to speak at an inauguration since Robert Frost for J. F. Kennedy in 1961. The sixth and final volume of her autobiography, *A Song Flung up to Heaven*, was published in 2002.

ARTHUR SCARGILL

miners' union leader

10 April 1988

'I think that the events over the past three
or four years have demonstrated that I was
absolutely correct'

Having succeeded Michael Parkinson as presenter
in March 1988, on only her third programme Sue
Lawley was able to put to the castaway a most un-*Desert
Island Discs*-like observation: 'You are something of a
bête noire to many.'

Her guest could hardly deny that, for few castaways
have been washed up on the island as widely vilified
as Arthur Scargill, leader of the National Union of
Mineworkers through the tempestuous strike of
1984–5.

Arthur Scargill was born in Leeds in 1938 and went
to work at the Woolley coal mine at the age of eighteen.
He soon became involved in politics, joining the Young
Communist League, then the Co-operative Party, and
then the Labour Party. He was also very active in the
NUM, becoming area president in 1973 and leading
the union through that year's national strike – a show
of union strength which contributed to Edward Heath's
defeat in the 1974 general election.

But it was the miners' strike of 1984–5 which established Arthur Scargill as – depending on your point
of view – either the devil incarnate or a champion of
oppressed workers. The core issue of this bitterly fought

ten-month dispute was the threat of widespread pit closures – with, in the wake of such closures, massive social disruption.

Sue Lawley tackles the issue of Scargill's unpopularity head-on and he responds with equal directness. 'It doesn't worry me. It sometimes saddens me that people can have an image of a person that's not true, and I suspect it's comparable with the soap operas on television . . . I think what happens is that the image of Arthur Scargill disguises the reality of the person.'

After playing 'The Entertainer' as Scargill's first record, Sue Lawley observes that there is something of the entertainer in her castaway. 'I think there is,' he agrees, 'particularly when I appear on a public platform and make a public speech. I think you see a completely different Arthur Scargill in those circumstances than you do, for instance, on television or on a radio programme. The fact is that you're able to give the complete picture in, say, a forty- or fifty- or sixty-minute speech, and you're able to throw pieces of humour into the speech, which you are not able to do when you are being very severely cross-examined by a television or a radio interviewer.'

An only child, Scargill had been 'a bit of a rebel' at school in Worborough, near Barnsley in Yorkshire. His father was a miner; his mother died when he was eighteen. The loss hit him hard: 'for three months, it literally rendered me unable to function properly'.

It had been an unusual family. 'My mother was strictly non-political. My father was very political indeed, and I was brought up in a household filled with love but also filled with this marvellous contradiction: my mother, who used to go to church, and my father, who used to go to the Communist Party meetings and to the meetings of the National Union of Mineworkers.'

Young Arthur followed his father down the pit. 'The first day at work was almost indescribable. I remember walking to the pit yard at Woolley, which is a colliery to the north of Barnsley. It was a dank, dark morning, and I was put into the engineer's office

Arthur Scargill and Tony Benn at a Nottinghamshire rally to protest against pit closures, May 1984

to await the big man coming along. There were about six of us waiting. And he duly came into the office about ten minutes to six . . . and he says: "What have we got here?" And what we'd got here of course was six young lads who were terrified. And he told his assistant to take us down into the screens. A screening plant was an area where you had a job picking out the rock from the coal as it went past on a conveyor belt, and we went across the pit yard and down some steps, under some very dark areas, and then down some more steps into an area which I can only describe as being comparable to Dante's Inferno. The dust was so thick you couldn't see more than a foot or two in front of you, and the noise was so intense that I learned within the space of three weeks to speak with sign language. I had to exist in that atmosphere for nearly a year, and it certainly had a tremendous influence on the way that I reacted towards other people . . . There is a degree of comradeship in the mining industry that you'll not find anywhere else – probably, apart from, say, the fishing industry.'

Early in his mining career he successfully represented a group of fellow pitmen in a dispute – 'and from that moment I was regarded as something of a champion in the pit'.

Fast-forward to the miners' strike of 1984–5, with Scargill as NUM leader in the thick of the action. 'The strike was created deliberately by both the National Coal Board and the Conservative government. And I had actually warned, in 1981, 82, that it was the Coal Board and the government's intention to bring about a pit closure programme. Tragically, not only were there many people outside the mining industry who didn't believe me, including the media; there were also sections of the miners' union who didn't believe me either. They thought I was scaremongering. They thought that I was just merely flying a kite. I think that the events over the past three or four years have demonstrated that I was absolutely correct.'

But something must have gone wrong, says Sue Lawley, because the miners had lost.

'I don't accept that in the end we lost. I think that if you look at the strike itself and take it into context, you'll see that it led to an inspiration as far as the labour and trade union movement is concerned. It's often been said in history that people have lost things. It was said the suffragettes lost, but as you and I talk here today, Sue, you know that the suffragettes didn't lose. It was said that the Tolpuddle Martyrs lost, but when we look back, we know that the trade union movement in this country, and in other parts of the world, flourished because of their sacrifice. I think that eventually we shall see not only the triumph of working people in establishing the right to work, but we shall see the establishment of socialism because of, and not in spite of, the miners' strike.'

Meanwhile there are *Desert Island Discs* choices to be made.

Arthur Scargill's book is one that has 'given me enormous pleasure, as I've read it and re-read it over the years': *Huckleberry Finn*.

And his luxury is nothing less than the *Mona Lisa*: 'a masterpiece – probably the greatest painting of all time.'

Arthur Scargill remained leader of the National Union of Mineworkers until 2002, when he stepped down and became Honorary President. In 1996 he founded the Socialist Labour Party.

ALFRED WAINWRIGHT

writer of guide books

4 September 1988

'If there's a chip shop on the island
I can go on for years'

'Few castaways have proved as elusive as A. Wainwright,' recalls Sue Lawley in her book *Desert Island Discussions*. 'Like a walker disappearing into a Cumbrian mist, he was a difficult man to track down. Our negotiations with him were more complicated and protracted than those with Joan Collins or the Archbishop of Canterbury.' Wainwright declined to go far from his Lakeland home, let alone anywhere near London (where he had been only once in his life), but eventually an arrangement was made: he agreed to be interviewed in Manchester, on condition that his journey home took in the famous Harry Ramsden's fish and chip restaurant on the edge of Leeds. (An additional incentive, according to Hunter Davies in his edition of Wainwright's letters, was that 'he wanted to see if Sue Lawley's legs were as good as everyone said'.)

Wainwright, eighty-one when cast away, had for years been the companion of any serious walker – in the Lake District and elsewhere – through the medium of his books, with text written in his own hand and accompanied by meticulously drawn maps and illustrations. As Sue Lawley wrote in her book: 'There are many who don't feel properly equipped unless they've got a "Wainwright" with them.'

Opposite: Lake Buttermere, and Wainwright's beloved Haystacks

Alfred Wainwright, suggests Sue Lawley, is something of a recluse, and dislikes publicity. 'I suppose it's true to some extent,' he concedes, 'because with one or two exceptions I do prefer my own company to that of other people. And during my walking years I always walked alone . . . I am antisocial, and getting worse as I get older. It started as shyness. It isn't shyness now. I can face anybody now, and not feel inferior to them. But I'd much rather be alone.'

So the prospect of being cast away on the desert island does not trouble him: 'If there's a chip shop on the island I can go on for years.'

Unusually for a castaway, Wainwright professes no special fondness for music: 'I prefer silence. I think I should make it quite clear that music has never played an important part in my life. It's never been an inspiration to me. Rather an irritation very often.'

Sue Lawley points out to her castaway that the consequence of producing those wonderful guide books is that people are attracted to the landscapes he loves, thus destroying the peace that he loves.

'I've often been charged with that, but I don't think so, and I certainly don't reproach myself about it. There's been such a change in leisure habits that when I started on the fells there were very few walkers there. Nowadays they walk in procession, and they would have come anyway, because they've more money to spend, they've more leisure time.' And if he does encounter another walker, 'You can strike off in another direction. There are boulders you can get behind.'

The walking bug can be traced back to Wainwright's childhood in a two-up, two-down in Blackburn. 'It was the only pastime we had when we were children in the 1920s – or earlier than that, even. Nobody ever had a penny to spend, so we amused ourselves in ways that don't seem to appeal at all to children these days. We'd play hide and seek, we'd play marbles along the gutter, kick a rag ball about, collect cigarette cards. It was a wonderful life, really.'

His father was an itinerant stonemason who spent long periods out of work, so the family was very poor. 'But so was everybody else. You never felt that you were poor, because everybody was in the same boat. People accepted their position. That's the way they were born. They'd to go in the mill and work for their living.'

But he was able to get a decent education. 'I did very well at the board school, and the teachers all said you ought to go to the central school in the middle of the town – which I did with considerable apprehension because

I had no decent clothes to wear and no shoes. But there I did extremely well and came first in every subject in the first year, and there were about twenty subjects. There wasn't much money coming in at all. I wanted to help out, and at the age of thirteen there was an advert in the local paper for an office boy in the town hall, and I applied for that and got it. Whereas everybody else that I knew was going into the cotton mill. I wouldn't have liked that . . . I started at fifteen shillings a week and I was only thirteen years old, and I remember running all the way home to tell me mother, who had a hard time. I used to wake up in the middle of the night and I could hear the mangle going in the kitchen downstairs, because to make things meet she had to take in washing from rather more affluent neighbours.'

In 1930, when he was twenty-three, he had his first holiday away from home. 'By that age I'd saved up five pounds, and I'd heard a lot about the Lake District, which until then had been a world away, although there were only sixty miles between us. I did as everybody told me, went up to Orrest Head, which overlooks Windermere. And I just couldn't believe that such beauty could exist. It made the whole world of difference to me. That did change my life. I decided then that this is a place I wanted to live' – and in 1941 he got a job in Kendal.

When did the guide books start? 'When I came to the Lake District I had a golden opportunity of getting out walking on the fells, and although there weren't many people walking in those days I was always coming across people who were lost. There were no guide books to the fells, and it was important that there should be. So more for my amusement than anything else I started to write the guide books. I thought: when I'm an old man and I can't walk the hills, these will be memories for me. I finished the first volume after two years of working every night. I really got obsessed by what I was

doing. I was able to illustrate them with drawings, I was able to give the natural features of a mountain and the routes of ascent, the ridge routes to the next one, the view from the summit.'

Friends encouraged him to have the book printed. 'At the time, although I'd only thirty-five pounds saved up, I went to a local printer and asked what it would cost to have two thousand copies made. And he worked it out and he said nine hundred pounds. I said I've only got thirty-five. Well, he said, never mind, this book will sell. Pay me off as you sell them. And he went ahead and printed them. Now that was a wonderful thing.'

Rex Allen

'There's an Empty Cot in the Bunkhouse Tonight'

'This is a tear-jerker'

Producing the books became an obsession – 'and nothing mattered to me except getting these books done. I had a single-track mind, and it ended finally with my wife walking out and taking the dog, and I never saw her again.'

'Did you blame her?' asks Sue Lawley.

'Not at all. Don't know how she stuck it for thirty-odd years.' A brief but telling pause, as if he is trying to push away a nagging demon, and then: 'Right, what's your next question?'

He has often slept out under canvas, and experienced the magic of waking up just before dawn. 'It's eerie. There's absolute silence, and all around the mountains are just black silhouettes, and then gradually you get the grey dawn and invariably in the Lake District at dawn the valleys are filled with a white vapour, and you watch as it gradually dissolves and reveals the fields and pastures below. Wonderful experience. Always alone. You know that you're the only person on the fells that morning. It's like being a king.'

Wainwright describes 'Oh, What a Beautiful Morning' from *Oklahoma!* as 'a wonderful, inspiring song. And you notice he talks about the sounds of the earth as like music. Now that's the sort of music that I really prefer: the tinkle of a mountain stream, the twittering of birds, the rustle of leaves in a forest in autumn, the sound of the wind sighing across the mountain tops. That's music to me. There's never any discord. It's harmony.'

Does he still walk, at the age of eighty-one?

'No, no. Unfortunately my eyes have gone in the last two or three years. I mean I always counsel people to watch where they're putting their feet on these rough mountain tracks. Now, the last time that I did a fell walk it was a pouring wet day, terrible wet day, and I was stumbling and slipping all over the place, and it wasn't because my glasses were misted, it was because I couldn't see where I was putting my feet. And that's the last time I did a fell walk, and the mountains wept tears for me that day.'

On the desert island, the castaway asks: 'Would there be anybody to look after me?'

'Nobody.'

'Because I can't look after myself. I've always been well looked after. Would there be chip shops on the island?'

'No.'

As for the book and luxury: 'You've told me there are no chip shops on the island so that I haven't a great deal of time to spend there before I faded away. I've always had an ambition to grow a beard and I've never been able to face people and their comments if I tried to do it now. But on a desert island it would be ideal, wouldn't it? So I'd like a mirror, a small mirror, just to see how it's getting on every day. And the other things that I would take would be two photographs, one photograph of the Blackburn Rovers football team that won the FA Cup in 1928 – that was really a highlight of my life. And the second would be of my wife Betty, who's been a treasure to me, and continues to be.'

This castaway clearly left his mark on the presenter. 'As we parted,' Sue Lawley wrote, 'he back to Kendal and I to London, I had a picture of this remarkable, enduring old man sitting alone on an island with only two pictures and an advancing beard for company. And then I thought of the visions that would fill his head: of sunny valleys and rolling mists, of happy bubbling streams and grim grey slabs of rock. All these and more would always be Alfred Wainwright's companions – wherever he happened to be.'

A couple of hours later, where Wainwright happened to be was in the world's most famous fish-and-chip emporium. His friend Andrew Nichol, who was driving him that day, told Wainwright's biographer Hunter Davies: 'He wolfed down his chips at Harry Ramsden's, twice as fast as me, then asked the young waitress what was for pudding. It was ginger pudding; he asked if it came with custard. "Is it hot custard?" The waitress nodded. "Does it come up to here, over the pudding, right up to the side of the bowl?" The girl nodded. "All right then, I'll have some." '

Alfred Wainwright died in January 1991, three days after his eighty-fourth birthday.

GERMAINE GREER

writer and academic

30 October 1988

'I've never said I've achieved anything, because if women have changed their lives, *they* changed them'

'The hope in which this book was written,' declared Germaine Greer in her seminal work *The Female Eunuch*, published in 1970, 'is that women will discover that they have a will; once that happens they will be able to tell us how and what they want.'

The book's core message was less about gender equality than about how women could be liberated from their subservience. It changed the way a generation – men as well as women – viewed the relationship between the sexes, and according to Sue Lawley's introduction, it made Germaine Greer 'unarguably feminism's most assured apostle'.

Sue Lawley asks Germaine Greer: Does she find men terrified of her?

'No, not at all. I find mostly they ignore me without very much difficulty, and they also patronize me, which amazes me still. I still can't get used to it . . . I change a tyre, because I have a house in the country in Italy where we do a tyre a week. I can change a tyre in about four minutes flat. But men are always elbowing you out of the way and then taking twenty minutes, which is so irritating.'

So what about surviving on the island? 'I had a very good training for it, because I was a very bored small child who – because my mother was very intent on getting a tan – was forced to spend long hours, eight or nine hours at a stretch, on the beach.'

Is she a good cook? 'I'm getting better, all the time. I used to be a coarse cook of lavish dishes of game and jugged hares and things of that sort, but with the onset of menopause I've become vegetarian. It's nothing to do with animals being hurt by my ministrations; it's to do with me being hurt by eating animals.'

How about a spouse? 'I would quite like a husband, but I only want one intermittently. I'd like someone who was rather good with the books and could tell me how to spend my money.'

'You had one once, didn't you?'

'For a minute, yes.'

'Three weeks.'

'Yes, but it wasn't really even three weeks. It was three weekends, and they were spent mostly fighting. He then went on and married Maya Angelou and stayed put for seven years. She's obviously a much stronger and more worthwhile person than I am.'

What did her parents do?

'My mother got a tan, mostly full time. My father sold advertising space, which has always struck me as quite the most meretricious occupation any human being could ever have. I feel more merciful about it than I did when I was a kid, I remember going to see *Death of a Salesman* and crying my eyes out because it seemed to me that Willy Loman was my father.'

'And was it a very happy home? Was there lots of music going on?'

'Nothing. Nothing. It was terminal sensory deprivation. We had no records, no pictures, no good food, no parties, no books, nothing. We had the beach – the dread beach.'

Deprived of sensory stimulation at home, Greer found it at her convent school: 'From the nuns, the divvy old nuns, who taught me to be immensely enthusiastic about painting, although they'd never seen any. In the best tradition of convents, they taught art without ever having seen a picture.'

From an early age, she was determined to leave Australia – 'because it was so *boring*. I just couldn't bear it, I just longed for beauty. The Australian ugliness

Germaine Greer, 1970

is pretty pervasive, and now that it's become kind of glossy American ugliness it's superficially more acceptable, but deeply more ugly.'

After university in Melbourne she moved to Sydney, and then in 1964 to Cambridge. She performed in Footlights – 'You had to do anything that came along: sing, dance, jump up and down, dress up, undress and so forth' – which led to co-presenting the television show *Nice Time* with Kenny Everett: 'I thought I was completely miscast and wrong and shouldn't have done it, because I thought it should be somebody with the common touch, and a much less complicated head than I've got.'

Sue Lawley sums up *The Female Eunuch*: 'You said that woman had become a stereotype sex object: she was a eunuch, she was weak, and she was passive, and she was debased. She was dependent on the male, and you were really calling on women to throw off the chains of marriage and trust in her true self. Is that fair enough?'

'Because I said, "Do what thou wilt", i.e. *want* to do what you do, and don't always let things *happen* to you, which was the role that women were supposed to play – it was taken as meaning that you should go out and be sexually active: i.e. another duty was imposed upon women, which was not my idea at all.'

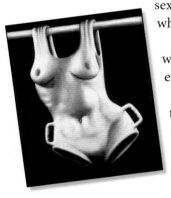

'It was your own personal quest, wasn't it, that you wanted to experience the total female experience and everything it had to offer?'

'Well, if I'd wanted to do that I should have made sure that I had a child . . . I don't know the sheer dreary slog that most women have. You know: get up; get the house organized; run to work; be terrific at work; run out at lunchtime and do the shopping; finish the day's work; run back home; get the kids organized; get the meal on and so on; and then be the perfect sexual partner with the candles lit at eight o clock when he comes in.'

John Holmes's cover image for The Female Eunuch, *1970*

What about another female experience, asks Sue: what about lesbianism?

'I think any sensible woman would be a lesbian. Women are so easy to love; they're *so* lovable. The only people who find them difficult to love are men, who never seem to know what's required of them: it's as if we spoke different emotional languages. I really envy lesbians, but I'm afraid I can't get it together.'

'It's not your thing?'

'No, but neither is the other now. I'm very happy to be free of both of it. It took such a lot of time, I seem to remember. I was always so concerned about it and him, and how it was working and whether we were doing it the right way and often enough, and it's such bliss to suddenly think, "Ah goodness, I don't have to do it any more." It hasn't left a gap in my life at all.'

How does she respond to the suggestion that, as Sue Lawley puts it, 'new woman has achieved everything that people like you were advocating, but in fact she's still not happy, because now she has the added tyranny of independence and strength and career as well as vulnerability and motherhood and marriage'? How far has there been revolution?

'I've never said I've achieved anything, because if women have changed their lives, *they* changed them. I didn't change them. And when women write to me saying you've changed my life, I write back immediately saying I did not, and don't foist that responsibility on me. If your life was changed, you changed it, not I.'

Germaine Greer's final record is 'bittersweet', as it recalls her visiting Ethiopia in the wake of the 1985 famine, 'having my life completely changed, my lens completely adjusted. So I now see life in a very different way, and take a different yardstick to absolutely everything, which has a good side and a bad side. It fills me with great tenderness for the vulnerability of things, as well as great grief for the massive amounts of human suffering that we really can't even begin to comprehend . . . This ridiculously jolly sound would come booming out in the *estaminets* of the filthy little towns without sewage, and it means something to me about the indomitability of the human spirit, this noise.'

Since being cast away on the desert island, Germaine Greer has written many more books, including in 1999 *The Whole Woman* – 'the book I said I would never write', in which she returned to some of the themes of *The Female Eunuch*. Her more recent books include *Shakespeare's Wife*, an acclaimed study of Ann Hathaway published in 2007.

In 1989 she went back to Cambridge as Special Lecturer and Unofficial Fellow of Newnham College, remaining there until 1998. She then returned to the University of Warwick, where she had started her academic career, as Professor of English and Comparative Literary Studies, where she remained until 2003. She continues to write and broadcast.

ENOCH POWELL

politician

19 February 1989

'I used to get up at five to work on my translation of Herodotus'

According to Sue Lawley, Enoch Powell had arrived at the studio with a firm instruction from his wife 'to show the warm side of his character'.

It was obvious where Mrs Powell's unease came from. Her husband was arguably the most controversial UK politician since the Second World War, principally on account of his notorious so-called 'Rivers of Blood' speech in April 1968 – at which point of his career he was shadow defence secretary on Edward Heath's Conservative opposition front bench. Essentially a warning about the possible consequences of immigration, the speech derives its name from the point at which Powell quoted Virgil's *Aeneid* in his climactic declaration: 'As I look ahead, I am filled with foreboding. Like the Roman, I seem to see "the River Tiber foaming with much blood".'

A man of legendary precision as well as conviction, Enoch Powell did not easily attract the word 'warm'.

Powell is not happy to be marooned: 'I think it's cruel of you to do this,' he complains in his curious reedy monotone, 'and probably leave me there for the few remaining years of my life. It's a cruel fate because man is a social animal, and to take him and put him, with whatever conveniences and commodities, in isolation is an affront to his humanity.'

His first four record choices are all Wagner: 'As far back as I can remember I've been under the influence of Wagner . . . *The Ring* after all is a gigantic work, in the sense that a whole cycle of thought and of events, a moral cycle and an intellectual cycle, is lived through as you witness and hear it. So that would be something to live on. So I'd like to hear something from each of the four parts of *The Ring.*'

Both Powell's parents were teachers, 'and my mother was my first teacher. I can remember standing by her as she worked in the kitchen, and she had the alphabet fixed up on the walls . . . She was the person who first taught me Greek.'

Had he been popular at school? 'I wasn't conscious of being unpopular, and certainly I enjoyed the company of my schoolfellows . . . I had a nickname at the secondary school which I attended before I went to King Edward's Grammar School [in Birmingham], and that was Scowlly Powelly, owing to my habit of frowning, which I think I probably still have.'

Then to Cambridge, where he took a double first. What kind of student had he been?

'Absurdly studious . . . I used to get up at five to work on my translation of Herodotus. I did an hour and a half before an early breakfast on that.'

Serving in the Second World War had a profound effect on him. 'Having anticipated the war as I did from 1934–5 onwards, and having regarded my existence as only provisional until it came – and having, when it did come, with such joy and relief, taken part in it, I emerged to my surprise into a full span of human existence. It was a different world to me in that sense, but I had not lived before in a world other than a world terminable by catastrophe. And here was a world which went on for ever. A normal world.'

Sue Lawley wonders whether he believed he would die in action.

'I assumed I would be killed in it. That was a natural assumption: after all, the average expectation of life of an infantry officer in November 1918 was three weeks, and as I was determined to be an infantry officer I assumed that was what would happen. And I suppose I've been lastingly ashamed of myself that it wasn't what happened.'

Powell vividly recalls the moment in 1944 when he realized he would survive: 'I was in India, and it was the night that the monsoon broke. And I did what everybody else does on the night that a monsoon broke: I walked out from under the veranda and stood in the rain and got soaked. And I

Enoch Powell during the 1970 general election campaign

suddenly said to myself, "What are you going to do, then? The chances now are that you will survive" . . . And it happened to me as I think it happens to most people: when what externally seems to be a major decision is taken, you don't actually take the decision, the decision was there. It's like hearing a knock on the door and you open the door, and there's somebody standing on the doorstep. And what was standing on the doorstep was: You will go into politics.'

Sue Lawley turns to the 1968 speech and his call for a reduction in immigrants coming into the UK, and repatriation for some who had immigrated earlier.

'That', says Powell, 'was official policy of the Conservative Party at the time.'

'Then why were you sacked by Ted Heath for saying it?'

'Because he didn't like the fact that it had been heard. It was the tone, not the content. He never claimed that the contents were incompatible with the policy of the party. He disliked the tone.'

Lawley quotes the passage about how the indigenous population found 'their wives unable to obtain hospital beds in childbirth, their children unable to obtain school places, their homes and neighbourhoods changed beyond recognition, their plans and prospects for the future defeated'.

'Yes,' says Powell. 'I'll stand by all that. It was a description of the circumstances in which many hundreds of thousands of people were already living – and many more hundreds of thousands were shortly to find themselves living.'

When asked how he responds to people who consider him a racist, Powell retorts: 'I always invite them to define the word. If you define it, I will say yes or no.'

The presenter suggests that in this case a racist would be 'someone who was not desirous of having people living alongside an indigenous population because of the colour of their skin'.

'Well, if it turns upon colour, then I shall return a negative. But for the rest of your question, I do not believe for example that the Indians wish to see forty million Europeans moving into the Republic of India, into the Union of India. And that's the relative proportion.'

In 1974 Powell left the Conservative Party (and thus Parliament) over the issue of Europe – 'One issue which overrides party is the independence of the nation' – but at the second general election of that year returned to the Commons as Unionist MP for South Down in Northern Ireland.

Back to the *Desert Island Discs* necessities. As for his luxury, 'I want what I believe is technically called a "smoker". You put fish into it and it comes out as smoked fish . . . I have an absolute passion – not merely a passion for fish but a passion for smoked fish. I could eat fish at every meal. There must be something about the genes derived from a remote period in humanity's history, when we lived by the sea shore and lived only on fish. Anyhow, the genes lodge powerfully in me, so a smoker, please.'

There had been little sign of the 'warm side' of Enoch Powell's character; but while Sue Lawley later reflected that 'there weren't many twinkly bits in our radio programme together', it is hard to disagree with her suggestion that 'he certainly sparkled – with an intelligence and clarity of mind that made this one of our most successful editions of *Desert Island Discs*'.

Seventy-six when cast away, Powell lived for nearly another decade, and continued making forays into political debate – especially on the subject of Europe. In November 1990, for example, he announced that were Margaret Thatcher to win the Conservative leadership contest, he would rejoin the party – but she did not do so, and he remained an exile from his old political homeland.

Enoch Powell died in February 1998 at the age of eighty-five.

DIANA MOSLEY

Mitford sister

26 November 1989

'He had extraordinary, sort of mesmeric eyes'

On 17 June 1989 Diana, Lady Mosley, one of the fabled Mitford sisters and widow of the Union of British Fascists leader Sir Oswald Mosley, wrote to her sister Deborah from her home near Paris: 'The D.I. Disc research girl came, so nice. Just a try-out . . . Of course the D.I. Discs girl went on about the Mitford girls, "It must have been quite something when you were all together." I pointed out that when you were three Naunce [Nancy Mitford] was eighteen. All such nonsense as though we were the same age.'

Diana was not the first Mitford sister to have been marooned on the desert island: her sisters Jessica ('Decca') and Deborah ('Debo') had both been cast away by Roy Plomley, the latter with her husband the Duke of Devonshire. But Diana's appearance in November 1989 was to become the most notorious episode in the history of *Desert Island Discs*.

In summer 1989, as soon as the programme was announced as part of that autumn's run, the press came alive with objections and counter-objections. At the core of the row was the timing of the broadcast, which was scheduled for 8 October, the eve of Yom Kippur: Greville Janner, Labour MP and a member of the Jewish Board of Deputies, declared that to interview Diana Mosley 'will be tasteless and offensive'. But

Mitford sisters Diana (left) and Nancy, 1932

a correspondent to the *Daily Telegraph* argued: 'If Lady Mosley can provide further insights into her husband and his times, that surely would be of great interest to those seeking to understand the historical background of the Europe now taking shape before us. For that reason alone, Lady Mosley should be allowed to have her say.'

Some took direct aim at *Desert Island Discs* itself, rather than at the BBC as a whole. 'That she has been invited to fulfil one of her long-standing ambitions to be on *Desert Island Discs* tells us something about the manner in which this once honourable if light programme is now being conducted,' declared a letter in the *Sunday Telegraph* in late July. The same issue of the paper carried a letter from Catherine Guinness, Lady Mosley's granddaughter: 'If the war was fought for anything, it was fought for free speech in a free country.'

In August the BBC announced that the programme would now go out on 1 October: this caused renewed outrage as that was the second day of the Jewish New Year. The date was changed again, to 19 November: 'No religious dates to worry about', wrote the *Sunday Correspondent*, ' – just the day when Jewish ex-servicemen march at the Cenotaph in remembrance of their dead.'

The broadcast went ahead on 26 November.

Diana Mosley speaking at a British Union of Fascists rally in the 1930s

'My castaway this week,' says Sue Lawley, 'is an exile. She is a Mitford girl, one of the six fascinating daughters of Lord Redesdale. This daughter married Sir Oswald Mosley, the man who was the leader of the British Union of Fascists. Like him, she was imprisoned during much of the war, and accompanied him abroad once it was over. Since his death, nearly nine years ago, she has lived alone just outside Paris. Today, fifty years after the events which changed her life for ever, she remains an example of the passions and tragedies of her family, as well as a reminder of things that were and those that might have been. She is Diana Mosley. I call you an exile, Lady Mosley, but that's a self-imposed state, isn't it?'

'Oh it is, yes,' replies the castaway in cut-glass tones. 'I don't consider myself an exile at all. I just prefer to live near Paris.'

They talk of the Palladian country house where Lady Mosley lives ('a *tiny* little house', says the castaway), and of the garden ('I don't allow any flowers near the house'), and of living in France ('Paris has kept its beauty in a way that I'm afraid London has not').

Lady Mosley's first record, Mozart's 'Jupiter' Symphony, is played: 'I chose that because it was the first really beautiful, sublime music I ever heard, and I suppose I must have been about fourteen. My brother was extremely musical, my brother Tom. He was a wonderful pianist himself and, although we only had a wind-up gramophone, we were able to listen to symphonies and so on, and I suppose he really introduced me to great music.'

They talk of life in that extraordinary Mitford household, where the key figure in Diana's young life was not her governess – 'When I was a child it was quite usual for gels not to go to school' – nor either of her parents ('We were quite in awe of them'), but Nanny: 'I really loved her more than my parents, as far as love goes.'

Lady Mosley brushes aside the suggestion that the Mitfords were a phenomenally talented family – 'We were bad at nearly everything' – but acknowledges that they were great readers: 'We had one very precious thing at home, which is a wonderful library, which had been collected by generations – not by my father, he never read a book. But he didn't mind us taking books out of the library, provided we put them back. And nobody censored our reading, and I think that probably was how we educated ourselves, because the governesses were fairly limited.'

She moved to London, did 'The Season' as a debutante, and at the age of eighteen married Bryan Guinness of the brewing family. They had two children – and then she met politician Oswald Mosley. 'You were both married to other people,' Sue Lawley reminds the interviewee, 'but you were both very strongly, mutually attracted, and not long after that you were to become lovers.' In 1936, after Mosley's wife had died and she had divorced, they married.

Now to approach the heart of the matter: 'It was, Lady Mosley, at about the time that you met Sir Oswald that he was founding the British Union of Fascists. Why was he so attracted by fascism?'

'It was just a name, then, which was given to a movement, which was more or less worldwide, or generally all over Europe, which embodied, I suppose you'd say, a great many of his economic ideas.'

'But it was a party which he decided should wear a uniform – the black shirt – and should have certain military overtones: the salute, and so on.'

'Well, the black shirt had various advantages. One was that it was extremely cheap – I think it cost a shilling – and therefore unemployed

Sir Oswald Mosley at a mass rally, saluting a group of women Blackshirts (female members of the British Fascist movement), Hyde Park, 1934

people could wear it. And so if you had that and grey flannel trousers, nobody knew what your background was and it made for a sort of comradeship, he thought. I think it probably did. And it was such a success that an Act of Parliament had to be passed to forbid them wearing it.'

'Was not that Act of Parliament passed for rather different reasons? That is to say, that when they wore that uniform and they marched through the inner cities of London and Manchester, great violence came in its wake.'

Lady Mosley shrugs that off – 'When there's a fight, people are injured, of course' – and continues to remain unruffled when asked whether her husband was anti-Semitic: 'He really wasn't. He didn't know a Jew from a Gentile himself. But as the Jews were so anti-him and attacked, as much as they possibly could, both in the newspapers and physically when there were marches in places like Manchester and so on where there were a lot of Jews, he, as it were, picked up the challenge, and then a great number of his followers, who really were anti-Semitic, joined him because they thought they would fight their old enemy.'

'But did he not call them an alien force? Did he not say in a speech once in 1936, they were "an alien force which rises to rob us of our heritage"?'

Procol Harum
'A Whiter Shade of Pale'

'I've chosen one pop record. It's partly because it's really based on Handel'

'Yes. You see, one of the things that horrified him was that we had this enormous empire, and he did think that the Jews and the City in general invested far too much in countries that had nothing to do with our empire.'

'And how did he and you feel when you discovered that Hitler's version of anti-Semitism was to end in extermination?'

'We didn't discover that for so long. First of all, after the war I simply didn't believe it, having been in Germany a good bit because my sister [Unity] more or less lived there, really . . . and it was years before I could really believe that such things had happened.'

'And do you believe it now?'

'I don't really, I'm afraid, believe that six million people were – I think it's just not conceivable – it's too many. But, you see, whether it's six or whether it's one really makes no difference, morally. It's equally wrong. I think it was a dreadfully wicked thing myself.'

Pregnant pause, then Sue Lawley suggests: 'Shall we hear your next piece of music?'

Unity had been fascinated by Adolf Hitler: 'She loved being with him. He was of course extraordinarily fascinating and clever, and you don't get to be where he was just by being the kind of person people like to think he was.'

Diana had met him often? 'Oh yes, several – many times really. Of course, at that moment he was the person who was making the news – what you might say – and therefore extremely interesting to talk to.'

Had she herself admired him? 'Very much. He had extraordinary, sort of mesmeric eyes – I think many people marked that. Blue eyes. And also he had so much to say, I mean he was so interesting, fascinating, perfectly willing to talk.'

Had not Hitler been at her wedding? 'He was a guest, yes.'

In May 1940 the Mosleys had been interned as security risks – he in Brixton and she in Holloway, where he was later allowed to join her: 'They kept saying one of the evil things we are fighting against is that there is no free speech in Germany, and here of course we have free speech. So, having been told that, he held meetings. He was always expecting to be told by the police now there are to be no more meetings, or by the government or whatever – but he never was. And he always said it would have been very cowardly, believing as he did that the war was a terrible mistake and that we could have negotiated peace before either England or the empire had been attacked in any way, he must speak his mind.'

Sue Lawley is in no mood to beat about the bush: 'To listen to you speak, Lady Mosley, sometimes when you're talking about those events of so long ago, it's almost – I think some people would say – as if you're rewriting history.'

'No, no, that's just how it was. I can remember it so well. It's very, very vivid in my memory.'

Released from prison in 1943 because of his ill health, in 1951 Sir Oswald and his wife moved to France, where she has lived ever since, and where they became very friendly with the Windsors – the Duke, who had abdicated the throne in 1936, and the Duchess, who had a reputation as a marvellous hostess: 'The food was too lovely for words.'

'You and Sir Oswald,' suggests the presenter, 'of course had something in common with them, in a sense, that you were both in a kind of exile.'

'Yes, well you say that, but they really were exiled because he refused, utterly, to go back as long as she was not given her proper title. But there was nothing of that sort for us, we went back constantly, and [Sir Oswald] never

Sir Oswald and Lady Mosley in retirement

considered himself an exile, he considered himself a European . . .'

Sir Oswald died in 1980 at the age of eighty-four.

The seventh record choice is a surprise – 'A Whiter Shade of Pale' by Procol Harum, that great pop anthem of the late 1960s: 'I've chosen one pop record. It's partly because it's really based on Handel, I think. Also because it's got such mysterious words, and also because it was such a favourite tune on the French wireless that whenever I was waiting for the news or something in French they used to play it, and it happened to be a very hot, delicious, happy summer at the Temple where I live, and so it's got memories for me. But it's not really my kind of music, otherwise – I'm not a great pop fan.'

Sue Lawley asks whether she has any great regrets about her life – such as her friendship with Hitler? 'I can't regret that – it was so interesting and fascinating.'

Her book? Proust's *À la recherche du temps perdu*: 'It's rather long. I've read it many times but each time one finds new beauties and new things to laugh at. It makes you laugh out loud.'

Luxury? A soft pillow and a soft rug.

'Diana, Lady Mosley, thank you very much indeed for letting us hear your Desert Island Discs . . .'

. . . and Sue Lawley had barely finished her sign-off before the reaction started. The day after first transmission, the *Daily Telegraph* ran a story reporting outrage at the BBC's putting out such an offensive programme, with a representative of the Jewish community declaring: 'There can be no whitewashing Oswald Mosley today . . . BBC listeners should not be exposed to apologia for Hitler and Oswald Mosley.'

Similar sentiments were expressed in the tabloid press. The *Sun* ran an editorial which read:

A PLATFORM FOR POISON

There was a rare treat for radio listeners this weekend – a glowing account of Adolf Hitler the man.

In the *Desert Island Discs* programme, the guest was Lady Mosley, widow of the unlamented Sir Oswald, who in the Thirties fancied himself as Britain's Fuehrer.

According to her ladyship, Hitler was 'interesting, clever and fascinating.'

And the horrors of war, the massacre of millions of Jews?

Lady M didn't quite believe it happened.

What a pity she could not have been marooned on a real desert island with her two dreamboats, Oswald and Adolf.

Along with the BBC nitwits who gave her a platform for her poison.

In the *Daily Mail*, a cartoon by Mac depicted hell in all its torment: soaring flames, clouds of toxic smoke, obese horned devils, the lot – and a naked figure suspended by chains manacled around his feet, half-submerged head-first in a boiling cauldron. A devil is holding a radio in one hand, while in his other hand is a trident with which he is prodding the rear end of the suspended figure. The caption has that devil shouting: 'Look up a minute, Adolph, it's *Desert Island Discs*! Oswald Mosley's wife says you've got mesmeric eyes . . .'

A BBC spokesman declared: 'We have every intention of repeating this programme in its usual slot this Friday', and the repeat was duly broadcast.

The furore ran its course, but that edition of *Desert Island Discs* remained part of Mitford folklore until long after Diana Mosley's death in August 2003 at the age of ninety-three. There can be no pithier summary of her performance than that made by her sister Jessica (Decca). In a letter to the novelist Herb Gold in June 1991, in which Decca talks about Diana's perpetuating the 'total lie' that Oswald Mosley had never been anti-semitic, Jessica Mitford wrote that Diana had been 'too ghastly for words'.

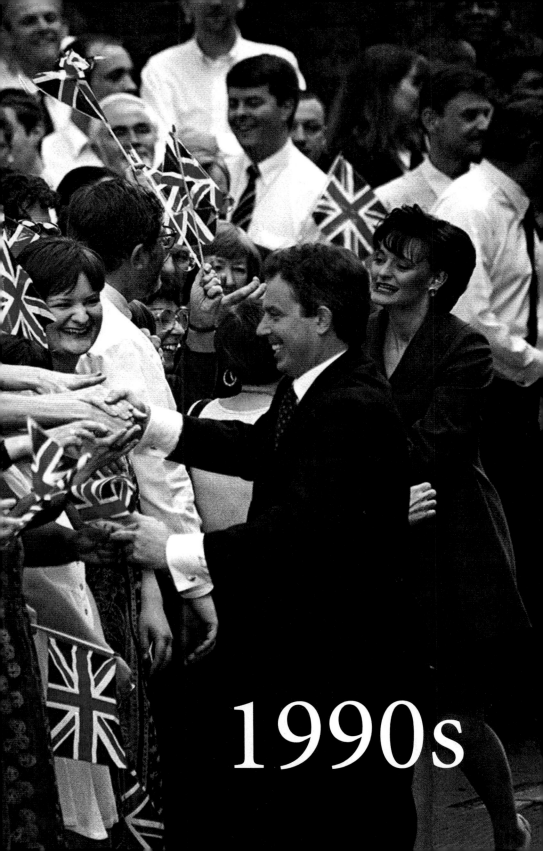

1990s

The Berlin Wall comes down, November 1989

FROM THE CASTING away of maverick politician Dennis Skinner in January 1990 to the marooning of Andrew Lloyd Webber in December 1999, Sue Lawley remained at the helm throughout the 1990s.

As usual, castaways included those who had been at the centre of great events. General Norman Schwarzkopf, commander of the allied forces in the first Gulf War, was marooned in 1992. Archbishop Desmond Tutu provided a wonderfully upbeat edition of the programme soon after the freed Nelson Mandela had become President of South Africa in 1994. Chris Patten, last Governor of Hong Kong, was cast away in November 1996, as the return of the former colony to China loomed.

And perhaps future castaways might shed fresh light on some of the other events of the 1990s: the collapse of the Soviet Union; conflict in the former Yugoslavia; the end of the Cold War; the opening of the Channel Tunnel; genocide in Rwanda.

On the domestic front, racehorse trainer Jenny Pitman was able, when cast away in 1995, to give a characteristically forthright view of the shenanigans at the 1993 Grand National, when her horse Esha Ness 'won' the race which was declared void after two false starts. Talking to Sue Lawley, Mrs Pitman summed it up nicely as 'a catalogue of incompetences'.

The very idea of interviewing a female racehorse trainer would have been unthinkable in the early decades of *Desert Island Discs* (women were not allowed to hold Jockey Club training licences until 1966), but the roll-call of 1990s castaways illustrated that women were now increasingly prominent in all sorts of fields. From the political world came Mo Mowlam and Ann Widdecombe (both marooned in 1999); from the fashion industry, Vivienne Westwood (1992); from journalism, Kate Adie (1994); from food writing, Prue Leith (1990); from theatre and film, actresses such as

Nicole Kidman (1998) and Judi Dench, who had been cast away by Roy Plomley in 1972 and returned to the island in 1998.

Some castaways had distinguished themselves in more than one field. Glenda Jackson had been interviewed by Roy Plomley in 1971 when at the peak of her acting career – she had been awarded the Best Actress Oscar two years earlier for *Women in Love* – and returned in 1997 to be interviewed by Sue Lawley as Transport Minister, having been elected Labour MP for Hampstead and Highgate at the 1992 general election.

'Stormin' Norman' – General Norman Schwarzkopf, 1991

And sometimes a programme was not broadcast, on account of momentous events engulfing Radio 4 – on no occasion more brutally than when on Sunday, 31 August 1997 the second *Desert Island Discs* appearance of singer Cleo Laine was cancelled following the death of Princess Diana in the early hours of that morning. The programme was first transmitted in the repeat slot the following Friday.

Sue Lawley had started making adjustments to the *Desert Island Discs* process as soon as she arrived in March 1988, and the changes were not limited to her insistence on proper cups and biscuits. Of major significance was the hiring of a researcher to prepare the ground well in advance of the studio recording, a role filled in the early 1990s by Rosemary Edgerley. In her book *Desert Island Discussions*, Sue describes the process which they then followed – a far cry from an amiable lunch with Roy Plomley at one of his clubs:

> I dislike talking to an interviewee in advance. I worry that it will spoil the spontaneity of our exchange. So I steer well clear of any meeting until the appointed hour. All of which makes Rosemary's task that much more important. She has to find out what reminiscences have prompted the selection of records, book and luxury. This is a more difficult ask than it sounds. Very rarely have people decided all these things. They're generally pleased to have been asked (hardly anyone refuses our invitation) and are looking forward to making their choices. The task of doing it, however, they often find very difficult.

One shift which might appear arcane to non-BBC insiders was that compilation of each *Desert Island Discs* programme was moved from the production unit of Radio 3 – to which it had long been entrusted, though always transmitted on Radio 4. But that shift reflected the changing nature of *Desert Island Discs*, from a record programme with added chat to an interview-based programme which under Sue Lawley was taking a robustly journalistic approach, on occasion producing a broadcast almost painful in its exposure of raw emotion.

In June 1991 the novelist A. S. Byatt spoke with immensely moving candour about the death of her son in a road accident in the week of his eleventh birthday: 'I know a lot of women whose children have died who do really believe that their children speak to them in some ways. But I myself feel that the dead are gone, and that this is a lesson one has to learn. This is the way my moral temperament takes me. But it was an extremely painful lesson.' She had recently used the experience in a short story, in which a man sees a boy's ghost, but the woman is adamant that 'There is no boy'. In as raw a passage as *Desert Island Discs* has produced, Antonia Byatt continued: 'I used to say to myself, waking up in the morning, "There is no boy." But you learn it very, very slowly. I worked it out with my intellect very quickly that you had to learn that somebody was gone, though actually it takes you years and years not to wait for them to come round corners and look down the street and see a child – you know, a small blond boy dancing – it's not a good thing, really.'

And then there was politics. In contrast to the 1960s, when senior management could warn the Gramophone Department that *Desert Island Discs* should steer clear of politicians, even the most cursory glance down the list of the decade's castaways shows that one very noticeable feature was a growing emphasis on politics, to the extent that the fiftieth anniversary in 1992 was marked by having on the island the programme's one and only current prime minister, John Major (see pages 318–22).

Politics has always been a potentially troublesome area for *Desert Island Discs*. From Tom Driberg in 1943 to David Steel in 1985, Roy Plomley marooned a few political figures but seemed to consider the theatre or opera house a more promising source of castaways – and conversation with those politicos whom he did bring in did not always prove comfortable. In November 1973, for example, he interviewed Vic Feather, former

A. S. Byatt at the Edinburgh International Book Festival, 2011

general secretary of the Trades Union Congress, and let his own guard down when referring to current industrial relations as 'diabolical'. Talk about a red rag to a bull. Feather responded instantly: 'Diabolical? Why should you say diabolical? What do you know about it? You know very little about it, if I may say so. Diabolical?' Feather pointed out that the current level of days lost to strikes was 0.2 per cent. 'Are you going to weep into your beer all day and all night and all through the future and rend your clothes and put ashes on your hair because we're only getting 99.8 per cent of possible? We're better than the United States and Canada, we're better than Australia, we're better than Japan. And why do you say that record is diabolical? . . . Throw

Gordon Brown, Shadow Chancellor of the Exchequer, 1993

rubbish at the TUC if you want – throw rubbish at the BBC if you want – but you must be sure of your facts.'

Aiming for safer ground, Plomley asks whether industrial relations are getting better. 'Well,' replies Feather, 'they're better if people like yourself, if I may say so, wouldn't keep saying they're diabolical.'

Plomley's interview with Margaret Thatcher was more amicable, and it is significant that, as we have seen on page 197, Mrs Thatcher had herself asked to appear on the programme. By the 1990s the opportunity for a politician to show his or her human side by appearing on *Desert Island Discs* was firmly embedded as a tenet of good political public relations, and the close proximity of the programmes with Gordon Brown (pages 374–80) and Tony Blair (pages 381–6) gave an opportunity not only to compare the styles of two men who were expecting within months to topple the John Major-led Conservative government, but also to assess Sue Lawley's style of questioning political figures.

It was one thing to interview a politician after their career was effectively over (Quintin Hogg, say, or Enoch Powell), but the chance to probe the mind and heart of someone aspiring to high office, albeit in the kindly and relaxed atmosphere of the *Desert Island Discs* studio, brought out the hard-nosed journalist in Sue Lawley. It was Sue's line of questioning about Brown's personal relationships which caused the post-programme ruckus, but she was even more persistent on other matters:

LAWLEY: Can we talk about a 'stakeholder society' for a moment, Gordon Brown? Is it simply a slogan, or is it a policy?

BROWN: It's a policy and it's a theme that matters, because if people don't feel they have a stake in society, if you've got 30 per cent youth unemployment in some of our inner cities, then you will have problems, and I think it's very important that we expect, in return for the opportunities that we create, responsibility is taken in turn by young people. And that's why having a stake carries not just opportunities, but carries responsibility.

LAWLEY: But when you put it like that, it does sound like a slogan, because it's applying to everything across the board . . .

BROWN: Well, I define a stakeholder in society and economy as opportunities for people to work . . .

LAWLEY: But none of those things, you see, sound particularly different from what the Tories tell us.

BROWN: I think they are different.

LAWLEY: That's the great problem with the new Labour, isn't it?

BROWN: No, I think they are different because the dividing line is . . . that I believe passionately that equality of opportunity for all is the key, not just to a strong society, but is also the key to a thriving economy.

LAWLEY: But nevertheless as we all know, ultimately, it's economic policy and pounds in your pocket that win elections, and you have not yet convinced this country, have you, that you are not a party of high taxation? There was a poll only the other day saying that 53 per cent of people still believe that the Labour government would end up putting up taxes in the long run.

BROWN: I don't think that is the general view of the population, and I think once people understand that I am building my tax policy from first principles, and that there is no desire on my part to raise people's taxes for the sake of it, then I think they do understand that Labour is different both from Labour of the past and from a Conservative government that has imposed very high taxes.

LAWLEY: But you consistently refuse to put the flesh on the bones of those policies, because that's what happened last time, isn't it? And in the end Labour didn't win because people felt they were going to be more highly taxed.

BROWN: No, what I've done is say . . .

She is similarly probing with Tony Blair, who (according to the diary of his then press secretary, Alastair Campbell) found the whole *Desert Island Discs* experience distinctly uncomfortable – evidence that the Lawley style was hitting home. No wonder she has written that on taking over the presenter's chair, one of her first thoughts was that politics was 'a rich furrow to be ploughed' – and it has remained fertile ground.

'How tickled I am': Ken Dodd

The first castaway of June 1990 was comedian Ken Dodd, whose Diddymen worked in the jam-butty mines of Knotty Ash and whose tattifilarious performances had made him for many years one of the most popular comic acts in Britain. The previous year he had been in court on a charge of tax evasion. He was acquitted; even so, his attitude towards the episode was a legitimate line of enquiry for his *Desert Island Discs* interview. 'I believed entirely that he was willing to talk about his problems with the Inland Revenue,' Sue Lawley recalls, 'and naturally I brought it up, but he simply refused to talk about the subject. I pressed and he refused point blank again.' That part of the conversation did not appear in the transmitted programme.

The issue was taken up in the *Sunday Times* by radio critic Paul Donovan, who compared the treatment of Ken Dodd with that of Lord Dacre, formerly Hugh Trevor-Roper. In 1988, castaway Dacre had been asked about his authentication of the supposed Hitler diaries and had replied that the episode was best left in the past. *Desert Island Discs*, wrote Donovan, 'reveals a person's life not only through their words but also their choice of music. But the Ken Dodd trial was one of the most important events of his life. As a result he has been "reborn", according to his publicist.' Donovan continued: 'Guests are selected, partly at least, for their news value. Obviously Dodd can refuse to discuss the past if he wants to, but it seems bizarre for the BBC actually to suppress Lawley's efforts, taken on behalf of the listeners and licence-payers, to get him to talk about it.'

The BBC conceded that editing out the exchange was an unusual step to take, but a spokesman said, 'Silences are not very good on radio.'

Even leaving aside the castaways' sensitive spots, it was not always plain sailing towards the desert island beach.

Very occasionally the programme was overtaken by events between recording and transmission. The edition planned to coincide with the running of the Grand National in 1993 was to feature Lord Oaksey, doyen of racing journalists and once a highly successful amateur jockey, whose programme included his account of being narrowly beaten in the 1963 National. But 1993 brought the mayhem of the void Grand National, so Oaksey had to return to the studio and record a fresh section covering that chaotic event.

A more remarkable example of the best-laid plans going awry came in spring 1995. It had been agreed that Sue Lawley and a small *Desert Island Discs* production team would go to the USA to record three American castaways: Buzz Aldrin, second man to have walked on the moon, playwright Neil Simon and blues legend John Lee Hooker. Buzz Aldrin had agreed in principle to do the programme, but as the date for their departure approached the team had still received no information about this highly distinguished castaway's choice of records.

John Lee Hooker at home with his daughter Zikiya, 1997

They flew over to the USA, and with Neil Simon and John Lee Hooker safely recorded made their way to Buzz Aldrin's house in southern California – where it became clear that either the astronaut's PR person had not passed on any information about the *Desert Island Discs* process, or Aldrin himself had paid no attention to whatever information he had been given. Shortly before the agreed date for recording they got a call asking to postpone, and shortly before the new date got another call asking to delay again. The producer reported back to London, and it was agreed that the team should try to salvage the situation in the only way possible. Sue Lawley takes up the story:

'This was becoming decidedly awkward as our time in the USA was very limited, but Buzz Aldrin was such a catch that we were extremely reluctant to give up on the idea. And we still didn't have his choice of music, so for once – as we were so desperate – we broke all the rules about not influencing the castaway's choices, and went to the local record shop and bought discs which contained "Fly Me to the Moon" and "Moon River" and various other lunar clichés! Eventually we had a list which we sent him.

'A new date was set, and this time we got as far as his house. As we set up the recording equipment I was talking him through what was involved – when he suddenly left us and went into another room at the back of the house. We were all set up – chairs in position, all the equipment primed – but for what felt like about fifteen minutes nothing happened. Then his wife emerged from the room into which he had disappeared and said, "I'm very sorry, but I think you guys are going to have to do this another day. Buzz isn't feeling so good."

'I said that it would be very difficult for us to come back another day, as our time was so restricted and we had already come thousands of miles to record this programme. Why didn't we just go for a walk for half an hour and see how he was when we came back?

'His wife went to put this suggestion to him, and through the door we could hear them shouting at each other. His wife then came out and told us he wouldn't do it. I decided that it was time to get tough, so I insisted – in a formal, BBC-ish kind of way – that we go ahead with what had been agreed, so she went back in to try and persuade him. But it was all to no avail, so we just packed up the equipment and left.'

It was a great shame that such a remarkable figure in twentieth-century history should have been, so far as *Desert Island Discs* was concerned, one that got away.

Handel
Zadok the Priest
*'This seldom fails to move
me to tears'*

'It's Over'
Roy Orbison

'Too Much'
Jimmy Reed

'Man Kind'
Misty in Roots

'Teenage Kicks'
The Undertones
*'I've always claimed that it was
my favourite record of all time'*

Rachmaninov
**Piano Concerto no. 2
in C minor**
Soloist: Peter Katin
Orchestra: London
Symphony Orchestra

'Eat Y'self Fitter'
The Fall

'Pasi Pano Pane Zviedzo'
The Four Brothers

**Dance to the Music of
Time by Anthony Powell**

Football

JOHN PEEL

radio presenter

14 January 1990

'I thought, what I'd really like is a job on the radio,
playing records that I like to other people'

It is a mark of the special position which John Peel enjoyed in British popular affection that when in 2002 the BBC held its poll for the One Hundred Greatest Britons of all time, he finished in the top fifty: in forty-third place, one below Sir Frank Whittle, inventor of the jet engine, and one above television pioneer John Logie Baird – remarkable company for a radio disc jockey to be keeping.

But of course Peel – born John Ravenscroft in 1939 on the Wirral (near but not in Liverpool) and educated at Shrewsbury School ('I was constantly in trouble') – was no ordinary DJ. More than any other of that calling, he was a test pilot for all sorts of musical genres, a man never content to go along with the trend but always exploring something new. He did not directly dictate taste, but he made clear what he liked and what he didn't, and his recommendation became a beacon for his followers. His radio shows provided a platform for live performance through regular 'session' slots, and the eclecticism of his choices and unforced intimacy of his presenting style – not the least attraction of which was his warm Liverpool-tinged accent – won him millions of fans.

Peel in festival mode, early 1970s

John Peel, Sue Lawley reminds listeners, has been with Radio 1 all its life: 'He was there when it started, twenty-two years ago, since when he's enjoyed an uninterrupted reign as the perceptive voice of pop. His enthusiasm for the new and the extreme has made him the champion of several generations of rebel, from flower power, through punk, to hip-hop and hardcore thrash.'

The young John soon decided he wanted to work in radio. 'I listened to Radio Luxembourg and to the American forces network in Europe, naively assumed that the DJs that I heard chose the records themselves . . . I thought, what I'd really like is a job on the radio, playing records that I like to other people. And that in essence is all I've ever done, really. People try to read more into it than that, but there isn't anything else to read.'

But before he could make a serious attempt at getting into radio he had to do National Service, after which came a move to Dallas, Texas. This was in the mid-1960s, the heyday of the Beatles, and one day he heard a local DJ talking 'a great deal of nonsense' about Liverpool – 'So I phoned him up and said that I was from Liverpool, and he immediately put me on the air, and we talked a bit about Liverpool and I set him straight on one or two things. I was then invited to go down to the station and become something of a Beatle expert – because the Americans in a rather charmingly naive way assumed that anybody who came from roughly the same area as the Beatles, even if they weren't blood relatives of theirs, would be an intimate friend. I never said that I did know the Beatles – but then again, I never said that I didn't.'

Back in England, he took a presenting job with the pirate station Radio London: 'They said that John Ravenscroft was too long a name for people to memorize, and one of the secretaries said, "Why don't we call him John Peel?"' – after 'the ghastly folk song'.

From Radio London he joined Radio 1 in 1967, where his show *Top Gear* (no relation to the later BBC television programme) aired music which was being passed over by the mainstream programmes: 'Of course, the irony of it is that a lot of the bands that we played then, people like the Pink Floyd and so forth, and Jimi Hendrix and Cream, people at the time said, "How can you possibly play this awful stuff?", whereas now they're pillars of the establishment, those that have survived.'

'But you were regarded as a bit of a late-night nutter, weren't you?' says Sue Lawley: 'You became a bit of a cult, and it's not a tag that you like, is it?'

'Not at all, no . . . ,' says her castaway, though he acknowledges it's hard to escape the label. 'The lack of image becomes an image in itself . . . People will try and make you fit into something that they've developed in their own mind.'

For all his cult status and large following, in the 1970s his relationship with many fans became strained by his interest in punk rock. 'You alienated a lot of your listeners,' says Sue Lawley.

Peel is unapologetic. 'The Ramones . . . were the first punk band I heard, and hearing them was similar to hearing Little Richard as a teenager – like Saul on the road to Damascus, a revelation . . . People phoned and said, "You must never do this again," and they wrote in afterwards and said, "Never play any of these records ever again," and of course I always find that quite exciting, so then I played a great deal more of them. It was terrific, and the whole audience changed in the space of about a month: the average age of the audience dropped by about ten years, and so all the people who wanted to go on listening to Grateful Dead records for the rest of their lives obviously got off the train at that point.'

'Do you champion the new for new's sake, or do you actually have to like the sound?'

'I do genuinely like it. I like it when people are making records because they have to be made. But if they are in any way successful at all, there comes a point very quickly at which they're making records to order, to the requirements not just of the record company and the accountants and so forth, but also to the requirements of the audience . . .

'It's rather like if you buy cornflakes or something, and if you like them, and you go to the supermarket to buy them again, you don't want them to be ginger flavoured or something whimsical like that. You want them pretty much as they were previously. And that's what happens with bands, I think. There comes a point, usually quite early in their career . . . at which they start to make things which just don't interest me any more. It's not elitism or any peculiar snobbery; it's that whatever the element was that attracted me initially is somehow bled out of them.'

At the Phoenix Festival, Stratford-upon-Avon, 1996

Sue Lawley observes how some bands have made it to the top thanks to Peel's encouragement. Does he enjoy such power?

'Not at all, really . . . People say there are certain bands, and obviously you kind of advance them a little bit and bring them to the attention of a slightly larger audience than they previously had, but at the same time there are numbers of bands whose records I've stoutly resisted playing and I've refused to have in session – like U2 and the Police and Dire Straits: all of them have applied for sessions at one time or another, and all were turned down by myself and the producer John Walters, and quite rightly so. So if ever I start to think of myself as sort of a king-maker, I can reflect back on those bands that have become stupendously successful. Bruce Springsteen was another chap—'

Aghast, Sue Lawley cuts in: 'What, you turned him down?'

'Not for a session, but when his earlier records arrived I thought they were absolute rubbish, and nobody could understand why I felt like this. I thought they were dreadful. I still think they are dreadful, as a matter of fact. It is really quite a good thing for me to turn against you because it's a guarantee of stupendous success.'

Some of John Peel's *Desert Island Discs* record choices are prompted by unusual personal reminiscences. He recalls being stuck in a motorway jam on his way to a football match in Liverpool, and hearing DJ Peter Powell playing the Undertones' 'Teenage Kicks' – 'which I had been playing for months, but to hear it played by someone else was a stupendous thing, and I actually burst into floods of tears in the traffic jam.'

But the reason for his choice of Rachmaninov's Second Piano Concerto must be one of the most affecting ever given by a *Desert Island Discs* castaway: 'When my daughter Florence was born about eight years ago, Sheila, my wife, was very, very ill, and it turned out subsequently that we both feared for her: she thought she was going to die and I rather suspected that she might as well. She lost a lot of weight, and was very ill indeed. I had to sleep in a different part of the house because she made so much noise when she was trying to sleep – it sounds selfish, but we agreed this was the only way I could get any sleep – and she came to me about four o'clock one morning and said that she thought the baby was about to be born. She climbed up on to the ledge where I had been sleeping – above the room where I played my records – and lay down. I went and made her a cup of tea and put on the Rachmaninov Second Piano Concerto, and when it had finished we drove off to the hospital, both of us thinking separately that she was going at least to be very ill, and possibly die. And in the event she was perfectly all right and Florence was born, the most healthy and pugnacious child – and so Rachmaninov's Second Piano Concerto means an immense amount to both of us.'

Change of gear: how practical a castaway would John Peel be? 'I'm hopeless about the house . . . I did once put up a corner cupboard and it's been there for something like fifteen years. It's held in place with wire coat hangers, but you can't tell that from the ground. I'm not a practical man at all.' Could he catch a fish or snare a rabbit? 'I don't eat meat anyway, so unless there is a great quantity of fruit and vegetables on the island, then I shall be in real trouble.'

To sum up his prospects as a castaway: 'I could cope for about twenty-four hours on my own.'

At the other end of the 1990s from his *Desert Island Discs* appearance, John Peel found a whole new audience when he became the host of *Home Truths*, the Saturday morning Radio 4 programme which put the spotlight on ordinary people with extraordinary stories to tell. It was a simple but brilliant concept, and ideally suited to Peel's unflashy style. A family man who embraced family values, he proved a wonderful interviewer, adept at bringing out the best in participants – and it was a terrible blow when in October 2004 he died suddenly at the age of sixty-five, suffering a heart attack while on a working holiday in Peru.

The London *Evening Standard* headline announcing his death was obvious but perfect: 'The Day the Music Died' – and at his funeral, the coffin was carried out to the strains of the Undertones performing 'Teenage Kicks', his record of records on *Desert Island Discs*.

BARBARA WINDSOR

actress

23 September 1990

'I'd have done anything to have got rid of those bosoms'

There is something indestructible about Barbara Windsor. Whatever life has thrown at her, she has thrown it back with added velocity. The busty beauty in nine *Carry On* films, she saw her career all but fall off the radar before reinventing herself – and reminding the watching public of her true acting credentials – as Peggy Mitchell in *EastEnders*.

Her private life has been a rollercoaster. She has had three husbands and more than one nervous breakdown, and on occasion has found herself in some very unsavoury company, yet somehow she remains the epitome of Cockney cheerfulness.

Barbara Windsor – born Barbara Ann Deeks in August 1937 – trained for the stage at the Aida Foster School and made her West End debut in 1952 in the chorus for the musical *Love from Judy*. She first made her mark on the silver screen in that enduring comic romp *The Belles of St Trinian's*, but it was her appearances in the *Carry On* films, starting with *Carry On Spying* in 1964, which established her trademark mix of innocence and sexiness – like a walking (usually tottering) version of a Donald McGill postcard.

Barbara Windsor was first washed up on the desert island by Roy Plomley in 1970. Second time round, Sue

Lawley introduces 'a woman whose honesty, determination and endless good humour have buoyed her up in often frightening circumstances'.

A startling fact about Barbara Windsor which Sue Lawley has unearthed is that as a child she wanted to be a nun. True, says the castaway. 'My mother said that she came home one day and I was prancing around the kitchen with a tea towel over my head, practising' – a charade influenced by her attending Our Lady's Convent in Stamford Hill, north London: 'It was very theatrical, and I quite liked it. I thought it very nice, the way they walk around in those black outfits, and I rather wanted to be a nun.'

That penchant for theatricality was steered in another direction by her appearance at the age of thirteen in *Madame Behenna's Juvenile Jollities*, prompting a talent scout to tell Madame Behenna: 'That little plump girl on the end, the little blonde one, she's got something.'

That the diminutive Barbara Ann Deeks 'had something' had long been obvious to those who had witnessed her impromptu performances: 'I was an only child, so I was always fantasizing. I'd get on the bus and show Mummy up, like I'd pull my skirts up behind and pretend I was Betty Grable, and look over my shoulder. . . I'd bring a little bit of hair over my eye and do a peek-a-boo Veronica Lake.'

Born in Shoreditch, 'in one of those typical little East End streets where everybody sat outside in their chairs shelling peas, and the key was in the door,' she did not enjoy a peaceful childhood. Her parents, she tells Sue Lawley, should not have married each other. 'My Dad was a typical East End Jack the Lad: lots of personality, loved the East End. Mummy was totally different. She was a very snobby East Ender. "Oh, I've got to get out of Shoreditch" – and she did. She got us up to Stoke Newington, which was considered big news in those days.'

Their arguing led all the way to the divorce court, where Barbara – 'a fifteen-year-old going on ten' – was called to give evidence regarding her parents' fighting. For years after that her father had nothing to do with her, but eventually they were reunited. 'It was lovely for just a few months, but there was always that thing about whether he could see Mummy in me, and then there was suddenly a row, and I just thought, "This is not meant to be."'

At the Aida Foster School, she was taught to speak posh – 'like a little plum in your mouth' – and be pretty and cultivate curls, whereas 'I was very short, fat and loud'. On her first day there she sat next to Shirley Eaton (later 'devastatingly beautiful' in the James Bond film *Goldfinger*), and Jean Marsh was in front of her. Why did she not lose heart? asks Sue Lawley, to which she gets a very direct answer: 'I didn't think that they could do it as well as me, at the end of the day.'

The Aida Foster School may have encouraged her to tone down the London accent, but 'the very first film job I got was in *The Belles of St Trinian's*, and I had to lean out the window and say, "Ta'rah, Mum, see you next hols!"' I had to be very Cockney, and my mother said, "I can't believe I've sat and done all that piecework to send you to Aida Foster's to get rid of your Cockney accent, and the first line you do is in a Cockney accent!"'

The musical *Love from Judy* was followed by *Fings Ain't Wot They Used t'Be* for Joan Littlewood's Theatre Workshop, *The Rag Trade* on television, and the film *Sparrows Can't Sing*. Composer Lionel Bart came to see a rough-cut of *Sparrows Can't Sing*, took her out afterwards 'for kippers and champagne', and promised to write her a song: 'Sparrows Can't Sing' is played as her next record.

Then comes a line of questioning that would have been considered ungentlemanly – indeed, inconceivable – during Roy Plomley's tenure. Sue Lawley is unashamedly direct:

'We talked about your height and your accent, Barbara. Your other trademark is, of course, the boobs. Your greatest assets, some would say.'

'It's so funny, because I went into *Love from Judy* when I was fifteen, four foot ten and a half, flat shoes, school uniform – and I came out two and a half years later teetering on high heels, with this 38C bust. I looked like I was falling over all the time, because I had this terribly little waist, eighteen inches.'

Frank Sinatra
and the Count Basie Band
'The Best Is Yet To Come'

'It just made me go all funny'

The boobs were strapped down while she continued in *Love from Judy*, 'but was there a time,' asks Sue Lawley, 'when you were embarrassed by them?'

'Yes, I hated it. I was very protected in *Love from Judy* . . . and suddenly I came out . . . I didn't know what to do with my evenings. I'd always worked in the evenings, and suddenly, going out and going to dances, and guys going, "Phwoar, look at that!" – and going past a building site and the whistling, and saying, "Seen your feet lately, darlin'?!" I hated it. I loathed it. I'd have done anything to have got rid of those bosoms.'

Barbara's bosoms have been the butt of endless jokes, especially in the *Carry On* films. Has she felt resentment that it was her body that people were giggling at?

The joke was not in the bosoms themselves, she says, but in the reaction of the men. 'Look at a scene. It's not me showing a left boob or whatever. It always pans on to the man's face going "Ooohh!", and that's what they laugh at. They laughed at Kenny Williams reacting to my boobs, and Sid James and Peter Butterworth. I never think it's the actual boobs.'

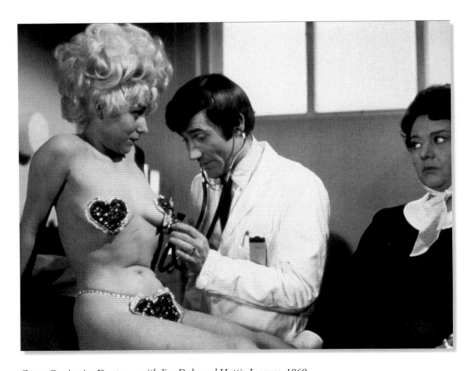

Carry On Again, Doctor – *with Jim Dale and Hattie Jacques, 1969*

Sue Lawley turns to the topic of Barbara's first husband Ronnie Knight, a man who knew the Kray brothers: 'But I didn't meet the Krays through Ronnie. I was in *Fings Ain't Wot They Used t'Be*, and it was all about gangsters and all the rest of it. Ronnie and Reggie and Charlie Kray came to see it and they asked to be introduced to me. They were thorough gentlemen, very nice.'

She has said that Charlie Kray was the most gentlemanly man she had ever met. 'He was charming, the handsomest guy I think I'd ever seen. He looked like Steve McQueen, and very sweet. And Ronnie and Reggie were charming.' The Krays were said to have governed the East End: 'If you're in trouble you go and see them, or they look after the people who can't look after themselves.'

With Reggie Kray, 1960s

Sue Lawley points out that the Krays had been found guilty of terrible crimes. Does she still have a soft spot for them? 'Oh yes. I write to Reggie and Reggie writes to me, and he always sends me flowers on my birthday. And Ronnie's made toys for me.'

Ronnie Knight, Barbara's husband of two decades, was jailed for his part in the Security Express robbery of 1983. The police, the press, the infidelities, the deceit: it is, as Sue Lawley says, a miserable history. How did Barbara stand it for so long?

She had had a nervous breakdown, but kept it to herself: 'I was very tough.'

Barbara subsequently remarried, and describes her second husband Stephen Hollings, twenty years her junior, as 'a joy – he's so sensible and so together'.

Inevitably, talk returns to the *Carry On* films, and Barbara Windsor relates how a taxi driver had said to her: 'All those lovely *Carry On* people – you're all dead, aren't you?' In particular she misses Kenneth Williams. 'I don't understand why Kenny's gone. He had an ulcer, and I can't believe that he died in the night in pain. Why couldn't he phone me up? I was only round the corner.' Her sixth record choice is Williams on the Tony Hancock radio show, with Hattie Jacques and Hancock himself.

Curiously, in the light of the path which Barbara Windsor's career was later to take, she confesses: 'I've never been very happy doing television, because I feel I'm terribly over the top. That's why it was good to do the *Carry Ons*, because they were all over the top as well. I'm a theatre person, I'm a big performer, and I always shudder when I see myself on telly!'

'What will you ponder about on your desert island?' asks Sue Lawley. 'What wisdoms will you decide you've won through your experiences?'

'I don't think negatively. I don't think about the rotten things and I won't think about those things. I will pick out all those wonderful things that have happened in my life and all the terrific people I've known and how lucky that I got paid – paid! – for doing something that I absolutely adored.'

Regrets? 'That I wasn't more together with my mother, that I didn't understand her . . . Every time she nagged, it was for her Bar. And that I didn't get that relationship with my father going.'

Would she endure being cast away? 'I'd like it, I suppose, just for a little while, and then I'd want to get back and see my mates, and have a walk around Soho!'

Barbara Windsor's last record? 'I'm very patriotic, and I can imagine me standing on that beach, tears flowing down, "Land of Hope and Glory" being played' – while she waves her luxury, the Union flag, to try to attract the attention of a passing ship.

Barbara Windsor joined the cast of *EastEnders* in 1994, taking over from Jo Warne as Peggy Mitchell – landlady of the Queen Victoria pub. For this role she won Best Actress at the British Soap Awards in 1999, and ten years later was given a Lifetime Achievement award at the same gathering. Peggy Mitchell left Albert Square in September 2010.

Barbara Windsor divorced Stephen Hollings in 1995, and married her third husband, Scott Mitchell, in 2000 – the same year she was awarded the MBE.

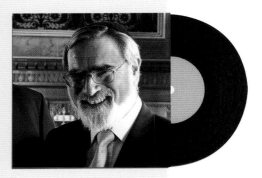

JONATHAN SACKS

Rabbi

21 April 1991

'There's a saying in Judaism: when nobody else is prepared to lead you have to try to lead'

When in September 1991, just a few months after being cast away, Jonathan Sacks became Chief Rabbi, he was only the sixth incumbent since that role was made formal in 1845. Prior to taking up that post, he had been Principal of Jews' College in London, rabbi of Golders Green and Marble Arch synagogues, and one of the most influential thinkers among Britain's Jewish population.

Jonathan Sacks is well known as a regular contributor to the 'Thought for the Day' slot on the Radio 4 *Today* programme, which has brought him a wide following as a speaker with a special skill at relating current events to his faith.

The themes of faith and family ran through the early part of Rabbi Jonathan Sacks's interview with Sue Lawley.

'I think we were a very happy family,' the castaway reminisces about his childhood as one of four brothers. 'My mother used to lay down limits, but they always used to be such broad limits that almost anything was possible within them. She used to say to me when I used to go off to college every time, "Jonathan, do whatever you like, but don't give up your Judaism," and since I had carte blanche to do almost anything, I did absolutely nothing.'

What Sue Lawley suggests was a certain complacency about Judaism did not survive the Six Day War in 1967. Sacks was nineteen years old, and vividly remembers his feelings at the time: 'In the weeks before the war, when Israel was surrounded by states who had declared their intention to drive Israel into the sea, the entire Jewish world was riveted on what seemed to be an unfolding tragedy. It looked as if a second, unthinkable Holocaust was about to take place, and it made a particular impact on those of my generation who were born after the Holocaust. It made us realize just what Jews had faced a generation before.

'We suddenly felt ourselves in the same situation again. And all through the university, people I'd never identified as Jews before suddenly turned up in the university synagogue, and there was an atmosphere that you could feel, that sent shivers down your spine. I mean, we were terrified. Of course, when the war was over in six days with a tremendous victory for Israel, the release of emotion was something that I don't think will happen again in my lifetime.'

After Cambridge, Sacks went to a religious seminary in Israel which was, as Dr Sacks puts it, 'a piece of eighteenth-century Europe transplanted into the middle of Israel'. It was a very intense environment: 'I came back with an enormous beard and a very, very pious look in my eyes. My parents came to meet me at the airport and they didn't recognize me at all. Eventually someone said, "That coat belongs to our son, therefore the person wearing it must be Jonathan."'

He then taught moral philosophy, and realized that he wanted the rabbinical life: 'There's a saying in Judaism: when nobody else is prepared to lead you have to try to lead, and in the end I said, that applies to me. And that's when I decided to become a rabbi.'

Sue Lawley turns his attention to the role of women in Judaism: 'They are excluded so much, as I understand it, from that which takes place in the synagogue.'

'I have a strong attachment to Jewish women. My mother was one, my wife is one, and my daughters are too. Therefore I feel for them, especially for my daughters, that they should have a Jewish education that is fully equal to that of my son; that Jewish girls and Jewish women should not feel excluded from the most fundamental act of all Jews, which is to study our own heritage, and to feel oneself to be a master of it. And that really is something that I'll work on very hard once I become Chief Rabbi.'

But Sue Lawley is not going to let him off so easily. 'Do you believe,' she asks, 'that Jewish women should be allowed to sit in the body of the synagogue?'

'I don't, for this simple reason. That there is a point at which men and women mixing or a certain kind of social atmosphere simply distracts from the unmediated intensity of prayer. In prayer I want to speak personally to God, and I don't want to feel that in some way I'm part of a social situation where I have to be self-conscious, and that's why Orthodox Jews have always believed that the sexes should pray, as it were, physically separately although as part of one congregation . . . The women will remain in the gallery, and I believe they will find that they can pray much more easily if they pray as women rather than as some hybrid that is neither male nor female.'

Another thorny issue: what does the Chief Rabbi Elect say to a young Jewish boy who has fallen for a Gentile girl? Would he try to convince the boy that marrying out is wrong?

'I would try and sit with him and just trace through that incredible line of ancestors, all of whom might have made the choice not to carry on their heritage to the next generation: two hundred generations of that young man's ancestors had against all odds survived and lived and had faith as Jews. And I would honestly ask him, would he want that two-hundred-generational tree to die with him?'

And if it were his own son . . . ?

'What would I say? That is the tragedy which I think is avoidable. If we educate our children so that Judaism is the most important thing in their lives, then it will surely be the most important thing in their marriages.'

Sue Lawley presses the point: 'So you don't believe – because of the education that you have given your son – that he would even arrive at that point? He would not allow himself to fall for a Gentile?'

'I would never want a child of mine to feel, "There is an act I couldn't do because it would give my father pain." I would wish him to feel, "There's an act that I can't do because it would give *me* pain", and that's what I've tried to teach my children – not very well, but I hope well enough for them to sense something of what I've sensed in Judaism.'

With regard to the dilemma of a liberal thinker like himself having always to take a line as Chief Rabbi: 'I try very hard to understand and respect positions that are different from mine, but that doesn't mean to say that I don't have an absolute conviction that there is truth and falsity, that there is good and evil. I don't think all things are true. I don't think all things are relative.'

As for the demands of the desert island, Dr Sacks declares himself 'severely practical when I have to be'.

Will the music be an escape? 'Music isn't an escape for me at all. Music is for me a way of re-engaging with the world. I quite often feel quite depressed at the sheer difficulty of some of the tasks that I've set myself. Whenever I fall into that kind of temporary despair, music just lifts me up and allows me to go back fighting into the world.'

Dr Sacks' final piece of music is the Jewish memorial prayer for the dead.

'This particular recording has a history to it. It's sung by a cantor called Sholom Katz, who was imprisoned and taken to a concentration camp during the Nazi regime. He along with two thousand other Jews was ordered to be shot and killed, and before that the Nazis ordered this group of two thousand people to dig their own graves. Katz stood with his colleagues in front of his own grave. He made one request of the German authorities, that he be allowed to sing a prayer, the memorial prayer for the dead. He sang it, and the camp officials were so impressed with his voice that they spared his life. He was liberated from Auschwitz and sang this song in memory of the six million Jews who had fallen. In it are all the tears and all the faith of Jewish history.'

Dr Jonathan Sacks was knighted in 2005, and became a life peer in 2009, sitting on the cross benches in the House of Lords as Baron Sacks of Aldgate in the City of London.

George Gershwin
Rhapsody in Blue
New York Philharmonic
Orchestra
*'A beautiful piece of music,
very haunting'*

'The Holy City'
June Bronhill

'The Happening'
Diana Ross and the
Supremes

Donizetti
**'O giusto cielo' (from
Lucia di Lammermoor)**
Soloist: Joan Sutherland

Popper
Elfin Dance
Mstislav Rostropovich

Cricket commentary
John Arlott
*'The greatest way I have to
relax is watching cricket'*

Elgar
**Pomp and Circumstance
March no. 1 in D major,
'Land of Hope and Glory'**
Conductor: Sir Malcolm
Sargent

**'The Best Is Yet
To Come'**
Frank Sinatra and the
Count Basie Band

***The Small House at
Allington* by Anthony
Trollope**

**Oval cricket ground
replica and bowling
machine**

JOHN MAJOR

Prime Minister

26 January 1992

'I'm a politician – perhaps I can build a hot air balloon'

Eight prime ministers have been cast away on the desert island: Margaret Thatcher, Tony Blair, Gordon Brown and David Cameron before their time in No. 10, and Sir Alec Douglas-Home, Edward Heath and James Callaghan after they had left office. Only John Major was marooned while serving as Prime Minister, and his presence on the island marked a very special occasion for the programme itself: the fiftieth anniversary of *Desert Island Discs*.

At the time of his casting away, John Major had been premier a little over a year, having emerged from relative political obscurity to thwart Michael Heseltine's leadership ambitions after the turbulent removal of Margaret Thatcher. He formally became Prime Minister on 28 November 1990.

His first year in office had included the Gulf War and negotiations leading up to the signing of the Maastricht Treaty in December 1991, but by early 1992 it was looking as if his stay in Downing Street might prove a short one. The Labour Party under Neil Kinnock was well ahead in the polls, and the general election was little more than two months away.

John Major's somewhat unusual beginnings are well documented.

His father was sixty-six when John was born, his mother in her mid-forties. They had two much older children, and lived in the south London suburb of Worcester Park, where his father made garden ornaments.

'It was bliss. It was a very close-knit family. People talk a lot about my father. He was a very colourful character, the best one-on-one raconteur I have ever heard, bar none. He was always immensely entertaining to listen to, and I was entranced as a small boy, listening to his many stories: going across the Atlantic in masted sailing boats, all sorts of things that he had done.

'But our family actually revolved around my mother. She was a formidable personality in her own right, and she was the centre of the family: she determined what we did. My father made the important decisions like what the government should do, and she decided where we went to school and where we lived.'

For many years his father had performed in music halls: 'He had his own small travelling show. He was a magician, he was a singer, he did a bit of acting. And my mother originally worked in his show.'

That blissful childhood was shattered when a business venture of his father's went awry, leaving the family deep in debt. They sold up and moved to Brixton: 'From a fairly pleasant, though modest, bungalow with a large garden and a pond and poplar trees at the bottom of the garden and a big lawn, we moved to the fourth floor of an old Victorian building. We had two rooms and a landing, and there were the five of us.'

The gas ring was on the landing, the toilet was on the ground floor, and the neighbours were as unsavoury as the surroundings: 'There was an elderly gentleman who had some very eccentric habits indeed. And I guess there were other people in the house whom I prefer not to remember.' But the experience had a lasting effect on his own outlook: it 'made me feel pretty strongly that I didn't want other people to live in the same circumstances. I think it did harden some attitudes in me that otherwise wouldn't have been there. I hate people who patronize. I dislike snobbishness. I don't like selfishness. I find those intolerable ways to behave.'

After *Rhapsody in Blue* and the singer June Bronhill – with whom his wife Norma had once shared a flat, and who had sung at their wedding

John Major, Tory councillor, at a Lambeth council meeting in 1967

– John Major's third record is 'The Happening' by Diana Ross and the Supremes. 'I worked in Nigeria in my early twenties, and whilst I was there I had a motor accident and spent some time in hospital, then quite a few months with a very serious leg injury in hospital in the United Kingdom – in Mayday in Croydon. I remember turning on the radio as I lay there in plaster up to my thigh, month after month, and this was the record that always seemed to be playing.'

Back to the early years. John Major left school at sixteen, and after a couple of lowly jobs found himself unemployed. 'It isn't pleasant, I think I can understand how other people feel. Though it has to be said, I was unemployed as a young single man. The real problem is when you're unemployed and you have family responsibilities, whether as a man or a woman, and you're older: I think it's much worse then.'

Sue Lawley reflects that 'impulsive' is not a word often ascribed to this Prime Minister – 'and yet apparently you proposed to Norma Johnson within three weeks of meeting her.'

'Yes, that's right! Many of the things I've done have been impulsive. The most important and worthwhile piece of impulsion was, as you say, Norma. But not only that. The house we live in – it took me two minutes to look at it and decide to buy it, yet it was infinitely the most expensive purchase I'd ever made.'

Sue Lawley relates Major's remarkable progress. 'You were, as we've heard, a young man with a fairly threadbare c.v. in your late teens, and you had no prospects. But by the age of twenty-six or twenty-seven you were chairman of Lambeth Housing Committee, you were vice-chairman of Brixton Conservatives, you were a governor of a few schools, you were a member of various voluntary organizations, and you had a proper job. You had a job in a bank, with prospects. Now, that transformation, if you like, from the wrong to the right side of the track was quite calculated, wasn't it?'

'I don't shrink from admitting that: yes, it was. I wanted to get into Parliament. It was perfectly clear that in many ways I didn't have a classic c.v. I hadn't been to university, I didn't have an Oxford double first, I didn't have many of the classic ingredients that one might look for in a parliamentary candidate. So I had to build up my curriculum vitae in another way: with work within the party, with experience in other ways.'

'So in that sense,' says Sue Lawley, 'you're a very good example of what you mean by the classless society, aren't you? A society in which people without money, without contacts, without the right qualifications, can win through and come to the top.'

'That's exactly what I mean by a classless society. When I use that phrase, I don't intend to damage the vivid tapestry of life that we have in this country, and the variety that we have in this country.'

But the politics of self-improvement does not benefit everyone, says Sue Lawley. 'For every one of you there will be hundreds of others who for whatever reason won't have the guts and the ability and the determination to get there. What about those people who fall by the wayside in your enterprise culture?'

'Well, not everybody would want to do that . . . They would wish to live their life in different ways, and I believe they should be entitled to. But if what underlies your question is the thought, do we need a proper welfare safety net in this country, then I believe very much that we do.'

'What are your eight favourite records?' 'Record bankruptcies, repossessions, interest rates, unemployment, VAT . . . er . . .'

By now Sue Lawley has the bit between her teeth: 'And yet one of the most striking images of the eighties were those people we saw who still do sleep in cardboard boxes, and already a telling image of the early nineties are the people whose homes are being repossessed. That doesn't quite fit, does it, with what you're saying?'

'Well, we stopped, if you recall, the repossessions just before Christmas. We took action which should stop most of the repossessions. There will always be some marriage break-up and problems of that sort that no government can wholly solve, so there will always be some repossessions, and always have been. I'm very concerned about the cardboard box people, but they're not there because there is no accommodation for them. In the areas where they actually sleep, you will actually find there is shelter available for them, and they simply will not go to that shelter . . . There are some people, for whatever reason, who stand outside the normal habits of society, and simply don't want to come inside, and it's a very difficult problem for a free society to cope with.'

To lighter matters. On the island, how practical would he be? 'I'd be pretty amateurish, I think, but I guess I'd have a lot of time to improve, so I think I'd be able to build a lean-to.'

He would try to escape, but how? 'Well, I'm a politician – perhaps I can build a hot air balloon.'

John Major outside No. 10 after winning the general election, 10 April 1992

And for one of the more unusual luxuries: 'What I'd really like to take with me is a full-sized replica of the Oval cricket ground . . . The sun will shine, the grass will grow, the pitch will be beautiful, and I will be able to bowl on it or bat on it – with the bowling machine that lives in the Ken Barrington Centre – to my heart's content.'

Against most predictions, the general election on 9 April 1992 saw John Major given another five years as Prime Minister. But his administration never really recovered from 'Black Wednesday' on 16 September 1992 – when the UK withdrew from the European Exchange Rate Mechanism – and was further buffeted by allegations of 'sleaze' made against Conservative MPs. At the 1997 general election the Tories were demolished by the Labour Party under Tony Blair. On the morning after polling day, John Major announced that he was going to Buckingham Palace to tender his resignation to the Queen: and 'after that Norma and I will be able, with the children, to get to the Oval in time for lunch and for some cricket this afternoon'.

BOB GELDOF

singer and activist

6 September 1992

'Though I know that this is a venerable British institution it is, after all, another radio show'

Bob Geldof divides opinion. Morrissey called him 'a nauseating character' and his charity group Band Aid 'diabolical', while others consider 'Sir Bob' – the knighthood is honorary, as he is not a British citizen – a secular saint on account of his efforts to relieve the suffering of famine-struck Ethiopia in the mid-1980s. Love him or hate him, Geldof defies pigeonholing. Rock star, political activist, thorn in the side of complacent authority – he is all those and much more.

Born in 1951 in Dun Laoghaire, on the southern edge of Dublin, he left Blackrock College without qualifications and worked in various jobs – including a stint as a music journalist in Vancouver – before founding the Boomtown Rats in 1975. The band's first UK No. 1 was 'Rat Trap' in 1978, and the following year it returned to the top spot with 'I Don't Like Mondays', a Geldof song based on an attempted massacre at an elementary school in San Diego, California.

What conferred sainthood upon his unkempt head was his response to television images of the Ethiopian famine. Along with Midge Ure of Ultravox, he commandeered a gallery of rock legends to record the single 'Do They Know It's Christmas?' under the name

Band Aid. The record was at No. 1 for five weeks, and in July 1985 Geldof built on it by organizing the Live Aid concerts in London and Philadelphia, which raised over £150 million. Backstage at the end of one of the most remarkable days in rock music history, he encountered a fan who asked, 'Is that it?' – a question which became the title of his bestselling autobiography.

Bob Geldof recalls a particular memory of the Live Aid concert in 1985. 'I was on stage with my band the Boomtown Rats, and the emotive quality of the day, which I hadn't predicted at all nor planned for, struck me. It was an electrifying moment, to be aware that there was someone in Shanghai or Tierra del Fuego or wherever watching that specific moment, and it was strangely calming. I felt very centred. And that was maybe the first time that I was aware of feeling that sense of being and place, of being right, was at that moment. Of course it passed very quickly, but just having experienced it the once, I knew that that must signify the greatest day of my life.'

Sue Lawley scolds her castaway: 'Let's get down to your eight desert island discs, which despite months of warning, you still only decided on in the past few days. Is that because it's such a weighty decision, or is it sheer laziness?'

If the question was provocative, so was the reply: 'It's not sheer laziness. It's because right at the moment I'm up to my neck with a million things, and it's the little minutiae of life that really bore me. I dismiss them until the last moment because they're not important. And though I know that this is a venerable British institution it is, after all, another radio show.'

Geldof's childhood in Dublin, suggests Sue Lawley, 'is the story of a child for whom life seemed to go wrong at a very early stage and who never really got quite back on the rails until adulthood, if I read it right. I mean, lots of despair, loneliness, misery, huge amounts of panic here and there.'

'That's how I remember it to be. My sisters have an alternative view and my Dad, despairingly, has another view. The background to it is your standard clichéd one.

The Boomtown Rats, 1978

We weren't well off. My dad was a commercial traveller – still is indeed, selling carpets and towels and things – and he'd go away to the country every Monday and come back on Friday.'

Bob's mother died of a brain haemorrhage in the middle of the night when he was very young. 'My father came to me in the morning, and he sat down and said words to the effect that "Your Mum's gone to Heaven." He started crying, and the fact that he was crying made me cry, because I'd never seen him cry.'

Geldof's first record is Van Morrison; his second is Loudon Wainwright III, which triggers more memories, from school in Ireland and from early adulthood in London. 'I started listening to Loudon Wainwright around 1970, and music was a big deal for me. I didn't play sport. I was interested in two things from about the age of eleven, politics and pop music, and pop music absolutely articulated for me everything I needed to say . . . I was scruffy even then, and I had floppy hair. You must understand that if you live by yourself and you're eleven years old, ironing your shirts is not one of your big priorities.'

This record choice takes him back to a particular period of his life. 'Wainwright always brings back to me the smell of dog piss and leaking gas, as that was what the squat and Tufnell Park smelt of . . . I'd been taking drugs and I was not well, and doctors were giving me uppers and downers and sideways and everything, and I thought, "God, I can't go on like this!" I didn't have a job, but Loudon Wainwright kept me going.'

Sue Lawley notes, 'You got beaten a lot by the priests at school, and by your father. What for?'

'Because I suppose I was iconoclastic. I wasn't doing at all well. They thought I was bright, and as a result would try and beat me into doing well.'

But in some ways his father stood up for him. When in 1968 it was discovered that Geldof had been importing copies of Chairman Mao's Little Red Book to distribute around the school, his father was called in. 'He thought, "Oh God, what's he done now?" and they said, "Your son, Mr Geldof, has been caught importing illegal books." My father hit the roof and said: "You've had him for twelve years, indoctrinating him with your Catholicism. If you can't put a rational argument up against him . . . !"'

Record number four is John Lennon's 'In My Life'. 'My world wouldn't have been possible without the Beatles . . . My sister took me to see them in 1964 or something, when I was very small, and I remember extremely well the sound of the screaming and the smell, which was girls fainting and peeing themselves as they fainted, and the urine running down the green marbled linoleum of the Adelphi Cinema in Dublin.' ('There's a lot of urine in these records,' observes Sue Lawley.)

In the mid-1970s Bob Geldof formed the Boomtown Rats: 'It was Halloween night 1975, Bolton Street College of Technology in a classroom. We were standing on the teacher's desk and there were about twenty-two people in the room . . . I didn't even think of the name until the last five minutes before the gig.'

Fame and fortune followed. 'It was so fantastic. Between being on the dole and eighteen months later, to be in Barbados, with a beautiful blonde girl in a villa on the beach, with an LP at number two in the charts and a single at number six . . . I lay back on that beach, and thought about my life as being something so improbable that it was laughable, but so enjoyable. I had a platform – the fame thing wasn't huge to me, except that I had some means to shout about things.'

But the appeal of lying back on the beach does not last long: 'I'm very afraid of boredom, so I stay frenetically busy, to the point of irritating myself to death and exhaustion.'

The Beatles
'In My Life'

'I seriously doubt if I'd have been able to conduct my life as I've conducted it without them'

Given the impact of Live Aid, says Sue Lawley, has he considered going into mainstream politics? 'Being a sort of single issue, Live Aid was relatively easy to get an idea across . . . Being one of six-hundred-odd voices in Parliament, subject to party whips, would be like being in school again, and I know I couldn't subject myself to that. I would inevitably be one of whatever party's rebels, and therefore I wouldn't get any promotion, and so what are you consigned to? A voice of impotence, howling in the wilderness of the back benches . . . If I could implement actual change, then that would be all right, but I don't think you can implement actual change even at national government level.'

As for his luxury, Geldof has narrowed his choice down to two: 'If it's not too grand,' he says, 'I'd bring the Metropolitan Museum of New York.'

'I'm not sure we can transport it,' says Sue Lawley: 'I'm worried about that one.'

'Well, it's completely impractical to have, so I thought I was conforming to the rules there. And of course, my other alternative was a packet of three.'

Bob Geldof on the Live Aid stage, Wembley Stadium, July 1985

'Which you can't have because that's not – well, it's too practical, basically.'

'Well, not really: I mean, you can never be too safe, Sue! And as I absolutely expect my Ursula Andress to rise Venus-like from the waves—'

'Would you like to choose between the Metropolitan Museum of New York or a packet of three?'

'I think a packet of three is nice because it represents hope over any possibility of salvation. But on the other hand, I'd probably prefer to look at the Metropolitan Museum of New York, so I'll take the latter.'

Throughout the 1990s, Bob Geldof continued to campaign, notably for debt relief for developing countries. He revisited the Live Aid concept in 2005 with Live 8, concerts staged around the world in the run-up to the G8 gathering of the world's eight richest nations. Part of the Make Poverty History campaign, Live 8 aimed to raise not only money but also general awareness of the grave problems facing the African continent.

Among numerous awards and distinctions – including the Lyndon Baines Johnson Moral Courage Award – in 2006 and 2008 Geldof was nominated for the Nobel Peace Prize.

Opposite: As Maria von Trapp in The Sound of Music, *1965*

JULIE ANDREWS

actress and singer

18 October 1992

'My legs were very bandy and my teeth were very bad'

She was Eliza Doolittle, she was Mary Poppins and she was Maria von Trapp; she sang in the Royal Command Performance at the age of thirteen; she was a Broadway star while still in her teens; and she won an Academy Award with her first film. And yet Julie Andrews, a global megastar if ever there was one, floats on to the desert island as charming, as unassuming and – it's hard to avoid the adjective always attached to her – as wholesome as ever. How *does* she do it?

Born in Walton-on-Thames in 1935 and renowned for her extraordinary voice as a child, she made her Broadway debut in *The Boy Friend* at the age of nineteen and starred opposite Rex Harrison in the original New York production of *My Fair Lady*, which opened in 1956. Five years later she played Queen Guinevere in the Broadway production of *Camelot*.

The Academy Award for Best Actress came for the title role in that perennial favourite *Mary Poppins* in 1964 – the year in which she was first cast away, by Roy Plomley. She was nominated for a second Oscar for her performance in *The Sound of Music* (1965). Nearly half a century after its original release, a special showing of *The Sound of Music* can still pack out movie-houses with worshippers, every one of them waving an edelweiss and most of them dressed as nuns.

Julie Andrews has just celebrated her fifty-seventh birthday, and, obviously impressed by her youthful vitality, Sue Lawley ventures to ask how hard this castaway works at her appearance.

'Only as hard as I absolutely need to, to get me by,' replies Julie Andrews. 'I'm not a fanatic about exercise, although I do do it. I have to be careful what I eat, I have a tendency towards low blood sugar so actually it's stood me in good stead, because it makes me eat sensibly.'

And she has to work hard at keeping the clarity in her voice? 'Yes, and as you get older particularly you do, because it just isn't as flexible and as pliant as it used to be . . . I do anything that will get me by. If I'm preparing for a concert or an album or something like that then I will absolutely disappear and go to the piano and do my really dedicated practice and technique and things like that. But it could be as simple as singing in the car on my way to work, or to the children's school.'

How about the music? 'In choosing my selections, I suddenly discovered that I'm fairly romantic in nature, certainly in my choices, I think – and also very British. I mean, a lot of the things I've chosen were to remind me of England.'

First off is 'Amberley Wild Brooks' by John Ireland. Young Julie's mother 'used to sit in our lounge when I was quite a young child and play it very beautifully . . . In her youth she trained to be a concert pianist, and then life really turned for her. She lost both her parents and had to take care of her younger sister, who is my aunt, and I'm afraid the concert platform just disappeared for my mother. But she played so beautifully.'

Young Julie had a 'freak' voice – 'freaky in the sense that it was very, very long and thin, and incredibly powerful and strong. I had about a four-octave range and a sort of adult larynx and could do the most extraordinary vocal gymnastics with it.'

Julie's mother and stepfather had a vaudeville act.

In BBC Television's Showtime, *1949*

'They were very successful. They were always touring, and at the beginning I would go on and stand on the sort of orange box to reach the microphone beside my stepfather, and then eventually when I was about twelve I did one broadcast and one show that kind of kicked me into public attention, and it was such a huge success that I took off from there.'

That show was a Vic Oliver revue at the London Hippodrome, which led to an invitation to appear in the Royal Command Performance, singing for the Queen Mother and Princess Margaret.

Sue Lawley asks whether it was Julie's step-father Ted Andrews who was the driving force behind her career. 'I think it was probably the combination of Ted Andrews and my mother, really: probably my mother was influential in getting him to do the driving, if you know what I mean. She probably was a bit of a stage mum in that respect, but a good one.'

'But did you ever resent it?' asks Sue Lawley: 'Did you ever think, "Why do I have to do this? Why can't I just be a child?"'

'You would think that I would have resented it but I didn't, and looking back on it, I think that I was unconsciously so grateful to have a talent that gave me an identity. Because being from a divorced family and being rather lost and somewhat – without any self-pity – just a little bit lonely, I think, it was wonderful to have something to hang on to, and this gave me something to do, and this made me feel special and important, and I could sing and wow people and things like that. So I thought myself at the time the luckiest little girl in the world and had all this fun, staying up late and going to shows and performing.'

'But looking back on it,' says Sue Lawley, 'do you think there was an element of your fulfilling someone else's ambitions – perhaps your mother's or your step-father's?'

'I probably did fulfil some of my mother's ambitions. It wasn't such a bad thing because I've come to love it so. I now so enjoy what I do, and I love giving pleasure to people and making them forget that there's a problem world out there, or that the taxman's waiting, or whatever. So I don't knock it at all.'

Sue Lawley has unearthed a quotation from Julie Andrews in which the castaway has described herself as 'plain, buck-toothed, boss-eyed and bandy-legged'. Can this be right?

'Absolutely true. You can't imagine – it was an awful combination. So it's a good thing I was able to sing, right!'

But was she really so bad?

'I had one eye that wandered right into the corner and seemed to have a life of its own, no matter what I wanted it to do, and my legs were very bandy and my teeth were very bad. But ballet helped straighten the legs, and a good dentist helped straighten the teeth.'

In 1954 she went to Broadway to act in *The Boy Friend*, which in turn led to the plum role of Eliza Doolittle opposite Rex Harrison in *My Fair Lady*. The role was 'tremendously taxing, and I certainly learned a great deal about my own ability to hold up under pressure during that show'. But for the film of *My Fair Lady* she was passed over in favour of Audrey Hepburn: 'At the time I really did understand why Audrey was chosen, because I was only known on Broadway in those days. I wasn't known across the country. I wasn't a film star. I had never made a movie . . . But then it wasn't so tough, because very shortly afterwards, almost as the most wonderful compensation, Walt Disney asked if I would like to do *Mary Poppins*.'

She took the role, and won an Academy Award.

The following year – 1965 – brought the other defining Julie Andrews performance, as Maria von Trapp in *The Sound of Music*. (The real-life Maria von Trapp had been cast away by Roy Plomley in 1983.) 'It was very hard work,' recalls Andrews of the filming. 'Nobody told us that in Austria they have the world's seventh highest annual rainfall, and so we sat for many hours on mountains under tarpaulins, waiting for the sun to come out.'

Sue Lawley is curious to know how she feels about her roles in *Mary Poppins* and *The Sound of Music*. 'Are you heartily tired of the world believing that you are crisp and efficient and wholesome, or are you all those things?'

'I suppose a certain amount of that rubs off in one's performances, and perhaps there is that in me. I think that one gets bracketed, you see, by the things that one has done that were the most popular . . . I hope that these days the body of work speaks for itself . . . But I don't knock that image, because it did give so much pleasure.'

And yet, as Sue Lawley points out, the Julie Andrews career has not all been playing wholesome roles: 'You've appeared naked in the shower with Rock Hudson, you've bared your breast in *S.O.B.*, you've changed sex in

Victor, Victoria: I mean, what does a girl have to do to appear unwholesome – well, less than wholesome?'

Julie Andrews is married to director Blake Edwards ('Between us we have five children, and we have raised them all'), and the choice of Aaron Copland's *Rodeo* brings in a family moment which could almost come from *The Sound of Music* itself: 'When we are together as a family we quite often put on music, and there is a kind of unspoken understanding that at a certain moment in the record the entire family, especially myself and the kids, get up and tear around the dining room at a fast pace because it's so joyous, and one can't help but do it. We never actually said, "Let's go!" or "Let's do it!", but we all of us one day just got up and did it, and it's become a sort of ritual ever since.'

Although the family lives in Los Angeles and spends some time each year in Switzerland, 'I do feel very English. I know it's terribly corny, but I do feel a sort of responsibility to take what's best of England with me wherever I go, and sort of speak for England – a sort of silent ambassador, if you will, or vocal ambassador, I'm not sure which. It's important to me that we reach out to each other, and I think, "Well, if I can give a good image of my country wherever I go, then I've helped a little bit." It does sound Pollyanna-ish: I'd better shut up!'

Julie Andrews must never shut up, for her appeal – in her best-loved films and on the recording of *My Fair Lady*'s original Broadway run – is timeless and universal; and her voice remains familiar as Queen Lillian in the *Shrek* films. She was made DBE in the 2000 Honours List, and over the next few years was showered with lifetime achievement awards.

There was clearly an iron fist in the velvet glove, and Christopher Plummer, who played opposite Julie Andrews in *The Sound of Music*, reportedly described working with her as 'like being hit over the head with a Valentine's card'. A more generous summary came from *Time* magazine: 'She's everybody's tomboy tennis partner and their daughter, their sister, their mum . . . She is Christmas carols in the snow, a companion by the fire, a laughing clown at charades, a girl to read poetry to on a cold winter's night.'

Her husband Blake Edwards died in 2010.

Poulenc
Gloria

Brahms
Violin Concerto in D major
'The first LP I bought'

Beethoven
String Quartet no. 15 in A minor, op. 132

Wagner
Die Walküre, **Act I**
'I turned to Wagner as someone who suited the dark and apocalyptic mood I was in'

'Please Please Me'
The Beatles
'A welcome breath of fresh air'

Mozart
Requiem in D minor

Puccini
'O Principe, che a lunghe carovane' (from *Turandot*)

'Non, je ne regrette rien'
Édith Piaf
'That just about sums up my life'

Middlemarch **by George Eliot**

Crème brûlée

STEPHEN HAWKING
physicist
25 December 1992

'I want to know what happens to a black hole when it evaporates'

Internationally acclaimed for his work on black holes and author of one of the best-selling science books of all time, Stephen Hawking is one of the few scientists to have become a household name – despite the fact that precious few households include anyone who can even remotely understand the nature of his work.

Non-physicists might have an idea that he is concerned with something called gravitational field theory, and how black holes emit particles of thermal radiation now known as Hawking's Radiation (and therefore are not wholly black), but that is about as far as it goes. It is a tribute both to Hawking himself and to the thirst for knowledge on the part of his readers that his book *A Brief History of Time* was a phenomenal success, spending a record 237 weeks on the *Sunday Times* bestseller list in the years after its first publication in 1988.

Hawking was born in January 1942, proved a good but not outstanding pupil at school, then took his first degree at Oxford. For his postgraduate work he moved to Cambridge, where in 1979 he was appointed Lucasian Professor of Mathematics. Not long after his arrival in Cambridge he was diagnosed with a form of motor neurone disease which has confined him to a wheelchair ever since. In 1985 a tracheotomy removed what was left of his ability to speak, and he was fitted with a voice synthesizer.

The first *Desert Island Discs* interview in which the castaway spoke with a computer-generated voice was broadcast on Christmas Day 1992.

Cut off from normal physical life and deprived of natural means of communication with others, is Stephen Hawking – wonders Sue Lawley – already familiar with isolation?

'I don't regard myself as cut off from normal life and I don't think people around me would say I was. I don't feel a disabled person, just someone with certain malfunctions of my motor neurones, rather as if I were colour-blind. I suppose my life can hardly be described as usual, but I feel it is normal in spirit.'

Hawking's interviewer suggests that, unlike most castaways, he is already mentally and intellectually self-sufficient: 'But what about emotional fulfilment, Stephen? Even a brilliant physicist must need other people to find that?'

'I couldn't carry on with my life if I only had physics. Like everyone else, I need warmth, love and affection.'

Hawking recounts how seven years earlier he literally lost his voice after a life-threatening bout of pneumonia while in Switzerland. Flown back to Addenbrooke's Hospital in Cambridge, he underwent an operation which saved his life but took away the power of speech.

'For a time after my operation, I was devastated. I felt that if I couldn't get my voice back it was not worth carrying on.' But help was at hand in the shape of a California computer expert named Walt Woltosz: 'His mother-in-law had had the same condition as me, so he had developed a computer programme to help her communicate. A cursor moves across the screen. When it is on the option you want, you operate a switch by head or eye movement, or in my case by hand. And this way one can select words. When one has built up what one wants to say, one can send it to a speech synthesizer . . . My youngest son, who was only six at the time of my tracheotomy, never could make me out before. Now he has no difficulty. That means a great deal to me.'

Édith Piaf
'Non, je ne regrette rien'

'That just about sums up my life'

His father was a specialist in tropical diseases. 'I modelled myself on him because he was a scientific researcher. I felt that scientific research was a natural thing to do when one grew up. The only difference was that I was not attracted to medicine or biology because they seemed too inexact and descriptive. I wanted something more fundamental and I found it in physics.'

Hawking went to Oxford to read maths and physics. He claims to have worked just one hour a day – 'the physics course at Oxford at that time was ridiculously easy' – and filled the rest of the time with traditional student activities like rowing and drinking beer.

It was at Oxford that he first noticed a problem with his hands and feet. 'The first thing I noticed was that I couldn't row a sculling boat properly. And I had a bad fall down the stairs from the junior common room. I went to the college doctor after the fall because I was worried that I might have brain damage. However, he thought there was nothing wrong and told me to cut down on the beer.'

But his mother realized that there was something seriously amiss, and Stephen underwent extensive tests in hospital. 'They didn't tell me what the prospects were, but I guessed enough to know that they were pretty bad, so I didn't want to ask.'

Eventually he was told that he had around two years to live. 'There didn't seem any point in doing anything, or working on my PhD, because I didn't know I would live long enough to finish it. But then things started to improve. The condition developed more slowly, and I began to make progress in my work, particularly in showing that the universe must have had a beginning and a big bang.'

Sue Lawley points out that Hawking has claimed to be happier since falling ill than he was before. 'I certainly am happier now,' he confirms. 'Before I got motor neurone disease I was bored with life, but the prospect of an early death made me realize life was really worth living . . . I don't think motor

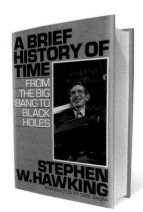

neurone disease can be an advantage to anyone, but it was less of a disadvantage to me than to other people, because it didn't stop me doing what I wanted, which was to try and understand how the universe operates.'

Hawking decided to write a book for a general readership – partly, but not primarily, because he needed the money. 'I thought I might make a modest amount from a popular book. The main reason I wrote *A Brief History of Time* was because I enjoyed it. I was excited about the discoveries that had been made in the last twenty-five years and I wanted to tell people about them. I never expected it to do as well as it did.'

'People buy it, obviously,' says Sue Lawley, 'but the question goes on being asked: do they read it?'

'All over the world, people tell me how much they have enjoyed it. They may not have finished it, or have understood everything they read, but they have at least got the idea that we live in a universe governed by rational laws that we can discover and understand.'

Back to basics. Sue Lawley asks: 'What would happen if you fell into a black hole?'

'Everyone who reads science fiction knows what happens if you fall into a black hole. You get made into spaghetti. But what is much more interesting is that black holes aren't completely black. They send out particles and radiation at a steady rate. This causes a black hole to evaporate slowly, but what eventually happens to the black hole and its contents is not known. This is an exciting area of research, but science fiction writers have not caught up with it yet.'

In his work, asks Sue Lawley, how far does he rely on intuition? 'I rely on intuition a great deal. I try to guess a result, but I then have to prove it. And at this stage, I quite often find that what I had thought of is not true, or that something else is the case, that I had never thought of. That is how I found black holes aren't completely black. I was trying to prove something else.'

Sue Lawley confesses that she is oversimplifying, but: 'You once believed, as I understand it, that there was a point of creation, a big bang. But you no longer believe that to be the case. You believe there was no beginning and that there is no end, that the universe is self-contained. Does that mean there was no active creation, and therefore there's no place for God?'

'Yes, you have oversimplified. I still believe the universe has a beginning in real time, at a big bang. But there's another kind of time, imaginary time, at right angles to real time, in which the universe has no beginning or end. This would mean that the way the universe began would be determined by the laws of physics. One wouldn't have to say that God chose to set a universe going, in some arbitrary way that we couldn't understand . . .

'You cannot deduce how one should behave from the laws of physics. But one could hope that the logical law that physics and mathematics involved would guide one also in one's moral behaviour.'

Stephen Hawking's story is an almost unbelievable one, as Sue Lawley comments: 'You've lived for thirty years longer than predicted. You've

Receiving the Presidential Medal of Freedom from President Obama, August 2009

fathered children you were told you'd never have. You've written a bestseller. You've turned age-old beliefs about space and time on their heads. What else are you planning to do before you quit this planet?'

'All that has been possible only because I have been fortunate enough to receive a great deal of help. I'm pleased with what I have managed to achieve, but there's a great deal more I would like to do before I pass on . . . Scientifically, I would like to know how one should unify gravity with quantum mechanics and the other forces of nature. In particular, I want to know what happens to a black hole when it evaporates.'

Back on *terra firma*, Stephen Hawking's item to bring him sheer pleasure is 'a large supply of crème brûlée: for me, that is the epitome of luxury'.

The year after his *Desert Island Discs* appearance, Stephen Hawking published a book of essays entitled *Black Holes and Baby Universes*, pushing further his attempt to make his ideas accessible. This was followed by other popularizing books such as *The Universe in a Nutshell* (2001), *On the Shoulders of Giants* (2002) and *A Briefer History of Time* (2005). In addition, he has written children's books with his daughter Lucy: *George's Secret Key to the Universe*, *George's Cosmic Treasure Hunt* and *George and the Big Bang* – at which many an adult has sneaked a look in the hope of finding complicated issues made simple.

He retired from the Lucasian chair in 2009, not long after Barack Obama had presented him with the Presidential Medal of Freedom, the highest civilian honour in the USA. But perhaps an even greater signal of Stephen Hawking's appeal is that he has made several appearances in cartoon form in *The Simpsons*.

FRANK BRUNO

boxer

6 June 1993

'Yes, boxing is dangerous, but lovemaking today is very, very dangerous'

Britain's most popular heavyweight boxer since Henry Cooper, Frank Bruno has endeared himself to the nation with his air of innocence, his wit and his trademark phrase 'Know what I mean?' (deployed twenty-seven times in the course of his *Desert Island Discs* interview).

The son of first-generation Caribbean immigrants, Frank was a wayward boy whose bursts of violent behaviour eventually got him sent to an approved school, where it was discovered that he had a talent for boxing. At eighteen he was national amateur heavyweight champion, and when he turned professional he won his first twenty-one bouts before eventually losing to James 'Bonecrusher' Smith in 1984. Thereafter he immediately started winning again, and in 1985 became European heavyweight champion. His first attempt at one of the three world heavyweight championships saw him lose to Tim Witherspoon in 1986, and in 1989 – after the three championships had been consolidated under one banner – he unsuccessfully challenged Mike Tyson for the undisputed world title: the referee stopped the contest in the fifth round.

When Bruno was washed up on the desert island shore, he had just those three blemishes on a professional record of thirty-nine fights. Such was the appeal of his personality, moreover, that he had already embarked on a parallel show-business career, with frequent appearances on television and in pantomime.

Sue Lawley remarks that Frank Bruno's sights are set on taking the World Boxing Council world heavyweight title from Lennox Lewis in a few months' time, before adding: 'Your life is a bit of a fairytale really. You left school with no qualifications, saying you wanted to be the heavyweight champion of the world and you wanted to be a multimillionaire. You're not the champion yet, but you're presumably a multimillionaire.'

Is the boxing ring, she asks, a terrifying place? 'Very much so, but – you know what I mean? – we've all got to do something in life. Boxing is very, very dangerous, but so are so many other sports, Sue . . . There's no room at all for fear. The fear is when you're training and leading up to the fight.'

Bruno has a strong religious faith – 'I believe in God, that's where I get most of my strength from' – and he makes the sign of the cross before each round.

'But isn't that really very difficult,' wonders Sue Lawley, 'to ask God to

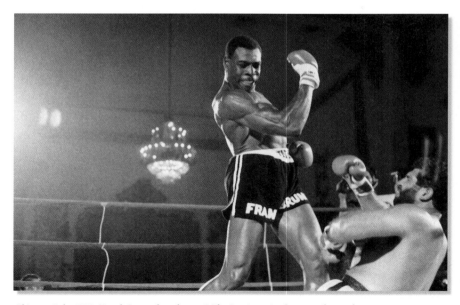

Chicago, July 1983: Frank Bruno knocks out Mike Jamieson in the second round

help you to beat the living daylights out of another man?'

'I'm not asking God for me to beat him up – just getting my strength from the man I believe in.'

Back to Bruno's childhood. He went to what he calls 'boarding school' at the age of eleven, and Sue Lawley notes that it was 'a special school – what we used to call an approved school.' Why was he sent there?

'My mum says that I was a bit of a bully, and that I just kept fighting a lot and I was just out of order.' If so, it is hardly surprising, as he was regularly beaten by his father: 'He beat me black and blue, and when I knew I'd done something, I would rather sleep out in the garden than go in and see him. But I deserved it, and I don't regret him beating me. I wished he would have beat me a little bit more – might have beat some sense into me. You know what I mean?'

'What did he beat you with?'

'He beat me with the curtain rail, his shoes, the belt, his hands: he really did steam into me. But it was a good cause he steamed into me for. He wasn't just beating me for the sake of beating me, but I was really out of order. I was big for my age, and thought I could throw my weight around. So I went to a boarding school and I got beaten up so badly that I knocked it on the head.'

At Oak Hall School they did all sorts of sport ('canoeing, walking, water-skiing, running, cricket, football, athletics, you name it, we'd done it'), but boxing proved his salvation, and Bruno became head boy. 'I think Oak Hall taught me about discipline, respecting people, getting up in the morning and looking after yourself, survival in life in general.'

His career as an amateur boxer was short and spectacular, but before he could turn professional he had to have corrective surgery on one eye – which made his eyes a target for opponents. 'People know you've had an operation and they try to go for that.'

How great is the fear of being knocked senseless? 'Sue, the fear is not there. Yes, boxing is dangerous, but lovemaking today is very, very danger-ous, buying a house is very stressful and dangerous, you know what I mean? – anything you do in life is very, very dangerous. It depends on how deep you want to go into the danger of what you're doing.'

'Well,' says Sue Lawley, 'I think you feel fairly deep into it when you're standing in the ring with somebody who is sixteen or seventeen stone – the same as you are. Boxing is a dangerous sport, and you can end up with your brain a bit addled.'

'Well, my brain was addled before I went in there, so it might do me a favour – you know what I mean – might put a little bit of sense in there, Sue – you know what I mean?'

The next piece of music is 'Tell Laura I Love Her', for his wife. 'I am married to a lady called Laura, and I think she's the best thing since sliced bread to me personally, if you know what I mean. And I'd like to dedicate the record to her, Sue' – and then a moment of self-mocking – 'if you know what one means'.

He met Laura at Battersea roller-skating park. She pinched his bottom – 'That's right, she pinched my big black ass!' – and they now have two daughters and have recently moved into a large house.

Sue Lawley observes that 'it's got stables' – which triggers a little teasing from her guest: 'It's got stables, it's got a toilet, it's got lights' – and a large garden: 'When the weather's nice you can get a wicked tan out there.'

As for his daughters: 'I try and be strict with them. You see, I was away from my family and my home, so I missed most of my childhood of growing up with my Mum and my family and all those sort of things.'

When in training for a fight he can lose as much as nine pounds of liquid in a session – 'I lost a stone once when I went to America, and that was the weirdest thing in a day' – and his diet is prodigious, though 'I try to eat common sense: pasta, fish, salad'.

Dennis Brown
'Wonderful World'

'We can live in a wonderful world'

What might he eat for an average breakfast? 'Some Alpen, some cornmeal porridge, egg, bacon, sausages sometimes, steak sometimes, liver and bacon, toast sometimes, water, a lot of fruit, grapes . . . It's a huge meal, but if you put a lot in, you know what I mean, you got to put something in the tank.'

Still on the theme of Bruno's training routine, Sue Lawley suggests: 'There comes a point, presumably, when you have to cut off relationships – personal relationships?'

This is an open goal for Bruno in mischievous mode. 'Are you talking about sex now, Sue? At the end of the day, are you beating about the bush?'

'I wasn't actually. I was meaning that you've got to stop even thinking about other people . . . You've got to be single-minded . . . We can think about sex now with the next record—'

'Oh, Marvin Gaye – "Sexual Healing"– but you know that's good at night time when you haven't got a headache, Sue – you know what I mean? Good record, Sue, that's all I've got to say – leave the rest to your imagination.'

Sue Lawley has rarely had a castaway stray into these waters, and it is a relief to get back to boxing. When he fought Mike Tyson, had he had a real chance?

'I had a chance. I think people didn't give me a chance one little bit, but I rocked him, and they said I should have followed up. I was trying to follow up, but it's not easy when you're in there with someone like him. It's easy to say from outside, but – and I don't want to make excuses – he beat me fair and square.'

After the Tyson fight Bruno was out of the ring for nearly three years: 'I was just trying to suss out my life. I had a few problems here and there and I didn't know what I was going to do, so I just chilled out for a little bit.'

Now back in action, he's changing his psychology: 'Be a bit more hungry, be a bit more vicious when I get in there. Because it's a vicious sport, boxing. It's show business with blood.'

Could he cope on the island? 'I think I could cope by myself. I used to cope before I met Laura. I used to do my washing for myself, I used to do a little bit of cooking for myself. Once I met Laura she spoilt me, but if I had to go back there I think I'd survive.' Is he good with his hands? 'Very, very good with my hands. I used to be a carpenter at school, and I could build with tree sticks, and light a fire and survive.'

Is he frightened of anything? 'I don't like mice or things like that.' What if a mouse came into his shelter? 'If I was hungry, I might season it up and cook it.'

As for the upcoming championship bout, 'I've got the tools, I've got the experience, and I've got the power to beat Lennox Lewis.'

When Sue Lawley suggests that Bruno has to say that – 'it's a bit like politicians' – her castaway becomes defensive: 'I haven't got to say that, Sue, because I haven't got to box at this moment . . . I'm comfortable in my life.'

Bruno becomes more edgy – 'I didn't have to come on this programme' – then apologizes for being aggressive: 'I have said things because I wanted to say them. I'm not saying them for hype. I'm not saying them because I'm trying to butter up someone. All I'm trying to do is talk from my heart and say it as it is.'

So he is genuinely confident about beating Lewis? 'Very, very confident. I don't have to say that, Sue, but I'm saying that because you asked me a question and I'm trying to relay, in my sort of way, as down to earth as much as possible – I'm not saying things because I have to say them.'

Were he to win, how long would he then continue? 'My ambition is to get it, defend it once and get the monkeys out of here.'

And were he to lose? 'I don't really think about losing – because losing is a very bad word.'

The fight between Frank Bruno and Lennox Lewis for the WBC world heavyweight title took place four months after Bruno's *Desert Island Discs* appearance. Lewis won on a technical knock-out in round seven. But Lewis then lost his title to Oliver McCall, and Frank Bruno finally got his hands on the WBC world heavyweight title when beating McCall in September 1995. Six months later his first defence of that title brought him up against Mike Tyson for the second time. Tyson won in round three, and Bruno did not fight again.

Frank and Laura divorced in 2001, and 2003 brought the revelation that Bruno had been suffering from depression – which may or may not have been related to the 'few problems here and there' referred to in his interview with Sue Lawley. He had been diagnosed with bipolar disorder – an uncomfortable flipside to the popular notion of Frank Bruno as the jolly innocent abroad, the champion boxer who teased Sue Lawley more than most *Desert Island Discs* castaways would have dared.

'Know what I mean, Sue?'

BETTY BOOTHROYD

Speaker of the House of Commons

13 June 1993

'I think I came out of the womb into the labour movement'

A star was born when in April 1992 Betty Boothroyd became Speaker of the House of Commons, the first female Speaker in history and the first from the opposition benches – she was a Labour MP, and the government was Conservative – since 1835. A passionate believer in the importance of the Commons in British public life, and blessed with a warm, generous and humorous personality, she was popular with MPs and the general public alike, and the strident tones in which she controlled the sometimes unruly chamber made hers one of the best-known voices in the land.

Betty Boothroyd was born in October 1929 in Dewsbury, Yorkshire. Interested in politics from an early age, she first stood for Parliament in 1957, but it was not until 1973 that she was finally elected – as Labour MP for West Bromwich. Fourteen years later in 1987 she became Deputy Speaker, and it was at this point that, on being asked by an MP how she should be formally addressed in the House, she famously replied: 'Call me Madam.'

The first duty of the Speaker is to control the House of Commons, and Sue Lawley wonders where her

At Westminster, 1959

castaway got her disciplinarian streak: 'Is there a lot of your mother in you? Do you handle difficult MPs like she might have scolded you – told you off for being stubborn or bloody-minded?'

'Not my mother,' replies Madam Speaker: 'I think my father was more the disciplinarian. I was brought up in a very disciplined household, and I think perhaps I follow my father in terms of being disciplined about timing, duty, that sort of thing.'

'People who get elected to the House of Commons', says the castaway of her fellow MPs, 'have been through very tough battles within their own party to get themselves established and with the electorate in order to be elected, and they come there with very robust views. They want to set the Thames on fire. They want to make themselves heard, so there is a lot of robust argument goes on, and I have to find a method of allowing them to do that while at the same time rein them in once they've gone a bit too far. And that's when the discipline comes in.'

Betty Boothroyd's career did not begin in politics. The first record choice – the Can-Can – leads inevitably to talk of the episode of Betty Boothroyd's life which has always intrigued people. 'Tell me,' says Sue Lawley: 'you did go south, and you did join a dance troupe?'

'Yes I did. When I was young and at home I'd always been at dancing class and thoroughly enjoyed it. I wanted to be a professional, and my mother took me to the Tiller School, where I was accepted. All you had to do was high kicks and the splits, and smile at the same time. And I was in pantomime [at the London Palladium] for the short winter season . . . I enjoyed it, but it was the very bad winter of 1947: cold, not much food around. I'd been cosseted at home, and I soon left and went back to Yorkshire.' But the experience was not wasted: 'I think it had prepared me for quite a lot later in my life, actually.'

Both her parents worked in the textile business – when there was work, that is. 'My father was unemployed a good deal . . . He did the housework for my mother. But what he would do, he would draw the curtains, so that the neighbours wouldn't see a man scrubbing the floors . . . In the winter, we all of us wanted snow. We would turn off the electric light, we would sit in the firelight and talk. We'd save a bit of money that way, and we would pray for snow so that my father got a job from the Corporation shovelling snow the next morning.'

Betty got a scholarship to Dewsbury College, 'where I was taught the things that enabled me to earn a living: shorthand, typing, mathematics, English grammar, all of those sorts of things'.

When had politics entered her life? 'I think I came out of the womb into the labour movement. My parents were involved very much at a local level, our front room was always given over to Labour Party meetings, as well as to wakes and weddings and things like that, and it was the committee room on polling day. So I was brought up in the labour movement and I was in the League of Youth as soon as I was fifteen or sixteen years old.'

After returning to London in the early 1950s she found a job working as a secretary in the House of Commons for Labour MPs Geoffrey de Freitas and Barbara Castle – 'they were enormously supportive' – and decided to try to get elected herself.

It took sixteen years, but eventually she became MP for West Bromwich at a 1973 by-election. 'I have today in the study in Speaker's House a wonderful photograph taken at two o'clock in the morning, where I certainly don't look tired and nor did my very aged mother, and she's giving me a spanking kiss on the cheek. It is a wonderful photograph . . . just full of sparkle and life, and I see it every day of my life, and remember that wonderful day.'

The Speaker must be above party politics, which means that Betty Boothroyd is denied the social cut-and-thrust of the gossip-laden Commons bars and tea-rooms. On the other hand, her tied cottage is the grandeur of Speaker's House. 'It's very fine and impressive,' says Sue Lawley, 'but it is very formal: you must therefore be really quite lonely on occasions?'

'The loneliness that I occasionally feel is in decision-making. At the end of the day when you've listened to all the advice – and it is very good advice that is given to me – I have to make the decision. The buck stops with me, and it's in that decision-making that I sometimes find a loneliness.'

In her pre-election speech, she had exhorted MPs: 'Elect me for what I am, not for what I was born.' What had she meant by that?

Plácido Domingo
'Dein ist mein ganzes Herz'

'This melts my heart and it brings me to order'

'"Elect me because you know me. I have been your deputy for a very long time. You know I am fair. You know I am just. Elect me for what I am, and what you know of me in that respect – not for what I was born, a woman."'

In her rise to the top, she is said not to have made enemies. 'I hope that is right. I don't set out to make enemies. I don't want to rise to stardom. I just want to do a job. I'm really terribly proud of the fact that I'm Speaker. It really is tremendous for womankind and it's wonderful for my constituency . . . It almost brings tears to my eyes with the pride I have in doing that job and the faith that people have in me, and therefore I have got to do it well. I don't want stardom. I just want to be known as a jolly good Speaker. And a nice girl, and somebody who has been very fair and just all round.'

Does she, wonders Sue Lawley, ever have moments of blind panic when the House is getting out of control? 'I do have moments like that, and all I can do then is to remain standing, to call order, to demand order – and of course if I didn't get it I would have to suspend, but I haven't had occasion to do that as yet.'

Betty Boothroyd lives alone; does she regret not having married? 'I didn't decide against it. I was very active when I worked in the House of Commons. I'd great opportunities to travel with parliamentary delegations, which I did, to most places in Europe and to the Far East and China and Vietnam, and of course I was fighting elections and by-elections. It's not every man who's going to wait until you've finished all that you want to do like that. They're going to find some other girl. So I think the timing wasn't right for me. I wasn't against it, it just didn't come at the right time.'

On the island, will she be able to look after herself? 'In terms of food, if there were any leaves around that I could chew on or grasses, that's what I would do.'

Sue Lawley helpfully suggests that 'you could always shout down a passing ship, you've had some practice at shouting'.

'I would yell – yes!' – and here comes the phrase which will forever be attached to Betty Boothroyd, and in those ringing Yorkshire tones: 'Order! Order!'

But she has a cleverer way of being found: 'My luxury is going to be the Mace of the House of Commons. I'm being rather cunning because I think that if I had the Mace with me, then the Serjeant-at-Arms would send out the navy and the air force to find the Mace, and I would be rescued.'

Betty Boothroyd stepped down as Speaker of the House of Commons and as an MP in October 2000, and in 2001 was created a life peer: she sits on the cross-benches of the House of Lords as Baroness Boothroyd of Sandwell. Her autobiography was published in 2001 to wide acclaim – none more complimentary than that of the *Times* reviewer, who noted that 'somehow Betty Boothroyd came to transcend politics . . . a British institution'.

JOAN BAEZ

singer

20 June 1993

'They figured as soon as I didn't salute the American flag I must be a pinko, a Commie'

A few weeks before being washed up on the desert island, Joan Baez had played in the besieged city of Sarajevo, the first major artist to perform in that stricken place since the beginning of the conflicts which followed the break-up of the former Yugoslavia.

It was an appropriate venue for a singer whose music has always been linked with her deep-rooted concern for human rights and social justice. In the 1960s she marched with Martin Luther King and withheld her taxes in protest against the Vietnam War, and she has remained committed to social and environmental issues ever since.

Joan Baez first came to prominence at the Newport Folk Festival in 1959, and from the early 1960s became an international star through songs such as 'There But for Fortune', 'Diamonds and Rust', Bob Dylan's 'Farewell Angelina' and especially that anthem of the Civil Rights movement, 'We Shall Overcome'. Her extensive covering of Dylan songs was instrumental in establishing his reputation through the mid-1960s, and they had a close though not always smooth relationship for many years. (According to an interview she gave to one of Dylan's biographers, on their first meeting after a Dylan gig, 'I said "far out" or "beautiful" and Bobby mumbled, "Hey, hey, too much"' – a curiously downbeat exchange between two of the great spokespeople for the 1960s generation.)

Having established that her surname is pronounced differently in different countries – it should be a monosyllable, but that is 'not in the priorities of things that concern me' – Joan Baez is asked by Sue Lawley whether she is a completely different person from her 1960s persona. Then she had 'long black hair and a very earnest, rather solemn face, and today you've got short stylish hair and you're all smiles'.

'I'm very different. Many people are stuck in some way in the sixties, and when they see me or hear me they identify immediately with their time in the sixties. I don't think I had that good a time in the sixties. I mean I was very, very serious about my work, and I was popping in and out of jail, and doing demonstrations and I was stimulated by it all and I'm glad I did all of it. But I didn't have a great deal of fun.'

Her mother was Scottish, her father – a university lecturer in physics – Mexican Spanish. Joan is the middle of three sisters.

Even at school, she knew her own mind. 'I had much more clarity about my feelings about non-violence and social political change than I did about music and about most other things in my life. By the time I was fifteen I had stopped saluting the flag – any flag, which of course nobody understood, because they figured as soon as I didn't salute the American flag I must be a pinko, a Commie. Then we had an air-raid drill in our high school . . . I went home to my father's physics books and found out how long it took for a mis-sile to get from Moscow to Palo Alto High School and realized it was a hoax! I'd suspected it was a hoax, but then I had proof in hand. So when the bell rang, and everyone went dashing home to have what they were calling their 'bomb parties' in their swimming pools, I stayed in school to protest, and that was really the beginning of a very visible career of non-violent action.'

She had been given a ukulele, and started entertaining her classmates. 'It was a way I could communicate with everybody . . . I know I was a terrific little flirt, but at the same time, what came to my mind was that girls' clique in junior high school that I wanted so badly to be a part of. And so it was pretty much to those girls that I started with my little ukulele at noon-time, entertaining them. I would do imitations of Elvis Presley and whoever else was currently being heard on the radio. And I was accepted in a certain way, which was better than not being accepted at all. It was kind of a little bit of a court jester but it was better than nothing.'

And she taught herself to warble: 'I wanted a vibrato in my little voice, which was straight as a pin.' So she experimented with manipulating her Adam's apple with her finger, and eventually the vibrato started to come – 'and then pretty soon after that, I couldn't sing without the vibrato.'

Her mother considered her voice a gift from God. Does she too see it as a gift? 'I do. Absolutely. I don't think it has the slightest thing to do with me. All I try to do is maintenance, and offer it in the most useful and soulful ways that I can.'

Joan Baez's appearance at the 1959 Newport Folk Festival in Rhode Island is one of the landmark occasions in the history of folk music. 'I was absolutely terrified! I could feel the leather thongs on my Jesus sandals and my knees shaking just above that. I had terrible stage fright for years, and I think if I were walking to the guillotine it wouldn't feel any different.'

Sue Lawley suggests that in the early 1960s, Joan Baez was the right person in the right decade. 'Absolutely right . . . I had started singing ballads and was known for that, and within two or three years, it was Bob Dylan, contemporary music, and then travelling around in the South and singing with Dr King . . . We reflect the times; the music reflects the times; the times reflect the music. It all bounces back and forth, and these radical changes happen when places are politically charged. The United States was as politically charged as I have ever known it in the early Sixties, with the Civil Rights Movement and then the war in Vietnam.'

How well had she known Martin Luther King? 'I knew him some. I was in on some of the fun times . . . He was terribly funny, and laughed and joked, but like other people in that kind of position, he was I think afraid to do that in public, so you don't see pictures of him, or see footage of him just smiling.'

But had her political position been compromised by her being rich and famous? 'I didn't have so much money. I just kept giving it all away. I didn't think I was supposed to have money. I can remember sitting in a house when I was about twenty-five years old, just writing out cheques. I mean, anybody who wrote and asked for money, I'd send them something. Anywhere from a five-dollar cheque to two thousand.' And she went through a phase of buying cars for people: 'It just made me deliriously happy to come tootling up in a new Whatever-It-Was and turn the keys over to somebody.'

She first met Bob Dylan in 1961, when they were both twenty – though Sue Lawley notes that 'you were a much bigger star than him at the time'. What were her first impressions of him?

Bob Dylan and Joan Baez, 1965

'People had told me about this incredible guy writing these incredible songs. He was just scruffier than I had pictured. He was very scruffy, but what they said about the songwriting to me was true. I guess I saw him for the first time in Gerde's Folk City, which is where one went in New York to hear local folk music. And he sang, "Blowin' in the Wind" that night, so history makes itself . . . I adored his music and I adored him.'

Were they in love? 'I don't know that I was capable of that, but it was certainly a happy match for a while. He was very creative during the short time that we were together – and I was going around stealing his songs. I mean literally. "Four-Letter Word" he wrote, then dropped behind a piano somewhere and forgot about it. And I retrieved it, in my own house, and I learned it, and I guess a year later was singing it, and he said, "Hey, that's a great song, where's that from?" – "You wrote it, you dope!"'

One of Joan Baez's record choices is herself singing 'Diamonds and Rust'. Is that song about her and Dylan? 'For years I wouldn't say who it was written about, and there was this funny moment when I went on the Rolling

Performing at an anti-Vietnam War demonstration in Trafalgar Square, May 1965

Thunder tour with Bob. "Diamonds and Rust" had come out fairly recently, and he said – we're all such egomaniacs, he said, "Are you going to do that new one, that diamonds thing?" I said, "Oh, you mean that one I wrote about my husband?" And it just stopped him dead in his tracks, and I burst out laughing. I said, "Only teasing, Bob!" I couldn't resist.'

Why had she gone to Bosnia earlier that year? 'I went to Sarajevo because somebody said, "The people in Sarajevo have asked you to come and try and lift their spirits after a year of siege" . . . and so of course I went, and they lifted *my* spirits! . . . It's *their* courage, it's their astounding behaviour in this disgusting situation that fed my spiritual, moral, all of my needs.'

Joan Baez says that how she will spend her time on the desert island depends on whether she has a horse or not, but Sue Lawley quickly squashes that idea. And since a horse cannot be her luxury, what inanimate object or objects will she take? 'There's a little amethyst stone from Mexico that reminds me about one part of my life. There's a patchy tear stone that my son gave me, and I carry in this little pouch. In fact, I would just take this pouch as it is, and I'd put those things there . . . It has a silver lion in it, and the lion will protect me on the beach.'

Joan Baez has continued performing throughout the two decades since she was cast away, her singing career now spanning half a century. In 2007 she received the Grammy Lifetime Achievement Award; the following year she appeared at the Glastonbury Festival; and in August 2009 she returned to Rhode Island to play at the Newport Folk Festival, fifty years after the performance which launched her career.

Blessed with a rare purity of tone, the voice of Joan Baez is one of the most distinctive of her generation. Her repertoire may have diversified considerably since her early days, but her commitment to social justice remains unchanged – like the crystal-clear glory of her singing.

KENNY EVERETT

comedian and DJ

24 October 1993

'There I was in Frinton railway station with my bag full of hankies and Y-fronts and toothpaste, off to board this tub'

'Wacky', 'zany', 'anarchic', 'surreal' – Kenny Everett has been described as all of these, and all fitted his unique style of broadcasting.

Born Maurice Cole in 1944 – his mother liked the name Maurice because it sounded posh – he was the son of a tug-boat captain on the Mersey. At a very early age he took to experimenting with his Kiddie-Gram record player, and later compiled comedy tapes for circulation among his friends – which in due course led to his joining the pirate radio station Radio London, then Radio Luxembourg, and then in 1967 the BBC: Radio 1 before television. His best-remembered television series was *The Kenny Everett Video Show* in 1978, which featured outrageous characters such as the movie star Cupid Stunt (who did everything 'in the best *possible* taste'), the hairdresser Marcel Wave, and one of Everett's old favourites, Captain Kremmen.

Kenny Everett – or at least the public Kenny Everett – was one of those people never more than a few seconds away from putting on a silly voice, and his interview with Sue Lawley crackles with shifts through the vocal

gears, from the way he booms out the name of the American evangelist who brought about his first sacking – 'GARNER! TED! ARMSTRONG!' – to the plummy tones of the BBC executive who has to inform him, 'Kenny, it's time for the parting of the ways . . .'

Introducing her castaway, Sue Lawley notes how Kenny Everett's personality has 'proved irrepressible' through various professional setbacks – and, much more seriously, through the experience of learning earlier that year that he is HIV positive. He faces the prospect of death philosophically: 'My sense of humour', he has said, 'will probably be the last thing to go.'

Does he worry every time he gets ill? 'Every now and then I think about the absolute end of everything, and that gets me for about a second, and then I say, "Stop it!" . . . I could get run over by a truck tomorrow. So could you, Sue. What's the point of thinking about it? . . . I think if I got a cold and it wouldn't go away, I would think, "Dear God, just please make it fast!" I think it's the lingering that goes with this that's the awful bit.'

As a teenager he became a big fan of radio, especially the BBC Home Service: 'I used to listen right up until the end, because that's when the announcer used to get intimate, when he thought the Director General wasn't listening because he was tucked up in bed, he'd sort of ad lib, and say, "Well, I can see the gas lamps are flickering in Portland Place, it's time to wrap up for the night." He'd have a little chat with the listener, and I always used to stay up for that bit because it sounded quite cosy. So I always wanted to be a DJ.'

Sue Lawley mentions that Kenny was something of a mechanical wizard: 'You were putting together tapes and things in your bedroom, weren't you?'

'Yes. I had a paper round, and with the proceeds I bought two tape machines, and used to make silly programmes for my friends.'

'You wired up the house with loudspeakers, and pretended to be the radio to your Mum?'

'Yes. I banned her from listening to the BBC. She had to listen to my channel. Only had an audience of two! Still have, actually!'

He sent one of his compilation tapes to the BBC, who – so he says – replied: 'Darling, come immediately!' He did. 'I said, "Wow, you've got carpets that go right to the edge! I want to work here!", but they said, "Well, we haven't got any jobs at the moment here, because there's Pete Murray and David Jacobs, and that's all we need really."'

Then he approached Radio London, one of the offshore pirate radio stations, and the next day, 'there I was in Frinton railway station with my bag

Opposite: *'Cupid Stunt' from* The Kenny Everett Television Show, *December 1981*

full of hankies and Y-fronts and toothpaste, off to board this tub'.

While bouncing around in the North Sea he had something of a coup: 'We got a little tug that used to come out and deliver records, and water, and food and things. One day, out came Brian Epstein's personal assistant with a freshly minted copy of "Strawberry Fields Forever" / "Penny Lane", and I was on the air at the time, and because Brian Epstein liked the pirates so much, he just gave it to me to play – and I was the first person in the world to play this glorious record!'

Sue Lawley takes Kenny back to his childhood on Merseyside, where one of his bad memories is how 'people want to thump you . . . You walk into a bar and you look at somebody for more than a split second and they'd say, "What the bloody hell are you looking at?" – and before you know it, your face is all over the floor.'

'You were shy and spindly, and worried a lot of the time. You were a loner – and worried about being bullied?'

'About everything – and how, if there was a God, why did he make me so thin and spindly?'

'And you were terrified of God?'

'Yes, well, I was brought up a Catholic. If you do something slightly naughty, you go to purgatory for an awful long time, and it's really awful! It's really bad. But if you commit one of this list of sins, and you don't get to Confession in time, you'll go to Hell for ever! And Hell is unimaginable agony, for ever! Fancy telling that to a kid. It's outrageous!'

'Sid Snot'

His great consolation was the radio: 'I used to love listening to the announcers. They were so friendly, and they didn't say, "What the bloody hell are you lookin' at?" They used to say, "Hello! What a lovely record this is!" They used to actually talk like nice people. So I thought that was very appealing.'

Also appealing for young Kenny was the prospect of being in bed: 'I think one of the great thrills of life is being in bed, gener- ally. But in the old days it was even more of a thrill, because the surroundings were not quite as fabulous as they are now, and so I used to look forward to going to bed madly, unlike most kids. I used to go to bed with my little transistor radio, which had just appeared then, and it was a little Philips red plastic thing, with a little grating on the front, and I used to take it to bed with me and listen to Radio Luxembourg. At the end of the broadcast, after David Jacobs had finished playing 'Da Doo Ron Ron' or whatever, they used to have this glorious piece of music to finish off the day's broadcasting. It was an English guy called Steve Conway with a very simple, beautiful tune called 'At the End of the Day' with a choir and everything. It was just like Ovaltine for your ears. It was such a lovely tune to end the day' – and to play on his desert island.

The Kenny Everett Video Show, *1985*

While at Radio London, observes Sue Lawley, Kenny 'developed a talent for getting sacked'.

His first removal concerned 'this taped thing from America, from a man called Garner Ted Armstrong. He used to have a show called *The World Tomorrow*. It was half an hour on tape, sent to radio stations all around the world, where you get the programme and he pays you, like, fifty pounds a night to broadcast it. It's an evangelical thing, and he tells you what horrors are in store on this planet if you don't buy his magazine.' Naturally enough, Kenny did not take kindly to his show being interrupted by this apocalyptic vision, and made uncomplimentary remarks about it on air. As luck would have it, Garner Ted Armstrong was in England, caught some of Kenny's remarks, and demanded he be sacked.

'It was a question of whether the radio station thought it was worth getting rid of me and keeping the fifty pounds a night, or vice versa, and they chose the fifty pounds a night. That was my first introduction to commercial thinking.'

He moved to the BBC – and was again sacked, after making what was deemed an inappropriate joke about a transport minister's wife having finally passed her driving test by bribing the examiner: 'People were so touchy in those days. I mean, nowadays you can get away with anything,

Bouncing back to the BBC, 1981

because the BBC softened up and people have become more outrageous.'

'Well, you told quite a dirty joke about Mrs Thatcher when you got sacked the second time,' says Sue Lawley about a later departure, 'which you needn't repeat now.'

Kenny says that he was handed that joke by his producer while on air, and had not read the punchline before speaking it. 'But,' asks Sue Lawley, 'did the adrenaline pump when you knew you were going to say or do something that was a bit risqué?'

'Oh, yes. When you're going to say something slightly naughty, half of your brain is saying, "Don't do it!" and the other half is saying, "Oh, but I'll get noticed! And then I might get a few job offers, because I'm bound to get fired." In fact, the first time I got fired from the BBC, the man rang me up, the General Director of Programmes, or something, and he said, [posh BBC tones] "Kenny, it's time for the parting of the ways." I said, "Oh, all right, cheerio!" – because I had just got a contract from London Weekend Television that very day, saying, "Why don't you come and do a huge series of television programmes for us?" So you see, one thing leads to another.'

The fourth of his record choices is one of his own 'Captain Kremmen' programmes: 'On commercial radio, I started doing a silly space serial, because since the days of the *Eagle* annual and "Dan Dare: Pilot of the Future" I'd always been a huge space fan. I used to make this silly serial in my Cotswold home studio, the night before I went on the air, which is Friday night. I used to think up a lot of silly space gags, stitch them together into a script and then go to bed. Next morning at seven o'clock, I would get up, go into the studio with a cup of coffee, do all the voices, put music on, edit it together and put it on to a tape. Then jump in the car about ten o'clock and drive hell for leather to London, to the radio station, and then stick it in the hole in the machine, and say, "Hello folks, it's twelve o'clock!", and press the button. I'd just done it, so it was nice and fresh and I'd actually sit there and laugh at it because I hadn't heard the jokes before.'

Kenny Everett was married for many years: 'I thought maybe if I married this jolly lady, with whom I was great friends, maybe one day I'd wake up and look at her and it would snap, and I'd think, "Oh, I get it!": you know, the shape and the lumps, the softness and everything, suddenly it would all fall into place. But I realized a lot later that you are what you're born. If you're born gay, then you're gay for ever.'

'But when you were first coming to terms with all of that, what were you feeling? Were you feeling shame, or fear?'

'Well, yes, because I'd been brought up to think that it was a huge sin. I thought I'm going to go to Hell for ever.'

In the 1980s he took his inimitable personality to television with *The Kenny Everett Video Show*. It had been hugely popular, but he found television uncomfortable – and besides, on radio 'you don't have to wear half as much make-up'.

Kenny Everett now lives on his own, and is impeccably tidy. Sue Lawley has read that 'you even hoover the plastic grass on the balcony'.

'Not only that, Sue, I found myself going a little too far a few weeks ago: I found myself polishing the hoover! It's got to stop!'

Kenny Everett's last record is Puccini's *Symphonic Prelude*, 'because it's just the most beautiful record I've ever heard. If I ever do die, I think as I'm hoiked aloft in a ray of God's lovely sunbeam, I'd like this to be on the gramophone as I go . . . I think I'd like to die serene. I haven't been very serene in this life. It's been a sort of a turmoil-ish sort of life, going on in front of cameras and being silly and potty. I think I'd like to try a bit of serenity.'

Kenny Everett's luxury is a bathroom suite – 'because I don't want to be dirty on my desert island. I feel very uncomfortable if I don't wash for at least a day. So I'll have to have a hot shower, limitless hot water and a lifetime's supply of Badedas, Sue.'

'It shall be done.'

Kenny Everett survived for only eighteen months after his unforgettable appearance on *Desert Island Discs*. He died of an AIDS-related illness in April 1995.

JEANETTE WINTERSON

writer

9 October 1994

'It was a fantastic shock to find out that some people thought that falling in love with another girl was not the thing to do'

"When my mother was angry with me, which was often, she said, "The Devil led us to the wrong crib."" Thus begins Jeanette Winterson's sparkling memoir *Why Be Happy When You Could Be Normal?*, published in 2011. Mrs Winterson is Jeanette's adoptive mother, a religious zealot convinced that the Almighty has brought her this child as a mouthpiece for his divine word – and one of the great offstage characters of *Desert Island Discs* history.

Castaways never come to the island completely alone. Each brings along an attendant retinue of family, remembered friends, ghosts and other influences, some of whom loom large in the interview – and few larger than Jeanette Winterson's mother.

As for Mrs Winterson's daughter, she is a writer, and one who – as is abundantly clear on the desert island – is self-possessed to a rare degree, unhesitatingly certain of her own abilities and destiny. She – and the ghost of Mrs Winterson – made for an unforgettable programme.

'My castaway this week,' announces Sue Lawley, 'is a writer. She grew up in Lancashire, the adopted daughter of Evangelical parents, who looked on her as a child they could dedicate to God. At fifteen, she fell in love with another woman, left home for good, and after working in a variety of manual jobs, including a spell in a funeral parlour, got herself into Oxford. Her first book, *Oranges Are Not the Only Fruit*, based on her childhood, was published when she was twenty-five, and won the Whitbread Award. More books and more prizes followed, each one attracting criticism and acclaim in equal measure. Her latest, *Art and Lies*, has been attacked with particular savagery in some quarters. She remains impervious. "As long as I am still being pummelled," she says, "I know I'm on the right track." She is Jeanette Winterson.'

Criticism, says the castaway, 'makes me surer of what I am about. After I published *Sexing the Cherry* in 1989, I decided that I would never again read any reviews, and I have stopped that. You can't peep around the corner. If you make that decision, you must read nothing. And so sometimes friends tell me that there has been something particularly insightful which can help me, and I read that. But the rest, it's either praise or it's blame, and they're both the same to a writer.'

Which said, she admits that on one occasion she went round to a critic's house and had it out with her. Does that indicate that she likes a scrap, asks Sue Lawley? 'I am a scrapper. I was brought up to stand up for myself. I had to. Otherwise I would have been entirely squashed, not least by the twenty-five stones of my mother, Mrs Winterson.'

There we have our first mention of Mrs Winterson, and after the first record (Kathleen Ferrier, who was born not far away from the Winterson household in Lancashire) Sue Lawley seeks more details of her castaway's adoptive mother. 'She was a woman of Rabelaisian dimensions,' says Jeanette Winterson, 'a woman for whom the Bible was a living, breathing, moving thing, and she lived inside it. She was Old Testament. She was one of the prophets, and she knew exactly what was right, exactly what was wrong, and for her a rod of iron was a gentle punishment.'

How had the young Jeanette coped? 'I learned to give as good as I got. It wasn't terrifying because I think many children, especially if they have a happy disposition, which I did, and have, really believe that the circumstances in which they are brought up are normal, and that everyone else is rather odd.'

As for her father, 'He was really an adjunct of my mother; he wasn't an individual in his own right.'

Mrs Winterson's religious zeal meant walking five miles to church every evening and five miles back – and for good measure Jeanette also walked the

Elim Pentecostal Church, Accrington

two miles to school and two miles back. There were no books in the house except the Bible and related titles – 'but also, strangely, Malory's *Morte d'Arthur* in two volumes, which to me was meat and drink in those days'.

Jeanette smuggled books home and hid them under her bed. 'You can fit seventy-seven paperbacks under a single bed in a single row. But of course after a while, my mother realized that the bed was rising visibly, and I was discovered and my books were taken away and burned.'

'But you found more?'

'I found more.'

The Wintersons had adopted their daughter for a very particular purpose. 'My mother always saw her life in operatic terms, in grand dramatic terms. She wasn't at all oppressed by being poor, by being nobody. She felt that she had a mission, that she'd been called by God to find a child, and that this child would fulfil all her ambitions for her.'

At the age of five Jeanette started preaching in church, 'because they thought that God was giving me messages'. But this bizarre early life had one advantage: 'I was given responsibility from a very early age and for a girl, that was helpful. It taught me to be self-reliant, to be self-trusting and not to be afraid to voice my opinions, to speak out . . . I have always believed that I would do something with my life. How could I not with Mrs Winterson telling it to me every moment of every day? And for a while I thought I would be a missionary and convert thousands and thousands of people. I was always a very good preacher and people were converted, and I think there are many souls even now that are still following the Lord, thanks to a Winterson sermon.'

But aged fifteen, she fell in love with another girl. 'It happened in the way it very often happens to girls – that there is someone a little older whom you admire and respect enormously and who is kind to you. And you fall for them, and obviously there are sexual feelings involved at that age, and it's silly to pretend that there are not. An involvement took place, because perhaps I was confident and I knew what my feelings were. I was self-aware. And I couldn't keep it a secret. I didn't know that it was wrong because nobody had ever told me . . . It was a fantastic shock to find out that some people thought that falling in love with another girl was not the thing to do.'

She was denounced in church, and given an ultimatum: give up the girl-friend or get out of the house. 'There was a fairly long period when I was supposed to be choosing, and trying to get back on the straight and narrow . . . I suppose there's a moment in every adolescent's life when they reach the point where they must decide whether they will carry on with the kind of received wisdom, or whether they will take the risk and set off on their own.'

She left home at sixteen, and among her early jobs were stints in a funeral parlour ('It was absolutely silent and I wanted to be able to think') and a mental hospital: 'They are quite restful, lunatics. I found them so – perhaps because we shared in common a sense of being outside and unregarded. At that time things were very difficult for me, and strangely I found a rest and a respite in that mental hospital.'

After initially being turned down by Oxford, she persuaded St Catherine's College to give her a place: 'The teaching was abysmal, but I didn't care, because I'd gone there to read, and read is what I did. And it filled in for me all of those things which I hadn't got in my formal education – although nobody knew the Bible as well as I did, and of course that's a great advantage if you're studying literature.'

Pause to play Maria Callas singing 'Vissi d'arte, Vissi d'amore' from *Tosca*. 'I am drawn to heroines who have achieved something against their own cir-cumstances – like Ferrier, like Callas – who get to a point where they should not be, but who do it anyway. So Callas, when I play this, gives me strength. I play it when I have been particularly upset by the idiot press, and the media, which always happens when I publish, and I think, "Yes, this is what matters, this is what I'm for." And of course, the great thing is that at the end of this scene she picks up the dinner knife and she stabs the bastard!'

When her first and semi-autobiographical novel *Oranges Are Not the Only Fruit* was published, 'My mother did write me a letter, and she said, "Oh, Jeanette, it's the first time I had to order a book in a false name," and she'd read it of course, and she said, "This isn't true, this isn't your life," and I said, "No, of course it's not! It's fiction." She was perhaps my most acute critic at that time.'

Sue Lawley suggests that the portrayal of the mother in that book is pretty devastating, but the author disagrees: 'I don't think so. I think it's a homage. I think she has gone into legend now, and with a woman like Mrs Winterson, legend is the best place for her.'

Jeanette Winterson has not tried to find her birth parents at the time of recording. 'We have no connection except a biological one, and we all know that families are often the most difficult places to find real love and real happiness. And I think in that instance, it would be unpleasant for everybody.'

She has been accused of arrogance when nominating one of her own titles as book of the year, or herself as author of the year, or comparing herself with Virginia Woolf. 'I think that I am a true writer, and I believe that my work will last. I do not believe that any artist, of any worth at all, has ever been modest about their abilities. I think they've always believed that what they're doing is absolutely essential and that they must do it. Otherwise, why would you carry on?'

'Then you're prepared to put up with being called arrogant and conceited for that?'

'Oh, I dare say I'll have to put up with a lot more than that as the years go by.'

As for Jeanette Winterson's desert island book, she wonders whether she can take the *Oxford English Dictionary*. 'I suppose so,' concedes Sue Lawley, but asks her for a single piece of work as well. The castaway opts for T. S. Eliot's *Four Quartets*.

Nor is the choice of luxury straightforward: a case of Krug champagne or a printing press? Jeanette Winterson does not need much persuading to take the champagne.

In her *Desert Island Discs* interview, Jeanette Winterson was adamant that she did not wish to trace her birth parents – but after the death of her adoptive parents she changed her mind, and met her mother, Ann. She recounts in her memoir with typical self-awareness: 'I notice that I hate Ann criticizing Mrs Winterson. She was a monster but she was my monster.'

Eight years after her appearance on the programme, Jeanette Winterson took up the post of Professor of Creative Writing at the University of Manchester – just twenty miles from where she spent her childhood with Mrs Winterson.

DESMOND TUTU

Archbishop and peace campaigner

6 November 1994

'You can even smell that it is different to be free'

While a select band of castaways have gone on from *Desert Island Discs* to be awarded a Nobel Prize, very few have arrived on the island already in possession of that lofty honour. One such was the irrepressible Archbishop Desmond Tutu, who had received the Nobel Peace Prize in 1984, when the citation acknowledged 'his role as a unifying leader figure in the campaign to resolve the problem of apartheid in South Africa by peaceful means'.

Apartheid – the political doctrine of racial segregation, in this case between the ruling whites and the oppressed blacks – had been the system of governance in South Africa since 1948. The African National Congress, dedicated to ending segregation, had been banned since 1960; Nelson Mandela, a leading figure in the ANC, had been imprisoned since 1964, but remained a unifying figure in the anti-apartheid movement, within which Desmond Tutu had long been a tireless campaigner.

Tutu was born in Western Transvaal in October 1931. His ambition to become a doctor was thwarted by his parents' poverty, so he followed his father into teaching, and was ordained as an Anglican priest in 1960. Later in the 1960s he studied in London, and by the early 1970s, back in South Africa, he was becoming increasingly active in the effort to overturn apartheid. Eventually the long and arduous struggle was crowned with victory. By the late 1980s apartheid was no longer sustainable, and South Africa started planning for a multiracial future. Nelson Mandela was released from Robben Island jail in February 1990, and became President of South Africa at the country's first fully democratic election in April 1994.

Little more than six months before his *Desert Island Discs* appearance, Archbishop Tutu had seen black South Africans queuing up to vote for the first time. 'Was that day a miracle for you,' asks Sue Lawley, 'or was it something you had always known would happen?'

'No words anywhere in the world would ever be able to describe adequately how we all felt on that day. And of course we recognize now – yes, it was a miracle.'

Was he always convinced that Mandela would lead South Africa? 'Most of the time, one had this as an article of faith. The issue is not in doubt. If God be for us, who can be against us? But there were times when you had to hold on to that belief by the very skin of your teeth, and sometimes you repeated things like, "We are going to be free," very much like whistling in the dark to keep your courage up.'

Not that everything had changed in those six months since the election, he points out: 'Before 27 April, the white people owned 87 per cent of the land. After 27 April they still owned 87 per cent of the land. But you are looking at some of these realities with different eyes. It's like when you are in love: suddenly this flower, which was beautiful before, is exquisite now. There is a texture in the atmosphere, you can even smell that it is different to be free. Not to have to pat your pocket when you see a police officer and wonder whether he's not going to ask you if you have your pass on you – it's "Hey! I'm a human being! And this has been recognized. I have a dignity!" It is fantastic.'

How had he felt at City Hall in Cape Town on 9 May, when he introduced President Mandela to the crowd? Was he not at that moment handing over the mantle? 'Absolutely, yes!', laughs the exuberant Tutu: 'I was hoping, "Hey now, take over, man!"' And beyond that moment, he wanted to assure other troubled countries, in Africa and beyond, such as Rwanda and Bosnia: 'You are going through a nightmare. South Africa had a nightmare, the nightmare of apartheid. It ended. Your nightmare will end.'

Opposite: Hail President Mandela, City Hall, Cape Town, 11 May 1994

Voting in South Africa's first multi-racial elections, April 1994

One of the key moments of Desmond Tutu's childhood came at the age of nine or so – by which time the family was living in Johannesburg – when he first encountered one of the great figures of the anti-apartheid movement. Tutu's mother was a cleaner and cook at a local home for blind women, and the local parish priest was Trevor Huddleston, the British clergyman well known as a vociferous opponent of apartheid. Desmond and his mother were standing on the veranda of the hostel, 'when this tall priest with a flowing cassock swept past – he was wearing a big black hat, and he doffed his hat to my mother. That was mind-blowing for me, a white man greeting my mother with such courtesy!'

'How aware were you as a small boy and then as a teenager,' asks Sue Lawley, 'that you weren't regarded as equal by the whites?'

The archbishop's answer produces a graphic image. 'I was probably the only black kid who had a bicycle, and my father sent me to town often to buy newspapers and things. I recall one occasion going past a school for white children, a primary school, and I saw black children scavenging in the waste bins of the school. They were picking out perfectly clean sandwiches and fruit which the white kids had thrown away, because they were being given free school feeding, which they didn't want; they wanted to eat what their mothers had prepared for them. And here were most of the black kids, whose parents couldn't afford – who didn't have free school feeding provided by the government. And maybe you didn't know then, of course, but this thing was etching itself on your consciousness – yet another thing you would remember in later years.'

One of his music choices is Glenn Miller's 'In the Mood', which brings out a different side of Archbishop Tutu: 'I can just still picture in my mind's eye the juke boxes that we had in a number of the stores in our townships. And I can just see all these young people: I was amongst them, jiving away like crazy on the stoop, on the veranda of the store!'

It was while Tutu was training as a teacher that the apartheid system was introduced: 'There was a deep sadness when General Smuts was defeated, because we thought: yes, things were bad, but this man was maybe the liberal. All these connections that he had with Great Britain meant that he wouldn't be nasty to us. And here were these people who were coming to power who were blatantly racist. They were saying, "We're going to put the black person in his place," and they meant it.'

The new government was proposing to introduce a new teaching regime: 'They were going to teach black children just enough English . . . for them to understand instructions that they were going to be given by their white employers – they were being prepared for perpetual servitude.' This was too much for Tutu, and he gave up teaching.

In the 1960s he came to England to study and to work. How did he find the contrast between being a fourth-class citizen in South Africa and being part of Swinging London?

'Unbelievable. Mind-blowing. To walk the streets of London, just to savour this thing of being free.' He and his wife Leah would deliberately stay out very late – 'which would have been curfew time in South Africa' – and ask policemen for directions, 'just for the incredible fun of having a police officer, and a white police officer at that, speaking to you courteously . . . He was not going to ask, "Why are you here? Where is your pass that gives you permission to be here at this time?" Incredible.'

In 1975 Tutu became Anglican Dean of Johannesburg, and not long after taking on that role wrote an open letter to Prime Minister B. J. Vorster. 'I just felt an incredible foreboding that things were going to explode unless the government did something pretty quickly, and pretty dramatic. It happened that I was in a retreat and it seemed like God was saying, "Maybe if you write this letter, this man may respond and this catastrophe may just be averted."'

Vorster never replied, and the following month Tutu's worst fears were realized with the Soweto riots, in which hundreds were killed. 'The children died. But you think now of what our Lord said about the grain – which if it does not fall to the ground and die it remains alone, but when it does fall to the ground and die, it germinates and blossoms. And it is in part because those children and others did what they did, that now the desert that was South Africa is blossoming.'

Glenn Miller
'In the Mood'

'I can just see all these young people . . . jiving away like crazy on the stoop, on the veranda of the store.'

From then on, Tutu became what Sue Lawley calls 'an extremely effective thorn in the side of the white South African government'. As a result, death

Bishop of Lesotho, 1977

threats were made not only against himself but against his family as well. 'I have said to people that I don't usually think that there are things that are unforgivable. But I am very close to saying the attempts by the apartheid system and those who supported it to get at me by getting at my family are near things that I find unforgivable.'

He believes that apartheid had a lot in common with Nazism. 'Here was a deliberate policy of the government, not only just to denigrate a people, they were seeking to destroy us! They may not have killed us off as in gas chambers, but when a child starves and they are stunted as a result of malnutrition, what are you doing? Maybe Hitler was more efficient, but these guys were determined to be setting out to do the same thing. And we said so to them!'

If violence were the only catalyst for change, would he advocate it? asks Sue Lawley.

'We said our last non-violent option was sanctions. And we came and begged your government here: "Please help us! Apply economic sanctions, to force the South African government to the negotiating table." They were not particularly impressed, but the people were marvellous! I doff my cap to them and say, "You are tremendous!" You should have seen it in 1988, when we were celebrating Nelson Mandela's seventieth birthday, you remember. A quarter of a million youngsters who had never seen Nelson Mandela – many of them had not even been born when he went to jail – they all converged on Hyde Park to celebrate the birthday of this prisoner. Incredible! Exhilarating!'

Amid this virtuoso performance on *Desert Island Discs*, Sue Lawley's next observation is spot-on: 'There is a lot of the showman in you, isn't there? I mean, you enjoy all that – being upfront, being popular.'

'I love being loved! And one of the most traumatic things for me was to be the ogre, the man most white South Africans loved to hate.'

To lighter matters. How about the practicality needed as a castaway? 'I'm totally useless.'

'But I'm sure you'll sit there on your desert island,' suggests Sue Lawley, 'and contemplate the tumultuous lifetime that you've had, and certainly the six months of true democracy that you've just experienced, the ongoing experiment in human relations that's going on in South Africa, and would you sit there and believe completely in its ultimate success?'

'Absolutely. The world wants us to succeed. There are not too many success stories around. God wants us to succeed as well, so that God can hold us up . . . and say: "Rwanda, you're not too many ethnic groups. Look at South Africa, man! Look at all the languages that they've got there! Look at the differences in culture! Et cetera, et cetera, et cetera. They're welding into one; you will too. Bosnia, look at the different faiths in South Africa, and extraordinarily, improbably, they're working together. Don't you think it can happen here in Bosnia?" . . . God has used us. God is using us, and all of you have been just marvellous, making it happen.'

And this castaway's luxury is more revealing than some. 'May I take an ice-cream-making machine? And one that produces my favourite, rum-raisin?'

'A rum-raisin ice-cream-making machine is yours!'

The end of apartheid did not mean the end of Desmond Tutu's campaigning. He remains deeply committed to building the new South Africa, which of course involved coming to terms with the nature of the old South Africa – in which he played a major role as head of the Truth and Reconciliation Commission.

When Tutu stepped down as Archbishop of Cape Town in 1996, Nelson Mandela saluted his 'immeasurable contribution to our nation'. Retirement brought no dilution of his passion, and he has continued to be involved in all manner of campaigns around issues of democracy and human rights – his zeal wonderfully complemented by his infectious laugh, so vividly pervading his *Desert Island Discs* interview.

Nelson Mandela again: 'Sometimes strident, often tender, never afraid and seldom without humour, Desmond Tutu's voice will always be the voice of the voiceless.'

John Goss and Edward Caswall
'See Amid the Winter's Snow'
Soloist: Jessye Norman

J. S. Bach
Orchestral Suite no. 3 in D major
'A very powerful tune of freedom'

'Hey Jude'
The Beatles

The 23rd Psalm in Gaelic
Kenna Campbell
'It was sung so beautifully at John Smith's funeral'

Runrig
'Loch Lomond'
'About the real Scotland as I see it'

George Fenton and Jonas Gwangwa
'Cry Freedom'

'Days'
Kirsty MacColl

'Jerusalem'
Liverpool Cathedral Choir

The Story of Art by **Sir Ernst Gombrich**

Tennis-ball machine and racket

GORDON BROWN
Shadow Chancellor of the Exchequer
3 March 1996

'It's just one of the things that may yet happen'

Sue Lawley's interview with Gordon Brown was to reverberate way beyond the Radio 4 airwaves – so far beyond that Paul Routledge, one of Brown's biographers, described the edition as 'the most controversial *Desert Island Discs* in the programme's fifty-four-year history.' While most castaway connoisseurs would dispute such a judgement – Diana Mosley in 1989 had caused considerably more fuss – the Brown programme ruffled a good few feathers.

Gordon Brown, then forty-five years old, was Shadow Chancellor of the Exchequer and, if the pollsters and bookmakers were to be believed, within a year or so of losing the word 'Shadow' from his job title, as New Labour was apparently cruising towards power at the general election likely to take place in spring 1997.

Brown was a 'son of the Manse' – one of three sons of a Church of Scotland minister – whose political career was based on a formidable intellect. He was elected to Parliament in the 1983 general election and became Shadow Chancellor under Labour leader John Smith in 1992. When Smith's sudden death in May 1994 changed the political landscape, Brown was clearly one of the two front-runners for the leadership. The other was his one-time House of Commons room-mate, one Anthony Charles Lynton Blair. After various discussions – most famously over dinner at the Granita restaurant in Islington, north London – Brown agreed to leave the way clear for his younger colleague. This was widely characterized as a 'deal' whereby Brown would in due course follow Blair into No. 10, but Blair wrote in his autobiography, *A Journey*: 'Though there was never a deal in the sense that his standing down was contingent on my agreeing to help him come after me, nonetheless there was an understanding of mutual interest.'

The Shadow Chancellor was certainly in need of showing the lighter, more rounded aspect of his personality, since he was perceived as deeply serious to the point of having tunnel-vision, and was widely lampooned when shortly before his party's annual conference in 1994 he told the press that Labour's new economic policy was rooted in 'post neo-classical endogenous growth theory and the symbiotic relationship between growth and investment in people and infrastructure.'

High time, then, for a rare glimpse of the human side of Gordon Brown.

The early exchanges suggest that the castaway has been well briefed in advance of his *Desert Island Discs* appearance, with 'team' and 'change' among his key concepts. The Labour Party, he says, has waited 'a long time and I think we work as a team. We've been working as a team for many years to get this result. We've had to make huge changes. I was one of the people advocating big changes . . . I think there is a tide in politics and I think people see the need for change and I'd like to be part of it.'

Brown's first music choice reflects his deep seriousness. 'The first record goes back very far to my youth, and of course I was brought up as a son of a Church of Scotland Minister. I don't think it was a Calvinist background as such. It was very much a social Christianity. But of course it revolved around Christmas and Easter and around hymns and churches, and that's why I've chosen a hymn, "See Amid the Winter's Snow".'

Although Gordon Brown was an academically gifted pupil, his childhood was dominated by sport: 'Football, rugby, tennis, running. I think I was a sports enthusiast right from the beginning and I remember running all the time . . . I loved playing rugby. I played a lot of tennis and played for my local team against all the clubs in Scotland, and I ran in the Scottish national schoolboy championships, as a sprinter.'

It was at the University of Edinburgh that he sustained the rugby injury which left him with sight in only one eye: 'I think people might be suspicious of my driving, but apart from that, it doesn't make any difference at all.'

He entered the House of Commons in 1983, the same year as Tony Blair. How close had they been in those early years? 'Very close, and still are.' Had he given thought to one day becoming party leader? 'I think that was always a possibility, but when the time came and John sadly died, it seemed the right thing that Tony [then Shadow Home Secretary] should be the leader. It would have been inconceivable that Tony and I would have stood against each other, and we didn't, and it was the right thing that he took the job . . . I feel privileged to be part of a team.'

But, presses Sue Lawley, how did they arrive at the decision as to which of them should step aside?

'I think that Tony had presented his case about the change that was necessary in a way that was very attractive to the public. Tony has got tremendous charisma and was very successful in presenting his Home Office brief, and had clearly a set of ideas that we both shared and that he could communicate very well.'

He means that Blair was more marketable? 'No, not at all. He was the man with ideas and vision . . . He also, I think, had a unique – and has a unique – ability to communicate with the public . . . What we've now seen in Tony Blair, a man of real steel and resolution and determination, is what I appreciated were the qualities that he did have.'

'Qualities that you don't have?' asks the persistent Sue.

'No, I don't say I don't have them, but Tony has them in tremendous abundance. He'll make a great Prime Minister.'

'How large was the fact that he is a family man and that the electorate on the whole might find it more appealing than the idea of a bachelor Prime Minister?'

'I don't know. That would have been something for the party to decide. I mean, I'm not married. It just hasn't happened. I hope it does, and it may yet and probably will do.'

Brown, suggests Sue Lawley, has a deal with Blair about taking over the leadership at some point – 'and no one would blame you if you had'.

'No, I don't, I wouldn't consider it a deal. We've got a strong friendship. It's a friendship that survives thick and thin. There's been obviously lots of occasions when we've had to make difficult decisions, but it's a friendship that survived, and I hope will be obvious to the country.'

From this the conversation moves on to a robust exchange, characteristic of the Lawley style with politicians – a style which had shifted the tone of *Desert Island Discs* over the previous decade. Then comes another record – after which she returns to a topic already aired:

Gordon Brown with (from left) *Peter Mandelson, Margaret Beckett, Alastair Campbell and Tony Blair: general election campaign, 1997*

'You're always asked, Gordon Brown, in interviews I've read, about women and marriage. Does that irritate you?'

'Not at all. It's a question that I expect, and is a question that I think I've already answered during the course of this interview – that it just hasn't happened. It's one of the things that I suppose I'm surprised it hasn't happened, but it hasn't.'

'It is interesting though, isn't it? That it would probably be less of an issue for you, if you'd been married three times. People don't remark on that, but they do remark on non-marriage.'

'I think that's true, and it certainly appears in all the profiles. I've got some very good friends obviously, and it just hasn't happened. It's one of the things that may yet happen.'

Sue Lawley, dogged as ever, will not let go. 'But do you understand people's curiosity? It is something that middle-aged men and women have to put up with. People want to know whether you're gay, or whether there's some flaw in your personality that you haven't made a relationship. You may feel, "Look, I don't have to answer these questions," but do you perhaps accept that as a public person it's a price you have to pay?'

'Well, I don't mind answering the questions,' replies Brown breezily. 'It's something that comes up, and certainly I think people have a right to know what their politicians do and what their arrangements are. There is a fascination. I'm not surprised at that.'

'Do they have a right to know?'

'It's different in other countries actually, but I think yes, people have got a right to know. I'm standing as a candidate at an election, I'm asking people to support me. They want to know what sort of person I am.'

'One of your colleagues I spoke to said the truth was that in fact, you're just a loner, and despite the fact that you say you'd like to get married, you rather like your life on your own.'

'I don't think that's the case,' replies Brown, laughing. 'It's very funny, because I've always assumed that I would be married. I actually don't think of myself as middle-aged and maybe I am, or maybe I'm not.'

'I suppose forty-five just about is.'

'I suppose it is, it's one of these things and it just hasn't happened.'

'But are you a loner?'

'No, I'm not a loner.'

'But we're back to this image thing again, and the contradiction. Because the image definitely is of the rather brooding, gloomy Celtic loner, and here you are sitting smiling broadly across the table, putting yourself forward as somebody quite different from that.'

'Well, I don't think I'm quite different in the image I put across from what I am.'

Irresistible force meets immovable object. Time to move on again.

Would he enjoy being cast away? 'I would enjoy perhaps the first month.'

Could he build a shelter, and forage for food? 'I think I could do that. I think I would just quickly get down to it and see what I could do, but I would always be secretly wishing for sort of a takeaway restaurant to appear!'

His luxury is a tennis serving machine. 'If you'd allow me an endless supply of tennis balls, plus a racket, that would be of great assistance in improving my serve and improving my game . . . My serve is not bad, but my returns are pretty poor, so that would be pretty helpful. And of course, if I got really desperate, I could send some of the balls out to sea with messages engraved on them.'

As a device to demonstrate the human side of Gordon Brown, the programme had been reasonably successful. For one thing, he often laughed – and laughed a good deal more than Tony Blair on *Desert Island Discs* a few months later. And his account of his amicable relationship with Blair – 'a friendship that survives thick and thin' – sounded plausible enough at the time, though before long commentators and political insiders would be queuing up to report how far Brown's assessment was from the whole truth.

What caused the post-programme fuss was Sue Lawley's remark that, 'People want to know whether you're gay, or whether there's some flaw in your personality that you haven't made a relationship.' Paul Routledge later wrote in his biography of Brown:

> Given the scale of editorial preparation, it is unlikely that the BBC was unaware that, for several years, rumours about Gordon Brown's sexuality had circulated in the bars and tearooms at Westminster. The suggestion that he might be gay was bandied about chiefly by political journalists, often reporters for Scottish newspapers who claimed to be 'in the know' about some dark secret from his years in Edinburgh. Not a shred of evidence was ever produced for these allegations, which those who know him well – and they are few in number – knew perfectly well were false.

Routledge had got hold of a transcript of the interview in advance of transmission, and on the morning of the broadcast had written a piece in the *Independent* which described how Sue Lawley 'gets extraordinarily personal' in the interview. After relaying the key exchange, Routledge had written: 'At this point Mr Brown snaps back: "Look, I don't have to answer these questions"' – and when later that day he heard the programme, the journalist was horrified to discover that those words had been spoken not by Brown but by Lawley.

Kenna Campbell

The 23rd Psalm in Gaelic

'It was sung so beautifully at John Smith's funeral'

Nor had Brown 'snapped back' at any part of the interview.

The BBC switchboard, traditionally reported as 'jammed' on such occasions, had had few calls on the Sunday of transmission, though more followed when the offending passage was granted a wider audience through the newspapers. Sue Lawley was dragged before the court of public opinion – to be specific, the court of *Feedback*, Radio 4's forum for audience reaction – and was unrepentant: 'It was a perfectly fair and proper piece of interrogation. It would not be responsible, even on a programme like *Desert Island Discs*, to give a politician a simple and easy ride.'

Official BBC reaction was equally unruffled. 'There is no question of anyone being reprimanded over it,' said a spokesman. 'We haven't a problem, and as far as we know, Mr Brown hasn't.' Indeed, Gordon Brown provided the best answer of all to what was in essence a storm in a desert island teacup when in August 2000 he married Sarah Macaulay. They have had three children, the first of whom – Jennifer Jane – was born prematurely and died aged ten days.

At the general election on 1 May 1997 the Labour Party under Tony Blair was voted in with a landslide majority, and Gordon Brown became Chancellor of the Exchequer.

Whatever the exact nature of the 'deal' with Blair, Brown was to spend a long time in the Green Room of politics, and it was not until June 2007 that Blair stood down and Brown, unopposed by any other candidate, became leader of the Labour Party and Prime Minister, remaining in office until Labour came off second best to the Conservatives at the 2010 general election.

In 2012 he was appointed United Nations special envoy for education by UN Secretary General Ban Ki-moon, with the aim of getting 61 million more children enrolled into education across the world by 2015.

TONY BLAIR

Leader of the Opposition

24 November 1996

'People can take me and like me or not as I am'

On the evening of Friday 20 November 1996, Alastair Campbell, chief press secretary to Tony Blair, leader of the opposition, wrote in his diary how that morning, 'I left early for TB's where he was preparing for *Desert Island Discs*. "Is this really wise?", he said. "I'm not sure." We went over the stories he might tell . . . He was very nervous and tense.' Campbell does not say whether Blair had got himself in the mood by listening to a tape of the Gordon Brown programme described on pages 375–9 . . .

Tony Blair, then forty-three, was almost within reach of 10 Downing Street. Educated at Fettes School and St John's College, Oxford, he had entered Parliament in 1983 and had quickly risen through the Labour ranks. Having taken the leadership in May 1994, by November 1996, with John Major's Conservative government in decline, Tony Blair looked a certainty to become Prime Minister at the forthcoming general election.

Sue Lawley asks whether Tony Blair's hinterland – he has a young family – will be a safety net, should the unexpected come to pass and the Labour Party lose the election.

'I don't know that it's a safety net,' replies her castaway, 'but I think it's important that you're not a political obsessive. I mean, politics is my life. I'm dedicated to the aims I've set myself in politics. But it's not all of life, and my family, my friends, other interests, are also important.'

Does he feel guilty, asks Sue Lawley, about not being able to devote more time and energy to his young family?

'I feel worried about it. It's a decision, once I decided to go for the leadership, that inevitably meant there were going to be strains on the family. But then it was what I thought was right to do and I wanted to do it. I think if you are in politics, and you decide it's the right thing to do, you've got to go for it.'

A few months ago Sue Lawley had Gordon Brown's take on how they came to an arrangement about the party leadership. Now she asks for Blair's.

'It was difficult discussing it, obviously . . . I'd always assumed that he would be the leader of the Labour Party and I've always had a huge and still have a huge admiration for him . . . Once John died and we had to come to the decision, then we did discuss, and I think it is a mark and measure of Gordon and the type of person he is, that in the end we were able to agree it.'

Tony Blair and Gordon Brown at the launch of the Labour Party's draft manifesto, July 1996

After Tony Blair's first record has been played – 'Cancel Today' by Ezio ('a group that no one will actually have heard of') – Sue Lawley gets down to the nitty-gritty, putting it to Blair that he has taken on the leadership of the Labour Party 'as a job that required discipline and dedication, but in the end you're doing it with your head, more than your heart'.

'Well, I hope I'm doing it with my heart as well. But I think there's a sense in which I really almost stood outside the Labour Party and looked at it and said, "Look, if you are an ordinary person looking at British politics, how would you want to see it develop? How should it develop?" And, ever since I've been in it, I've thought we had to change. But I think it would be wrong to see this merely as a sort of, you know, as a rational expedition, rather than an emotional one.'

Sue Lawley presses the point: 'But it is more of a rational expedition than an emotional one, isn't it? Because, as I say, you're not bound up with those thousands of people in the Labour Party who would, you know, live and die by Clause Four [of the party constitution, stipulating common ownership of the means of production]. You were able to say "It's not doing us any good, we've got to get rid of it."'

'Yes, but I think more than that though. What I would say to you is that the true emotional attachment to the Labour Party is not to cling on to something long past its sell-by date. It is actually to say, "But what is this party about? What do we feel? You know, why do we join the Labour Party?"'

'Why did I join the Labour Party? The sense of justice. The single greatest difficulty we've had in changing has been this belief that if you change, you become unprincipled. That is absurd! Principles are for all time, but policies and practical programmes will vary from generation to generation . . .

'I didn't sort of sit there and say, "Well, how do we get the Labour Party into power? Ditch everything it believes in?" I mean that's just rubbish. That is what has kept the left back for so, so long, that it has confused principles with their application.'

Sue Lawley sticks to her line. 'But the point of mentioning all of that is that people have called you rootless in the past, but this is what's quite important in the shaping of Tony Blair, that you don't bring that emotional baggage of the Labour Party with you. You're not a child of the welfare state, you're not the son of a miner, you didn't struggle through the seventies, did you? You're a man with a job to do, simply that. Get the party elected.'

'I hope that I'm also someone with a vision for both the Labour Party and the country. But you're right in this sense, that it's not a question of being rootless. It's being part of my own generation.' The Labour Party 'stands for certain key values. It does not stand for rigid economic policy prescriptions that may be good for one generation but aren't good for another. And therefore it's not a question of, as it were, not carrying the emotional baggage of the Labour Party; it's that my emotions are grounded in something different.'

From reading law at Oxford he went to study in the legal chambers of Derry Irvine, where he met another young pupil, Cherie Booth, who was to become his wife.

After the fourth record – Bruce Springsteen: a reminder of the tracks the young couple used to listen to together in Tony's 'extremely grotty flat' – Sue Lawley suggests: 'You don't like talking about all this personal stuff, do you? You lose your fluency, almost?'

Bruce Springsteen
'Fourth of July, Asbury Park'

'One of the tracks that Cherie and I used to listen to together'

'I don't like it very much, no,' concedes Blair. 'I think it's difficult for people sometimes to understand, as well. Politicians are normal people, most of us, and we came into politics because there were great policy ideas that we had, and ideals that we wanted to implement and see through. And it is difficult, because you then get to a stage in your political life [when] people are more interested in what you are privately than your public position. You know the press – it's a tiger – and whether you like it or not in politics, you're put astride it, but it's a pretty fearsome beast.'

Blair has been MP for Sedgefield since 1983, and has chafed at spending thirteen years in opposition. Sue Lawley quotes her interviewee as having said in the past that being in opposition is a matter of 'waking up every day thinking of what you've got to say, not what you're going to do.'

'I think, whether we win or not, we have now created what is plainly an electable party . . . Yes, it was extremely frustrating – *is* very frustrating – because if you're in politics and you've got anything about you at all, you want to *do* something.'

One of Tony Blair's most memorable soundbites in opposition has been that his three policy priorities are 'education, education, education' – and he must have been prepared for Sue Lawley's next line of questioning. Does he think, she wonders, that with hindsight it had been a mistake sending his son Euan to a grant-maintained school rather than the local comprehensive?

'No, I don't, because I think it was important to do the right thing for him. And had I not done that, that would have been a betrayal of his future.'

'But he was in a sense selected wasn't he? You had to be seen by the headmaster.'

'Well, you do in all the church schools, but that happens because, since it's a church school, they wish to be clear that you share the religious convictions of the school . . . I think everyone wants to do the best by their children. Our task is not to stop people doing the best by their children; it is to make the state education system excellent.'

The atmosphere between castaway and presenter cools when she wonders whether others in the Labour Party would consider that their leader is 'being a bit of a hypocrite here'.

'I don't accept that. But in relation to whether it's right to make this choice, because there's going to be a political outcry, I've got an obligation to my boy as his father, and we've got an obligation to him as parents . . . We're not going to put him in a particular school because it happens to be convenient to do so . . . I think what is important in the end is that we actually do try and raise up the standards of all the schools, not say to parents, "We've got to send your child to a particular school even if it's not a good school for him."'

Tony Blair's next record – blues legend Robert Johnson – shifts the mood, but then the presenter opens another line of enquiry. According to the opinion polls, Tony Blair has a problem with female voters: 'They think you're smarmy, too smooth – and they don't like your hair.'

'People can take me and like me or not as I am. I always thought at the time with this publicity that it was the most extraordinary and gratuitous insult to women to believe they were going to change their vote on the basis of my hairstyle . . . I'm not going to change. There's no point in pretending.'

'And you can't flatten the hair.'

'I've got no intention of doing anything like that . . . In the end, what I think is that people should make up their minds on some slightly more serious topics – and indeed, I'm sure that they will.'

How would he survive on the island? 'The DIY is not good . . . The cooking I can just about manage. I cook occasionally for the kids – but they're not very flattering about it, I have to say . . . I'd miss the family, and I hope that my party would miss me – that the Labour Party National Executive would pass a resolution by twenty votes to five, asking me to return.'

Alastair Campbell's diary relates that during the recording, 'I sat in the cubicle and it felt like it was getting worse and worse. He allowed her to put him on the defensive.' And at the end of the programme, 'TB hadn't taken to her at all. Lots of press and TV came in at the end and I said to her, "Sorry, he didn't open up for you, like he has with other interviewers." She got the message. I felt the whole thing had been a lost opportunity on both sides. TB knew that he had not been on form but he said there was no point him going hard on her because of the sort of programme it was.'

Tony Blair became Prime Minister with Labour's landslide victory at the general election of 1 May 1997, and remained in 10 Downing Street through the elections of 2001 and 2005 before standing down in June 2007, finally handing the key to No. 10 to Gordon Brown.

BENJAMIN ZEPHANIAH

poet

8 June 1997

'I had this energy, and I just found a way of channelling it'

Nothing about Zephaniah is predictable or orthodox. He had a turbulent childhood in the Handsworth area of Birmingham, got into trouble with the law, and by the age of thirteen had been expelled from school, unable to read or write. Within a few years he found himself convicted of burglary and sent to prison. At that point in his life he already had a reputation as a performance poet, and this reputation grew considerably when after coming out of prison he became ever more deeply involved with the local rap and blues scene. He decided to try his luck in London, and there he became involved with a writers' cooperative in the East End. In 1980 he published his first book of poetry, *Pen Rhythm*.

And somewhere along the line he became a fan of George Formby – as Sue Lawley is to discover.

Sue Lawley quotes Benjamin Zephaniah's aim: 'I'd like to be counted as one of the people who popularized poetry again' – but what sort is his own poetry? Not the sort you can sit and read in the corner. His poetry has to be performed. But is it rap or dub – or even both?

'It's called dub poetry . . . The word "dub" comes from reggae. Just going back in time a bit, when reggae was being created in Jamaica, most of the producers couldn't afford to record a B-side, so they would record the A-side with the singer and the normal reggae song, and on the B-side they would have what was called the dub version: the vocals taken out of it, the kind of drum-and-bass part of it mixed a lot heavier, and lots of echo and sound effects on it. And then you may have someone speaking over it . . . This is how you can tell a true dub poet: if you listen to them without music, you should still be able to hear the music.'

Sue Lawley asks for an example, and her castaway reads in his wonderfully rich Caribbean tones 'a poem where I politically correct the English language from a black point of view, and it's called "White Comedy"':

I waz whitemailed
By a white witch,
Wid white magic
An white lies,
Branded a white sheep
I slaved as a whitesmith
Near a white spot
Where I suffered whitewater fever.
Whitelisted as a whiteleg
I waz in de white book
As a master of the white arts,
It waz like white death.
People call me white jack
Others call me white wog,
So I joined de white watch
Trained as a white guard
Lived off the white economy.
I was caught and beaten by de whiteshirts
and condemned to a white mass,
Don't worry,
I will be writing to de Black House.

Zephaniah's poetry is usually humorous: 'You can reach a lot of people through humour; you can tell them something very serious through being humorous.'

When his first book was published he was in his early twenties, but could hardly read or write. 'First of all I wrote it the way it sounded to me: phonetically. But then, when I gave it to someone else to look at I also kind of made sure that they didn't just translate it to standard English. I always knew what I wanted to say, so I didn't have that problem at all.'

His first experience of performing words had been in church as a ten-year-old child: 'I just stood in front of the audience and I went: "Genesis, Exodus, Leviticus, Numbers, Deuteronomy, Joshua, Judges, Ruth, First and Second Samuel, First and Second Kings, First and Second Chronicles" – and just went through the books of the Bible. And everybody just went, "My gosh, we have a prophet amongst us!" And it was strange, because for the next couple of months they really thought I was something special, and I was trying to tell them that I wasn't.'

'That you'd just learnt it like a poem,' says Sue Lawley.

'I made it worse for myself, because then I had a dream one day that a hand came from the sky and was picking people up from the High Street, and I went and told my pastor, and they were convinced that they had this prophet in their midst.'

But rather than dedicate himself to the church, Benjamin Zephaniah turned to crime. Sue Lawley skips over the details to the nub of the matter: 'Do you think that your poetry saved you from a life of crime? Would you go as far as to say that?'

'I'm not sure. No, I think what really saved me from a life of crime is, and it's going to sound like a bit of a cliché now – I mean a lot of people say this and it's probably been overused – but I had this energy, and I just found a way of channelling it. It was as simple as that . . . Deep down in my mind, I knew I wanted to do something with words and be a poet. But I was in that climate where young black kids just didn't say that.'

Cue George Formby, with his little ukulele in his hand – and not so incongruous a choice after all: 'I just love the comedy in it, and I love that kind of northern humour. I have one of these old sports cars and I take it out, just on good weather days, and I took the top off and I remember driving around East Ham blasting this out, and all the police looking at me in complete

Leonard Cohen
'Last Year's Man'

'His words are so crucial and the music just hangs on the words'

confusion. You know: why is he not listening to Public Enemy or something like that?'

Sue Lawley spools back to the castaway's early life: eldest of nine children; parents had come over from the Caribbean; terrible poverty.

'I must say I didn't see many rich people. It was all poverty, even for the white people around me. We lived in those houses with the toilets at the back of the yard. I don't want to go on about people leaving their doors open, but that's exactly what people used to do, and I remember playing in communal yards, having baths together in tin baths. We did it because we were poor, but there was something really nice about it: something that bonded the community together.'

When his parents split up, his mother took Benjamin and his eight siblings remained with his father, and he was drawn towards a life of crime. 'I hated authority. And like many young kids, I wanted to keep up with the kids around me. I did bow a lot to peer pressure, especially in the teenage years.

'As for my poetry, I always describe it as like being gay: I didn't tell anybody. It was something that I kind of kept to myself. Okay, they knew I was doing a bit of rap and a bit of toasting' – a kind of fast Jamaican rap – 'and musical things, but I didn't use the word "poet". I remember coming across somebody once who actually admitted to writing poetry, and we kind of got together and I said, you know, "You show me yours and I'll show you mine." It was a real secret that we had.'

While confined in various places of detention, he concentrated on his writing. 'It was mainly writing in my head. What I did, especially in my last prison sentences, was I did a lot of thinking. And it was then that I think I got kind of political. I started to realize that I wasn't really being a rebel by going out and stealing something. In fact I was playing into the hands of the law.'

Years later, a policeman stopped him in a Birmingham street. 'He said to me: "I remember you. I remember I used to kick you. I'd love to do it now, but I can't, can I, because you will write a poem about it and you'll be on television. And you'll earn more money from me beating you up." And he realized he was in a situation where he couldn't touch me unless he had a good reason to.'

After listening to Leonard Cohen singing 'Last Year's Man' – 'His words are so crucial and the music just hangs on the words' – Sue Lawley refers to Zephaniah becoming a rapper after leaving prison. Her castaway corrects her: 'I was a toaster, which is like the Jamaican form of rap. It's rap but it's to a different beat . . . At first I performed just for Rastafarians, and I can remember a time when I started performing for black people who were not Rastafarians. And I can remember a time when people said to me, "Hey, your message is for everybody – go and perform for white people as well."'

Zephaniah explains about Rastafarianism. 'There's three things, I think, all Rastafarians have in common. One is that they recognize Haile Selassie and his lineage as the lineage of David and Solomon – an unbroken lineage. Two: that they recognize Ethiopia, or Africa, as their spiritual homeland. And three, that they recognize a person called Marcus Garvey as a kind of prophet, as a kind of modern-day John the Baptist. Marcus Garvey was the founder of the Pan-African movement, and quite an amazing person. I mean when you think of Malcolm X and Martin Luther King: two kind of black freedom fighters who came from completely different perspectives, but they both called themselves Garveyites because Garvey taught self-pride, black pride.' And his next record is 'Marcus Garvey' sung by Burning Spear, 'a kind of Rastafarian anthem'.

When he was twenty-two Benjamin Zephaniah moved to London, where he encountered the National Front: 'I remember walking down the street in the middle of the night and just meeting a group of skinheads and having to run for your life.'

But then he was contacted by Nelson Mandela, still imprisoned on Robben Island. 'Somebody gave him a parcel of my work – some of my books and poetry and tapes, and things like this. The reason was because I'd done a fundraising tour round Europe to pay for a radio transmitter that the apartheid regime had smashed when we'd gone to South Africa and Tanzania. So he read it and listened to it. I'm told that he passed it around his little government that was in prison. So the next time he came to England – he was actually coming to meet Mrs Thatcher – he contacted me and said that he wanted to meet me. And I'll never forget it because it was seven o'clock in the morning, and I said, "That's ridiculous, can't you meet me after you've seen Mrs Thatcher?" And he said, "No, I need you to brief me."'

He does a lot with children. 'My so-called workshops are performances where I allow the children to talk to me and question me about poetry and I try and inspire them to go away and write poetry. I never wanted to become like a teacher. Not that I'm against teachers, but I don't want to be like a teacher by saying, "Right, now boys and girls, sit down and we've got half an hour and we're going to write a poem." I want to inspire them to write poetry and then let the teachers do the work afterwards.'

But he has publicized the fact that he cannot have children himself. 'There was a moment not too long ago,' he recalls, 'where I was just watching people playing with their children. For some reason it just struck me then. I really just felt like crying. I've always wanted these very simple things in life and one of them has just been a baby, and it's like the one thing that I can't have no control over really: I can't order it; I can't ring a friend and get him to organize it or something like this. And it's very difficult for me to talk about, and that's why I write poems, because I express myself easier through poetry. I'm going to start getting tearful now. Can we talk about football or something?'

In 1989 he was nominated for the Oxford Professorship of Poetry, but lost out to Seamus Heaney, 'a writer I really do admire and really do love'.

Benjamin Zephaniah – vegan, non-smoker, non-drinker – will be in his element on the desert island, but: 'I need an audience. I'd miss an audience. I think I'd have to get the animals to sit down so I could perform to them or something, because I would need to preach to somebody.'

His book? 'At home I have a book published in 1853 by Edward Moxon, and it's *The Poetical Works of Percy Bysshe Shelley*. I've always loved Shelley. I don't claim to fully understand him, but he's a poet that I really, really love.'

And then comes one of the most unusual luxuries in *Desert Island Discs* history: 'The rules of the island. The law of the land – so I could break it at least once a day, because I believe that it's quite healthy to break the law at least once a day. Especially when you're hurting nobody.'

In 1999 Benjamin Zephaniah published his first novel, *Face* – in separate children's and adult editions – which was followed over the next few years by *Refugee Boy*, *Gangsta Rap* and *Teacher's Dead*. However, he remains best known for his poetry, much of which has been set to music and issued in audio form.

He has received honorary doctorates from several universities, among them, in 2008, the University of Birmingham – the city where he was born and raised.

SIR PETER O'SULLEVAN

horseracing commentator

28 September 1997

'I think I might have just made it pay'

No sports commentator has provided the soundtrack of his sport so definitively and for so long as Peter O'Sullevan. Most of the landmark moments of racing since the 1960s, and most of its equine heroes – Arkle, Nijinsky, Red Rum, Desert Orchid – are recalled through those inimitable (though frequently subjected to poor imitation) honeyed tones. The voice has been described in many ways over the years, none better than Russell Davies' description of it as 'perhaps the only "hectic drawl" in captivity'.

Known within racing as simply 'The Voice', Sir Peter – he had been knighted earlier in 1997 in recognition of his charitable work – was due to hang up his binoculars two months after being cast away.

Sue Lawley's introduction is perfectly pitched: 'My castaway this week is a sports commentator. For the past fifty years he's been the voice of racing for the BBC and for thirty-six of those years was also the racing correspondent of the *Daily Express*. When he retires in November this year, he estimates that he'll have provided the commentary for fourteen thousand races. To hear him now, it's hard to imagine that this refined and urbane gentleman had a childhood dominated by asthma and acne, which isolated him and drove him for companionship towards a love of horses. He still loves them, he's owned them, bet on them and he's only giving up commentating on them because of his age. Almost eighty, he says he doesn't think he'll get any better, so he can only guard against getting any worse.'

That trademark voice: how did he cultivate it? 'Frankly, Sue, not at all. It's just my voice. Maybe I've modified my pace a bit. I'm told that I used to speak very much too quickly and so I tried to slow down, but of course you have to talk quite fast to keep pace with a racehorse . . . I think one has to remember that as a commentator on a sport in which so many listeners or viewers have a pecuniary interest, you're inevitably a purveyor of ill tidings to the majority – and not only a purveyor of ill tidings, but you're held partially accountable for them.'

He is known as an enthusiastic punter himself. Does that affect his commentary? 'Once the race is in progress then I think you go into a mode in which it is your responsibility to interpret the action, and I find that so exciting that I don't really find it too difficult to be impartial.'

He has been commentating on the Grand National since the race was first televised in 1960. Is it the hardest race to call? 'It's not necessarily the hardest, Sue, but it's the most fraught. It's the one that one's most anxious about.'

How does he prepare for it? 'I make a colour chart, and make notes about, for instance, how many Nationals a jockey has ridden in, his age, where he's finished in his previous efforts – and naturally I learn as much about the

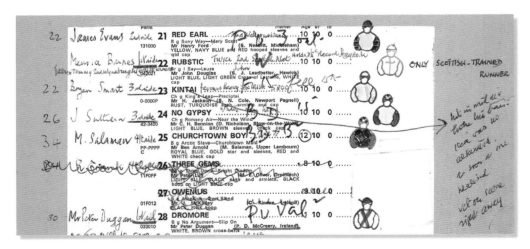

Part of Peter O'Sullevan's colour chart for the 1979 Grand National

horses as I can . . . I paste up the colours, but even having done so, and having hopefully learned them, I still like to see them in the weighing room before they go out on to the field of action . . . Currently there are fourteen thousand eight hundred registered colours. Now they've made it slightly easier in the last few years by reducing colour variations or basic colours to eighteen. But in the 1970s I was writing a foreword to a book about colours, and I noticed that there were twenty shades of green alone: almond, apple, bottle, dark, emerald, grass, Irish, jade, leaf, light, lime green, Lincoln Green, moss, myrtle, olive, pale, pea, rifle, sage and sea green. And it's very difficult to distinguish when they're going forty miles an hour and they're coming at you!'

He keeps the colour charts, and often offers them at charity auctions: 'This year's Grand National card, absolutely amazingly, was auctioned at a dinner the following week and it fetched thirty-five thousand pounds!'

Conditions were primitive during his early commentating career, as is clear when he recalls his first Grand National commentary, for radio in 1949. 'The BBC, bless them, felt that if you were at a racecourse then you could commentate. The vantage point really didn't enter into it at all. I was supposed to stand down by the first fence on the ground and commentate on the fallers. And there was a little latrine nearby with a sloping corrugated iron roof. Because you'd slide, I took my shoes off, and then I had to take my socks off because you slide just as much in socks – so I was there in my bare feet.' He was assisted by his 'race reader' in the shape of friend and *Daily Express* colleague Clive Graham, who agreed to take his shoes off but not his socks – 'and he made his only contribution to the broadcast, he said, "I'm going to fall off this something roof!"'

O'Sullevan has loved horses from an early age. Given the choice, asks Sue Lawley, would he have preferred to be a jockey? 'I think so, really. I can't think of anything more exciting, because you're closer to the horses, and I've always wanted to be close to horses.'

'But you were too tall, too big?'

'And too incompetent!'

Born in County Kerry, O'Sullevan was brought up by his grandparents in Surrey. One day, prompts Sue Lawley, he went missing. 'I was very indignant, because the weekend guests had brought their horses with them, and my pony was turned out of his box. It was raining very hard. It was a filthy day and he was absolutely miserable, so I went out to see him with an umbrella – to talk to him – and nobody could find me. My grandfather contacted the local police and everybody was sent out to find me – and a member of the constabulary rang to say that a small boy had been seen just off the Reigate road with a chestnut pony, holding an umbrella over it. One of my journalistic colleagues who wrote a piece about me said rather nicely, "He's been metaphorically holding an umbrella over horses ever since."

His childhood asthma triggered a virulent form of acne – 'very unsightly, and to me it was much worse than the asthma. It limited the scope of one's life comprehensively, and I suppose drove me more into myself, as it were, and detached me from my fellow creatures . . .

'It affected my outlook. It was painful in the sense that it was a very, very severe skin eruption, but of course it made one so unsightly that you felt a pariah. I came back to England' – from Switzerland, where he had been sent for treatment – 'and I was treated by all sorts of people and nothing really helped me. I was in such a poor state that I was treated in the Middlesex Hospital, where I stayed for several months, and they realized they couldn't do very much for me so they encouraged me to leave. But I wouldn't go out in the daytime. I stayed on there and used to go out at night, and ultimately when I went racing I would only go to the Silver Ring and to the periphery where there weren't people, and I'd even sometimes watch from the roadside . . .

Yehudi Menuhin & Stéphane Grappelli
'The Lady Is a Tramp'

'One of the most felicitous marriages in music'

'At the outset of the war, before the war really even started, I was medically graded out of the services. So I changed my car for a four-seater and I evacuated families to the country. Then when I had run out of my slender resources, I joined the Rescue Services in Chelsea. I found when the raids started that most people were very apprehensive, but I wasn't in the least bit apprehensive and was absolutely impervious to danger – thought to be amazingly dare-devil and courageous on that account, but it was just that I didn't really care. And while everybody else was apprehensive, my condition improved enormously. It was psychological.'

O'Sullevan is known to have enjoyed a bet ever since his school days. Does he have rules for his punting? 'I think it's mad to restrict oneself – as long as you follow the basic tenet that you don't play with money you can't afford to pay.'

But his interviewer wants more. Has he had a four-figure bet in his time? 'Yes, I'd have to say that.' And over his betting career, is he up or down? 'I don't think I've come out too badly – but mind you, any punter will tell you that!'

'Quite,' she follows up – 'but I'm trying to get to the truth!'

'I think I might have just made it pay.'

Even in his venerable old age, Peter O'Sullevan is waging campaigns on various racing and animal welfare fronts. One such is the use of the whip in races: 'It began to offend me, the extent to which it appeared to be used as an instrument of chastisement rather than encouragement. And I felt that this should be brought home not just to riders but to owners and trainers, because after all it is they who give instructions.'

Another cause is the fairness of the Grand National course, and especially its most famous fence, Becher's Brook. 'I felt that it was very unfair that the ground on the landing side was so much lower than the take-off side, so that it was a trap. The Brook fulfilled no purpose other than it was a part of history, and horses used to fall back into the Brook and it was very difficult to get them out.' Such is Peter O'Sullevan's status in the racing world that his concerns – shared by other influential racing figures – were taken very seriously, and alterations to Becher's Brook were duly made.

Sir Peter's final record is part of Beethoven's 'Emperor Concerto', played by Vladimir Ashkenazy: 'Having heard that, if I'm not going to develop a musical appreciation after listening to it, there's no hope for me.'

Luxury? 'I'm very susceptible to mosquitoes, and so I would very much like to take a spray that would inhibit their activity, without obviously upsetting the ecological balance of my island.'

Sue Lawley has reservations: 'It's a bit practical for us really, Peter. Wouldn't you like a nice bottle of Calvados instead? I mean, you wouldn't feel the bites if you drank that.' The castaway agrees.

Sir Peter O'Sullevan made his final race commentary in the Hennessy Gold Cup at Newbury at the end of November 1997. Since then he has spent much of his energy raising funds for a range of animal welfare charities, and even though he is well into his nineties his passion for horses and for racing remains undimmed.

2000s+

THE FIRST TWELVE years of the new millennium have seen momentous events around the globe: the attacks of 9/11; war in Afghanistan; the invasion of Iraq; the Indian Ocean earthquake and tsunami; the London attacks of 7 July 2005; the Haitian and Japanese earthquakes; the Arab Spring. Three prime ministers of the United Kingdom held office during this period, and all three have been cast away: Tony Blair and Gordon Brown in 1996, David Cameron in 2006.

While television screens in the UK showed ever more reality shows and talent competitions which offered aspirants the chance of fame and glory, *Desert Island Discs* not only remained a staple of the Radio 4 output but, under Sue Lawley, steadily increased in popularity.

At the heart of its appeal lay the continuing variety of the castaways. The year 2000 alone saw a diverse island intake which included Dr Jane Goodall (who had undertaken ground-breaking work in the study of chimpanzees), Clive James (previously marooned in 1980), actress Sheila Hancock (ditto 1965), biographer Claire Tomalin, Colin Montgomerie (first golfer since Peter Alliss in 1987), Harry Potter creator J. K. Rowling (pages 409–12), musical theatre legend Stephen Sondheim (pages 413–17), and two very different actors: Hollywood star Donald Sutherland and Norman Painting, who had played Phil in *The Archers* since that programme's birth half a century earlier.

Just as enduring as that variety was the programme's continuing ability to excite emotions, as when in 2006 the appearance of Daniel Barenboim took the *Desert Island Discs* team to Israel. Sue Lawley asked the conductor about the decline of his wife, the great cellist Jacqueline du Pré (cast away with Roy Plomley in 1977), whose glittering career as a performer was cut short by multiple sclerosis. 'The cruelty about the illness,' said Barenboim, 'is not only what it does, but it took in her case four and a half years to diagnose . . . She stopped playing before it was diagnosed. She had lost all sense of touch, and therefore when she would pick up the bow she didn't know whether it weighed five kilos or five milligrams. She couldn't feel it.'

In spring 2006 Sue Lawley and Mark Damazer, who had become Controller of Radio 4 two years earlier, were in a café at Berlin airport waiting to board a plane

Jacqueline du Pré in BBC Two's In Rehearsal, *January 1965*

back to London after attending one of Daniel Barenboim's Reith Lectures, when Sue dropped her bombshell: she intended to vacate the *Desert Island Discs* presenter's chair later that year. Initially Damazer tried to persuade her to rethink, but she was adamant. 'Had I had my way she would have continued,' he recalls, 'but it was clear that she had made up her mind. She felt that it was time to move on, and that was that.'

Sue Lawley had been fronting *Desert Island Discs* since March 1988, and by the time she finally left the desert island she had presented nearly 800 editions of the programme. 'I've had more than eighteen very happy years,' she told the *Guardian*, 'and have talked to some extraordinary people as they revealed themselves through their choice of music. It is one of the best jobs in broadcasting. But it has dominated my professional life and I feel the time has come to concentrate on other aspects of broadcasting and maybe a bit of business too.'

Mark Damazer told the same newspaper: 'She started her career as a journalist and is still a journalist at heart. She also has an enormous interest in people. Put these two attributes together and you end up with fascinating and entertaining interviews that are now the hallmark of *Desert Island Discs*. She will be a tough act to follow.'

Indeed, and as another mark of the programme's place in the national psyche, the bookmakers were immediately offering odds about the succession. 'Whoever takes over will be inheriting a much-loved position and an opportunity to become a broadcasting institution – if they are not one already,' said Graham Sharpe of bookmaker William Hill, and he priced up a large field of candidates:

3/1 David Dimbleby
5/1 Andrew Marr
6/1 Sue MacGregor, Michael Parkinson
7/1 Jenni Murray
8/1 Michael Palin
10/1 Sarah Kennedy, Jeremy Vine, Johnny Walker
12/1 Jeremy Paxman
14/1 Victoria Darbyshire, Terry Wogan, Fi Glover
16/1 Jonathan Ross
20/1 Ken Bruce, Nicky Campbell, Simon Mayo, Kirsty Young
25/1 Clive Anderson, Tony Blackburn, Steve Wright
33/1 Alan Partridge
50/1 Chris Evans
66/1 Johnny Vegas, Joanne Goode

Three things about that list immediately catch the eye. The first is the suggestion that Michael Parkinson might have been up for a return to the desert island. The second is the skimpy 33–1 against Alan Partridge being lured away – even by *Desert Island Discs* – from his spiritual home on the 'Mid-Morning Matters' show on North Norfolk Digital. And the third is a reminder, were one needed, that outsiders often belie their odds . . .

The William Hill run-down of the prices lists twenty-five runners, but within days of Sue Lawley's departure being announced, more than four times that number of pitches from would-be presenters had landed on Mark Damazer's desk. 'Pretty well anybody you might have considered wrote in,' he recalls, 'or applied through their agents. A real *Who's Who* of broadcasting applied, plus a huge cast of characters who had appeared on other radio networks down the ages. And there were plenty of members of the general public with no broadcasting experience who thought they were just what *Desert Island Discs* needed.'

Damazer had already had first-hand experience of the fierce resistance to change of some Radio 4 listeners when he altered the station's early-morning schedule, and in so doing consigned to the scrapheap the 'UK Theme' which was the network's own dawn chorus. So he was well aware that appointing a new *Desert Island Discs* presenter required extreme care.

One person who had not rushed to apply was a well-known broadcaster whose chance was assessed by William Hill as 20–1. After cutting her teeth with BBC Scotland, East Kilbride-born Kirsty Young had worked for

Channel Five and ITN – where she was much praised for her coverage of the 9/11 attacks – and was now back at Channel Five as the principal news-reader. In addition, she had been standing in for Michael Parkinson on his Sunday-morning programme on Radio 2, and had occasionally presented the satirical television game show *Have I Got News for You*.

The more he ruminated, the more Mark Damazer thought how well Kirsty Young fitted the bill, not least because of her voice. 'She has a fabulous broadcasting voice. No matter how good your message is, on radio there is nowhere to go. It doesn't matter what you look like, it doesn't matter how clever you are, it doesn't matter what graphics you've got – if you don't have the voice, it's not going to work. Kirsty has a fabulous vocal instrument: rich, warm, clearly articulated and with a great range – and you can sense when she's smiling. Furthermore, she's intellectually curious about people, and empathetic with them. She understands when to press the button and when to release it – when to ask the question and when not to ask it.'

The final decision was to be his, but he very discreetly sought the opinions of the two people he needed on side: Jenny Abramsky, Director of Radio, and Mark Thompson, BBC Director-General. Neither took much persuading, and soon after Kirsty Young's agent eventually threw her hat into the ring Damazer met his quarry at a London hotel and came straight to the point: he wanted her to be the next presenter of *Desert Island Discs*. Stifling her surprise, she accepted, and the news was broken to an expectant public in late June 2006 – when she herself was on maternity leave after the birth of her second daughter.

The announcement caused quite a stir. The *Daily Telegraph* called the appointment 'an entirely unexpected move', while the *Daily Mail* quoted an unnamed Radio 4 source as declaring, 'People are worried about the future of *Desert Island Discs* as they see her as too lowbrow for Radio 4's audience.'

The fourth presenter, Kirsty Young

Kirsty Young herself told the press: 'I've loved *Desert Island Discs* as long as I've been listening to radio. Its enduring success is testament both to the brilliant format and consistently fascinating guests. There isn't a show on radio I'd rather present. I'm completely thrilled to be doing it and can't wait to get started.'

That start came on 1 October 2006, and in the early weeks with the new presenter at the helm, one thing became apparent: there was no danger of the variety at the core of the programme's appeal being compromised. Kirsty's first ten castaways were illustrator Quentin Blake; *Little Voice* actress Jane Horrocks; journalist Robert Fisk; charity leader Camila Batmanghelidjh (pages 450–3); chef Heston Blumenthal; musician and *I'm Sorry, I Haven't a Clue* treasure Humphrey Lyttelton (who had previously appeared fifty years earlier); former Metropolitan Police Commissioner Lord Stevens; block-buster author Stephen King; comedian Matt Lucas (below, as Vicky Pollard); and impresario Raymond Gubbay.

Over the decades, *Desert Island Discs* fans had been recording their favourite programmes on reel-to-reel tape machines and then on audio cassettes. But advances in digital and internet technology in recent years brought with them hitherto unthought-of possibilities for giving listeners access to previous programmes, and early in 2010 a team of production wizards got down to work on the programme's website. When launched in April 2011 by the recently appointed Radio 4 Controller Gwyneth Williams, the website offered a wholly new chapter in the life of the programme, and indeed in the way Radio 4 uses its archive. It provided the facility to play with the programme, to search for every track, book and luxury choice made by every castaway, and to listen to previous editions then and there, or download and save them for ever. Since the launch the scope of the archive has been steadily increased, and by mid-2012 it was offering all complete editions of *Desert Island Discs* in the BBC's possession, going back to Margaret Lockwood's recording in 1951 – some 1,500 in all. So keen were listeners to take advantage of the availability of this cornucopia of riches that by mid-2012 over 8 million episodes had been downloaded.

In planning the website, a key issue was what to do with the data on offer, for 2,800-odd castaways had between them chosen over 22,000 pieces of music – not to mention the books and luxuries that would accompany them on to the desert island. (Sometimes the website entry cannot tell the whole story. For example, according to the transcript of the programme Sir Basil Spence opted for a supply of spaghetti only after Roy Plomley had advised him that he could not take his wife.)

After labouring away for some time, the website team produced what they called their 'dirty spreadsheet', which listed all the data that could be mustered from the BBC Written Archives – plus other sources such as books, back issues of the *Radio Times*, electronic systems and dusty paper files.

Jane 'Little Voice' Horrocks

The availability of audio recordings of *Desert Island Discs* programmes is patchy for the early decades. There is nothing at all from the 1940s. For the 1950s there are currently two complete editions (Margaret Lockwood and Jimmy Edwards) in 1951, then two more in 1955 (Sir Malcolm Sargent and Emlyn Williams), and for the rest of the decade only short fragments of sound. It is a similar picture with the 1960s; it was not until the mid-1970s that – with a few exceptions – all programmes were routinely kept. (For rights reasons the music items are currently shortened in the downloadable versions.)

One particularly fascinating option offered by the website is the 'Others Who Chose This' facility. For example, 'A Whiter Shade of Pale' by Procol Harum was a musical choice of Diana Mosley, actress Gemma Jones, photographer Lord Lichfield and politicians David Blunkett and Michael Howard. Former Radio 4 Controller Mark Damazer points out that both Shami Chakrabarti, head of the pressure group Liberty, and Jeremy Clarkson of BBC's *Top Gear* had 'Heroes' by David Bowie among their record choices, and comments: 'If you want to define the two people least alike in the United Kingdom, it would be Shami Chakrabarti and Jeremy Clarkson.'

In June 2011, with the seventieth anniversary of the first *Desert Island Discs* programme coming up the following January, Kirsty Young presented a ninety-minute special on Radio 4 called *Your Desert Island Discs*, in which – assisted by composer Howard Goodall, music journalist Miranda Sawyer and 'general pop know-it-all' Paul Gambaccini – she analysed listeners' own accounts of how music had defined the key moments of their lives. Over 25,000 people had responded to the invitation the previous month to send in their contributions, and the result was not only fascinating, but an illustration of how *Desert Island Discs* now relates to its listeners. Being a fan is no longer just a question of turning on the radio and listening placidly; it is a two-way affair.

And in their way, the accounts of the 'ordinary' listeners were no less engaging than those of many celebrity castaways. For example, John Cunliffe listened to the programme from Baghdad, where he was working as director of Save the Children in Iraq. His first choice of record was a Bob Dylan track which took him back to an earlier posting in Zaire, where he was surrounded by 'murder, looting, pillage, rape'. His colleague Tim had a guitar and would play for the other charity workers in the evenings, and one night performed 'Shelter from the Storm': 'It was the first time we'd heard or seen anything that beautiful for a long time. Since then it's stuck in my head and never gone away. For me, it's a story of a person who is struggling, or a people that are struggling, and it seemed to sum up the moment in Zaire at the time.'

The Top Twenty musical choices among those listeners who had partici-pated are as follows:

1 Vaughan Williams – *The Lark Ascending*
2 Elgar – *Enigma Variations*
3 Beethoven – Symphony no. 9, 'Choral'
4 Queen – 'Bohemian Rhapsody'
5 Pink Floyd – 'Comfortably Numb'
6 Elgar – Cello Concerto in E minor
7 Handel – *Messiah*
8 Holst – *The Planets*
9 Vaughan Williams – *Fantasy on a Theme by Thomas Tallis*
10 Mozart – Requiem in D minor

11 Led Zeppelin – 'Stairway to Heaven'
12 Pachelbel – Canon in D Major
13 Pink Floyd – 'Wish You Were Here'
14 The Beatles – 'Hey Jude'
15 Mahler – Symphony no. 5 in C sharp minor
16 Parry – *Jerusalem*
17 The Kinks – 'Waterloo Sunset'
18 Rachmaninov – Piano Concerto no. 2 in C minor
19 The Rolling Stones – 'Gimme Shelter'
20 Simon and Garfunkel – 'Bridge Over Troubled Water'

The leading ten artists/composers were the Beatles, Bob Dylan, Beethoven, Mozart, Pink Floyd, J. S. Bach, the Rolling Stones, Elgar, Vaughan Williams and Queen.

After a good deal of speculation and rumour, it was announced that the castaway for the seventieth-anniversary programme on 29 January 2012 would be Sir David Attenborough (pages 489–95), who had previously been on the programme in 1957 and 1979 with Roy Plomley, and in 1998 with Sue Lawley – making Sir David only the second person, after Arthur Askey, to appear on *Desert Island Discs* four times. A National Treasure for a national institution.

Opposite: *Daniel Radcliffe in* Harry Potter and the Chamber of Secrets, *2002*

J. K. ROWLING

children's writer, creator of Harry Potter

5 November 2000

'I had never been so excited by an idea in my life'

Every cloud has a silver lining. When in 1990 the train taking Joanne Rowling to King's Cross was badly delayed and she had nothing to do but let her mind wander, into her head came the idea for a book about a boy attending wizard school. Ten years later when she appeared on *Desert Island Discs*, that boy had become one of the best-known characters in literary history, and bore one of the most familiar names on the planet: Harry Potter.

At the time of J. K. Rowling's being cast away, Harry had been the hero of four books (starting with *Harry Potter and the Philosopher's Stone*, published in 1997), which between them had garnered an array of awards and sold over 40 million copies. The fourth, *Harry Potter and the Goblet of Fire*, sold over 370,000 copies on its first day alone, and over three million copies in two days in the USA – figures which must make uncomfortable reading for the numerous publishers who turned the original book down.

Sue Lawley kicks off with the explanation of her castaway's name: 'J. K. in case the boys didn't like reading what a woman had written, according to your publisher. A very sexist thought?'

'It was. I argued, and then what it came down to was that I was so grateful to be published, they could have called me anything. They could have called me Graham if they'd wanted.'

How close to the truth, asks Sue Lawley, is the image that has been perpetuated of Rowling as the down-at-heel single mother pushing the buggy round Edinburgh, writing in a café because her flat was unheated?

Marianne Faithfull
'Guilt'

'An emotion I am not unfamiliar with'

'It's like most newspaper stories. It's about fifty per cent true and fifty per cent embroidery. It's true that I lived entirely on benefits for nine months, and mostly on benefits for about eighteen months. It's true that I wrote in cafés with my daughter sleeping next to me. And that sounds very romantic, but of course it's not at all romantic when you're living through it. The embroidery comes where they say, "Well, her flat was unheated": I wasn't in search of warmth; I was just in search of good coffee, frankly, and not having to interrupt the flow by getting up and making myself more coffee. I did also meet an American journalist who said to me: "So, you wrote your first novel on napkins" – and I laughed myself stupid, and said, "No, I could afford paper."'

So was it a case of Harry Potter coming into her mind and demanding to be written?

'Absolutely it was – yes. I was twenty-five when I had the idea for Harry, and I had been writing (if you include all the teenage embarrassing rubbish) for years and years, and I had never been so excited by an idea in my life. I'd abandoned two novels for adults prior to that. Actually the second novel I was still writing when I had the idea for Harry, and for six months I tried to write them both simultaneously, and then Harry just took over completely . . .

'I knew that his parents had been killed, I knew he was a wizard and he didn't know he was. It wasn't until I got off the train that I started going back and thinking, "Well, how can he not know?" and "What happened to his parents?" – and it took me five years to work out this very long plot.'

What was she like as a child, Sue Lawley wonders?

'A real daydreamer, very vivid fantasy life, very freckly, squat, thick National Health glasses, bit of a know-it-all, underneath very nervous, very, very insecure' – and always reading: 'Anything, absolutely anything. The great thing my parents did, nothing in the house was banned, so I read a lot of adult novels young, but I also read Enid Blyton, and I read Barry Hines, and Noel Streatfeild, and then pretty much anything else.'

A sense of family, Sue Lawley ventures, is important to Rowling. She agrees: 'There is an innate desire in every child to have a family, and Harry goes out and makes his own family. I think I possibly put some of my feelings about my mother's illness into Harry, in that sometimes home was a difficult place to be, because my mother was very ill . . . She had MS, and I do want to emphasize she did have a galloping form of it. Someone can have multiple sclerosis and have a normal lifespan and not be tremendously affected. My mother was unlucky: she died at forty-five . . . I was twenty-five. I started writing Harry six months before she died, so she never knew.'

What about all those strange words in the Harry Potter books?

'Dumbledore came straight out of Thomas Hardy. Dumbledore is used in *The Mayor of Casterbridge* as a dialect word meaning "bumblebee", and I loved that word' – and 'Parselmouth' was an obsolete slang term for a cleft palate. 'It's as though, subconsciously, for years I had been preparing for writing Harry Potter, because I had just been storing weird words . . . just as you would collect useless objects, really.'

After her mother's death she moved to Portugal, to teach English as a foreign language. While there she married, had a baby, and spent some time teaching. But her marriage broke up and she returned to Britain. *Harry Potter and the Philosopher's Stone* was accepted by an agent, who eventually found a publisher for the book: hearing that news was, after the birth of daughter Jessica, 'the best moment of my life.'

'Part of the secret behind the success of Harry Potter', suggests Sue Lawley, is 'that it is actually very simple. It does touch an awful lot of things we know about: orphan children, they're at boarding school—'

'There's a reason why the orphan is a recurring figure in children's literature.

The children are instantly on that hero's side or heroine's side: you haven't got your mum and dad. But more than that, it's very liberating to be an orphan. You don't have to keep anyone happy, and I think even happy children love to be able to explore – through a fictional orphan – the possibilities of that situation . . .

'I do think this is so funny. There are two groups of people who think I'm wholeheartedly with them. One are people who believe passionately in the boarding school system, and the other group are practising witches. I think rarely has anyone united those two groups, and I have to say I'm not on either of their sides . . . If you spend a minute looking at what I have to do to get Harry to the places he needs to be, it's apparent he really has to stay at school at night, and that's why it's a boarding school. And as for the practising witches, I don't believe in magic in that sense, but people come up to me in signing queues and whisper, "I'm trying the spells."'

The Harry Potter phenomenon, already astounding at the time its creator was cast away, has continued to grow. The film of *Harry Potter and the Philosopher's Stone*, with Daniel Radcliffe as Harry, was released in 2001, to be followed by hugely successful films of all the other six books, and globally the Harry Potter brand is now estimated to be worth some £7 billion.

Plenty of adults have lost themselves in the world of Harry Potter, but autumn 2012 saw publication of J. K. Rowling's first novel for a specifically adult readership, *The Casual Vacancy*.

STEPHEN SONDHEIM

composer and lyricist

31 December 2000

'I consider myself a playwright who writes in song'

Stephen Sondheim, a giant – many would say *the* giant – of modern musical theatre, was first washed up on a desert island by Roy Plomley in August 1980. At that point he was familiar to British audiences through his lyrics for *West Side Story* and *Gypsy*, plus a string of innovative shows for which he also wrote the music, including *A Funny Thing Happened on the Way to the Forum* (starring Zero Mostel in New York, Frankie Howerd in London), *Company*, *Follies*, *A Little Night Music* (which contains his best-known song, 'Send in the Clowns'), *Pacific Overtures* and that louring masterpiece *Sweeney Todd*.

The twenty years between his first and second appearances on *Desert Island Discs* had added to the Sondheim canon, among others, *Merrily We Roll Along* and *Sunday in the Park with George* – and to the Sondheim mantelpiece, already groaning with trophies, an Academy Award for Best Song in 1990: 'Sooner or Later (I Always Get my Man)' from the film *Dick Tracy*.

Sue Lawley understands that Sondheim is not bothered if an audience does not go away humming his tunes.

'That whole thing about hummability, it's vastly exaggerated. First of all, when an audience leaves a theatre

Sondheim's Sweeney Todd – the Demon Barber of Fleet Street, *Adelphi Theatre, March 2012: Michael Ball as Sweeney Todd and John Bowe as Judge Turpin*

humming a tune, it's because they were humming it when they came in. Or it's a tune that has been exposed. I think sometimes, particularly in the old days, tunes were reprised many times during the course of the evening . . . I remember at the end of the first act of *A Little Night Music* there's a song called "Weekend in the Country" which has six or seven choruses, and sure enough the audience – you know, supposedly I write "unhummable" music – they're all humming it at the interval because it had just been drummed into them.'

Why had he trained his sights on Broadway-style musical theatre?

'Oscar Hammerstein was my mentor and he came from Broadway, and I wanted to be what he was. I suspect if he had been an opera composer, I might have become an opera composer. I've often said that if he were a geologist, I would have been a geologist.'

Hammerstein has been a huge influence on Sondheim: 'Oscar was using music to establish tone, rather than merely to entertain' – and Sondheim's work would follow the master's example.

The castaway's second record – after 'the finest American musical', *Porgy and Bess* – needs a preamble: 'I decided to throw modesty to the winds and take to the island some of my own pieces. Not just because I enjoy them but because they bring memories back. Good memories. Memories of working on the shows. The first of these is *Sweeney Todd*, which is probably the show that was easiest for me to write. It just flowed.'

Back to Oscar Hammerstein, and what Sue Lawley calls 'this ongoing masterclass that you enjoyed for so long'. How did Sondheim first meet him?

'My parents were divorced when I was ten years old. My mother got custody of me and she bought a farm in Bucks County, Pennsylvania. Three miles from the house she bought lived the Hammerstein family. They had a son named Jimmy, my age, and we became close chums . . . My mother was a difficult woman, and I spent more and more time over at the Hammerstein house . . . By the time I was twelve or thirteen years old I was in the Hammerstein house much more than I was in my own, so Oscar became a surrogate father for me and encouraged me to be a songwriter, although I had only been moderately interested in music before that . . . Movies were my thing.'

Under Hammerstein's tutelage his interest in music grew. At the age of fifteen he wrote his first musical and took it to show his mentor – 'absolutely convinced', says Sue Lawley, 'that it would be on Broadway within the year'.

'Within the week, I think! . . . I went to a school called George School and I wrote a show called *By George!* with two classmates and brought it to Oscar and asked him to judge it – not as if I were a friend of the family, but as if it were a script that merely crossed his desk. I came over to his house the next day to sign the contract, and he said, "If you really want me to treat this as if it were from a stranger, I must say it's the worst thing I've ever read." I was shocked beyond belief, and he said, "It's not untalented, but if you'd like to know why it's terrible, I will tell you" – and he proceeded to tell me, starting from the first sentence of the first stage direction.'

When writing for the musical theatre, is there what Sue Lawley calls a 'central trick'?

'It's not a trick, it's a central principle, which is to treat songs like little one-act plays, where you present a situation and then either resolve it or, if you don't resolve it, move forward so that by the time you've finished the song you're at a different point than you were – in terms of the story, of the show, of the play – so that each song has a function.'

Sondheim wrote the lyrics for *West Side Story*, to Leonard Bernstein's music. 'He wanted the show to be important, and therefore he thought the lyrics should be poetic. Well, his idea of poetry is my idea of purple prose – I mean, we just don't agree . . . I was only twenty-five years old, and I was the mascot of the group, so to speak. Though I had my own principles and opinions, I was trying to please everybody. So in trying to please Lenny I pushed myself to write some fairly purple passages. "Today, the world was just an address" is not, I think, what a street boy who's an ex-gang member would say, and "I Feel Pretty" of course is my *bête noire*: the idea that Maria would sing a song of such elegant phrasing is deeply embarrassing. No, the lyrics I like in that show are few and far between, but "Something's Coming" is a lyric I like, because that sounds like a boy being excited. And the Jet song I like – and now I'm running out of moments I like!'

After *West Side Story* and *Gypsy*, he decided that writing lyrics was not enough. 'I was trained as a composer, and that's what I wanted to do. I went to my friend Burt Chevelove, who suggested that we do a musical based on Plautus' plays, and we all started to work on *A Funny Thing Happened on the Way to the Forum* . . . Plautus invented situation comedy as we know it. It was domestic comedy – cuckolded husbands and things like that – and Burt said, "We can make a musical farce" and so that's in fact what we did. That was my first big hit . . . It ran just under a thousand performances. It supported me for many, many, many, many, many, many, many years, the income from various productions all over the world and particularly from schools, universities – although there have been schools in the United States who've refused to do it because it uses the word "virgin".'

Sondheim does not like defining himself, but Sue Lawley persists: 'Are you as much a playwright as you are a songwriter, a writer of musical theatre? Does your theatre happen to be musical?'

'Oh yes: I consider myself a playwright who writes in song. I get attracted to stories. I do not get attracted to themes, or theses.'

'But there are themes and theses, aren't there?'

'Yes, but they are never in the forefront of my head, and I never think of anything except telling the story, creating suspense, making laughs and dealing with character. Because playwrights are essentially actors and when I write a song, I'm really an actor.'

What brings him the greatest joy from his work?

'I think it's the universal one: I think you'd find the same answer from virtually everybody. First, there's the joy for the composer when you hear the orchestra reading down the score and you hear the instruments for the first time. Then the look on the faces of the cast when they hear the orchestra

Sondheim's Sunday in the Park with George, *Wyndham's Theatre, London, 2006*

for the first time is like the look on the faces of children on birthdays and Christmas. It is unalloyed joy, and whatever the problems of the show, they disappear for that day.'

To desert island business: this castaway would be 'helpless' at the practicalities, and as for his luxury, 'it would have to be a piano, because I get such pleasure out of playing the piano. Thinking about the luxury, I thought, "Well, is there electricity on the island? Because then maybe a VCR and a lot of old movies would be terrific!" But I think, for eternity, or for a long stay, it would have to be a piano.'

Stephen Sondheim's eightieth birthday in March 2010 was the trigger for widespread celebration of one of the all-time greats of American musical theatre. The New York Philharmonic played a birthday concert and the New York City Center staged a glittering tribute evening – and a few weeks later came a special Sondheim evening at the Royal Albert Hall in London as part of that year's BBC Proms, with Judi Dench singing 'Send in the Clowns'.

'**Dancing in the Street**'
David Bowie and
Mick Jagger

Beethoven
**Piano Sonata no. 23
in F minor, op. 57,
'Appassionata',
2nd movement**

'**I Got You Babe**'
Sonny and Cher

Brahms
**Concerto for Violin
and Cello in A minor,
3rd movement**
*'The very first classical record
that I had'*

Handel
**Recorder Sonata
in F major, op. I/II,
2nd movement**

'**Just the Way You Are**'
Billy Joel

Britten
*A Midsummer Night's
Dream*, **Act 3 finale**

Mozart
'**Soave sia il vento**'
(from *Cosi fan tutte*)
*'I shall be playing that piece as
I'm rescued, and sailing away
into the sunset'*

. . . .

📖 *The Ascent of Man*
by Jacob Bronowski

♡ Telescope

SIR PAUL NURSE

biologist

10 February 2002

'I think I went quite wild!'

S ue Lawley's interview with the biologist Sir Paul Nurse was nothing if not educational. Indeed, it was one of those memorable editions of *Desert Island Discs* in which a complicated subject – in this instance, how cancer spreads – is illuminated for a lay listener through the medium of an articulate castaway. No one who heard the programme would ever look at yeast in the same way again. And, as so often, it is the castaway's sheer enthusiasm which lubricates the process: early on, Paul Nurse declares that the discovery process in science 'is like being an explorer in the Amazonian jungle or in the Arctic'. His own work on the protein molecules which control the division of cells led him to the ultimate accolade of the Nobel Prize.

Born in Norwich in 1949, Paul Nurse studied at the universities of Birmingham and East Anglia. As a research scientist he became interested in gene division, a field in which he carried on working when he moved from his academic base to the Imperial Cancer Research Fund, which in 2002 – just a week before he was cast away, in fact – merged with the Cancer Research Campaign to form Cancer Research UK. In 1999 he was knighted, and in 2001 he shared the Nobel Prize in Physiology or Medicine with Leland H. Hartwell and R. Timothy Hunt.

The road to that accolade began with the humble medium of yeast. Does he mean, asks Sue Lawley, 'ordinary common-or-garden yeast that we use to make bread?'

Yes, says her castaway, 'the yeast that makes bread and beer and wine'. It's also useful for research, he goes on, 'because it acts as a good model for understanding how processes work in more complicated living things like our cells . . . [There are] only five thousand genes in yeast and it's very easy to manipulate and grow, whereas human beings have forty or fifty thousand genes: much more complicated.'

His breakthrough came when he discovered the gene that causes cells to divide and create more cells. 'How long then,' asks the presenter, 'did it take you to show that the gene that you had isolated in yeast was, in fact, pretty much the same in human beings – because that was the great leap, wasn't it?'

'I first identified this gene in the mid-1970s, and then my work and of course the work of many others – because science is truly a social activity – led to the physical isolation of the gene in the early 1980s, from yeasts, and then another five or six years before we made the link with humans – so quite a long time.'

'That must have been quite a moment, when finally you realized that it was – forgive me if I get it wrong – practically the same gene.'

'It's practically the same gene, despite the fact that it's been one thousand million years or maybe one thousand five hundred million years since yeast and human beings diverged. That was a "Eureka!" moment. We don't have many of them in science, and I remember I was sitting there with my colleagues in the lab looking at the computer screen, waiting to see whether they were the same or not – and out it printed. I still see the letters in my mind, and we knew we'd got it.'

'What did you do?'

'I think I shouted. I think I ran round the lab. I think I ran into the next lab. I think I went quite wild!'

Paul Nurse grew up in north-west London, where his interest in science was triggered in the late 1950s by the appearance of Sputnik 2 – the Soviet space capsule that carried Laika, the first dog into space – in the night sky.

Laika, the first dog in space

'The English were very interested in it

because they all worried about what would happen to the dog. Of course, it died on re-entry. I waited up at my front door and there was this bright "star", moving across the sky. It was truly amazing. I got so excited, running down the street, my mum calling after me – I was in my pyjamas, and I didn't have any shoes or socks on – telling everybody I saw, "Just look at that! Look up there, it's a satellite! It's Sputnik 2!" They obviously thought I was barmy.'

Having elegantly dispatched the story of just what brings about the division of a cell, Paul Nurse is asked the big question: 'If you know what it is that causes cells to divide, and we know that cancer is the uncontrolled division of cells, why haven't we already arrived at a drug that can simply zap those defective cells?'

'The problem is that cell division isn't simply important for cancer, but it's important for nearly every other growth process in the body. We were all once a single cell, when we were an egg in our mother's body: you and I were once single cells. But to produce us we had to go through many, many divisions, and when we damage ourselves – cut our hand, say – we have to get cell division to repair that. Now, we could easily stop that with a drug against the genes that I, or many other people have identified, but we wouldn't simply kill the cancer: we'd kill all the dividing cells as well. So the real key for cancer is actually to try and identify something that's specifically different about the cancer cell compared to the normal cell.'

Sue Lawley moves to the next big question: 'Do you think we in our lifetime are going to see a cure for cancer?'

'We'll never see a *cure* for cancer, because there's just too many different types of cancers out there. But I confidently predict that we're going to see a major attack on many of those cancers in the coming generation.'

In the mid-1990s Paul Nurse became Director of the Imperial Cancer Research Fund. 'Two-thirds of all cancer research in this country', Sir Paul points out, 'is funded by the charities . . . The British public are very generous. They give to us and I suspect that the government thinks, "Well, if it's going to be looked after by direct contributions, it's less of a priority" . . . You understand where they're coming from because they're well pressed for money, but it can't be said to be right.' And as for the current government's not yet having banned cigarette advertising: 'This is an utter disgrace. We are killing a hundred thousand people a year due to tobacco, and the tobacco industry has been almost evil in how it's dealt with this in the past by covering up what they knew before – that we know a ban on advertising will have a huge effect: it would save many lives, and it's a disgrace it continues.'

At a workshop on DNA for schoolchildren in Birmingham, 2010

Sir Paul's current research is into the shape of cells: where is that leading?

'A very important feature of all living things is their shape, their form. You look at a tree, you look at a dog, you look at a human being, and we all have characteristic shapes. That's seen in its simplest way at a cell, a single cell . . . My yeast cell is just like a little cylinder, but I can change its shape using mutants again, and so they grow like bananas – they're curved – or like a ball, like a sphere or T-shaped cells because they have more than one growing side. Cancer is really dangerous when it spreads throughout the body, and for cells to spread through the body they have to change their shape and creep through the tissues to escape from where they are, to go somewhere else. How this is controlled is just not understood, and I'm starting with that to see whether we can get some clue as to how it might work.'

On the desert island, how readily would he be able to engage in abstract thinking?

'I quite like the idea of being on a desert island. I am very sociable so I am a bit worried about being alone. That bothers me, but I'm going to sit on the beach and contemplate.'

And with his luxury, a telescope, 'I can look at the stars at night, and I can look at the birds during the day, and I can look for the ship that's going to rescue me.'

Later in 2002 Sir Paul Nurse was awarded the *Légion d'honneur*, and in 2006 became a Foreign Honorary Member of the American Academy of Arts and Sciences. In 2010 he became President of the Royal Society, and in January 2011 was appointed the first Director and Chief Executive of the UK Centre for Medical Research and Innovation (now the Francis Crick Institute).

But post-castaway life has not all been plain sailing. In the *Desert Island Discs* interview there had been little mention of Sir Paul's family background, though he did mention that he was the youngest of four children – 'by far the youngest of four, and probably a mistake'. In 2007 he discovered that one of his older sisters (by then deceased) was in fact his mother, and the couple he thought were his parents (also deceased) had been his grandparents. The family had arranged this deception to protect his unmarried eighteen-year-old mother from the disgrace of having borne an illegitimate child.

In an addendum to his Nobel Prize autobiographical statement in February 2008, Sir Paul wrote: 'I regret not having had time with my real mother or the opportunity to discuss my origins with her later in life, and then there is the final irony that even though I am a geneticist my family managed to keep my genetic origins secret from me for over half a century.'

SISTER FRANCES DOMINICA

pioneer of the hospice movement

8 February 2004

'It's not about dying – it's about living fully until you die'

'**M**y castaway this week is a nun' is one of the rarer opening sentences in *Desert Island Discs* history, but this castaway was a very special nun: Sister Frances Dominica Ritchie, moving spirit behind hospices for sick children – and, for good measure, adoptive mother of a boy from Ghana.

Born in Inverness in 1942, granddaughter of an elder of the Church of Scotland, she was educated at Cheltenham Ladies' College after her family moved south, before going on to train as a nurse at the Hospital for Sick Children in Great Ormond Street, London. She joined the Anglican order of All Saints Sisters of the Poor, and in 1982 founded Helen House for sick children in the grounds of her convent in Oxford.

As a small girl, asks Sue Lawley, had she had any idea that she would grow up to be a nun? 'No – no idea at all . . . I wanted to be a nurse from the age of three.' Later, while working towards qualification, 'I hoped that when I had completed my training I would be able to work with one of the agencies abroad. Some of my senior colleagues had gone to Vietnam and were looking after children affected by the war. That was the sort of thing that really fired me.' Prompted by Sue Lawley that she might have intended to marry, she admits: 'I was going to meet the perfect man and I was going to have five children and adopt five more – it was all quite straightforward.'

It was while she was at the Middlesex Hospital that she nursed a vicar from the Church of England, and 'for some reason best known to God, certainly not known to me, I started going to church regularly'.

'It's one thing to get involved in the Church,' Sue Lawley suggests; 'it's another thing to decide that you want to become a nun.'

'It happened very dramatically, and I hate God to be dramatic.' At a retreat, 'at two minutes to eleven, just before the service began, with the sun streaming through the windows, in a split second I knew that none of my ideas were for me . . . What God was asking of me was to be a nun, and there was just, from that moment on, a conviction that this was what I had to do.'

Howard Blake
'Walking in the Air'

'The theme song of Helen House for a number of years'

How did her family feel about this sudden vocation? They were devastated: 'It was less painful, they said, not to see me at all than to see me in a habit.'

'So they didn't see you?'

'So they didn't see me for a long time.'

'How long?'

'Oh, several years. But the community was very good in allowing me to go and spend a day a month with my grandfather, which was a special concession – and we used to have lovely days together. But I didn't ever see any other members of the family when I saw him.'

Her grandfather lived with her parents – who made sure they were out on the days that she visited.

'You didn't see your mother?'

'No. It was too painful for her . . . It is hard, I suppose, to see your daughter do something that you just hate. She would have been proud to have said, "My daughter's working with the Save the Children Fund," and so on. It was rather different to say I was, as she once described it, "holed up in some godforsaken place an hour's drive from home".'

Sue Lawley takes the conversation back to schooldays at Cheltenham Ladies' College. Young Frances never felt she excelled at anything, which meant she was overlooked. 'My school reports always used to say, "She'd do better if she concentrated more" . . . I'm really glad now, looking back, that I experienced that sense of failure because I think it gives you a whole other dimension to your character and to your understanding of other people.'

Her mother – who had herself been at the school – was disappointed at this failure to shine: Frances had once come across a letter Mrs Ritchie had written to one of her daughter's best friends at school, asking, 'Why is Frances such a failure?'

'I never admitted to having read it but it was quite an experience.' Happily, in her mother's last years 'we became the best of friends and she was my greatest supporter, and just wonderful to me'.

For the newcomer to the convent, accommodation was a cell: 'It had a small window which was so high that you couldn't see out – and that was deliberate. It had a wrought-iron bedstead with a mattress which had been slept on for a few years, I think, and kind of dipped in the middle. It had a high-backed chair. It had a washstand with a bowl and a jug and cold water, and it had a prayer stool and a crucifix.'

As part of her daily routine she peeled potatoes, scrubbed floors and dusted choir stools, but she saw such tasks as 'the most wonderful gift, because it didn't require very much concentration. It offered the opportunity to enter into whole new worlds in relationship with God, and so door after door opened to me in the silence and through the work.'

After eleven years at the convent she was elected Mother Superior – 'I would have ninety-five-year-old nuns describing themselves as my child!' – and it was while holding that office she founded Helen House.

'It happened through a friendship with a little girl, Helen, and her parents. Helen tragically was taken very ill when she was two and was in hospital for six months, and at the end of the six months, when her parents knew she wasn't going to get well, they took her home and cared for her with tremendous love and devotion. And they were good enough to trust me, so they lent her to me sometimes, just to give themselves a very short break. It didn't happen very often, but they would say it was knowing that I loved her and would care for her – in as much as possible the same way as they cared for her at home – that enabled them to carry on through weeks and months. It was thinking about that that led me to wonder if there were other desperately sick children and families out there, experiencing tremendous stress and distress, without very much support.'

So the hospice is not necessarily a place where children will see their days out, suggests Sue Lawley, but rather a home from home.

Sister Frances in BBC Two's Children of Helen House, *January 2007*

'It's a home from home, and families would be welcome too. Mothers, fathers, squads of brothers and sisters, Golden Labradors and terrapins and all the rest have come to stay!'

The death of a child is unthinkable, says Sue Lawley. How can she make it easier for parents to bear? 'What I can best offer is companionship – the ordinary, everyday coming alongside, sharing the joys and sorrows . . . It isn't all tears . . . If you live through the immensity of grief and sorrow, you somehow become capable of experiencing the same amount of joy and wonder . . . It's not about dying – it's about living fully until you die.'

And when a child does die, 'We have a little room in Helen House which is like a bedroom, which they can arrange as they like with furniture and toys and candles and pictures – whatever they want to bring into the room.'

Time and again, parents must have asked Sister Frances, 'Why would God do this to us?'

'Yes, but almost always there is also a sense in which life has somehow emerged. This isn't an end – it can't be an end – but there is the pain of separation.'

There is also the joy of coming together, and Sister Frances tells how she came to adopt a little boy from Africa:

'I was helping with the Clergy Conference in Ghana in 1988. One Sunday I visited the hospital, and among many other people met a very tiny, very frail little boy. He was ten and half months, weighed just under nine pounds and was very poorly. It was a year of terrible drought in Ghana, and a lot of people were suffering extreme malnutrition . . . I talked with the doctor, who didn't hold out very much hope for him. So I said in one of those moments of madness, "May I take him and care for him?" – and he's now sixteen and five foot eleven.'

The other nuns agreed to her scheme and the little boy was duly brought to Oxford, but how are they now able to live together as mother and son? 'The community owns a house just across the road from the convent, just an ordinary house in the road, and so that's been our home since he was three . . . We try to be as normal as we can! He's passionate about moto-cross racing, and so we trundle off with motorbikes and end up in muddy fields or incredibly dusty fields . . . He races and I stand in the middle of the field with my eyes shut, absolutely terrified.'

'It is an incredible story,' remarks Sue Lawley. Does Sister Frances think she has had her cake and eaten it?

'Oh yes, I've been incredibly blessed.'

Later in 2004 a second hospice (or 'respice') named Douglas House was founded to accommodate people between sixteen and forty years old – and was opened by the Queen.

Sister Frances Dominica was appointed OBE in 2006, and in 2007 she was named Woman of the Year 2007 in recognition of her work.

TRACEY EMIN

artist

28 November 2004

'I think I'm getting happier, and then something always happens'

The work of Tracey Emin provides heavy-duty ammunition for both sides of the debate about modern art. For one camp, her uncompromising confrontation of her own experience represents a ground-breaking new category of the visual arts. For the other camp, it is the epitome of vacuous mediocrity masquerading as artistic expression.

Tracey Emin first came to public prominence – some would say notoriety – in 1997 when *Everyone I Have Ever Slept With 1963–1995* was exhibited at Charles Saatchi's *Sensation* exhibition at the Royal Academy. This exhibit was a tent, inside which were appliquéd the names of everyone who qualified, including Emin's grandmother Granny Hodgkins. Traditionalists huffed and puffed, but Tracey Emin's name was made.

Emin became even more controversial with *My Bed*, which was nominated for the Turner Prize in 1999. On show the previous year, it was described in the following terms by the Saatchi Gallery: 'Tracey shows us her own bed, in all its embarrassing glory. Empty booze bottles, fag butts, stained sheets, worn panties: the bloody aftermath of a nervous breakdown. By presenting her bed as art, Tracey Emin shares her most personal space, revealing she's as insecure as the rest of the world.'

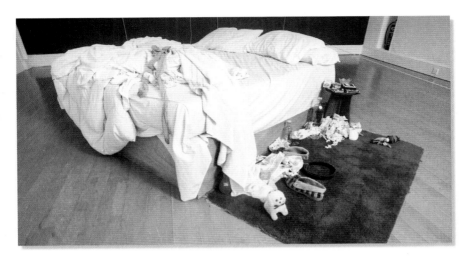

My Bed, at the Scottish National Gallery of Modern Art, Edinburgh, 2008

Tracey Emin, says Sue Lawley, 'takes, not unreasonably, some delight in the controversy that her art engenders'. Has her art been a kind of therapy for her 'complicated life'?

'I think it started off like that. I always say I'm not the best visual artist in the world, and I really mean that. What I like about my art and what's kept me going is the fact that it's about communication . . . While I'm making my art and I'm communicating then I'm obviously not alone, and that's what's important to me.'

Sue Lawley mentions the Tracey Emin watercolours which had accompanied the unmade bed in the Turner Prize exhibition: 'They were very beautiful.'

'They were very tiny watercolours, about four inches by four inches, and they were scenes of myself sitting in a bath. They were very traditional, very dainty, beautiful little watercolours.'

'And did they give you the same pleasure to do as creating a kind of mussed-up bed and the detritus of sexual activity?'

'When I was making those watercolours I was actually crying at the time, so yes, it comes from the same place. It's an emotional thing.'

'But you wouldn't have achieved what you've achieved, and the fame and the recognition, if you'd just done watercolours. Is that the point?'

'We don't know, do we? . . . As an artist, to get some kind of notoriety or some kind of credit or fame, then you have to make a seminal piece of work, you have to change the face of what people understand is art or is contemporary art. I've done that with two pieces of work. I've done it with my tent

and I've done it with my bed. Most artists, no matter how successful they are and even if they earn a really good living, the majority of them don't make anything seminal in their life. I've done that with two things. Whether people think it's good or bad or rubbish, I have done it. That's what the difference is.'

Back to her years growing up in Margate. 'When I was about fourteen I would have liked to have been a dancer.' So why did she not pursue that ambition? 'In Margate the best dancers were men, and there was a lot of pressure from them, older men. The fact that I'd slept with most of them just wasn't conducive . . . In a way there was a lot of unhealthiness about the sex thing and all that kind of stuff, but actually the dancing was pretty good. We weren't going around smashing things up or breaking into houses, we were danc-ing and having sex. It wasn't the most unhealthy thing in the whole world really when I look back on it.'

She was raped when under-age: 'I had sex against my will, but it was called "being broken into". You were "broken into", you went to school the next day and you said, "I was broken into last night." You didn't complain, you didn't go to the police; it just carried on and on and on . . . You kind of expect it to happen because that's what happens.'

Life changed in 1972 when her father went bankrupt and lost the hotel he owned. 'He lost absolutely everything and with it everything that my mum owned as well. So from one minute having this hundred-bed hotel and staff – my friends say this explains the "princess and the pea" factor – the next minute we're squatting in a cottage where the staff used to live, with abso-lutely nothing and with no dad around either. Not at all. And a very, very upset, angry, frustrated mum who then had to go out to work every hour God sent so she could provide stuff for us.'

Sue Lawley suggests: 'This is where it all began, isn't it – Tracey Emin flouting the rules of convention, just doing what she felt like when she woke up that morning.'

'Maybe I have a problem with authority or something, but also in some ways I was quite mature, and I think that's why I started having sex when I was quite young. Every time that I slept with someone, I used to call it the "springboard effect". I used to think by sleeping with someone it was like travelling to a new country or to a new world. It was good. It was free. It wasn't hurting anyone. It was great. What was the problem with it?'

She enrolled at Maidstone College of Art, where she graduated with first class honours. 'My personal life was an absolute mess of course, but I just loved every single day at college.'

What sort of art did she produce there?

'A few Edvard Munchs. A few Egon Schieles. A bit of German Expressionism. It was really bleak, but lots of self-portraits as well.'

Next came the Royal College of Art: 'The best thing about the Royal College of Art is that letter saying that you got in. After that it goes downhill.'

Tracey Emin's life hit a new low, with one abortion being followed by another, and her response was to destroy every piece of art she had created: 'I smashed it all up and I threw it in rubbish bins and I got rid of it all, and said, "Well that's it – art's over!" Because after being pregnant I understood the true essence of creativity for myself. So then I couldn't justify the art that I was making. It was just more objects filling up the world – more rubbish, more stuff.'

But in time she returned to her art, and her reputation rose to the point where she staged an exhibition at the influential White Cube Gallery. This featured a crumpled cigarette packet which had belonged to her uncle. 'Explain that to me,' prompts Sue Lawley.

'My uncle Colin got killed in a car crash in 1982. He was at a traffic lights and a lorry came down and pushed his car underneath a bus, and he was about to light a cigarette at the time. The cigarette pack that he was holding was a Benson & Hedges packet, which is gold, and you can see where the imprint of his hand was at the time when he was killed.'

This hoarding of 'bits and pieces' intrigues Sue Lawley – 'It's all genuine, is it?' – as does the fact that Tracey Emin employs people to sew together her creations.

'Of course other people have to sew for me,' replies her castaway, 'but I do the cutting, I do the placing, I do the laying. No one does anything without my say-so. I believe in the distribution of wealth really strongly, and if I'm in a point where I can

The Beach Boys
'Good Vibrations'

'We used to listen to the Beach Boys and pretend that Margate was California'

employ six people, that is really brilliant. I don't see what's wrong with it.'

'But I'm really talking about the art,' says Sue Lawley, 'as to whether it matters whether it really was a bit of blanket that you slept with when you were nine.'

'I don't know if it matters so much to other people but it really matters to me.'

Is Tracey Emin getting happier? 'I think I'm getting happier, and then something always happens, and I realize that it's still really difficult. We all have our crosses to bear, but money can't buy you love and it can't buy you health – but it can get you really, really good health insurance, and it can buy you a round-the-world air ticket at any given moment that you need it . . .

'I swim every day and I never eat bad food. The only thing I do which is really, really, really negative and bad, is I drink too much and I'm going to have to do something seriously about this . . . I stopped smoking on my own, after smoking for twenty-seven years, last Christmas – Christmas day – and I want to give myself another gift. I want to be free. I want to break away from the alcohol. I can't stand it.'

'How', asks Sue Lawley, 'would you like to think that art historians might place you? Let's say they're writing about you fifty years on, what would you like to feel that they would say about your contribution, and you?'

'That I was consistent, that would be a good thing. So when I'm eighty or ninety and I'm still making art, they're going to have to rethink the things that they've said about me. And a few of them are starting to rethink it, and they are starting to use words like, "Whether you like it or not, she's still here, she's still around." And I will be for a really long time.'

In March 2007 – the same year as a major exhibition of her work at the Venice Biennale – Tracey Emin was made a Royal Academician (joining fellow castaways such as David Hockney (pages 165–8), Peter Blake and Anthony Caro). In 2008 an exhibition of her work broke Scottish National Gallery attendance records for a living artist, and in 2012 she staged an exhibition at Turner Contemporary in her home town of Margate as part of the London 2012 Cultural Olympiad.

RONALD SEARLE

artist and cartoonist

10 July 2005

'You never escape from your island prison'

One word dominates Ronald Searle's 2005 interview with Sue Lawley: 'prisoner'. It sets the tone for one of the most powerful editions of *Desert Island Discs* ever.

Ronald Searle is perhaps best known for his inspired cartoons depicting the anarchic goings-on at St Trinian's girls' school from the late 1940s and the life of Nigel Molesworth at St Custard's prep school in the 1950s. Both are comic classics – but there was a very dark side to Searle's life.

Born in Cambridge in 1920, Ronald Searle was the son of a Post Office worker. Money he earned from singing in the church choir went on drawing materials, and in 1935 he started producing weekly cartoons for the *Cambridge Evening News*.

He was called up for military service on the very first day of the Second World War, and in 1942 was sent to the Far East, where he was captured by the Japanese. 'I never really left my prison cell,' he wrote in his volume of war drawings published in 1986, 'because it gave me my measuring stick for the rest of my life.'

Searle published dozens of his own books as well as illustrating for other authors, and his work remained hugely loved in Britain even after he had moved to

France in the early 1960s. It was to his house in rural Haute Provence that Sue Lawley took her microphone in summer 2005.

> Johann Strauss II
> **'Champagne Song'**
>
> 'It rather sums up exactly the vision of Monica and myself in the kitchen'

'I don't miss any particular country,' says Ronald Searle when Sue Lawley asks whether he misses Britain: 'because the point is, if you're a freelance artist and you're commenting on the world around you, you've got to live on an island. I have the advantage, perhaps, of having been captured and put into prison, and one curiosity is that once you've been a prisoner, you never escape from your island prison.'

This idea of prison is present even in his first record choice, *Fantasia on a Theme by Thomas Tallis* by Ralph Vaughan Williams: 'If you're a prisoner and you want to recreate England, your childhood, or the history, the actual smell of the country in which I was born, this particular record is perfection.'

So, says Sue Lawley, 'you found yourself as a young man in his early twenties a prisoner-of-war in the tropical misery of South-East Asia. You did hundreds of drawings during your four years of captivity. How much was the anarchic cruelty of the St Trinian's drawings fed by that experience?'

'Perhaps to a certain extent, but I think basically what changed was the fact that there'd been a war, and war is nothing but killing. A soldier is there to kill, that's all. You're trained to kill. So the mentality of everyone who was involved in the war was that no longer the politeness of prewar existed, but horror, misery, blackness, the horribleness that one saw.'

Throughout his childhood in Cambridge, Searle had been keen on drawing, and it was in the 'sixpenny box' at Heffers bookshop that he came upon a book about the German satirical artist George Grosz. 'I suddenly realized that graphic satire could be so explosive, so disastrous. And I thought, "My God, I want to become a great man like George Grosz." When I went into the army, officially we were fighting Germany, but I had in my pocket that little book, someone that represented the best of what Germany could possibly be.'

In 1942 the 22-year-old Searle was posted to Singapore with the Royal Engineers. 'Did you have any idea at all what you were being sent to?' asks Sue Lawley.

'Our commanders simply said to us, "No problem – they're slit-eyed, they can't shoot straight, they're just a lot of yellow dwarves." That sounds really rather horrible, but that was the attitude in that epoch.'

'How long before you were captured?'

'We had a month fighting in the jungle, and of course the Japanese, if one can say so, were brilliant at guerrilla warfare. They sat up in the top of every palm tree and as you walked down below, they shot you. And suddenly we found ourselves – pathetic little territorials, who'd never seen a Japanese before – taken prisoner. And you were in a temperature, on the Equator, of about 90 degrees all the time . . .

'What happened to us very frequently was that we were very badly beaten. A Japanese carrying a bamboo pole for beating you is like being beaten with an iron bar. The only people who were executed were the people who tried to escape. And you dug your own grave and that was it.'

A group of prisoners, including Searle, were sent to work on the Thai–Burma railway. 'I was on the River Kwai and all the building of the bridges. And there I lost all of my friends . . .'

'Every morning you woke up,' says Sue Lawley, 'and more of your friends had died. You obviously felt that was what was going to happen to you. What was the nadir for you? How bad did it get? How ill did you become?'

'We were all ill. You can't be in the jungle without being ill. The problem with the jungle is that it's very beautiful, but in it you've got insects, and those insects bring life or death. We were eaten alive, all the time we were work- ing. Most of the time we were working eighteen hours out of twenty-four a day breaking rock, constructing a railway through a jungle which was sup- posed to be probably the most impenetrable jungle on this planet. But the terrifying thing was that you were with your friends – people you grew up with, people you had joined the army with, and you wake up in the morning and find that each side of you one of your friends was dead. Inevitably you were covered in miserable, irritating, painful skin diseases – apart from the fact that you were working physically and your food was almost non-exist- ent. You still have to retain some sort of optimism, and curiously enough the thing that kept me going was that if I could only draw and show people what it was like, I would have achieved some sort of object in the short life I was probably going to have. But I was convinced I was coming back with those drawings . . .

'People could be reduced to nothing and still have the will to survive. And what's so fabulous is that the human body can suddenly revive. You can

Ronald Searle at his desk, 1956

go through all this, and you can still come out of it, so that when you come
back to England, your sister says, "Oh, you haven't changed much."'

Sue Lawley notes that we have a vivid picture of what life was like for
the prisoners from Searle's three hundred drawings. How had he got the
pencils and paper? 'Everyone had a book, and in every book there was a fly-
paper, and people would tear out the fly pages of the book . . . I had to let
people know what was happening. I was convinced that someone had to put
down on paper exactly what was happening, but what was never explained
to us, what was never apparent, was that this was a clash of two cultures. The
Japanese culture is so removed from our little territorial culture, under the
Japanese culture, Japanese military tradition, to be a prisoner was the lowest
of the low. They died before they were taken prisoner.'

Searle survived to return to England. He married and had two children.
But despite working hard he was 'in a state of panic . . . When you've come
out of the sort of world that I came out of, a world of total unreality, into a
postwar Britain, the whole thing was not only transitory, it was ephemeral.'
When the rest of the family was away, he decamped.

'It was survival again, if you like – it was a question of survival – and I decided that, I'm sorry, but I had to abandon my wife, abandon my children, abandon my house, abandon my career, abandon my reputation – the lot – and start from zero.'

He moved to France to live with 'marvellous Monica' and the two of them have been together ever since. Does he, asks Sue Lawley, keep in touch with his fellow prisoners-of-war? Yes – although there are only about a dozen of them still alive – but they never discuss details. 'Because no one else could ever understand?' asks Sue Lawley.

'If all your generation,' replies Searle, 'if everyone you knew died when they were nineteen and twenty, you've got the biggest present in the world. I should have died when I was nineteen. I'm eighty-five now. How many presents can one have in one's life? Every day is a present, and I'm making the best I can out of every second of my life.'

His final record choice is inspired by 'one of the great pleasures of living in France. The day is over and the glass of champagne is bubbling, and the champagne song from *Fledermaus* rather sums up exactly the vision of Monica and myself in the kitchen.'

And his luxury is predictable: 'I'd have the best possible bottle of champagne, and then I'd write a note, put it into the bottle, and then throw it into the sea: "Please send another one."'

Although in his mid-eighties at the time of the *Desert Island Discs* interview, Ronald Searle continued to be very active after it, still drawing for newspapers and magazines in many countries. Among his late works was a 2006 collaboration with Jeffrey Archer (*Cat o' Nine Tails and Other Stories*) and two books of rhymes with Robert Forbes (*Beastly Feasts* and *Let's Have a Bite*).

He died on 30 December 2011, at the age of ninety-one.

Nigel Molesworth: scourge of St Custard's

Opposite: *With Fanny the Wonderdog*

JULIAN CLARY

entertainer

25 September 2005

'God bless the BBC! – beautifully put!'

'There's nothing he likes better, he says, than a warm hand on his entrance.'

When Sue Lawley introduced her castaway in such terms, *Desert Island Discs* listeners might have thought that they were in for forty-five minutes of the unrelenting camp which has given Julian Clary such a following – an army of fans who delight in his stream of innuendo and double entendre. Not for nothing was his 1993 stand-up tour named *My Glittering Passage*.

The programme did indeed contain a fair amount of vintage Clary, but this was to prove one of those classic editions of *Desert Island Discs* which went much further than expected, and provided a fresh perspective on the personality of the castaway: as well as the outrageous gay comedian, a diffident, ruminative, reflective person.

Sue Lawley's introduction credits Julian Clary with being 'the man – or one of them anyway – who brought camp out of the closet and on to mainstream television'. With his garish costumes, full make-up and endless innuendoes, he enjoyed great success with shows such as *Sticky Moments* on Channel 4. 'He had a conventional upbringing in south-west London,' she continues, 'but

was teased at school for being effeminate. He enjoyed some success as a drag artist, worked the alternative comedy circuit, and then glittered into television.' Clary's rising profile has recently been given a further boost by his reaching the final of *Strictly Come Dancing*.

Before getting down to the Clary life story, Sue asks for word of Julian's stage partner Fanny the Wonderdog – and the news is not good.

'She's passed away to the Great Behind. She was my co-star – a small mongrel that came from a dogs' home. Her first ever appearance was when I was doing a club where there was no dressing room. I told her to sit quietly by the side, and she started to get laughs and upstage me. But she did seem to have comic timing. Night after night, she'd deliver the goods.'

What exactly did Fanny do?

'It's quite hard to describe. She used to do impressions. She did a very convincing Sarah Ferguson, and the Queen Mother. She wore a wig for Sarah, and for the Queen Mother you would just lift her gums up – she had rather brown teeth, and facial hair. But her main gift was giving withering looks to the audience. If I was playing a rough club, people would heckle, and to protect me she would stare people out.'

Clary, the son of a policeman and a probation officer, says that when he was a child there was always comedy at home – for instance, his mother would routinely walk round the house with a pair of knickers on her head. 'It was a very proper, very moral upbringing, but they did have a laugh.'

Barb Jungr
'Peace in the Valley'

'A very dear friend and a very wonderful singer'

Young Julian won a scholarship to St Benedict's School in the west London suburb of Ealing – 'very posh' – an establishment run by Benedictine monks, one of whom was responsible for teaching him a particularly harsh lesson.

'I was quite a chatty eleven-year-old, into my guinea pigs; quite extrovert, quite friendly. There was one monk I liked in particular. I was very religious: I used to go to Mass a lot, and I used to pray a lot. That's what I was like until it all went horribly wrong.'

How?

'I was suddenly disillusioned by this favourite monk of mine. He used to beat naughty boys – that was part of the Rule of St Benedict – never me,

In the final of BBC One's Strictly Come Dancing, *2004, with Erin Boag*

because I never did anything wrong. But one day I forgot my swimming things. He said, "Get up to my office!" – where he beat me very hard with his strap. I was terribly shocked by the violence of it – and the humiliation, and the transformation of this holy man. His whole face changed. I hadn't done it deliberately – I quite liked swimming, so it was my loss. After that my religious fervour rather evaporated.'

In the upper school he teamed up with friend Nick. 'The two of us became increasingly theatrical and deliberately provocative, reading Quentin Crisp and Muriel Spark and wanting to be *la crème de la crème*. We enjoyed provoking people. Obviously we were bullied, but I don't like to portray myself as being a victim, as we enjoyed our celebrity status . . . It was the time of David Bowie and Marc Bolan, and there seemed to be some glimpse of a life outside St Benedict's which attracted us . . . It was a very boring life there, and we were highly amused by each other.'

As a student of English and drama at Goldsmiths' College, University of London, Clary flourished. 'You were allowed to be an individual, grow your hair, wear make-up and put on shows. I was constantly acting in plays and putting on cabarets at lunchtime.'

Here were born two of the most striking of Clary's alter egos. 'Gillian Pieface was a sort of Mother Earth figure. She wore a kaftan, wooden beads and plimsolls. She was kept in a holdall which was stolen from the back of my van – I was doing singing telegrams and balloon deliveries at the time . . . I loved the make-up and the glamour but didn't want to become a female impersonator, so I thought black rubber would be good: it doesn't crease and you rinse it under the tap. Joan Collins was everywhere at that time, so I called myself The Joan Collins Fan Club and suddenly felt much more comfortable being a glamorous man than being called Gillian or Glad or May.'

At Goldsmiths' there had been a heterosexual affair – 'and very successful it was, too,' he assures Sue Lawley: 'I wasn't just dabbling; I was quite accomplished at heterosexual goings-on, I'll have you know.'

In 1987 Clary appeared on television in *Friday Night Live*: 'One seven-minute slot on that show and a whole different world opened up. I was perfectly happy on the cabaret circuit and with my self-sufficient life of writing my own act and negotiating my own fees and taking the dog and getting the train and going to do gigs, and it was a very pleasant life. That slot led to my having my own show on Channel 4, *Sticky Moments*.'

How does the Julian Clary camp act differ from those who had come before, such as Larry Grayson?, wonders Sue. 'I suppose what had changed is that I was allowed to be an out gay man and Larry Grayson wasn't. He did everything but. I don't think he could say, "I'm a gay man" and carry on working. I didn't feel I was on any great crusade . . . Obviously I was a gay man, and there was no point in saying I wasn't.'

Behind his increasingly successful career was private tragedy. His partner Christopher was dying of an AIDS-related illness, and Clary nursed him until he died. 'I don't think I dealt with that bereavement very well. I carried on working and then I had another relationship which went horribly wrong, and then everything seemed to conspire to turn around and bite me. Everything just spiralled out of my control.'

At the 1993 British Comedy Awards, Clary made what Sue Lawley delicately describes as 'an obscure reference to a particular sexual act performed by sado-masochistic gays' – 'God bless the BBC! – beautifully put!', interrupts her castaway – in connection with the then Chancellor of the Exchequer, Norman Lamont. The ensuing hoo-hah saw Clary taken off live television.

'That infamous joke haunts me still. I was very depressed and drugged at the time, mixing Valium and alcohol . . . and probably if I'd been sober I'd have had some restraint.'

He returned to live with his parents, underwent counselling and was treated for depression. 'I had to be very tenacious and start all over again.'

He had panic attacks triggered by his fear of being recognized, a contradiction quickly picked up by the presenter: 'Panicking at the idea of fame is such a contradiction, because you are an arch-exhibitionist.'

'I'm not really,' replies her castaway. 'I'm quite introverted. If I'm on stage and being paid to be an exhibitionist that's fine, but most comedians are quite introspective, and are busy observing people.'

Suggesting that underneath the outrageous stage presence there was an orthodox man trying to get out, Sue raises Clary's attempts to have a child. Adoption was still a possibility: 'I've got a spare room, and could give a child a very nice life.'

He is writing a novel, and loving it: 'You can do what you like. I killed a couple of people off last night as they were getting on my nerves. Perhaps I'll go and live in Nicaragua and write books . . . But I'll probably just carry on with tired old innuendoes, playing smaller and smaller venues.'

Julian Clary's response to the prospect of being cast away is that 'I'd absolutely hate it', but admits that island life might be made more tolerable by his selected luxury – one of the more unusual choices in the programme's history – an all-purpose prosthetic arm: 'Very useful for cracking open shellfish and things to do with trees, and it would glint in the sunshine, so a passing ship might come and rescue me.'

Since being cast away in 2005, Julian Clary has enjoyed enduring popularity and public affection. His many television appearances include hosting the BBC One quiz show *Have I Got News for You*, making a cameo appearance in the Australian soap opera *Neighbours*, and co-presenting ITV's *This Morning*, while he remains a regular on the BBC Radio 4 game *Just a Minute*.

DAVID CAMERON

Leader of the Opposition

28 May 2006

'A political party should be like a well-tuned orchestra'

When David Cameron was cast away in May 2006 he had been a Member of Parliament for only five years and leader of the opposition for just six months. The fifth leader of the Conservative Party in the space of nine years, he had inherited, in the words of Sue Lawley's introduction, 'an organization only just beginning to revive after three thumping election defeats'.

Across the House of Commons Dispatch Box he faced the still formidable figure of Tony Blair (pages 381–6), who had declared that he would not be seeing out the whole term as premier, and against whom at Prime Minister's Questions the new Tory leader was undergoing a crash course in the parliamentary hurly-burly – his gibe to Blair that 'You were the future once!' being an early indication that he could give as good as he got.

Born into a prosperous Berkshire family and educated at Eton and Oxford, Cameron seemed a throwback to an earlier sort of Conservative leader, but the party responded to his tone and style, and the climax of his conference speech during the 2005 leadership campaign sealed what had long looked a very unlikely victory: modern compassionate Conservatism, he argued, was 'right for our times, right for our party and right for our country. If we fight for it with every ounce of passion, vigour and energy from now until the next election, no one and nothing can stop us.'

Stirring words for the party faithful; but he had yet to submit himself to the smiling yet steely Sue Lawley, whose interviews with leading politicians always had a particular edge. Intriguingly, the sentiments expressed by David Cameron about his 'hinterland' echo closely the opening gambit of another charismatic young party leader a decade earlier: one Tony Blair.

Sue Lawley quotes David Cameron's assertion that 'I probably have more hinterland than front land. For me, family, friends and home are the most important thing in my life. If politics interfered with that too much, I'd call it a day.' Then she addresses her castaway in challenging terms: 'That's very noble New Man stuff, David, but it can't last, can it? Because this kind of job eats you alive' – producing a characteristically smooth response: 'I hope it doesn't, and I don't think it's impossible to combine a high-profile job and a family life. You just have to lay down some clear boundaries.'

Like what?

'I try not to leave home in the morning before about a quarter to eight, because I help get our children up, one of whom goes to school, and I try to make sure that a couple of nights a week – or one night a week – I'm back in decent time to bath the kids. You've got to try and keep a balance, and not just for the family – also, I think, it helps you make better decisions. If you're permanently exhausted and frazzled, and going from one meeting to the next, you'll forget what you're trying to do.'

With a working wife, Samantha, three children under five, a house in the country and a vegetable patch on which he grew prize-winning tomatoes ('Digging a garden is a good way of switching off – and good fun, and good for you,' he observes), had it not been a huge decision to stand for the leadership?

With Samantha after his first Conservative Party Conference speech as leader, 2006

'It was a big decision and I didn't do it lightly. I always thought there was a fair prospect of winning the competition to become leader. That might sound arrogant, but I thought it was very important to think it through, and think: can I cope with it, can my family cope with it, is it the right thing to do?'

So is it amazing that he was elected leader?

'I suppose it is in a way, but I think I had a very clear campaign saying what needs to change in the party, and being quite uncompromising about that, and not trying to please everybody by saying what they wanted to hear, but saying some of the things that I think they needed to hear. And being clear, that's why my campaign struck a chord.'

Taking a handy cue from the Bob Dylan song which provides Cameron's first choice of record, Sue Lawley observes that 'your ancestors have been tangled up in blue down through the ages': his great-grandfather on his mother's side was a Conservative MP before losing his Berkshire seat in 1905, 'and there were quite a few before him'.

And then there was the royal connection, though from the wrong side of the blanket – or, as Sue Lawley puts it, 'Royal bastardy is a bit of a theme in your family.' Soon after becoming party leader, Cameron learned

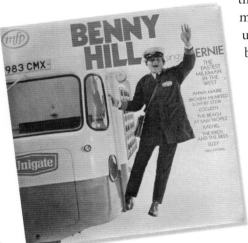

that he was descended from Mrs Jordan, a mistress of William IV; and for good measure his wife Samantha turned out to have been descended from Nell Gwyn.

While not overtly political (his father was a stockbroker and his mother a magistrate for many years), the Cameron household in which David grew up at The Old Rectory, Peasemore, was one in which a wide range of issues were discussed. On a more personal note, one morsel of revelation was that as a child he had been so pudgy that a friend nicknamed him 'Pavarotti'. And a better childhood revelation comes before his second record choice is played: 'Ernie: The Fastest Milkman in the West' by Benny Hill was his party piece. Enthusiastically egged on by Sue Lawley, he recites the first two lines from memory; then comes the music itself, prompting him to declare: 'I haven't heard it for ages, and that was bliss.'

Coverage of his Oxford days inevitably raises the matter of his belonging to the notorious Bullingdon Club – 'Yes,' he laments, 'I was hoping we might not come on to that!' – and he plays it with a straight bat: 'Oxford is quite a clubby place and quite a drink-fuelled place, and I suppose like others I probably drank too much and did things I shouldn't have done – but nothing too heinous, I hope . . . It was just a dining club—'

'It was more than just a dining club, wasn't it?' interrupts Sue Lawley: 'There's an initiation ceremony, isn't there, when your rooms get wrecked?'

Her castaway agrees that there had been 'rather stupid things' done – 'but as I say, nothing too heinous . . . We drank too much and fell over, like lots of people do.'

'Is this where you smoked the spliff or snorted the coke?' the fearless Lawley asks, but again her delivery is fended off: 'I think it's fair in life to say you're entitled to a private past that can be both private and in the past – whereas as a politician today, people are entitled to poke around and have a look at my life.'

Working in Conservative Central Office, he had a ringside seat at the downfall of Margaret Thatcher – 'It was a very sad time' – and worked for such senior Tories as Norman Lamont and Michael Howard. Then he left the Westminster bubble for a while to work for Carlton Communications, because 'I wanted to get some experience of business life'. And then, in 2001, he was elected to the House of Commons.

At this point comes a complete change of mood. 'Yours is an altogether very blessed story, for the most part,' says Sue Lawley: 'conventional, rounded, happy, high-achieving, undramatic. And then in 2001 you and Sam had your first child, Ivan. How long was it before you realized something was wrong with him?'

'It was only a few days. We went home to Sam's parents' house in Oxfordshire, and we just noticed he was having these strange movements – very sudden jerky movements. You obviously worry about everything as a parent. You start asking questions. Initially we were told that he was fine, but then we took him to hospital, and they ran some tests, and said that he had this very rare condition, which has very poor outcomes. It means you're very disabled, and can't really do a lot of things – a combination of epilepsy and cerebral palsy. It was a complete shock.'

Ivan needs round-the-clock care. 'He's a wonderful boy, with the most lovely eyes. He definitely interacts with us, in the way he looks at you, and the way he moves his head, but he often is in a lot of pain. The thing that worries us is his quality of life, and trying to make sure he has a good quality of life, but we're very positive, optimistic people; we're determined to give him all we can, and to make sure he's part of a happy family . . . It hits you almost like mourning: you're mourning the gap between your expectation and what has happened, and it does take a lot of time to get over.'

Ivan was followed by two siblings. 'When Arthur and Nancy were born, obviously we were watching them like hawks . . . Are they going to make a strange movement? Is everything going to be all right?'

Sue Lawley moves from the personal to the political. David Cameron is a proponent of so-called 'compassionate Conservatism'. 'You've emphasized the compassion, but people say: when are you going to address the Conservatism? Which of the fundamental Conservative beliefs ring bells for you?'

Her castaway claims to have two overriding guiding principles: the first is trusting people; the second is sharing responsibility.

Now the fabled Lawley political antennae are twitching. 'But in not mentioning the key policies that are so close to the heart of the diehards, the Tory grass roots, are you in fact willing to alienate them? Can you manage without them? Is that the strategy?'

'I don't want to alienate anybody. The way I think about it is, a political party should be like a well-tuned orchestra – it's got to have a brass section and a string section – and I think the problem in the past is perhaps we just emphasized some points and some policies more than others, and there was a danger that the Conservative Party was becoming the tax-cut, crime and immigration party. What people want is balance. They want to see that your concerns mirror their concerns.'

So are the green policies and the compassion a bid for what Sue Lawley jokingly calls the 'middle-ground swingers'?

'I look at it in a slightly different way,' replies Cameron. 'I think what you ought to do in politics is take your values – trusting people, sharing responsibility – apply them to the big problems of the day, and just say what you think, say what you believe – and if that means that sometimes you're going to agree with your opponents, be relaxed about that.'

The general election is probably four years away, but Cameron's prospects of getting the keys to 10 Downing Street are naturally high on the agenda. When Sue Lawley asks whether coalition with the Liberal Democrats might bring 'real hope of office', her castaway takes care not to rule it out: 'I don't think it profits politicians at all to try and posit ideas like that. I hope a lot of Liberal Democrat supporters and voters will come and support *us*, particularly now the Conservative Party is back in the mainstream, and has got a big commitment to the environment.'

The Smiths
'This Charming Man'

'I probably don't agree with their lead singer Morrissey about anything'

'But do you rule out coalition?'

'I want to win the election outright, and I don't think it's sensible—'

'But if you didn't, would you consider it?'

'I don't want to speculate on what might happen if there was a hung parliament.'

'So you're not ruling out coalition – or the possibility of it?' persists Lawley.

'I'm ruling in the attempt to win the next election outright.'

To the desert island practicalities. David Cameron's book is Hugh Fearnley-Whittingstall's *River Cottage Cookbook* – 'I love food and I'm very greedy.' And his luxury? 'I've had real trouble over this. I'm a very practical person, so I thought: perhaps a fishing rod? And then I thought: I love a little drink late at night, reflecting on the day, and I love drinking whisky, so I thought I'd take a crate of whisky, possibly from Jura – we go there every year, total peace, lovely sandy beaches – so I'd sit, supping away, looking out to sea, and thinking of my friends and Sam and all the people I'd be missing.'

Sue Lawley was right to badger David Cameron about a possible coalition government, for the general election of 2010 produced a hung parliament, and after five days of feverish activity her castaway entered 10 Downing Street as Prime Minister, leading a coalition with the Liberal Democrats.

Ivan Cameron died aged six in 2009. In 2010 David and Samantha Cameron had another child, whom they named Florence.

'**Mockingbird**'
Eminem
'These kids taught me about rap'

Rimsky-Korsakov
Scheherazade, **2nd movement**

'**Ne me quitte pas**'
Jacques Brel
'Poetically he's brilliant'

'**Amazing Grace**'
Choir of Cregagh
Presbyterian Church,
Belfast
'Sends chills up my spine'

Elgar
Cello Concerto in E minor
Soloist: Jacqueline du Pré

'**Dance with My Father**'
Luther Vandross
'The thoughtfulness of a child looking back on his history'

★ '**Redemption Song**'
Bob Marley
'This is the person that kids admire the most – here you are, these criminal kids have some sense of quality'

Brahms
Cello Sonata no. 1 in E minor (for piano and cello)

Being and Nothingness
by Jean-Paul Sartre

Yo-yo

CAMILA BATMANGHELIDJH

children's campaigner

22 October 2006

'No child is born a criminal or a killer'

Kirsty Young's first month in the *Desert Island Discs* presenter's seat brought to the island a castaway who had been described as 'Britain's most colourful charity leader' – and few who had encountered Camila Batmanghelidjh would quibble with that description. In public, the founder of the children's charities The Place2Be and Kids Company stands out both for her dress – she is usually swathed in a kaleidoscope of flowing multicoloured robes topped with a turban – and for her inspirational approach to her work with disadvantaged children.

Born in 1963 into a well-to-do Iranian family, she moved to England at the age of eleven to attend Sherborne School in Dorset, where 'everybody thought I was completely odd'. Although severely dyslexic – she cannot use a computer – she took a first-class degree from the University of Warwick.

In 1994 she founded the charity The Place2Be, which works inside schools to improve the emotional wellbeing of children and their families. And in 1996 she started Kids Company, which now operates from three centres in London.

Those are the bare facts, but for the essence of the Camila Batmanghelidjh story we can do no better than Kirsty Young's introduction to their interview.

'My castaway this week has dedicated her life to the children that most of us would cross the street to avoid . . . The children she works with are the stuff of newspaper headlines: feral teenagers who don't go to school, run drugs and don't know a stable family life. The product of a privileged background herself, she decided early on to set aside her own thoughts of motherhood and devote her life to those she calls "urban child warriors". Today the project she set up in disused railway arches in South London has spread to help around eleven thousand young people every year. Such is her notoriety that she's feted by celebrities, courted by politicians and visited by Prince Charles, who was reputedly moved to tears by what he saw.'

And then, directly to her castaway: 'Camila, let's be clear: the people who are actively welcomed through your doors are the ones that most of us would be terrified of even encountering?'

'Yes, possibly, because I think they can be quite frightening. They can be quite dangerous, they can harm people. I can understand why people would be frightened of them. I love those children very much, but I'm fully aware of the fact that when they first arrive they can be very dangerous, so we take precautions in case they lose it . . .

'They need what every child needs: they need loving care, they need nurture, they need somewhere safe to stay, and this is the thing that people often forget: the humanity of these children. A typical arrival is maybe a thirteen-year-old boy. He's been run by drug dealers, couriering drugs, he's got health issues, he's not been in school since he was ten years old – and what he wants is somewhere safe. And then after a few days of trusting us, he will go and bring his younger siblings, and the younger siblings are usually in households where maybe the parent is suffering from mental health difficulties or drug addictions. What's really moving is these children's loyalty – total loyalty – to their parent.'

Is there an element of romanticizing these children battling against the odds, wonders Kirsty Young, 'because for a lot of us on the receiving end of their behaviour, they are the most unpleasant people to be around?'

'I don't think that it's romantic, I think it's realistic. I acknowledge that they're really unpleasant. Remember, I have to look after my staff and protect them against the unpleasantness of these children. You know, the debate

is divided into demons and angels, and civil society perceives itself as angelic and these children are the vehicles for demonic feelings – whereas the truth is that civil society is just as responsible for the way these children behave in damaging ways.'

The contrast between the lives of the children she takes into her centres and her own childhood could not be greater. She recalls being accompanied everywhere by two police bodyguards, with cooks and maids at home, and summers spent at the 'Ice Palace', where her father had built skating rinks, swimming pools and even a ski resort. Although 'I had no idea we were wealthy', the family clearly was: 'I walked into St James's Palace, looked up, and thought the chandeliers were rather low-key compared with the ones in my house!' And it was her relationships with the staff that opened her eyes to poverty. 'I remember being shocked that the maid lived in another room somewhere, with five of her children in the same room.'

At Sherborne School she struggled academically, but once the dys- lexia had been recognized, 'I started breathing' – and then, while she was at Sherborne, the Iranian revolution took place. 'It was a very strange envi- ronment to be in, because school life was carrying on as normal, and on the news I was watching the flags being burnt and the beginnings of the revolu- tion. I got news that my father had been executed, and then they came back and said, "No, he's been imprisoned," and I couldn't get any news.'

Her mother was in France at the time, and Camila was queuing for lunch at school when she heard that she had been granted political asylum: 'I just didn't know how to react. Was I supposed to be happy that I had political asylum? I'd lost my country. What was I supposed to feel?' Her sister became very disturbed and eventually took her own life, while her father, released from prison, escaped by walking over the mountains from Iran into Turkey, by which time she was studying at Warwick University.

She started looking after children in the affluent area of Kensington and Chelsea: 'There were children who were biting their fingers, drawing in blood on the wall; there were children who were smearing their faeces – so there was a lot of disturbance. There was also a huge amount of love: they were taking their children to ballet classes, cello classes, whatever class there was. There was a great effort to look after the children, but in some ways it had a thoughtlessness about it too.'

The moment when she decided to set up her own charity was when she realized that 'the central flaw in the care for children . . . is the assumption that behind every child is a responsible carer who's going to take them to an appointment . . . I don't think anything could have prepared me for the underbelly of children that I discovered.'

At the core of her philosophy is one simple fact: 'No child is born a criminal or a killer. Something happens to that child, and my anger is that society's not there when these children are being abused behind closed doors. The making of a criminal child is five, six, seven, eight, nine years. Where was civil society all that time? . . . The science of it is there for everyone to see – that compassion and love develops the brain, and develops control.'

Children are at the heart of Camila Batmanghelidjh's existence, and there must still be something of the child in her, for she becomes the first person in *Desert Island Discs* history to take as her luxury object . . . a yo-yo.

The work of Kids Company and The Place2Be continues to embody the energy and conviction – the 'vocation', as she puts it – of an extraordinary character.

YOKO ONO

artist and musician

10 June 2007

'I have an incredible sense of myself'

On his *Imagine* album, John Lennon sang of how Yoko's love would turn him on. But millions of Beatles fans in the late 1960s were distinctly turned off by Lennon's love for the avant-garde artist Yoko Ono, to the point that she was blamed by some for the break-up of the Fab Four.

And those fans had to suffer the further aggravation of having 'The Ballad of John and Yoko' reach the No. 1 spot in 1969 under the name of the Beatles, though later songs such as 'Give Peace a Chance', 'Power to the People' and 'Happy Xmas War is Over' were credited to Lennon, Ono and the Plastic Ono Band.

Yoko Ono was born in Tokyo in 1933, and after the war moved to the USA, where she established a reputation as an avant-garde film-maker.

Kirsty Young remarks that, after her castaway had started dating John Lennon, 'depending on who you listen to, she either stole him from the nation or helped him to focus on what was important to them both. For a long time she was publicly reviled, but now, more than twenty-five years after John's murder and with Yoko herself aged seventy-three, the public perception of her is, at last, shifting.'

Did Yoko Ono find that initial attitude hurtful? 'It was hurtful in a way, but I had John beside me, which did help – and also it seemed almost as if those things were happening in a distance.'

That ability to distance herself proclaimed an independence of spirit which was nurtured in her childhood. 'You were born into a very wealthy family,' says Kirsty Young, 'indeed, with aristocratic lineage, and yet your mother was very determined that you would become an independent little girl.'

'Yes,' says Yoko Ono, 'it is amazing when you think about it, because when I was evacuated into the countryside – most kids were evacuated – that time was very difficult. We didn't have enough food and the war was going on, and there were planes coming and bombing places, and my mother was saying, "You have to write about this –

Yoko, aged two, with her parents

just think about writing, because you are a good writer. Somehow I think it taught me to be objective about the situation, and that way of thinking about life probably made it easier for me to cope with the situation where the whole world was against me.'

It was in New York that she became a prominent avant-garde artist, but 'my inspiration comes from Asian culture, and I was influenced by that a lot, by Zen Buddhism a lot. I was really an avant-garde artist before I went to the United States.'

Kirsty wants to know more about her castaway's art, especially the so-called 'happenings': 'One of them was called "Cut Piece", where you invited members of the audience who had come to see you to cut your clothes off – you gave them a pair of scissors. That's a very brave, bold statement to make. Did you feel like a brave and bold artist as you did it?'

'It was a bit scary. I just thought that this is the kind of work that has to be done – and for that, I didn't mind taking the risk.'

Yoko Ono earned money from lecturing, mostly about classical Japanese art. She worked as a typist and as a waitress, 'but also I had my pride as being an artist and it was great that way. I felt very good because I was doing what I wanted to do.'

It was at her exhibition *Unfinished Paintings and Objects* in London that she met John Lennon.

'I had a show in the Indica Gallery, a one-woman show, and just after I finished putting everything together, John Dunbar, who was the owner, came in with John. But I didn't know it was John . . . People always say, "You must have known," but I didn't.'

What did John make of her art?

'He came in and he just went downstairs, and I saw that they were standing in front of the "Hammer Nail In" painting . . . There's a small nail in a glass jar, and there's a hammer dangling on the side of this white block of wood – and by many people hammering in the nail, gradually the painting will become a different painting than just a block of white wood.'

'And did John Lennon engage in this? Did he hammer the nail into the wood?'

'No. He said, "Could I hammer a nail in?" and I said, "No, because this is before the opening and I want to keep it clean." Then I thought, "No, no: you can do it if you pay five shillings." That's because the night before I was thinking about the opening, and I thought, "What am I going to do? Because my work is conceptual, so nobody's going to buy them. So how am I going to justify my existence as an artist or whatever?" Then I thought, a good idea to make them pay to do these things. He didn't pay five shillings: he said, "Well, is it all right if I hammer an imaginary nail in, and I pay in imaginary money, an imaginary five shillings" . . . I thought, "All right, he's playing the same game I'm playing." I thought he was very beautiful and very elegant.'

'He was already married when you met,' observes Kirsty Young, 'and it was eighteen months before you became a couple . . . It happened extraordinarily over one night: you recorded a whole album over one night, which became *Two Virgins*?'

'He invited me and I went up to his house, and already by then we knew that we were madly in love with each other . . . I felt scared about it.'

'What were you scared of?'

'About the fact that he was in the Beatles, and it started to dawn on me that this was a little bit different situation and I might lose my freedom, and then everybody was so upset with us so that they made stories.'

Kirsty Young wonders if there was an element of racism or misogyny in people's reaction to John and Yoko.

'The racism was always there, but it was more than that. It was something about John being their treasure or something. It seems like I stole that from them, or something like that. It was so shocking. I just didn't understand why that was happening.'

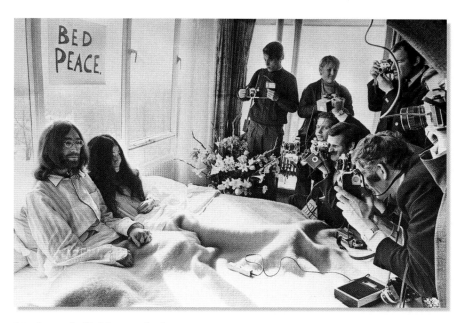

March 1969: bedded down with John Lennon

In 1969 John and Yoko held the famous 'Bed-in for peace', while on their honeymoon in Germany. 'You invited the world in to share your honeymoon,' says Kirsty Young: 'Why on earth would somebody do that?'

'Well, for world peace! We thought we were doing a good thing, and we were very narcissistic about it.'

Later Kirsty Young turns to the events of 8 December 1980, when Lennon was shot outside their home in New York's Dakota Building: 'He was returning from the studio with you that evening, going to your apartment building. Are you able to tell us what you remember of that evening?'

'It was a slightly warm night, and I said, "Shall we go and have dinner or something before we go home?" and he said, "No, let's go home because I want to see Sean before he goes to sleep." It was like he wasn't sure whether we could get home before he goes to sleep – maybe he's already gone to bed or something. He was concerned about that – but that's the last thing he said then, that he wanted to see Sean.' (Sean Lennon was five years old.)

'As you were entering the building he was shot. Did you have any time to talk to him? Did he have time to say anything to you?'

'No.' And after a long pause: 'It was a very hard time for me. But I was concerned about how it would affect Sean. I just couldn't tell him that night.'

Kirsty Young confesses: 'It's a curious experience talking to you, because you seem to have an innate optimism, you seem to be somebody who has taken life on your own terms. But at the same time, there has been this great circus, this great sideshow that has travelled along with you because of the Beatles and because of your love affair with John Lennon. How much are you realistically able to retain a sense of self when all this criticism comes your way?'

'I suppose I have an incredible sense of myself, and that's the only reason why I was able to survive. I'm not surprised if I'm vilified again when I pass away . . . I just like to believe that he's working up there for us and I'm working here with him still.'

After the final record has been played, Yoko Ono asks to give her 'affirmation':

'Thank you for the beautiful planet we live on and enjoy, in the most interesting, exciting and enlightening time of the history of the human race. Each of us was born at this time to fulfil a mission. Together we are in a process of healing and creating a better world for the lives of the planet. Our work is not yet done, but it will be done soon. For good of all concerned, so be it.'

'Beautiful,' responds Kirsty Young before moving on with the essential *Desert Island Discs* business. Yoko Ono's book is *Sai-Yu-Ki* – 'It's a very profound and fun Chinese story and it really changed my life when I was a little girl.'

Her luxury is nothing less than 'my life for the next thirty years'.

'I don't have the heart to turn that down,' responds Kirsty Young, 'although I don't know if it would be possible to give you it!'

Shortly after her appearance on the programme she joined Paul McCartney and Ringo Starr on *Larry King Live* in the USA. She continues to work, often combining music with performance art. Among many high-profile concerts in recent years was a benefit in New York in March 2011, when she performed with her son Sean to raise money for the victims of the Japanese earthquake and tsunami, while in June 2012 there opened at the Serpentine Gallery in London her exhibition *To the Light*, a retrospective collection of – in the words of *Daily Telegraph* critic Richard Dorment – 'her elusive, uneven but by no means negligible art'.

MORRISSEY

singer

29 November 2009

'Life leads me – I follow it'

In a poll of September 2011, *Radio Times* readers voted Kirsty Young's *Desert Island Discs* interview with Morrissey the second greatest broadcast interview of all time – attracting nearly 12 per cent of the votes cast and beaten only by David Frost's interview with Richard Nixon. Trailing in its wake came such encounters as Jeremy Paxman and Michael Howard, Melvyn Bragg and the dying Dennis Potter, and Martin Bashir with Princess Diana. Whether you consider Morrissey's gnomic utterances to be deeply meaningful or empty verbiage, that was some achievement.

Born in May 1959, Steven Patrick Morrissey reached global fame as lyricist and lead singer with the Smiths, the highly innovative band who first hit the upper reaches of the charts with 'Heaven Knows I'm Miserable Now' in 1984. The Smiths stayed together less than five years, and in 1988 Morrissey embarked on a solo career which was to make him one of the biggest draws in the world. The *NME* went so far as to call him 'one of the most influential artists ever'.

Morrissey has long had a reputation for not being the most straightforward of celebrities, and Kirsty Young's introduction sends out signals that this might not be the cosiest *Desert Island Discs* chat ever. He is, she says, 'the outsider's outsider . . . an intensely private person' of 'awkward grace and spiky reflections'. She then offers him one of his own quotes about his work: 'It's one hundred per cent a calling, it really is, because unfortunately I don't really exist anywhere else in life.' Does he mean that he does not exist anywhere else in life apart from the moment that he's on stage performing?

'No, I mean geographically. I don't exist anywhere else. I can be found in Yellow Pages, but nowhere else.'

'The quotes come back to haunt you,' says Kirsty Young, 'because you do give a good quote.'

'Lots of them were never mine, astonishingly.'

'Was that one?'

'That was, yes. The ones that were mine I stand by.'

Forty-five minutes is looking like a long time, but Kirsty persists, and asks about his time with the Smiths.

'I heard you say in an interview that you are a consonant away from the person you were then. Who are you now? Who do you feel yourself to be – as a performer at least?'

'That's unfair. I have absolutely no idea. I really do not. Life leads me – I follow it . . . I think I see the poetry in everything, and I see the sadness in everything, and I take that and I carry it with me and that's quite difficult. I think it's very difficult being in the world of music to begin with, because it's all about artificial responses. But life is terribly serious, I find, and I think it's much better when you face it head on.'

The Smiths play The Tube, *1984*

'What is it that moves you, then? What are the things that you feel profoundly touched by?'

'I feel profoundly touched by people's sadness. That's the thing I most see
in other people. Does that sound ridiculous?'

'I don't think it does at all, no—'

—and then she surprises him by asking about Paul Marsh's record shop.

'Good grief! Well, any education that I now have was gained at this
record shop in Moss Side in Manchester in the sixties, where I was raised.
I was fascinated by this little record shop with wooden floorboards exposed
with sawdust on the floor, and I would go there as often as I could as a five-
year-old, six-year-old, and I would simply stand and examine everything
and read everything . . .

'I was completely entranced by recorded song, and the emotion that
came from people's singing. I found it so beautiful. And the recorded noise,
the recorded song, I thought was the most powerful, beautiful thing, and I
still believe that.'

'Was home a musical place?'

'Yes, it was. I came from a very large extended family and there were lots
of young people, and there was constant pop music. I knew that I wanted to
sing, even then, and I knew there was nothing more powerful than singing,
nothing at all.'

Kirsty quotes Morrissey again, this time on his teenage years, 'constantly
waiting for a bus that never came'.

'Yes, that's true. I think that's typical of teenage frustration, though. You
don't want whatever's on offer. I knew I didn't want to be there. I knew I
didn't want anything that I had . . . I wanted a completely different life, and
whatever that entailed.'

His had been a Catholic family – 'very religious, then we had a couple of
horrendous family deaths and everybody turned away from the Church for
a while, but returned.'

'Does it comfort you?'

'Nothing comforts me – no, nothing at all. Nothing comforts me at all. I
think the world is a mesmerizing mess and I think human beings are mesmerizing messes and there we are.'

His fans are incredibly dedicated to the cult of Morrissey, says Kirsty:
'You seem to find a lot of things uncomfortable. Is that another thing you
find uncomfortable?'

'No, not really. I understand the reasons why. I think they feel I've been slighted generally, and I'm disregarded and I'm overlooked and so forth, and I think they're quite right. Nothing's ever easy. I release a new single and it's very hit-and-miss whether anybody will play it, and most people don't play it.'

In 1998 Morrissey went to live in Los Angeles. 'You were forty – was that a midlife crisis?'

'Yes, obviously. Why else would anybody go to Los Angeles?'

He sold out the Hollywood Bowl faster than the Beatles. How much influence did that have on the record companies?

'Absolutely none. I don't think they pay attention to anything like that. They are a strange breed of people. But it just so happens that naturally I am quite separate. I'm not a celebrity. I'm not a part of anything. And the music industry has never grabbed me, in the way that the sea might grab a sailor . . . Am I talking rubbish now?'

'I wouldn't dare say, even if you were – but no, I don't think you are. Shall we have some more music?'

'That means that I am talking rubbish!'

'No, it absolutely doesn't. But we've got to get in the eight tracks in the scripted amount of time.'

'Well, Kirsty, do you know "Your Pretty Face is Going to Hell"?'

'You're not the first person to say that!'

Then comes the music: Iggy and the Stooges with 'Your Pretty Face is Going to Hell', after which Kirsty, now relishing every moment with her awkward interviewee, adds: 'I won't take it personally, Morrissey.'

And then she takes herself back in time: 'I was fascinated like so many people of my generation by the young Morrissey, and part of the fascination was in your discomfort with the world: the angles emotionally and often physically that poked out from you. When I meet you today, you seem somebody at fifty entirely at home with themselves. You seem so – I'm not going to use the word "Zen" because it's ridiculously cheesy – but you seem entirely unspiky and thoughtful.'

'Well, I think if you reach fifty and you're not at one with yourself, whatever that may be, then you're in serious trouble, because you've had time to work things out, and there isn't that much time left.'

'Do you struggle with the proximity of death, about how little time we all have?'

'I'm fascinated by the brevity of life and how people use their time, because we all know the actual fall, it's inevitable as you and I are sitting here now that the Tuesday will arrive when you, Kirsty, are not here. Nobody can reach you by telephone. Nobody can write to you. Nobody can email. You just won't be here. So we all know this fact, and with that at the forefront of our mind in everything that we do, I find it fascinating how people spend their time ...

'I think the world is quite dark and I think it is quite mad and I think to be a human being is quite a task. Everybody dies screaming. They don't die laughing their heads off, as far as I know.'

'Have you thought about being in control of your death? Have you thought about shuffling off this mortal coil at a time of your choosing?'

'Yes, I have, and I think self-destruction is honourable. I always thought it was. It's an act of great control, and I understand people who do it.'

'You can't really stand other people's company. I'm imagining you'll be very happy on your desert island, all by yourself.'

'I can't wait.'

Morrissey's book is the complete works of Oscar Wilde. And his luxury? 'I would either take a bed, because I like to go to bed, or I would take a bag of sleeping pills, because I might want to make a quick exit.'

'OK – so which is it? You have to decide.'

'I would really take the bed I think; because going to bed is the highlight of everybody's day. I like to be hidden and I like to sink and I think we all love to go to bed and we love to go to sleep. It's the brother of death. It means we can just switch our brains off when we go to bed and forget about ourselves, hopefully ... Desert island or not, what's the point without a decent bed?'

'Fair enough. And if you had to pick just one of the eight tracks that you've chosen today, which one would you pick?'

'Good grief! There has to be one question I can't answer.'

'You're not allowed – I won't let you out the studio – I may padlock the door if you don't answer this.'

'I'm used to that. I would say track number one.'

'OK – that's the New York Dolls and "There's Gonna Be a Showdown". Morrissey, thank you very much for letting us hear your Desert Island Discs.'

'Young, thank you very much.'

The particular chemistry of this edition is cranked up by the fact that the teenage Kirsty Young had herself been a big fan of Morrissey. At one point in the programme she remembers 'running through the school playground after seeing you on *Top of the Pops*' and exulting with her friends that 'somebody's talking about me, and my experience'.

MAGGIE ADERIN-POCOCK

scientist

7 March 2010

'It was very nice using my scientific knowledge and applying it to a problem that's so emotional'

'Science is a wonder,' declared Maggie Aderin-Pocock in an interview with the *Independent* newspaper in March 2012: 'It's like poetry and music, and yet people don't see it in that way.' Many of them do, though, after experiencing the infectious exuberance that shone through as upbeat an edition of *Desert Island Discs* as you could imagine.

Born in London, daughter of Nigerian parents who divorced when she was four, Maggie yearned to travel into space throughout her childhood. Despite dyslexia, she enjoyed an excellent academic career – with a PhD from Imperial College, London – then worked on landmine detection for the Ministry of Defence before specializing in satellite technology. Always a keen believer in popularizing science, in 2006 she was awarded a grant which allows her to tour schools, spreading the word about the magic of science – and in 2009 she received the MBE in recognition of her work.

Maggie Aderin-Pocock is fascinated by the moon. 'I think I am a bit of a lunatic, literally! I find it mesmerizing. It's probably a nasty place to live – there's no atmosphere and you'd have to walk around in space suits all the time – but at the same time it's so beautiful.'

To study the moon and places way beyond you need a decent telescope, and as a teenager Maggie made her own: 'It's not very hard at all. It takes a while but you can make your own telescope. I think mine took probably of the order of six months. What you do is, you grind your own mirror, and that was what made it so wonderful: this is something I'd made myself . . . To look at the moon and see the craters jump out, it was just magical.'

She has recently spent time at the Gemini Observatory in Chile, which has one of the largest telescopes on earth – eight metres.

'When you say eight metres,' Kirsty Young asks, 'is that the diameter of the lens?'

'The diameter of the mirror. With lenses, because the light passes through them, you can get corruption of the light. If you use a reflective surface, because the light bounces off you can get a much better image. So most of the big telescopes we talk about these days are mirrors. Telescopes are like gathering buckets, and the bigger the bucket the more light you can get, and so the fainter objects, and the further you can see out . . .

'With a telescope that large you get so much light, what you actually want to do is analyse that light.' At University College, London, she was working with a spectrograph: 'Effectively it just makes rainbows. It takes the starlight from billions of miles away, puts it through various optics, and then stretches the light out into its rainbow colours. From that you can actually work out what's happening in the heart of a star. You can see chemical reactions, you can actually see clouds of gas between us and the star. And so it gives us very detailed analysis by looking at its rainbow light.'

Cue an entirely appropriate record choice for this castaway: 'Moondance' by Van Morrison. 'Music for me comes into different categories: music that evokes strong emotion in me, and music I like to bop to. When I was up on the mountain' – in Chile – 'I was very isolated and I really missed my husband, and that's our song we played at our wedding. When I hear it, I think of us, sort of dancing in the moonlight.'

'Looking at the edge of the universe': star HD148937, three or four million years old

Back to her childhood. Her parents had moved to England from Nigeria as her father wanted – but failed – to study to be a doctor. 'I think he had two main disappointments. He wanted to come and study medicine, and he wanted a boy – so I decided that I would be a sort of scientific boy for my father . . . I wanted to demonstrate that even though I was a girl I could be just as good as any boy. It probably drove me further than I would have gone anyway.'

Her parents broke up when she was four, which meant a succession of schools for young Maggie – thirteen in fourteen years – as she and her three sisters were buffeted about by custody battles, and school fees went unpaid. 'I don't see it as bad at all, I think it made me very adaptable.'

What about being the new girl who's black?, asks Kirsty Young. Did that matter?

'When I was a child I'd never call myself British. I would always say I was Nigerian. I've never been to Nigeria but I wanted to be seen as Nigerian because I thought too many people wouldn't accept me if I said I was British. "You're black, you're not British!" So there was that barrier.'

In one of those many schools she attended, a key moment came in a science class: 'There was a very simple question. If a litre of water weighs one kilogram, if you had a cubic centimetre of water how much would that weigh? All of a sudden, "Oh, it's one gram!" I could scale it up, and no one else in the class got it. How come I know that, and all these bright people, far brighter than me, don't? Suddenly science was quite appealing . . .

Receiving the MBE, February 2009

'I was advised that I should go into nursing instead, because that was quite scientific . . . I have a stubborn streak. Because someone says, "You can't do that," I think, "Oh, can't I?" And I'll focus and try and get it done. I had lots of support from my father and we studied science together . . . It became like a hobby as well as doing it at school, and so I saw my marks going up and up and up.'

She studied at Imperial College, since when, says Kirsty Young, 'your career path has not been straightforward . . . Your doctorate was in engineering, and you went on to work in rather practical areas, landmines and so on?'

'I like to describe myself as an "instrumentationalist" – as a dyslexic I can get away with making words up! – because from building my telescope I loved the practical side of things. For landmine detection I was working for the research arm of the Ministry of Defence. I started off working on missile warning systems using optics there, and we had a group looking at landmine detection, and it was very prominent in the news then . . . Landmines are such a devastating problem all over the world . . . It was very nice using my scientific knowledge and applying it to a problem that's so emotional.'

'Is it important to you that your science is applicable?' asks Kirsty.

'Yes, I like that. Understanding science or having a knowledge of science just for science's sake is fantastic, but if you can use that science to understand climate change, to detect landmines – I think for me that just gives it an added dimension.'

Her current specialization is satellite technology – science with a highly practical role to play. 'With Hurricane Katrina, for instance: there was extensive flooding throughout New Orleans and they wanted to get help in, but they couldn't work out the best route to take. By looking at it from space you'll have a real application on the ground and it means you can get help to people a lot quicker.

'I'm in a very lucky position,' she concludes, 'because I work on many projects that are looking at planet Earth, monitoring carbon dioxide emissions, things like that, but I also get the opportunities to look at missions that are looking at the edge of the universe.'

For her luxury, this castaway wants . . . yes, a telescope. 'I'd like to sit on the beach – I'm assuming that the beach is in the southern hemisphere so you'd then look at the heart of the Milky Way – and I'd be there with my telescope, and every night I'd pick a new star, lie down on the starry beach, look at that star and say, "Okay, that's where I'm going to make my mind journey tonight."'

Maggie Aderin-Pocock's *Desert Island Discs* was shot through with the energy and enthusiasm which have characterized her whole career, and it is easy to forget the obstacles she has had to overcome to reach her present eminence. But as she said in her *Independent* interview: 'Albert Einstein allegedly suffered from dyslexia and didn't start speaking until he was four years old, so his parents probably thought he was quite slow. You don't need a big brain the size of a planet, or mad hair. You need a passion to understand things.'

TONY ADAMS
footballer

27 June 2010

'You're flirting with me!'

In stature as well as achievement, Tony Adams was a giant among footballers. Captain of Arsenal for fourteen years and anchor of the fabled Highbury back four in the late 1980s and 1990s, he was a legend in his own time for his unyielding discipline and control. The paradox of his story is that off the pitch his life was far from controlled – with grave consequences that brought him to the brink of disaster.

Adams signed for Arsenal on his fourteenth birthday in 1980 and spent his entire playing career at the club, with whom he won four championship titles and the FA Cup twice (among many other trophies) before retiring in 2002. In addition, he made sixty-six appearances for England between 1987 and 2000, fifteen as captain.

After his retirement from playing, Adams made several forays into the managerial ranks without conspicuous success, and shortly before his *Desert Island Discs* interview in 2010 it was announced that he was moving to Azerbaijan to manage Gabala FC in that country's Premier League.

In 1996 he publicly admitted that he had had serious alcohol problems since his teens. His remarkably candid autobiography *Addicted*, published in 1998, was a bestseller, and his *Desert Island Discs* interview with

Kirsty Young – transmitted during the 2010 World Cup – again shone the spotlight on the brittle vulnerability behind the tough-guy image.

Kirsty Young introduces her castaway as a man whose 'journey of recovery is as remarkable as anything he ever managed on the pitch'. But that's beginning in the middle: what about his earlier journey through life? Where did that begin? What is his family background? 'Working-class. The East End. My father was evacuated during the war up to the north-east. After the war had finished he came back to the East End with a northern accent, and his family disowned him because of it.'

There were two older sisters. 'As the youngest of three and the only boy, how were you treated?' asks Kirsty.

'I was completely spoilt rotten. I was the golden child – and especially because I could keep the ball up many, many times.'

His skill with a football had first become apparent when he was six. His father played regularly – 'He always thought he was better than me' – and one of Tony's first memories is of 'standing over Hackney Marshes, watching my dad play central defender – heading it, kicking it – raining so hard and I was so cold and so frozen, but I wasn't moving. And the whole team picked me up at the end of the game and put me in the showers to thaw me out. I got my sister to take me to Romford Juniors, my first club. I was physically a tall boy. Even at that age, at six, I could play for the under-nines.'

At that tender age, he already had inner confidence in his ability. 'I couldn't vocalize it at that point, but inside I knew that this was for me . . . I knew that I was good at this. Driven – totally and utterly driven.'

Choosing Neil Diamond's 'Sweet Caroline' in memory of his mother, who died of bone cancer in 2000, brings tears to his eyes: 'Oh wow, I'm going!' Composure is restored as he explains how footballing drive eclipsed his school work: 'I had the worst attendance record at the school. I used to make out every morning that I was a little bit unwell, and by the time it was eleven o'clock I was up over the park and kicking a ball against a brick wall. So my education definitely suffered. My teachers used to say: "Tony Adams at school? It must be games lesson!"'

School frightened him, to the extent that reading aloud would bring on a panic attack: 'My schooling days came at the wrong time for me. I wanted to be a footballer.'

Soon he would be.

'When I was about thirteen I went round all the clubs and had a look with my dad,' who qualified as a coach so that he could teach his son properly. 'He could see how addicted I was to the game.'

Did his sisters resent the attention he was getting? 'I'm sure they did . . . Maybe it was a family joke. I could do nothing wrong – and going forward into my drinking days . . . when I used to wee the bed and things like this, drinking too much alcohol, my mother used to put the mattress out the window to dry it. Her son could do nothing wrong – instead of saying, "Oh Tone, you've got a real problem here" . . . They loved me and they did the best that they could.'

Signing for Arsenal with manager Terry Neill, January 1984

He signed for Arsenal on his four-teenth birthday, at which point his father stepped back and left the coaching to the professionals – mostly: 'Occasionally he would whisper something in my ear, and I always listened.'

But life changed when at seventeen he broke a foot and spent weeks in plaster.

'Football was the drug that I loved. It fulfilled me. But I couldn't get that when I had the plaster on and the crutches, and it got to about eleven in the morning, and I was feeling really insecure and scared and frightened and panicky, and I used to hobble up to the local pub and get smashed.'

The situation was not helped by a typical teenage awkwardness: 'Around girls in that period it was just so cripplingly painful. I just didn't know how to deal with life outside football, so I drank.'

Drink was to remain part of the fabric of Tony Adams's life for much of his Arsenal career, but on 6 May 1990 he hit a brick wall – literally.

He was due to go on Arsenal's post-season tour of Singapore – and 'obvi-ously when football's finished during those days I got drunk'. Trying to get to the airport on time he drove too fast: 'I went straight over an A-road, and I remember looking back, going "Jesus Christ, I've just crossed an A-road there!" – and completely lost control. It was over in seconds.' The car went 'bash, bash, bash – and ended up over this brick wall. The rest is history.'

Convicted of drunk driving, he was sent to prison. 'People that do know me know that I'm quite insular and quite a loner. In prison I got a little bit of sport, a little bit of exercise three times a day. I dropped about seven, eight pounds, eating well, sleeping well, reading a couple of books of an evening, on my own, I loved it – when that door shut, it was heaven. I know you're shaking your head here, but for some people the outside world was scary. In there I was happy because my world outside was hell.' But he wasn't oblivious to the consequences for his family. 'When I went to prison, they were the ones I felt really sorry for. I was stuck in a prison and I was out the way, but they had to deal with the shame and the disgrace I brought upon their family.'

The demon was not easily overcome. Adams had been England captain when the national team was beaten on penalties by Germany in the semi-final of the 1996 European Championships. How did he deal with the devastation of losing?

'I drank. I drank for the next six-odd weeks, ending up on 16 August, which was my last drink.'

Rewind to the beginning of that year. 'There was a big change for me in the January of that year, 1996: it was the first time in my life that I didn't want to drink and I was finding myself drunk. That was the big shift for me. In the January my wife was in treatment; my mother-in-law had come round and taken the kids off me; my park bench was my sofa. It was a mess. I couldn't blame anybody. I couldn't blame the wife, my family, the football, the fame or whatever. I couldn't blame anything else. I stayed sober through Euro '96, just focusing on football, that was my only thing.'

And then semi-final defeat by Germany – and it was back to the bottle.

'For most people,' says Kirsty Young, 'six days would be a binge, but you go on this six-week binge. Where does it lead you at the end? What happens?'

'I can't remember – a lot of black-outs in there. I can't remember most of it: a lot of time wetting the bed, the pigsty which was home, passing out, getting up and going to drink again.'

But he sobered up – and this time he stayed sober. After a couple of years of people asking him how he had done it, he set up the Sporting Chance clinic, for – as Kirsty Young puts it – 'sportsmen and sportswomen who are recovering addicts of any sort – it could be drugs, it could be gambling, it could be alcohol.'

Now life is getting better on all fronts. He has a second wife, Poppy, and they have three young children together. And he is about to move the family out to Azerbaijan, where he will be coaching Gabala FC. 'For me it's a no-brainer. There's a group of guys that need to be coached, need to be led, and they've just said to me, "Go and build a football club," which is extremely exciting – and the wife said, "Let's go for it!"'

When Kirsty asks Tony Adams about how much of the recent, happier part of his life he has been able to share with his parents, the tear ducts start twitching again:

'My father and mother were Tony Adams fans, so anything I did was good enough for them. They knew me better than anybody. I got loads of time with them. I had four years sober with my mother, six years with my father, and I made a lot of amends.' Together, he and his father built a house in southern France: 'It was the closest that I've ever got to my father, and on his deathbed I shook his hand. He said, listen—' and then: 'You're going to make me go again! – We just loved each other – Please move on! – I'm a tough big guy here, come on!'

Kirsty tries to come to the rescue:

'It's funny that, isn't it, because there you are, tough big guy, handsome big guy—'

'Oh, I like the handsome bit!'

'It's true.'

'You're flirting with me!'

'You mentioned, a minute ago, fear. How can this high-achieving, talented sporting hero, who has turned his life around, be still propelled by a sort of fear?'

'I like to think that I'm not motivated by fear today. But fear is still with me. All these feelings don't go away. I just don't suppress them

any more; they're still with me, and fear is a big one . . . I'm very comfortable with who I am today, and that's a massive shift.'

Tony Adams's final record choice – and his record of records – is 'Always Look on the Bright Side of Life.'

The castaway's attempt to build the 'Tony Adams side' in Azerbaijan proved short-lived, and he left Gabala FC in November 2011.

Shortly afterwards a statue of Tony Adams was unveiled outside the Emirates Stadium, now home of Arsenal, a fitting tribute to one of the club's all-time greats.

In bronze – and in the flesh

KATHY BURKE

actress, comedian, director

15 August 2010

'No, I don't think they ever told me I was gorgeous!'

There are many sides to Kathy Burke. Appearances in priceless television comedies, notably her wonderful collaborations with Harry Enfield (most famously as the teenage slob Perry to Enfield's Kevin) but also in other shows such as *French and Saunders* and *Absolutely Fabulous*, made her a familiar face on television. But she also made her mark as a film actress, beginning with her appearance in the 1983 Mai Zetterling film *Scrubbers* and rising to her brilliant performance as the battered wife in *Nil by Mouth*, which won her the Best Actress award at the 1997 Cannes Film Festival and one of her six BAFTA nominations. And in 2001 she started to concentrate on directing, at the partial – though not complete – expense of her acting.

Her *Desert Island Discs* is another of those classic editions in which a great comic talent reveals the grim reality behind the laughs.

No beating about the bush. Kirsty Young asks Kathy Burke: 'Do you not mind presenting yourself in a way that most actresses would shy away from, somebody who's got snot hanging out their nose or dressed as a boy – all that sort of stuff – warts on your face?'

'No. When I was acting I didn't mind at all, really. To me it was more fun, putting some scabs on and greasing the hair rather than washing the hair, and distressing the clothes, rather than making sure the clothes were nice and pristine.'

Born into a family of Irish immigrants in Islington, Kathy Burke had a testing childhood. Her mother died when 'I was coming up for two', and her father had such a bad drinking problem that there was always the risk that the motherless child 'could end up in a home . . . Even though I was quite a naughty girl, I wasn't so naughty that I was a bad girl.'

Through the local church, a temporary fostering arrangement was made for her with a neighbour: 'A woman called Joan Galvin looked after me Monday to Friday and then at the weekends I would go home. This was up to about the age of seven or eight, I think.'

She had two elder brothers, John and Barry. 'John, the eldest, was more like Dad to me, really . . . He'd get me up in the morning, he'd make me my breakfast, he'd get my clothes ready. He and Barry were both quite brainy, so they went to the London Oratory in Chelsea. So not only was John taking care of me and Barry, he was also then going over to Chelsea from Islington every day to go to school – which I look back on now and I'm astounded.'

Their mother was never talked about. 'I was a minx. I was a horrible little so-and-so, because I learned very quickly how to use not having a mother. If I was upset about something, like I wanted a Mars Bar, I knew I had to turn on the waterworks and say, "I miss my Mum!"'

Kirsty brings up 'the comic masterpiece that is Perry, of Kevin and Perry'. Where, she asks, did that sort of characterization come from? 'Were you thinking about your brothers?'

'No, I was thinking more of myself! I think Perry is probably the closest I've ever played to myself, really, because I was quite an awkward teen. I hated being a teenager, I really hated it. I just didn't know what was going on or what I was turning into. I think when I hit thirteen I looked forty-five. Something happened to my hair, my face. I don't know what went on – it was just something out of the Black Lagoon came emerging . . . I was just miserable and moody and spotty and fed up and I hated school. But my saviour, I think, was punk. I was looking at people and I thought, "Well, they look like a mess, they've got spots and they're not pretty and they're not glamorous people!" I felt a bit male-ish rather than female, so then it was great and I could suddenly shave my head and

Kevin and Perry Go Large,
2000

wear army trousers and DM boots, and then everything sort of evened out for me.'

She preferred the company of boys to that of girls. Did none of the women in her life, wonders Kirsty Young – such as her foster-mother Joan Galvin – ever sit her down and tell her she was a gorgeous girl, and everything was going to be all right?

'No, I don't think they ever told me I was gorgeous! But that isn't their fault. I mean, I wasn't really. My hair was always in rats' tails, my teeth were bad. Punk was a great help. I was part of something new. Oh, it was so empowering!'

At the suggestion of her English teacher she enrolled at the Anna Scher Drama School, which, she says, saved her. 'By the time I got there I was hanging around with people that were not that great, and there was a real aggression in the air in the late seventies. The atmosphere was really hardcore.'

Sex Pistols

'Pretty Vacant'

'This music, I really do think it changed my life'

And then in her twenties she got angry, 'which wasn't very good because I started drinking a lot. I'd get really angry in pubs and suddenly turn over tables and go nuts for no reason. I just needed a "check-up from the neck up", and I didn't get around to doing that until I was in my early thirties. So it took me a long time to sort myself out emotionally . . . I was drinking a lot. I was drinking every day, every night. I suddenly thought, "I've got to put a stop to this!" . . . So I knocked it on the head. I still have a drink now, but I'm sort of in control of it.'

'You have moved away in recent years from acting to directing,' says Kirsty Young. 'Do you find that you have, if you like, a louder voice than you had as an individual actor? Do you feel that you've got more power, and that it's better used?'

'It's more satisfying for me personally. Whereas I should have been getting more and more happy with these acting roles – and suddenly I was on a list for films, I was a film actress – I was actually getting more and more miserable and depressed, and didn't like it . . . There were too many other people involved. I kept getting touched and prodded and fiddled about with, and you're being a grumpy eejit with these people that are always up three hours at least before you are, and then I'd come in and be all miserable – "I don't really want to be here" – and I just thought: "Well, if you don't want to be here, get out of here and let somebody who does want to be here, be here!"'

Kathy's father had lived long enough to see some of her success, and 'was very proud of what I was doing'. He had given up drink for ten years: 'It was a bit sad that he realized that he'd wasted a lot of money on drink, and a lot of time. A lot of his life was just wasted, with no memories, and then when he was finally in hospital, when he only had a couple of days to live and he knew he was dying, I have to say he was extremely brave . . . He was sixty-three, so he was young, but still I was quite amazed he'd lived as long as he had, because of the countless times when we were kids that he'd fall over and crack his head open . . .

'His own childhood was a bit rubbish. He had an extremely strict father, and he told me a story that his mother tried to kill herself, and Dad found her and saved her. Then she was put in the local mental institution, and that's where she died, and Dad never saw her again.'

'How old was he when he found her?'

'He told me he was about twelve.'

'How had she tried to kill herself?'

'She tried to hang herself.'

Kathy learned that her father's father had been 'a tyrant . . . Sadly it took him dying to then tell me about this and I was very glad to know it, because when I was a little girl I spent the majority of my time really hating him, and really wouldn't have cared if he'd have died. So when it finally came round to the fact that he was dying, I'm just really pleased that I'd got to know him as a person and that I did love him.'

Although she had not talked about her mother in childhood, later she learned more. 'When I was a little girl growing up, my mum was talked about, if she ever was talked about, like she was an angel. She was an angel, because she'd died. And it was only as I got older that I heard: no, she had a bit of a mouth on her, and she'd shout at anyone that dared talk to John and Barry in any way that wasn't lovely and kind. She was very strong, and I think, "Oh God! I'd much prefer

With Imogen Bain in Scrubbers, *1983*

that than some angel." But the one thing I carried into my thirties about her was the way she died . . . She already knew she had cancer when she was pregnant with me, but she was determined to have me, no matter how sick it made her.'

Kirsty brings up the subject of relationships. 'One of the other things that you've said that you are is very sort of bossy and uncompromising. Do you find it difficult to have relationships? Are you somebody's who's – you know – awkward?'

'Yeah, I wasn't made for relationships, really.'

Kirsty asks how she can write herself off like that, when she could enrich the life of somebody else and have her life enriched in return?

'Yes, but I want to enrich my own life. I'm not here to sort out somebody else's bleedin' life!' . . . I spend ninety per cent of my time on my own and that's the way I like it. I'm a very solitary person.'

As, of course, she will be on the desert island – where, she says, she would like to take a luxury which no one else in all the years of *Desert Island Discs* has come close to requesting: 'I need something nice to look at, and I don't know how to say this without sounding salacious. I find deeply attractive James Caan [left] from *Dragons' Den*. I think he is adorable. What I would like is a life-size photograph of him, and I'd like it laminated so I can body surf on him!'

The year after her *Desert Island Discs* appearance Kathy Burke showed that, notwithstanding her new focus on directing, she remains a notable character actor, giving a superb performance as Connie Sachs in the new film adaptation of John Le Carré's *Tinker, Tailor, Soldier, Spy*.

Kathy Burke's career is ample witness, as her own website rightly notes, that 'it doesn't matter who you are or what you might look like, that talent, honesty, hard work and a basic level-headedness is more than enough to progress in this world. And it will even get you loved for it.'

JOHNNY VEGAS

comedian

3 October 2010

'I'd play my nose in class'

Kirsty Young found herself interviewing two people in this compelling programme. One was the squeaky-voiced Lancashire comic Johnny Vegas, whose aggressive drunkard act had thrilled the comedy circuit for so long before he started to concentrate on straight acting. The other was a young boy named Michael Pennington, who had heart-rending stories to tell of an impoverished childhood in Lancashire, who had so convinced himself that he had a vocation to the Catholic priesthood that he had spent four unhappy terms in a seminary, and who was still weighed down with accumulated guilt decades later.

Johnny Vegas – the name he took for his stand-up career – was born in St Helens in September 1971. After his brief stay in the seminary he completed his education in a local school, then enrolled at Middlesex University to study art and ceramic design. He became compère of comedy nights at the Citadel Arts Centre in St Helens before moving down to London, and his career took off at the 1997 Edinburgh Festival. But inside the stand-up grotesque there was a seriously good straight actor – as he showed in roles such as Krook in the 2005 BBC adaptation of *Bleak House*.

Johnny Vegas, quotes Kirsty Young, once said: 'I always consider myself creatively at my best when at odds with the world.' Does he still feel that it's always better to be the grit in the oyster? Had there come a time with his stand-up act that his life had started to imitate his art?

'Yes. I found a popularity through self-destruction. Suddenly, the more you damage yourself, the more people are drawn to you, and that can be quite addictive.'

Kirsty takes her castaway back to childhood. His father was a joiner, his mother 'stayed at home or did various cleaning jobs' – and times could be very hard, as illustrated by the terrible episode which later found its way into his act, but at the time was not funny at all.

'It was one of those mornings that my dad got us up for school, and as we were leaving for school he went, "Right, whose rabbit's going in the pot today?" I genuinely thought he was joking because it was such a ridiculous concept. But I came in from school and he was out in the back, cleaning out the hutch – and I sort of looked round the garden and asked my dad where it was, and he went, "It's there!" – and I looked behind me and it was skinned and hanging up. I couldn't quite believe it. There were no tears. I didn't react, but my sister went absolutely berserk, and my mum. And my dad had always claimed that rabbits were livestock, but we'd never eaten one before. My dad had been laid off: that might have not in itself been a break-down or something, but I just wonder if it was a man at the end of his tether.'

'How aware were you then, throughout your childhood, that lack of money was a big shadow?'

'I was very aware. There was a definite incident one day when I was nagging my dad over an ice-cream, and nagging and nagging. He took me outside, to the end of the street, and just said to me, "I got laid off today." There'd been other children at school whose dads had been laid off, and there was that little bit of dread – kids coming back in the same school uniform, pants getting shorter, and the nicknames: "Pov" and things like that. And then he said, "Look here's some money. Get an ice-cream, but do me a favour, don't ask me for a while." . . . I just felt awful. I felt like this spoilt brat who'd been nagging and nagging and nagging, and I should have understood and I didn't.'

From an early age he thought he wanted to be a priest, and aged eleven was enrolled at a nearby seminary: 'I enjoyed the reaction that it got . . . It was fantastic. The ambition of every parish is to produce its own priest, but I know for certain that my mum really didn't want me to go . . . With a lot of the negative press of late [regarding abuse], I think it's something that my mum suspected . . .

'I left in the fourth term. I stuck out my first year, and for me the place had very little to do with religion and a lot more to do with regime. I'd come home for Christmas and we'd gone to Benediction, and we were due to drive back that evening – and I turned to my dad and told him that I didn't want to go back, and my mum was in floods of tears – and the worst thing is that at the time I thought I'd broke her heart by leaving. And it was quite the opposite as it turns out. It was such a relief for her . . .

'I felt that I'd let a lot of people down . . . There were things that went on at that school, and it was very difficult to come back at weekends and people would say, "What you're doing is a wonderful thing," and you're quietly going, "It's not a wonderful thing, and it's not a wonderful place."'

'Were you abused there?'

This is clearly a difficult area of his life to discuss, and it appears to be an effort for him to get through the next few seconds: 'I wasn't, no. And it's a very difficult thing to talk about in public because for people who are, or were, is it really up to me to drag that into the spotlight?'

'I suppose what I am asking,' says Kirsty Young, 'is: there was a level of activity there that even as a young boy you were aware of, that other people were going through?'

Her castaway struggles to answer, before saying: 'When I left, I wanted to take everybody else with me.'

Time to change the subject. At that stage, did he make people laugh? There were 'little bits of entertainment: I'd play my nose in class' – as if it were a musical instrument: 'I played a Hawaiian tune and I had a quiet ambition to get on *That's Life*.'

Given a place on the ceramics course at Middlesex University, he was warned by his father to try and save money while he was there, as he would be surrounded by students from better-off backgrounds. 'I ran up a lot of debt in my first year. But then in the second year the party was over. There was no money . . . When I first went there I resented my parents for not being able to support me. But I graduated, and then realized it wasn't the most commercially successful move I'd ever made. A degree in ceramics! When have I ever gone into the dole and they've had a card up saying, "Teapot mender"?! I sat on the train with my dad, and I just went, "I've made

As Krook in the 2005 BBC production of Bleak House

a huge mistake!" – which after four years of putting them through all that financial pressure is not really what you want to hear from your graduate son, is it?'

His ambition to become a stand-up comedian took him from early appearances in St Helens to London, and in 1997 to the Edinburgh Fringe – where he won a Perrier nomination and recognition as Most Promising Newcomer. Was he conscious of that as a breakthrough moment? 'I think so, and I think it established me outside of the north-west. As a festival it was brilliant. Within three days we'd pretty much sold out the run. I loved it: it was just one long very hard party, with the gigs thrown in for good measure. Everything came together and people got it. Everybody was getting it, critics were getting it, audiences were loving it. Perfect.'

The stand-up act was Vegas as the overweight comic with a drink in his hand, and he threw himself into the role enthusiastically: 'My usual approach was just to get as drunk as possible. I mean I can count on one hand the times that I've gone on stage as Johnny without a drink.'

'At its worst,' asks Kirsty Young, 'how badly did the drinking affect your life? What were the points at which things were out of control?'

'I think there was a period in my life after college when I became so resentful, even towards friends. There was nothing happening in my life, but I wasn't making anything happen. I'd always drunk to socialize . . . Everything centred around the pub, but this was drinking in a room on your own, and blaming the world for you not being where you thought you should be.'

Later, 'I thought I could go out and play the hell-raiser, but then put Johnny back in his box. Within my personal life I went through a separation and a divorce, and I think I was just burning bridges with people because I wanted people to know I was desperately upset.'

'What sort of a husband were you?'

'I don't honestly think it lasted long enough to find out.'

Johnny Vegas is now a well-respected actor. 'It was something I quietly wanted to do, but without having the formal training I didn't really feel very confident about putting myself out there and saying I wanted to act.' And his parents, who would not have gone to his stand-up shows, could watch him on television: 'It's really nice to finally do something, like with *Benidorm*, something that my Mum can discuss without bringing shame upon the family!'

Johnny Vegas's seventh record is 'There She Goes'. 'For some reason I've probably come across so melancholy while I've been talking to you. I love love songs, I live for love . . . I now have a lady in my life that just – that smile makes the day. Somebody that can come along and make you realize that my life isn't best lived on my own. And I'll love my son till the day I die; nothing can ever change that. Whether I've struggled through my faith, through drinking, through anything, just that one guarantee has made the world of difference to my life. And I'm not a misery guts.'

Johnny's book is *The Ragged Trousered Philanthropists* – 'I learn something from it every time I read it' – and his luxury an unusual one, but one which might at last justify that ceramics degree: a kiln.

'Let's hope it's a clay-based soil, then,' says Kirsty.

In 2007 Johnny Vegas had presented his play *Interiors* at the Manchester International Festival, and he returned there in July 2011 with *And Another Thing*, a play about television shopping channels.

'This man', wrote the *Guardian* of Johnny Vegas, 'is one of the true comic greats' – but it was the more sombre side of his life which produced such an affecting edition of *Desert Island Discs*.

BETTY DRIVER

actress

23 January 2011

'I was the meal ticket for the entire family '

One figure dominates Kirsty Young's interview with the ninety-year-old *Coronation Street* actress who as Betty Turpin (later Williams) for more than four decades had been dispensing beer, hotpot and homespun wisdom to regulars in the Rover's Return: Betty Driver's mother.

Plenty of castaways have unpacked difficult relationships with one or both parents – underlining the programme's ability to reach emotional parts that other interviews cannot reach – but listeners have rarely heard of a character like Nellie Driver.

Betty Driver was born in Leicester in 1920, and her family moved to Manchester two years later. Urged on by her mother, Betty first appeared on stage at the age of six, and joined the Terence Byron Repertory Company at nine, becoming a professional actress at ten. She went on to appear on the stage and in films until the 1960s, when problems with her voice – for years her mother had insisted that she sing out of her natural range in order to sound like Gracie Fields – forced her retirement.

She started running a pub in Derbyshire, and it was after she moved from there to another pub in Cheshire that she was visited one day by the executive producer of *Coronation Street*, six years into its stride and already

embedded in national culture. 'You're pulling pints here,' she remembers his saying: 'why don't you come and pull pints in the Rover's Return?' Thus began a new – and by far the happiest – phase of Betty Driver's life.

Greeting her castaway, Kirsty Young can scarcely contain her admiration: 'Betty Driver, welcome. You are, unbelievably, ninety now, rude with health, and you've been working for the past eighty years.' There must be something about *Coronation Street*: 'What is it about the work that you love so much?'

'I think I just love people, you see, and I love the cast. I've made tremendous friends. When you're in the theatre, when you're doing variety, you work for a week and you meet somebody, you may never meet them again – so you don't really make friends. When I joined the "Street" I made friends, and I'm the happiest person in the world. It's just like a big family and I just love it.'

'That is lovely to hear you say that there is a great sense of happiness,' says Kirsty, 'because I know in your early life there wasn't a lot of happiness around. So now you think you've found a sense in which you feel fulfilled?'

'We had no happiness when we were little, me and my sister Freda. We went to a different school each week, which was horrendous, so you never really caught up on any education. It was awful. We had a mother that was a matriarch, and she just wanted me to be in the theatre, irrespective of whether I wanted to or not.'

Betty Driver's first piece of music is herself at eighteen years old singing the Oscar Hammerstein song 'I'll Take Romance' – a choice which she calls, in a most un-castawayish fashion, 'this piece of music which I can't stand'. She explains:

'I can't bear my voice. I hated it when I did it, when I was eighteen, and I'm ninety now and I just can't bear it . . . I did it when I was making a film. I got a contract to do three films, and this song was in one of the films. It did quite well, and I thought, "Oooh, I'm going to be a big film star, lovely!" I finished the three films and then the war broke out, and all the contracts were cancelled – so that was the end of my filming career. I've hidden these really old records right at the back of

Aged eleven

the wardrobe so nobody would find them at all. But my friends, they're like little squirrels – and they found this.'

After the record has been played, Kirsty Young observes: 'I noticed all the way through that you were grimacing and you were huffing and puffing—' and is interrupted by her castaway: 'I can't bear it. It's no good. I sound like an old tin can' (a verdict which does not accord with Kirsty's).

'By that time,' says the presenter, 'you had already starred in a West End show, you'd taken on your first film roles, spent a good number of years in rep – and all because Mummy wanted you on the stage?'

'Yes. I did a season in rep when I was about eleven. But it was very good for me, because it taught me how to learn lines and how to enter on to a stage.'

'Probably, but did you say to your mother, "I don't want to do this"?'

'Yes, every day, and she said, "You're going to do it, no matter what." No love attached at all, nothing. We never got a kiss, we never got a present, nothing.'

With Mitzi and Tina, 1955

'What did your father have to say about this?'

'Well, my mother was so strong that I think my dad just gave up: he was a sweet person but he just gave up. She was so domineering, there was nothing you could do about it.'

'Why did she want you to do it? Was it the money?'

'I don't know. I will never know. It was just a very, very sad little life for me and my sister.'

'It's an unusual degree of cruelty, though, that doesn't allow a child to celebrate Christmas, or birthdays, or give them a hug. Where did that come from?'

'We don't know. We always had a Christmas tree and Daddy used to put lights on it, and it was lovely. Freda and I used to put our little presents all around, which we'd bought during the year for them, but there was never one from my mum or my dad. Never. The age of seven was the last time we ever had a present . . .

'And we never got a kiss, only on New Year's Eve. The bells would go for New Year's Eve and my dad would say, "Happy New Year!" – then a kiss on the cheek – and my mum would grudgingly say, "Happy New Year!" then "Right, that's it" – that was the love for the year.'

When Betty Driver was in her mid-thirties, her mother died. Freda was with her as she passed away, and Nellie Driver asked her for forgiveness. 'What do you say? You say yes, of course you do,' and that is what Freda did.

'Could you forgive her in your heart?' asks Kirsty Young.

'No – she never asked me to forgive – oh no, no, no, no, no. I was the meal ticket for the entire family: my mother, my father, my grandma, my granddad, my aunts, everyone. They all had a nice little share of my money.'

During the war Betty Driver worked with ENSA, performing for the troops in Europe. One occasion has stuck in her mind. 'It was the last place the boys went to before they came home, a de-lousing centre. There were hundreds of them in this hall and they all looked dead, these boys. The commanding officer said, "Well, I don't know whether they'll respond at all." Their faces were covered in white powder all over, and they looked like ghosts.'

She tried to cheer them up with some of the old songs, and eventually they started to respond: 'I sang to them for hours, and by the end of the time they were cheering, and the commanding officer said, "I don't believe it. I've never seen anything like that in my life – from dead people to alive." We danced until the early hours of the morning and they all were normal boys

Filming in the Rover's Return

by the time we left, and to me that was the most fantastic achievement. If I never do anything else in my life, I think I've done something wonderful there, by bringing those boys back to life.'

But there were also nervous breakdowns and bouts of agoraphobia, until sister Freda took the situation in hand while Betty was performing in London: 'My mother had had to go home, as she had very bad asthma. The day she went home, my sister said: "Right, we're changing all your music, we're changing your act, we're changing your gowns – that's it!" And we did – gradually, together, we changed. She was wonderful, my sister. An angel. She began to tell me I was good – I'd never heard that word in my life. And it was through Freda that I blossomed out.'

Kirsty Young asks Betty about her fan mail. She gets 'tons – a heck of a lot of it from little children . . . I had one the other day from a little boy. "I am six. My Nana is very poorly at the moment and I think she's going to die, so will you be my Nana – because I love you." You can imagine the mess I'm in when I'm reading that.'

Betty Driver died less than a year after her *Desert Island Discs* appearance – in October 2011, at the age of ninety-one.

SIR DAVID ATTENBOROUGH

naturalist, broadcaster

29 January 2012

'You know perfectly well that what they do
is pee on their hands'

The seventieth anniversary of Roy Plomley's encounter with Vic Oliver in 1942 required a very special castaway – and the BBC secured someone so exceptional that he had already appeared on *Desert Island Discs* three times. David Attenborough had been interviewed by Roy Plomley in 1957 and 1979 and by Sue Lawley in 1998, and when cast away by Kirsty Young in January 2012 became only the second person to notch up four appearances.

Born in 1926, Attenborough (younger brother of the actor Richard – himself cast away in 1952 and 1964) displayed his early passion for natural history when collecting fossils, and went on to win a scholarship to read zoology at Cambridge. In the early 1950s he joined the BBC and became a producer in the Talks Department. He started to specialize in natural history with the three-part series *The Pattern of Animals*, which he produced with London Zoo in 1953 and presented himself, and followed that in 1954 with the series *Zoo Quest*, monitoring the collection of wild animals. After a foray into management he returned to the screen and to a stellar broadcasting career, the finest glories of which were the ten series which began with *Life on Earth* in 1979 and included *The Living Planet, The Private Life of Plants, The Life of Birds* and *The Life of Mammals.*

Combined with spectacular filming, David Attenborough's depth of knowledge and pitch-perfect presentation produced some of the most fascinating programmes in television history. From the North Pole to the South Pole and at all points in between, his infectious enthusiasm for the natural world brought huge viewing figures and, for the presenter, a shoal of awards and honours, including a knighthood in 1985 and the Order of Merit in 2005.

David Attenborough's other career, in senior BBC management, saw him become Controller of BBC2 in 1965 and Director of Programmes in 1969. In these roles he commissioned classic documentaries such as *Civilisation, The Ascent of Man* and Alistair Cooke's *America* as well as lighter fare such as *The Old Grey Whistle Test* and *Monty Python's Flying Circus.* He returned to full-time programme-making in 1973. 'I spent all my time sacking people,' he tells Kirsty Young: 'it's not my game really, and I decided to go back to making programmes' – for which generations of viewers are indebted to him.

David Attenborough, suggests Kirsty Young, 'has seen more of the world than any person who has ever lived'. You can see what she means. For nearly sixty years he has been making unforgettable natural history programmes in remote places, and 'from sitting hugger-mugger with the mountain gorillas of Rwanda to describing the fragilities of the flightless kakapo, the wonders of the world are his stock-in-trade'. So does it come as a staggering thought to him that – she repeats – he has seen more of the world than anybody else?

'I suppose so, but then on the other hand it's very salutary to remember that perhaps the greatest naturalist who ever lived and had more effect on our thinking than anybody, Charles Darwin, only spent four years travelling and the rest of the time thinking.'

'Professionally,' observes Kirsty Young, 'it was fortunate for you that your career coincided with commercial air travel. That was one of the reasons why you've been able to reach all of these points around the globe. But you were certainly, in the beginning, seeing an unspoilt planet. Were you conscious that you were treading in places that people had never trodden before?'

'Very much so – though in fact, fifty or sixty years ago the world was known pretty well. I did manage to do that every now and again, but not often.'

Opposite: *Close encounter with an orangutan, 1982*

David Attenborough's passion for the natural world is reflected in his first record choice: a folk tune called 'The Bell Bird', played on Paraguayan harps – to remind him of the song of the real bird: 'a two-note song which drives you mad; walking through the forest you hear this noise coming at you all the time'. (He returns to the forest for his fourth choice: 'I would like a reminder of the richness of the natural world, of the rain forest, and one of the nicest ways to do that would be a recording of the lyre bird which lives in southern Australia and mimics other birds, as well as many other things that it hears.')

Does he take music away with him on his travels?

'I used to take a lot, yes. I take less now, partly because in the old days travel involved a lot of sitting around in tents and in railway carriages. These days we're very much more streamlined, and I don't have as much time to myself as I did.'

His first expedition to far-flung places was to Sierra Leone in 1954, for his television series *Zoo Quest*: 'We were just going to film the operations of a collecting team set up by the London Zoo. I had no experience about collecting animals. I had taken a degree in zoology, it's true, but that doesn't involve and explain how you jump on a boa constrictor, and we were just there to see how it was done.'

To the young zoologist, what was that first experience of Africa like? 'The sheer abundance of it, the superabundance of it, the variety of form, the chameleons here, snakes there, wonderful birds there, sun birds – it's just breathtaking.'

The first time he had appeared on *Desert Island Discs* – when 'a young slip of a thing', says Kirsty – David Attenborough had told Roy Plomley that his ambition was to climb Mount Everest. She asks, 'Have you ever done that?'

'No, I won't make it to base camp now, but as a teenager and in my early twenties I thought that the only thing that a red-blooded Englishman should do was to climb Everest.'

David Attenborough was born in 1926 and brought up, along with his two elder brothers, by 'formidable' parents in Leicestershire. His father was principal of the college that became Leicester University, and his mother was a suffragette – though 'she didn't jump in front of racehorses' – who became a JP and made arrangements for refugee children coming from continental Europe: first young Basques, then Jews from Germany.

With the Jewish children, 'what happened was that we had to provide guarantees about looking after them and so on, and then they'd be on their way to relatives in America or somewhere. A number came through that way, and two of them arrived, in theory going on to New York. Then about a month after they arrived there was a sinking of a ship which contained a lot of children, and [their passage] then was cancelled, and they stayed with us for the rest of the war. So they were, in fact, our sisters.'

'So you were three brothers with two new sisters. How did that go?'

'Interestingly!' The boys were not sure that they wanted to share their parents with anybody, but their parents 'soon sorted that out: "You're lucky you've got your parents. These two girls haven't got their parents at all, so you'd better pull yourself together, Attenborough!" . . . We came to like them. They were two very nice girls, and I'm sorry to say that both of them are no longer alive. After five or six years with us, after the war they went to America, where they got married and so on, and we went out to see them for the rest of their lives.'

Attenborough's enthusiasm for the natural world began with a collection of fossils. Kirsty wonders if the attraction was scientific, or just that 'they looked jolly good and you knew they were old?'

'The romance of it was very vivid: the possibility that there is in front of you a rock the size of a football, and there is quite a good chance that that will contain a shell – a perfect shell – which nobody in the world has ever seen before, and which the light of the sun hasn't shone on for 350 million years. You are the first person to see that – that's the thing.'

As a young boy he set up a little museum, with ammonites and fossils, and bits of Roman pottery: 'I had a grass snake's skin from a whopping grass snake. It was getting on for two and a half feet long.'

At Cambridge University he met his wife Jane, without whom, he insists, he could never have achieved what he has: 'If you go away for three or four months of the year you can't just abandon children, so she looked after the children and devoted her life to doing that . . . She turned out to be a brilliant carer for animals, particularly mammals and particularly primates. We had little bush babies, charming little primitive primates, and we had a whole room in which they lived and bred.'

With Prince Charles and Princess Anne at the BBC's Lime Grove studios, 1958

'Yes,' says Kirsty. 'How do they mark their territory, I'm wondering?'

'You know perfectly well that what they do is pee on their hands, and go around plonking their urine all over the place. That's why they have to have a house of their own. But she really looked after them.'

Jane's skills were recognized at London Zoo, and he fondly recalls the time when she was asked to take in a gibbon which had been imported illegally. 'It was dying of chronic indigestion and diarrhoea and one thing and another,' and needed tender loving care. 'Jane brought this little creature in, which simply wanted to hang on to her, and she made a sort of sling for it, so he lived permanently on her, and used to talk to her in gibbon language, a sort of eructation' – at which point the great man gives his unreproducible impression of how a gibbon would have talked to his wife.

Life on Earth, says Kirsty Young, 'changed the way we watch television' – and this 1979 series included one of the greatest TV moments of all, when David Attenborough found himself on very close terms with mountain gorillas in Rwanda. How much of his mind was occupied by fear and how much by fascination?

'Oddly, no fear at all. You might think it was silly, but I knew perfectly well that we were not in an aggressive situation. The first physical contact was with a female with her twins, and she put her hand on the top of my head and turned my head towards her, so that we could look in one another's eyes! And then she stuck her finger, which was huge, like a great sort of articulated banana, and put it in my mouth – lowered my jaw and looked inside my mouth! It was extraordinary. But as that happened, you knew perfectly well that she was amiably inclined.'

Was she assessing him as a potential mate?

'I have no idea. I'm just reporting it as I wrote it in my diary. The encounter I had with the gorillas seemed to go on for ever, and I was kind of in paradise. I lost all sense of time, and when I eventually emerged and went back, I said to the team, "God, wasn't that extraordinary?" – and the producer, poor chap, said, "I think we've got a few seconds of it." I said, "A few seconds?! I've been there for ten minutes," and he said, "Yes, but I was waiting for you to say about the zoological point" – which was why we were supposed to be there – "and if I'd started doing this other stuff, I didn't know when you were going to start your serious bit."'

It had only been when the cameraman had suggested that they shoot 'some of this stuff with David rolling around with gorillas, if only to make the people in the editing room laugh,' that they started filming.

Filming for the BBC's Living Planet, *1984*

Fast-forward to the present. Kirsty asks: 'What about the role of work now in your life? You spoke very tenderly about Jane, to whom you were married for forty-seven years, and you've written that she died fourteen years ago, and you've written that "the focus of my life, the anchor had gone". Is work the thing now that helps to anchor you?'

'Yes, I'm very lucky that I'm able to go on working . . . Quite a lot of people my age are liable to be sitting in a chair and saying, "What do I do with the next hour?", and I at the moment have got more than I can properly deal with.'

David Attenborough's castaway book is the same as he chose on two of his previous *Desert Island Discs* appearances: *Shifts and Expedients of Camp Life and Travel*, published in 1871: 'It's about four inches thick, and every conceivable disaster that you can think of that might happen to a traveller is there, together with the solution. It says things like, "An unmanly fear of fever is inclined to bring on the symptoms." Good stuff, you see! But it also tells you, to use its own phrase, "How to baffle an alligator".'

Neither David Attenborough's energy nor his commitment shows signs of flagging. In May 2012 he started presenting a botanical series, *Kingdom of Plants*, for Sky, based in Kew Gardens and transmitted in 3D, while *Sixty Years in the Wild* for the BBC looks back on arguably the greatest television career of all.

Into the eighth decade

Beyond the fourth appearance on the programme of Sir David Attenborough, the seventieth birthday was marked with other broadcasts on Radio 4: *Vic Oliver: the First Castaway Remembered*, presented by David Baddiel, and, in the *Archive on 4* slot, a celebration entitled *Castaway: 70 Years of Desert Island Discs* presented by Kirsty Young. Both programmes were transmitted on the eve of the anniversary itself, and it was announced that in September 2012 there would be a special *Desert Island Discs* concert at the Royal Albert Hall as part of the BBC Proms.

An additional celebration nationwide took place. Radio Scotland, Radio Wales, Radio Ulster, Radio Foyle and Radio nan Gàidheal joined forces with all the BBC local radio stations in England and broadcast – simultaneously at noon following the Attenborough programme on Radio 4 – their own, very special, editions of *Your Desert Island Discs* – the programme where the listeners were invited to be the castaways.

The *Archive on 4* programme (which together with other special programmes can be heard on the *Desert Island Discs* website) told the story of those seven eventful decades through interviews with Sir Michael Parkinson and Sue Lawley, as well as with others involved in producing the programme over the years, and includes many memorable clips. In

Barbara Woodhouse with her heifers, 1945

1980, for instance, Roy Plomley reminded dog-trainer Barbara Woodhouse that 'as a child, you used to ride a heifer', prompting the airy response: 'I never see why poor cows should be left to end their days just grazing – why shouldn't they come out and see the world? I only had a heifer when I was a little girl, that's all. We didn't have ponies – so I saddled the heifer up, and she jumped beautifully.'

A far grimmer memory in 2001 took actor Joss Ackland back to the night when his house in south-west London was destroyed by fire. 'You lost everything,' says Sue Lawley, to which the actor replies, 'We lost everything except life' – and he goes on to describe his wife Rosemary's terrible experience. At the time they had five children, and Rosemary – Ackland himself was not at home – managed to get three of them out of the house, then went back inside, where she 'saw this smoke coming from under the door. She opened the door and the house exploded, and she caught on fire. She ran through the flames up the stairs, and one of the children was unconscious – she threw them out, and by the time she jumped they couldn't see her because of the smoke, and she plummeted down twenty-five feet and broke her back.

'She was five months pregnant and they said the baby would come away straight away. They didn't think she would live. And she was in Stoke Mandeville for eighteen months. That baby which they said was going to come away straight away has now got five children of her own. They said that Rosemary would never walk again – and she's the only person with that injury to have walked away from Stoke Mandeville.'

'So you didn't lose everything at all?' says Sue.

'We didn't lose anything.'

In addition to reviewing seven decades of such soul-baring moments, the *Archive on 4* programme took the opportunity to ask a recent castaway how it felt to be on *Desert Island Discs*. In her interview with Kirsty Young, retail guru Mary Portas (right) had given a graphic description of her traumatic teenage years, and Portas acknowledged how the intimacy of the *Desert Island Discs* studio can unlock doors in the memory: 'It felt the right place to do it. It just felt right. But it was probably the first time that I had really articulated it and really deeply thought about it.' It had proved a cathartic experience. On stepping outside Broadcasting House after the interview, she said, 'I just felt exhilarated, but at the same time like some enormous other life I had, had been lifted and set free, and I got outside and I just sobbed. I just sobbed. It was really meaningful.'

The *Archive on 4* hour concluded on a stirring note with Kirsty's *Desert Island Discs* credo: 'For me, the programme's strength lies where it always has, in the unique blend of a castaway's life and the music that forms its soundtrack. At best it displays the frailties and strengths of the human condition, how our creativity, grit and humanity can see us through.'

There was a fair bit of creativity, indeed, in the widespread press comment on the seventieth anniversary – in the sense that some of the old *Desert Island Discs* urban myths were wheeled out. The *Guardian* reported how Brigitte Bardot had asked for 'happiness' as her luxury, a request which according to that paper 'caused Plomley momentary consternation; it sounded as if she was asking for "a penis".' This claim would have more authority had BB ever appeared on the programme. The *Daily Telegraph* repeated the same old chestnut, and for good measure exhumed another: namely, that 'Margaret Thatcher was ridiculed for choosing the Rolf Harris hit "Two Little Boys Had Two Little Toys" as her favourite song.' (Any Thatcher anorak will confirm that she did indeed once make that claim, but in an interview with Radio Blackburn in 1979, and not on *Desert Island Discs* in 1978.) The *Telegraph* also offered a lesser-known myth – the source of which is unclear – that Yoko Ono (page 454) 'chose "The Cheeky Song" as her favourite piece of music'. But the paper hit the right note when Gillian Reynolds, doyenne of radio critics, declared of *Desert Island Discs* that 'Something magical is at work here.'

However hard it may be precisely to define that magic, the editions which launched the programme into its eighth decade in the first half of 2012 read like a taster menu for the whole history – and a demonstration that, even at the grand old age of three score years and ten, the show was far from set in its ways.

In late March the team left Broadcasting House and made for Bristol, where the interview with jazz pianist and singer Jamie Cullum (left) was recorded in front of a highly enthusiastic audience as part of Radio 4's More Than Words festival. This proved a real success, and he thrilled those in the hall when he performed three of his musical choices on the piano, winding up the programme with his own haunting version of Randy Newman's 'I Think It's Going to Rain Today'. (Randy Newman himself appeared on *Desert Island Discs* with Kirsty Young in October 2008.)

For the year of the London Olympics the sporting castaways included Denise Lewis, who had taken the gold medal for the heptathlon in the 2000 Games in Sydney; rugby player Brian Moore, who like fellow sporting legend Tony Adams before him (pages 469–73) gave a moving account of the pressures of top-level competition; and Martina Navratilova, whose inter-

view was first broadcast on the final day of the Wimbledon championships which she had graced for so many years of her long career.

The transatlantic thread which runs through *Desert Island Discs* history brought comedian Jackie Mason into the studio; the literary world was represented by the prolific Peter Ackroyd; and from the medical realm came Baroness Sheila Hollins, Professor of the Psychiatry of Learning Disability at St George's, University of London.

For the June weekend of the Diamond Jubilee celebrations, *Desert Island Discs* shipwrecked the Queen's first cousin (and bridesmaid) Margaret Rhodes, who gave her assessment of how her regal relative had adapted for the role of monarch: 'You have to squash the self out of you, in order to give yourself whole-heartedly to the job. Spontaneity has to

Castaway Margaret Rhodes, with her cousin Princess Elizabeth, 1947

leave your life. You know six months ahead what you're going to be doing every day, and that demands quite a lot of sacrifice – and she has done that, and I think she's just been a perfectly marvellous queen.'

In the tradition of a senior politician creating a desert island stir, Labour peer and former Deputy Prime Minister John Prescott caused a ripple with what was perceived as lukewarm support for party leader Ed

Miliband – though more interesting was his piece of advice to Miliband: 'Put your bloody jacket back on, because leaders shouldn't be walking around with no jacket, in my view.' And Prescott's private side was poignantly exposed when he talked of his family. He had experienced difficulties when his parents divorced, and being the eldest child had had to take on fatherly responsibilities within the family. Did he, asked Kirsty, try to be closer to his own sons than his father had been to him? Yes, but he had suffered from a 'kind of detachment' that came, he thought, from his background and culture. 'I've got two brilliant sons. I love them to death. But to my great regret I cannot somehow put my arms round my sons . . . I'm sad about that.'

The recurrent idea of marooning a castaway who is perhaps not a household name but none the less has a gripping story to tell brought to the island Ahdaf Soueif, novelist (the first Muslim woman to have been short-listed for the Booker Prize) and political activist in her native Egypt, who gave a riveting eye-witness account of the events in Tahrir Square in 2011: 'There was a moment when we were at the mouth of Tahrir and ahead of us there was smoke and the gunfire, and just thousands and thousands of people, and every once in a while there would be a surge of a few metres forward, as your friends, who were being killed at the front, gained you those three metres and your job, as the masses, was to move forward and hold the three metres. And that was, I suppose, when it really, really did sink in that this was a battle for the country and that we were all part of it, and I was there.'

Another profoundly moving personal account was that of Doreen Lawrence (below), whose son Stephen was murdered in a racist attack in

south-east London in 1993. Mrs Lawrence, who has been applauded (and decorated) for her tireless work to improve community relations, spoke frankly about her loss nearly twenty years on: 'My son was special and I think, what happened to him, I just wanted everyone to know and learn about him. But all the other things, the OBE – I'd swap all of that just to have my son back. When your children are young you take them for granted, because you think they're going to be there for ever.'

Nor did the supposedly lighter castaways always bring unrelenting sunshine to the island. Kirsty's interview with actor James Corden – about to conquer Broadway with the transfer of the West End smash hit *One Man, Two Guvnors*, which was to bring him the 2012 Tony Award for Best Actor in a Play – produced one of the most affecting recent editions.

James Corden and Ruth Jones in a 2008 episode of Gavin and Stacey, *the television show they wrote and starred in*

After a brisk rise to fame through Alan Bennett's play *The History Boys* and then *Gavin and Stacey* on television, James Corden had experienced difficulties in coming to terms with his fame and had seen his reputation suffer following a less than gracious acceptance speech at the 2008 BAFTA Awards. His account of this decline switched *Desert Island Discs* into full confessional mode. Was there, wondered Kirsty Young, 'a moment of epiphany'?

There was: the morning when a hung-over Corden was visited by his parents. 'They sat on the tiny two-seater sofa and I sat on the floor, and we didn't have any milk. I had half a bottle of vitamin water in the fridge and a Lindt chocolate bunny – I remember that – and we sat, and I'd had such a great relationship with my parents, but over the last year it seemed like I'd done all I could to try and sever that. I was just looking at the floor. I felt embarrassed that they were seeing me like this. I felt embarrassed at so many things, at the way I had behaved or acted at points over that seven- or eight-month period.

'My Dad just stood up, and he walked across to where I was and he just put his arms around me, and said, "You've got to get through this, son." And I just started to cry, as you do when your Dad hugs you when you're thirty, and my Mum came over and joined us, and we sat there, and my Dad said, "I'm going to say a prayer for you." The only way I can describe it is, it felt like every, every tear that was leaving my eyes was making me feel a bit lighter, because it started as like a light cry and then it became like a real sob.'

But sometimes gloomy stories have happy endings. Liverpool comedian John Bishop (left) spoke of how he had drifted into stand-up in his mid-thirties during a messy separation from his wife Melanie. Living on his own except when his children came to stay at the weekends, drinking too much and getting lower and lower, he found himself at a 'open mic' evening in a Manchester comedy club: £4 entrance, free if you did a turn. He tried his hand and was so well received that he gradually got more work on the comedy circuit of the north-west. By now he and his wife Melanie were talking only through lawyers, but then one gig turned everything around: 'I used to do a joke about splitting up with my wife. The joke was that we've split up but it's not that bad; we're not divorced or anything. I've just killed her, but I knew I'd miss her so I kept her head in the fridge. Now, that was not a brilliant joke, but as I said that joke I looked to the left, and the head that was meant to be in the fridge was sat in the audience.'

After the show they met in the bar, where Melanie told him, ' "You're back to the person I fell in love with" . . . We got back together after being apart for two years. I regard the relationship as the second marriage – because we're two different people now.'

'We should have the theme to *Love Story* now,' says Kirsty with the perfect reaction, 'but we don't . . .'

On which romantic note we set sail from the desert island, leaving behind on the beach a car boot sale's worth of luxuries, including a head of garlic, the Oval cricket ground, Michael Palin's stuffed body, a prosthetic arm, the Albert Memorial, a stick of marijuana, the law of the land, the *Mona Lisa*, a laminated life-size photograph of James Caan and a supply of acid drops.

Stacked under a nearby palm tree is an extensive library of books – including the *Eagle* annual and the *Beano* annual, copies of *Exchange and Mart*, the New York and London telephone directories, *Das Kapital*, the National Hunt form book and *Fun in a Chinese Laundry* by Josef von

Sternberg – in addition to those makeshift shelves groaning under multiple copies of the Bible and the complete works of Shakespeare.

And scattered among the seagull droppings in the sand dunes are some 22,000 records, from Arne to Zelenka and from Abba to Zappa.

As we steam away from the island we see, a mile offshore, a ship breaking up on the rocks – and a solitary figure clambering on to a plank of wood from the disintegrating vessel and striking out for the shore, eight records clamped under one arm and a book and something else wedged beside them on the plank – just as there will be next week, and the week after that, and the week after that, for at least another seventy years . . .

THE COMPLETE CASTAWAYS

ABBADO, Claudio (1980)
ABBOTT, Diane (2008)
ABBOTT, George (1984)
ABBOTT, Paul (2007)
ABICAIR, Shirley (1956)
ABRAHAMS, Harold (1959)
ABSE, Dannie (1977)
ACCARDO, Salvatore (1980)
ACKLAND, Joss (1982, 2001)
ACKROYD, Peter (2012)
ACOSTA, Carlos (2005)
ADAM, Sir Ken (2004)
ADAMS, Douglas (1994)
ADAMS, Richard (1977)
ADAMS, Tony (2010)
ADDAMS, Dawn (1965)
ADERIN-POCOCK, Maggie (2010)
ADIE, Kate (1994)
ADLER, Larry (1951)
ADRIAN, Max (1969)
ADSHEAD, Dr Gwen (2010)
AFSHAR, Lady [Haleh] (2008)
AGATE, James (1942)
AGUTTER, Jenny (1982)
AHLBERG, Allan (2008)
AITKEN, Maria (1989)
ALAGNA, Roberto (2009)
ALDA, Alan (1991)
ALDISS, Brian (1982, 2007)
ALEKSANDER, Igor (1999)
ALI, Tariq (2008)
AL-KHALILI, Prof. Jim (2010)
ALLBEURY, Ted (1979)
ALLCARD, Edward (1955)
ALLEGRO, John (1962)
ALLEN, Dave (1975)
ALLEN, Joseph (1985)
ALLEN, Sir Thomas (1982, 2001)
ALLENDE, Isabel (1993)
ALLISS, Peter (1987)
ALLSOP, Kenneth (1971)
ALSTON, Rex (1964)
ALVAREZ, Al (2000)
AMADEUS STRING QUARTET
   (1978)

AMBLER, Eric (1955)
AMBROSE, [Bert] (1965)
AMELING, Elly (1985)
AMIES, Hardy (1958)
AMIN, Mohammed (1992)
AMIS, Kingsley (1961, 1986)
AMIS, Martin (1996)
ANDERSON, Gillian (2003)
ANDERSON, Lindsay (1980)
ANDERSON, Moira (1969)
ANDREWS, Anthony (1987)
ANDREWS, Archie (1952)
ANDREWS, Eamonn (1958)
ANDREWS, Julie (1964, 1992)
ANDREWS, Wilfred (1966)
ANGELOU, Maya (1987)
ANNAN, Lord [Noel] (1990)
ANNIGONI, Pietro (1961)
ANSELL, Col. Sir Michael (1973)
ANTONIO (1961)
APRAHAMIAN, Felix (1995)
ARCHER, Jeffrey (1981)
ARCHER, Mary (1988)
ARDIZZONE, Edward (1972)
ARLOTT, John (1953, 1975)
ARMATRADING, Joan (1989)
ARMSTRONG, Karen (2006)
ARMSTRONG, Louis (1968)
ARMSTRONG, Richard (1982)
ARMSTRONG, Lord [Robert]
   (1988)
ARMSTRONG, Sir Thomas (1989)
ARNAUD, Yvonne (1951)
ARNOLD, Doris (1967)
ARNOLD, Eve (1996)
ARNOLD, Malcolm (1959)
ARRAU, Claudio (1960)
ASHCROFT, Peggy (1957)
ASHDOWN, Rt Hon. Paddy (1991)
ASHER, Jane (1988)
ASHKENAZY, Vladimir (1978)
ASHLEY, Lord [Jack] (1993)
ASHTON, Sir Frederick (1959,
   1981)
ASKEY, Arthur (1942, 1955, 1968,
   1980)
ASPEL, Michael (1972)
ASQUITH, Anthony (1955)
ATHILL, Diana (2004)
ATKINS, Eileen (1998)
ATKINS, Robert (1956)
ATKINSON, Rowan (1988)

**ATTENBOROUGH, Sir David
   (1957, 1979, 1998, 2012)**
ATTENBOROUGH, Richard (1952,
   1964)
ATWELL, Winifred (1952)
ATWOOD, Margaret (2003)
AWDRY, Rev. W. (1964)
AYCKBOURN, Alan (1974)
AYER, Sir Alfred (1984)
AYRES, Pam (1979)
AYRTON, Michael (1955)
AZNAVOUR, Charles (1978)

BACALL, Lauren (1979)
BADDELEY, Angela (1974)
BADDELEY, Hermione (1959)
BADER, Sir Douglas (1981)
BAEZ, Joan (1993)
BAILEY, Bill (2008)
BAILEY, David (1991)
BAILEY, Norman (1976)
BAILLIE, Isobel (1955, 1970)
BAILY, Leslie (1964)
BAINBRIDGE, Beryl (1986, 2008)
BAKER, Danny (2011)
BAKER, George (1965)
BAKER, Hylda (1969)
BAKER, Dame Janet (1968, 1982)
BAKER, Richard (1968)
BAKEWELL, Dame Joan (1972,
   2009)
BALCHIN, Nigel (1954)
BALCON, Jill (1945, 2007)
BALCON, Sir Michael (1961)
BALL, Michael (2008)
BALLARD, J. G. (1992)
BAMBER, Helen (1999)
BANHAM, John (1991)
BANKHEAD, Tallulah (1964)
BANKS, Iain (1997)
BANKS, Capt. M. B. B. (1954)
BANNATYNE, Duncan (2010)
BANNISTER, Sir Roger (1992)
BARABAS, Sari (1970)
BARBER, Chris (1959)
BARBER, Lynn (2010)
BARBER, Noel (1976)
BARCLAY-SMITH, Phyllis
   (1974)
BARENBOIM, Daniel (2006)
BARKER, Eric (1957)
BARKER, Pat (2003)

BARKWORTH, Peter (1979)
BARNARD, Dr Christiaan (1976)
BARNES, Dame Josephine (1989)
BARNES, Julian (1996)
BARNETT, Isobel (1956)
BARRINGTON, Jonah (1942)
BARRY, John (1967, 1999)
BARSTOW, Josephine (1979)
BARSTOW, Stan (1964, 1986)
BART, Lionel (1960)
BARTLETT, Vernon (1971)
BARTOK, Eva (1963)
BASELEY, Godfrey (1969)
BASIE, Count (1957)
BASS, Alfie (1968)
BASSEY, Shirley (1960)
BATES, Alan (1976)
BATES, H. E. (1962)
BATH, Marquess of [Alexander
    Thynn] (1975, 2001)
**BATMANGHELIDJH, Camila
    (2006)**
BATTY SHAW, Patricia (1978)
BAWDEN, Nina (1995)
BAXTER, Beverley (1943)
BAXTER, Raymond (1963)
BAXTER, Stanley (1970)
BEACHAM, Stephanie (1988)
BEADLE, Sir Gerald (1961)
BEALE, Simon Russell (2007)
BEARD, Mary (2010)
BEARD, Paul (1960)
BEATON, Sir Cecil (1980)
BEATTY, Robert (1952)
BEAUX ARTS TRIO (1981)
BEDFORD, Sybille (1998)
BEDSER, Alec (1960)
BEECHAM, Sir Thomas (1957)
BELAFONTE, Harry (1958)
BELITA (1953)
BELL, Martin (2001)
BELL BURNELL, Prof. Jocelyn
    (2000)
BELLAMY, David (1978)
BENINGFIELD, Gordon (1985)
BENN, Tony (1989)
BENNETT, Alan (1967)
BENNETT, Jill (1969)
BENNETT, Joan (1963)
BENNETT, Richard Rodney (1968,
    1997)
BENNETT, Tony (1972, 1987)
BENSON, Ivy (1971)
BENSON, Mary (1997)
BENTINE, Michael (1963)
BENTLEY, Dick (1957)
BERBERIAN, Cathy (1978)
BERKELEY, Sir Lennox (1978)
BERKOFF, Steven (1992)
BERLIN, Sir Isaiah (1992)
BERNARD, Jeffrey (1991)
BERRY, Mary (2012)
BERRY, Owen (1957)

BERRYMAN, Gwen (1972)
BETJEMAN, Sir John (1954, 1975)
BEVERLEY SISTERS (1961)
BHASKAR, Sanjeev (2008)
BIELENBERG, Christabel (1992)
BIFFEN, Rt Hon. John (1990)
BILIMORIA, Karan (2004)
BILK, Acker (1962)
BILLINGTON, Rachel (1983)
BINCHY, Maeve (1990)
BIRD, Dickie (1996)
BIRD, John [satirist] (1968, 2000)
BIRD, John [*Big Issue* founder]
    (1998)
BIRTWISTLE, Sir Harrison (1994)
BISHOP, John (2012)
BISHOP, Stephen (1966)
BLACK, Cilla (1964, 1988)
BLACK, Conrad (1994)
BLACK, Don (1995)
BLACK, Stanley (1958)
BLACKHALL, David Scott (1980)
BLACKMAN, Honor (1964)
BLACKMORE, Susan (1998)
BLACKSTONE, Lady [Tessa] (1993)
BLADES, James (1977)
BLAIR, Betsy (2005)
BLAIR, Lionel (1975)
BLAIR, Rt Hon. Tony (1996)
BLAKE, Peter (1979, 1997)
BLAKE, Quentin (2006)
BLAKEMORE, Prof. Colin (1996)
BLANC, Raymond (1992)
BLANCH, Stuart (1976)
BLANCHFLOWER, Danny (1960)
BLAND, Sir Christopher (2002)
BLASHFORD-SNELL, Lt-Col. John
    (1976)
BLEASDALE, Alan (1991)
BLESSED, Brian (1995)
BLETHYN, Brenda (2005)
BLISS, Sir Arthur (1959, 1972)
BLOFELD, Henry (2003)
BLOOM, Claire (1955, 1982)
BLOOM, Ursula (1960)
BLUE, Rabbi Lionel (1988)
BLUEBELL, Miss [Margaret Kelly]
    (1988)
BLUMBERG, Prof. Baruch (2003)
BLUMENTHAL, Heston (2006)
BLUNDELL, Tom (2007)
BLUNKETT, Rt Hon. David (1990)
BLYTH, Sgt Chay (1966)
BLYTHE, Ronald (2001)
BOARD, Lillian (1969)
BOE, Alfie (2011)
BOGARDE, Dirk (1964, 1989)
BOGDANOV, Michael (1987)
BOLAM, James (1977)
BOLET, Jorge (1985)
BOLT, Robert (1971)
BOND, Michael (1976)
BONFIELD, Sir Peter (2000)

BONINGTON, Chris (1973, 1999)
BOORMAN, John (1993)
BOORNE, Bill (1968)
BOOTH, Webster (1953)
BOOTHBY, Lord [Robert] (1960)
BOOTHROYD, Basil (1963)
BOOTHROYD, Betty (1993)
BORGE, Victor (1957)
BOSTRIDGE, Ian (2008)
BOSWELL, Eve (1959)
BOTHAM, Ian (1989)
BOTTOMLEY, Virginia (1993)
BOUCHIER, Chili (1996)
BOUGH, Frank (1987)
BOULT, Sir Adrian (1960, 1979)
BOULTING, John and Roy (1974)
BOURNE, Matthew (2004)
BOWEN, Elizabeth (1957)
BOWMAN, James (1995)
BOYCE, Max (1983)
BOYCOTT, Geoffrey (1971)
BOYER, Ronnie (1959)
BOYLE, Rt Hon. Sir Edward (1967)
BRABAZON of Tara, Lord [John]
    (1959)
BRABHAM, Jack (1966)
BRADBURY, Malcolm (1983)
BRADDON, Russell (1968)
BRADEN, Bernard (1955)
BRADFORD, Barbara Taylor (1985,
    2003)
BRADLEY, Helen (1975)
BRADY, Karren (2007)
BRAGG, Melvyn (1976)
BRAIN, Dennis (1956)
BRAINE, John (1971)
BRAITHWAITE, Bob (1968)
BRAMBELL, Wilfred (1964)
BRAMWELL-BOOTH,
    Commissioner Catherine
    (1980)
BRAND, Jo (2007)
BRANDRETH, Gyles (2011)
BRANNIGAN, Owen (1965)
BRANSON, Richard (1989)
BRASHER, Chris (1957)
BRATBY, John (1964)
BREAM, Julian (1961, 1983)
BREARLEY, Mike (1977)
BREASLEY, Scobie (1963)
BREMNER, Rory (2003)
BRENDEL, Alfred (1971)
BRENTON, Howard (1998)
BREWSTER, Yvonne (2005)
BRIERS, Richard (1967, 2000)
BRIGGS, Prof. Asa (1968)
BRIGGS, Barry (1967)
BRIGGS, Raymond (1983, 2005)
BRIGHTWELL, Robbie (1964)
BRITTAIN, Sir Harry (1964)
BRITTAN, Sir Leon (1993)
BRITTEN, Valentine (1956)
BRITTON, Tony (1973)

CONRAN, Jasper (1995)
CONRAN, Shirley (1977)
CONRAN, Sir Terence (1996)
CONSTANDUROS, Mabel (1944)
CONSTANTINE, Sir Learie (1963)
CONTEH, John (1975)
CONTI, Tom (1980)
CONWAY, Russ (1960)
COOGAN, Steve (2009)
COOK, Robin (2002)
COOKE, Alistair (1962)
COOKSON, Catherine (1984)
COONEY, Ray (1984)
COOPER, Alice (2010)
COOPER, Lady Diana (1969)
COOPER, Dame Gladys (1952, 1967)
COOPER, Henry (1966)
COOPER, Jilly (1975)
COOPER, Joseph (1973)
COPLAND, Aaron (1958)
COPLEY, John (2010)
CORBETT, Harry (1965)
CORBETT, Ronnie (1971, 2007)
CORDEN, James (2012)
COREN, Alan (1978)
CORNWELL, Bernard (2004)
CORNWELL, Patricia (2002)
COSTA, Sam (1956)
COSTELLO, Elvis (1992)
COTRUBAS, Ileana (1979)
COTTEN, Joseph (1981)
COTTLE, Gerry (1984)
COTTON, Billy (1959)
COTTRELL, Leonard (1966)
COTTRELL-BOYCE, Frank (2010)
COURTENAY, Tom (1967)
COURTNEIDGE, Cicely (1951, 1957)
COUSINS, Robin (1981)
COUSTEAU, Capt. Jacques (1982)
COUTTS, Gen. Frederick (1965)
COWARD, Noël (1963)
COWDREY, Colin (1968)
COWELL, Simon (2006)
COWLES, Fleur (1983)
COX, Josephine (2005)
CRADOCK, Fanny and Johnnie (1962)
CRAIG, Charles (1966)
CRAIG, Michael (1966)
CRAIG, Wendy (1971)
CRANBROOK, Countess of [Caroline] (2009)
CRAVEN, Gemma (1988)
CRAWFORD, Anne (1951)
CRAWFORD, Michael (1971, 1978, 1999)
CREWE, Quentin (1984, 1996)
CRIBBINS, Bernard (1963)
CRITCHLEY, Julian (1987)
CROFT, David (1993)
CROFT, Michael (1977)

CROSBY, Bing (1975)
CROSS, Joan (1957)
CROWTHER, Leslie (1962)
CRUICKSHANK, Andrew (1966)
CRYER, Barry (1987)
CULLEN, Bill (2003)
CULLUM, Jamie (2012)
CULVER, Roland (1974)
CUMMINGS, Constance (1951)
CUMMINS, Peggy (1953)
CUNEO, Terence (1972)
CUNLIFFE, Prof. Barry (1972)
CURLEY, Carlo (1982)
CURRIE, Finlay (1961)
CURRY, John (1977)
CURTIS, Richard (1999)
CURZON, Sir Clifford (1978)
CUSACK, Sinead (1983, 2002)
CUSHING, Peter (1959)
CUTFORTH, Rene (1967)

DACRE, Lord [Hugh Trevor-Roper] (1988)
DACRE, Paul (2004)
DAHL, Roald (1979)
DAHRENDORF, Prof. Ralf (1991)
DALBY, Barrington (1942, 1960)
DALLAGLIO, Lawrence (2011)
DANCE, Charles (1988)
DANE, Clemence (1951)
DANGERFIELD, Stanley (1975)
DANIEL, Prof. Glyn (1981)
DANIEL, Paul (1998)
DANIELS, Ann (2007)
DANIELS, Bebe (1956)
DANKWORTH, John (1957, 1986)
DANZIGER, Nick (2003)
DARE, Zena (1957)
DARZI, Ara (2008)
DAUBENY, Peter (1971)
DAVIES, Andrew (2007)
DAVIES, George (2006)
DAVIES, Prof. Dame Kay (2009)
DAVIES, Rupert (1961)
DAVIS, Andrew (1986)
DAVIS, Carl (1982)
DAVIS, Colin (1967)
DAVIS, David [broadcaster] (1970)
DAVIS, David [politician] (2008)
DAVIS, Joe (1961)
DAVIS, Steve (1983)
DAVIS, William (1988)
DAWKINS, Dr Richard (1995)
DAWSON, Les (1978)
DAY, Edith (1962)
DAY, Frances (1955)
DAY, Sir Robin (1969, 1990)
DAY LEWIS, C. (1960, 1968)
DE BEER, Sir Gavin (1970)
DE BURGH, Chris (1998)
DE CASALIS, Jeanne (1952)
DE GURR ST GEORGE, Vivian (1954)

DE JONG, Florence (1973)
DE LOS ANGELES, Victoria (1978)
DE MANIO, Jack (1964)
DE PEYER, Gervase (1973)
DE VALOIS, Dame Ninette (1966, 1991)
DEAN, Basil (1973)
DEEDES, Lord [Bill] (2001)
DEELEY, Michael (2008)
DEIGHTON, Len (1976)
DEL CONTE, Anna (2010)
DEL MAR, Norman (1963)
DEL MONACO, Mario (1962)
DELDERFIELD, R. F. (1962)
DELFONT, Lord [Bernard] (1991)
DELYSIA, Alice (1972)
DENCH, Judi (1972, 1998)
DENHAM, Maurice (1965)
DENIS, Armand and Michaela (1960)
DENISON, Michael (1952)
DENNING, Rt Hon. Lord [Alfred] (1980)
DENNIS, Felix (2007)
DENT, Alan (1944)
DESMOND, Florence (1952)
DETTORI, Frankie (2006)
DEVI, Gayatri (1984)
DEVONSHIRE, Duke and Duchess of (1982)
DEXTER, Colin (1998)
DI STEFANO, Giuseppe (1981)
DIAMAND, Peter (1966)
DIBNAH, Fred (1991)
DICKENS, Monica (1951, 1970)
DICKSON, Barbara (1995)
DICKSON, Dorothy (1952)
DICKSON WRIGHT, Clarissa (1999)
DIETRICH, Marlene (1965)
DIMBLEBY, David (1974, 2008)
DIMBLEBY, Richard (1958)
DINGLE, Capt. A. E. (1942)
DISTEL, Sacha (1971, 2004)
DIXON, Reginald (1954)
DJERASSI, Carl (2002)
DOBSON, Anita (1988)
DODD, Ken (1963, 1990)
DODWELL, Christina (1994)
DOLIN, Sir Anton (1955, 1982)
DOLL, Prof. Sir Richard (2001)
DOMINGO, Placido (1980)
DON, Monty (2006)
DONALD, Athene (2009)
DONALDSON, Julia (2009)
DONLAN, Yolande (1953)
DONLEAVY, J. P. (2007)
DONOHOE, Peter (1988)
DONOUGHUE, Lord [Bernard] (1988)
DOONICAN, Val (1970)
DORATI, Antal (1960, 1980)
DORITA (1964)

FREUD, Clement (1967)
FRINK, Elisabeth (1974)
FROST, Sir David (1963, 1971, 2005)
FROST, Sir Terry (1998)
FRY, Christopher (1978)
FRY, Stephen (1988)
FULLER, Rosalinde (1968)

GABLE, Christopher (1972)
GALBRAITH, Prof. J. K. (1982)
GALLICO, Paul (1961)
GALWAY, James (1976)
GAMBACCINI, Paul (2002)
GAMBON, Michael (1988)
GAMLIN, Lionel (1955)
GANDER, Marsland L. (1969)
GANNON, Lucy (1998)
GARDINER, John Eliot (1992)
GARDNER, Frank (2005)
GARRETT, Lesley (1993)
GASCOIGNE, Bamber (1987)
GASKIN, Catherine (1980)
GAVIN, Dr Catherine (1978)
GEDDA, Nicolai (1969)
GELDOF, Bob (1992)
GEMMELL, Prof. Alan (1977)
GENN, Leo (1953)
GEORGE, Boy (1989)
GEORGE, Susan (1987)
GERALDO (1958)
GERHARDT, Elena (1958)
GERVAIS, Ricky (2007)
GHEORGHIU, Angela (2004)
GIBBERD, Sir Frederick (1983)
GIBBONS, Carroll (1952)
GIBSON, Alexander (1973)
GIBSON, Wg Cdr Guy (1944)
GIBSON, William (1999)
GIELGUD, Sir John (1962, 1981)
GIELGUD, Val (1962)
GILBERT, Lewis (2010)
GILBERT, Martin (1982)
GILL, A. A. (2006)
GILLARD, Frank (1970)
GILLESPIE, Dizzy (1980)
GILLIAM, Terry (2011)
GILLIAT, Sidney (1962)
GILMOUR, David (2003)
GINGOLD, Hermione (1952, 1969)
GIULINI, Carlo Maria (1968)
GLADSTONE, Sir William (1976)
GLENDENNING, Raymond (1962)
GLENNIE, Evelyn (1993)
GLITTER, Gary (1981)
GLOVER, Brian (1980)
GLOVER, Jane (1986)
GLUBB, Sir John (1978)
GLUCKSTEIN, Sir Louis (1971)
GOBBI, Tito (1958, 1979)
GODDEN, Rumer (1975, 1996)
GODFREE, Kitty (1987)
GODFREY, Isidore (1970)
GODWIN, Dame Anne (1968)

GODWIN, Fay (2002)
GOLDBERG, Whoopi (2009)
GOLDSCHMIDT, Berthold (1994)
GOLDSMITH, Harvey (2009)
GOLLANCZ, Victor (1961)
GOMBRICH, Sir Ernst (1992)
GONELLA, Nat (1966)
GOODALL, Howard (2008)
GOODALL, Dr Jane (2000)
GOODALL, Reginald (1980)
GOODHEW, Duncan (1992)
GOODISON, Sir Nicholas (1987)
GOODMAN, Lord [Arnold] (1991)
GOODMAN, Len (2011)
GOODWIN, Denis (1955)
GOODWIN, Ron (1984)
GOOLDEN, Richard (1945, 1967)
GOOSSENS, Léon (1960)
GOOSSENS, Sidonie (1955)
GORDIEVSKY, Oleg (2008)
GORDON, Richard (1971)
GORE-BOOTH, Sir Paul (1968)
GORING, Marius (1957)
GORMLEY, Antony (1998)
GOWER, David (1984)
GRACE of Monaco, Princess (1981)
GRADE, Lew (1987)
GRADE, Michael (1992)
GRAHAM, John (2011)
GRAHAM, Winston (1977)
GRAINER, Ron (1963)
GRANGER, Stewart (1945, 1981)
GRANT, Duncan (1975)
GRANT, Hugh (1995)
GRANTHAM, Leslie (1989)
GRAPPELLI, Stéphane (1972)
GRAY, Dulcie (1952)
GRAY, Linda Esther (1983)
GRAYLING A. C. (2008)
GRECO, Juliette (1963)
GREEN, Benny (1986)
GREEN, Felicity (2011)
GREEN, Hughie (1962)
GREEN, Lucinda (1987)
GREEN, Michael (1999)
GREENE, Sir Hugh (1983)
GREENFIELD, Dr Susan (1997)
GREENSLADE, Bill (1952)
GREENWOOD, Joan (1952)
GREER, Germaine (1988)
GREGG, Hubert (1966)
GREGORY, Richard (1993)
GREGSON, John (1955)
GREIG, Tony (1976)
GRENFELL, Joyce (1951, 1971)
GRENFELL, Stephen (1964)
GREY THOMPSON, Tanni (2001)
GREY, Anthony (1969)
GREY, Dame Beryl (1958, 2002)
GRIFFITH, Hugh (1967)
GRIFFITHS, Richard (2006)
GRIGSON, Geoffrey (1982)
GRIGSON, Jane (1978)

GRIMSHAW, Nicholas (2003)
GRINHAM, Judy (1959)
GRISEWOOD, Frederick (1945, 1960)
GROSSMAN, Loyd (1997)
GROVES, Charles (1972)
GRUNWALD, Anatole (1965)
GRYN, Rabbi Hugo (1994)
GUBBAY, Raymond (2006)
GUBBINS, Nathaniel (1942)
GUEST, George (1976)
GUINNESS, Sir Alec (1960, 1977)
GUNN, James (1962)
GUNTER, John (1983)
GUTHRIE, Gen. Sir Charles (2000)
GUTHRIE, Tyrone (1959)
GUYLER, Deryck (1970)

HACKER, Alan (1994)
HACKETT, Gen. Sir John (1980)
HADOW, Pen (2004)
HAENDEL, Ida (1970)
HAGUE, William (2001)
HAILEY, Arthur (1986)
HAILSTONE, Bernard (1975)
HAITINK, Bernard (1974)
HALE, Binnie (1952)
HALE, Kathleen (1994)
HALE, Lionel (1958)
HALE, Sonnie (1952)
HALL, Adelaide (1972, 1991)
HALL, Dr Elsie (1969)
HALL, Sir Ernest (1998)
HALL, Henry (1952, 1968)
HALL, Sir Peter (1965, 1983)
HALL, Prof. Stuart (2000)
HALSEY, Prof. A. H. (2003)
HAMBLING, Maggi (2005)
HAMILTON, Andy (1997)
HAMLISCH, Marvin (1983)
HAMMOND, Joan (1951, 1970)
HAMMOND, Kay (1951)
HAMNETT, Katherine (1989)
HAMPSHIRE, Susan (1968)
HAMPTON, Christopher (1996)
HAMPTON, Lionel (1983)
HANBURY-TENISON, Robin (1984)
HANCOCK, Sheila (1965, 2000)
HANCOCK, Tony (1957)
HANDL, Irene (1962)
HANDLEY, Vernon (1984)
HANDS, Terry (1981)
HANFF, Helene (1981)
HANSFORD-JOHNSON, Pamela (1962)
HANSON, John (1965)
HARBEN, Philip (1955)
HARDCASTLE, William (1974)
HARDING, Gilbert (1952)
HARDING, Mike (1982)
HARDWICKE, Sir Cedric (1955)
HARDY, Prof. Sir Alister (1973)

HYTNER, Nicholas (1993)
IANNUCCI, Armando (2006)
IBBETT, Cdr (1957)
IDLE, Eric (1976)
IFIELD, Frank (1965)
ILLINGWORTH, Leslie Gilbert
  (1963)
IMRIE, Celia (2011)
INGHAM, Sir Bernard (1995)
INGLEFIELD, Sir Gilbert (1968)
INGLIS, Brian (1974)
INGRAMS, Richard (1972, 2008)
INNES, Hammond (1972)
IRONS, Jeremy (1986, 2006)
IRONSIDE, Virginia (1997)
IRVINE, Lucy (1984)
ISAACS, Jeremy (1988)
ISHIGURO, Kazuo (2002)
ISSERLIS, Steven (2007)
IVES, Burl (1979)
IVESON, Tony (2011)
IVORY, James (1983)

JACKSON, Betty (2002)
JACKSON, Sir Geoffrey (1972)
JACKSON, Glenda (1971, 1997)
JACKSON, Gordon (1975)
JACKSON, Jack (1960)
JACOB, Naomi (1958)
JACOBI, Derek (1978)
JACOBS, David (1964)
JACOBSON, Howard (2011)
JACOBSON, Maurice (1969)
JACQUES, Hattie (1961)
JACQUES, Dr Reginald (1963)
JAEGER, Lt-Col C. H. (1968)
JAFFA, Max (1958)
JAFFREY, Madhur (1985)
JAFFREY, Saeed (1997)
JAMES, Clive (1980, 2000)
JAMES, Geraldine (2004)
JAMES, P. D. (1982, 2002)
JAMES, Polly (1974)
JAMES, Sidney (1960)
JAMESON, Derek (1994)
JASON, David (1994)
JAY, Joan (1942)
JEANS, Isabel (1953)
JEANS, Ursula (1955)
JEFFORD, Barbara (1961)
JEFFREYS, Alec (2007)
JENCKS, Charles (2012)
JENKINS, Clive (1990)
JENKINS, Rev. David (1992)
JENKINS, Karl (2006)
JENKINS, Rae (1965)
JENKINS, Lord [Roy] (1989)
JENNER, Heather (1967)
JENNINGS, Elizabeth (1993)
JENNINGS, Paul (1975)
JEWEL, Jimmy (1975)
JOAD, Dr C. E. M. (1945)
JOFFE, Lord [Joel] (2007)

JOHN, Barry (1978)
JOHN, Elton (1986)
JOHNS, Glynis (1976)
JOHNS, Stratford (1964)
JOHNSON, Alan (2007)
JOHNSON, Bill (1951)
JOHNSON, Boris (2005)
JOHNSON, Celia (1945, 1954, 1975)
JOHNSON, Hugh (1984)
JOHNSON, Linton Kwesi (2002)
JOHNSON, Paul (2012)
JOHNSTON, Brian (1974)
JOHNSTON, Sue (2002)
JONAS, Peter (1990)
JONES, Alan (1981)
JONES, Sir Digby (2006)
JONES, Freddie (1980)
JONES, Gemma (1976)
JONES, Gwyneth (1983)
JONES, Paul (1983)
JONES, Peter (1962)
JONES, Philip (1976)
JONES, Dr Steve (1992)
JONES, Terry (1983)
JONES, Tom (2010)
JONES, Tristan (1980)
JORDAN, Neil (2000)
JOYCE, C. A. (1971)
JOYCE, Eileen (1945, 1955)
JULIUS, Anthony (2009)
JUROWSKI, Vladimir (2007)

KAHN, Percy (1958)
KALMS, Sir Stanley (2001)
KARLIN, Miriam (1967)
KARSAVINA, Tamara (1957)
KATIN, Peter (1956)
KAVANAGH, P. J. (1974)
KAVANAGH, Ted (1951)
KAYE, Gorden (1991)
KAYE, M. M. (1983)
KAYE, Stubby (1984)
KAZAN, Elia (1979)
KEANE, Molly (1990)
KEARTON, Ada Cherry (1956)
KEATING, Tom (1983)
KEEGAN, John (1998)
KEENAN, Brian (1990)
KEILLOR, Garrison (1994)
KEITH, Alan (1971)
KEITH, Penelope (1976)
KELLINO, Pamela (1953)
KELLY, Barbara (1955)
KELLY, Jude (2002)
KEMP, Rosea (1968)
KENDAL, Felicity (1978)
KENDALL, Henry (1951)
KENEALLY, Thomas (1983, 2007)
KENNEDY, Charles (2003)
KENNEDY, Helena (1998)
KENNEDY, Ludovic (1971)
KENNEDY, Nigel (1986)
KENT, HRH Duchess of (1989)

KENT, Jean (1951)
KENTNER, Louis (1962)
KENTON, Stan (1956)
KENWARD, Betty (1974)
KENWRIGHT, Bill (1998)
KERMODE, Sir Frank (1997)
KERR, Deborah (1945, 1977)
KERR, Graham (1971)
KERR, Judith (2004)
KERSHAW, Andy (2007)
KHAN, Akram (2012)
KHAN, Imran (1991)
KIDMAN, Nicole (1998)
KIDSTON, Cath (2011)
KILLANIN, Lord (1987)
KING, Dave [comedian] (1960)
KING, David [scientist] (2005)
KING, Hetty (1969)
KING, Lord [John] (1991)
KING, Stephen (2006)
KING-HALL, Cdr Sir Stephen
  (1961)
KING-HAMILTON, Sir Alan
  (1983)
KINGSLEY, Ben (1986)
KINNOCK, Glenys (1994)
KINNOCK, Neil (1988)
KIPNIS, Igor (1976)
KIRBY, Gwendoline (1966)
KIRKWOOD, Pat (1942, 1955)
KITT, Eartha (1956)
KLUG, Sir Aaron (2002)
KNAPP, Jimmy (1995)
KNIGHT, Esmond (1952)
KNIGHT, Maxwell (1965)
KNOX-JOHNSTON, Robin (1970,
  1990)
KOCH, Dr Ludwig (1958)
KOHN, Ralph (2004)
KOLTAI, Ralph (1998)
KOSSOFF, David (1964)
KRETZMER, Herbert (2003)
KROTO, Sir Harry (2001)
KUCHMY, J. (1982)
KUMAR, Satish (2005)
KUREISHI, Hanif (1996)
KWEI-ARMAH, Kwame (2011)

LA FRENAIS, Ian (1979)
LA PLANTE, Lynda (1994)
LA RUE, Danny (1966)
LABBETTE, Dora (1956)
LADENIS, Nico (1997)
LAINE, Cleo (1958, 1997)
LAIRD, Gavin (1992)
LAKER, Jim (1956)
LAMB, Charlotte (1983)
LAMBTON, Lucinda (1989)
LANCASTER, Sir Osbert (1955,
  1979)
LANDAUER, [Walter] (1957)
LANDEN, Dinsdale (1978)
LANDESMAN, Fran (1996)

MALLALIEU, Ann (1968)
MANDER, Raymond (1978)
MANILOW, Barry (2009)
MANNING, Olivia (1969)
MANNINGHAM-BULLER, Eliza (2007)
MANSFIELD, Michael (2010)
MANSFIELD, Peter (2006)
MANTOVANI (1957)
MAPANJE, Jack (2004)
MARCEAU, Marcel (1972)
MARGARET, HRH Princess (1981)
MARGOLYES, Miriam (2008)
MARK, Sir Robert (1976)
MARKOVA, Dame Alicia (1958, 2002)
MARKS, Alfred (1959)
MARRINER, Neville (1980)
MARSH, Dame Ngaio (1968)
MARSHALL, Arthur (1974)
MARSHALL, Sybil (1993)
MARSHALL, Wayne (2002)
MARTIN, George (1982, 1995)
MARTIN, Mary (1977)
MARTIN, Millicent (1963)
MARTINELLI, Giovanni (1962)
MARX, Robert (1965)
MASCHLER, Fay (1999)
MASCHWITZ, Eric (1956)
MASEKELA, Hugh (2004)
MASKELL, Dan (1968)
MASON, Jackie (2012)
MASON, James (1961, 1981)
MASON, Dame Monica (2012)
MASSEY, Anna (1961)
MASSEY, Daniel (1981)
MASSINE, Leonide (1972)
MASTERSON, Valerie (1975)
MATHIESON, Muir (1951)
MATHIS, Johnny (1987)
MATTHEWS, A. E. (1951)
MATTHEWS, Denis (1967)
MATTHEWS, Jessie (1954)
MATTHEWS, Very Rev. Dr W. R. (1967)
MAUGER, Ivan (1970)
MAUPIN, Armistead (2007)
MAXWELL, Robert (1987)
MAXWELL DAVIES, Peter (1983, 2005)
MAY, Brian (2002)
MAY, Lord [Bob] (2002)
MAYER, Sir Robert (1965, 1979)
MAYERL, Billy (1958)
MAYLE, Peter (1993)
MAYNARD DENNY, Adm. Sir Michael (1963)
MAYS, Raymond (1969)
MEHTA, Ved (1984)
MEHTA, Zubin (1984)
MELACHRINO, George (1959)
MELCHETT, Peter (2000)
MELLOR, David (1992)

MELLY, George (1973)
MELVILLE, Alan (1957)
MENDOZA, June (1979)
MENOTTI, Gian Carlo (1978)
MENUHIN, Hephzibah (1958)
MENUHIN, Yehudi (1955, 1977)
MERCHANT, Ismail (1986)
MERRILL, Robert (1967)
MERRIMAN, Percy (1964)
MERTON, Paul (1993)
MESSEL, Oliver (1958)
MEYER, Sir Christopher (2003)
MICHAEL of Kent, HRH Princess (1984)
MICHAEL, George (2007)
MICHELL, Keith (1970)
MIDDLETON, C. H. (1943)
MIDGLEY, Mary (2005)
MILES, Bernard (1953, 1982)
MILES, Sarah (1990)
MILLAR, Sir Oliver (1977)
MILLER, Dr Jonathan (1971, 2005)
MILLER, Max (1953)
MILLER, Mitch (1966)
MILLER, Ruby (1958)
MILLIGAN, Spike (1956, 1978)
MILLS, Barbara (1993)
MILLS, Cyril (1961)
MILLS, Freddie (1951)
MILLS, Mrs [Gladys] (1971)
MILLS, Hayley (1965)
MILLS, Sir John (1951, 1973, 2000)
MILNE, Christopher (1976)
MILNES, Sherrill (1976)
MILNES-WALKER, Nicolette (1971)
MINCHIN, Tim (2012)
MINGHELLA, Anthony (1997)
MINTER, Alan (1980)
MIRREN, Helen (1982)
MIRVISH, 'Honest' Ed (1984)
MITCHELL, David (2009)
MITCHELL, George (1962)
MITCHELL, Leslie (1974)
MITCHELL, Warren (1967, 1999)
MITCHELL, Yvonne (1961)
MITCHENSON, Joe (1978)
MITCHISON, Naomi (1991)
MITFORD, Jessica (1977)
MOFFO, Anna (1976)
MOISEIWITSCH, Benno (1958)
MOLONEY, Paddy (1999)
MONKHOUSE, Bob (1998, 1955)
MONSARRAT, Nicholas (1955)
MONTAGU, Lord [Edward] (1987)
MONTGOMERIE, Colin (2000)
MONTGOMERY of Alamein, Viscount [Bernard] (1969)
MONTGOMERY HYDE, Harford (1963)
MOODY, Ron (1975)
MOORE, Brian (2012)
MOORE, Christy (2007)

MOORE, Dudley (1969)
MOORE, Gerald (1951, 1967)
MOORE, Patrick (1963)
MOORE, Roger (1981)
MOORHOUSE, Geoffrey (1983)
MORE, Kenneth (1956, 1969)
MORECAMBE, Eric (1966)
MORGAN, Cliff (1969)
MORGAN, Piers (2009)
MORLEY, Robert (1962)
MORLEY, Sheridan (1974)
MORPURGO, Michael (2004)
MORRIS, Bill (1998)
MORRIS, Desmond (1968, 2004)
MORRIS, Jan (1983, 2002)
MORRIS, John (1959)
MORRIS, Johnny (1960)
MORRIS, Sir Peter (2002)
MORRISSEY (2009)
MORTIMER, Harry (1960)
MORTIMER, Sir John (1968, 1982, 2001)
MORTON, J. B. (1943)
MOSER, Sir Claus (1988)
MOSHINSKY, Elijah (1993)
MOSIMANN, Anton (1988)
MOSLEY, Lady [Diana] (1989)
MOSS, Pat (1963)
MOSS, Stirling (1956)
MOTION, Andrew (1998)
MOTTRAM, Tony (1955)
MOULT, Edward (1959)
MOUNT, Peggy (1968, 1996)
MOUSKOURI, Nana (1979)
MOWLAM, Mo (1999)
MUGGERIDGE, Malcolm (1956, 1981)
MUIR, Frank (1960, 1976)
MULLEN, Barbara (1946, 1971)
MULVILLE, Jimmy (2010)
MUNRO, Matt (1975)
MUNROW, David (1974)
MURDOCH, Richard (1952, 1961)
MURPHY O'CONNOR, Abp Cormac (2001)
MURPHY, Delia (1952)
MURPHY, Dervla (1993)
MURRAY, Barbara (1968)
MURRAY, Les (1998)
MURRAY, Simon (2009)
MUTTER, Anne-Sophie (1986)

NAIPAUL, V. S. (1980)
NAPIER, John (1976)
NAVRATILOVA, Martina (2012)
NEAGLE, Anna (1952)
NEAL, Patricia (1988)
NEEL, Boyd (1952, 1963)
NEGUS, Arthur (1967)
NEIL, Andrew (2007)
NERINA, Nadia (1965)
NESBITT, Cathleen (1973)
NESBITT, James (2008)

PRICE, Alan (1982)
PRICE, Annie (1983)
PRICE, Dennis (1956)
PRICE, Leontyne (1973)
PRICE, Margaret (1975)
PRICE, Vincent (1969)
PRIESTLAND, Gerald (1984)
PRINCE, Hal (1986)
PRIOR, Allan (1979)
PRIOR, James (1975, 1987)
PRITCHARD, Sir John (1983)
PROOPS, Marjorie (1963)
PRYCE, Jonathan (1990)
PULLMAN, Philip (2002)
PUTTNAM, David (1984)
PYKE, Dr Magnus (1974)
PYM, Barbara (1978)

QUASTHOFF, Thomas (2009)
QUATRO, Suzi (1986)
QUAYLE, Anthony (1957, 1976)
QUENNELL, Peter (1976)
QUINN, Michael (1984)
QUIRKE, Pauline (1996)

RABBATTS, Heather (2011)
RACE, Steve (1959, 1971)
RADICE, Vittorio (2003)
RAEBURN, Anna (1978)
RAINER, Luise (1999)
RAMBERT, Marie (1960)
RAMPLING, Charlotte (1976)
RAMSAY, Gordon (2002)
RANDALL, Derek (1977)
RANKIN, Ian (2006)
RANTZEN, Esther (1975)
RAPHAEL, Frederic (1981, 2006)
RATCLIFFE, Hardie (1964)
RATTIGAN, Sir Terence (1974)
RATTLE, Simon (1978, 2008)
RAVEL, Jeanne (1959)
RAWICZ, [Marjan] (1957)
RAWLINGS, Margaret (1958)
RAWSTHORNE, Noel (1972)
RAY, Cyril (1974)
RAY, Robin (1974)
RAY, Ted (1952)
RAYNER, Claire (1977)
READ, Al (1965)
READ, Miss (1977)
READER, Ralph (1944, 1961)
READING, Bertice (1984)
REARDON, Ray (1979)
REDGRAVE, Lynn (1970)
REDGRAVE, Michael (1945, 1955)
REDGRAVE, Lady [Rachel
    Kempson] (1989)
REDGRAVE, Vanessa (1964)
REDHEAD, Brian (1986)
REDMOND, Phil (1995)
REECE, Brian (1953, 1961)
REED, John (1972)
REED, Oliver (1974)

REEMAN, Douglas (1983)
REES, Sir Martin (1997)
REEVE, Ada (1952)
REEVE, Christopher (1984)
REEVES, Vic (2003)
REGO, Paula (1997)
REID, Beryl (1963, 1983)
REILLY, Tommy (1961)
RENDALL, David (1984)
RESNIK, Regina (1964)
REVNELL, Ethel (1964)
REYNOLDS, Fiona (2002)
REYNOLDS, Quentin (1963)
RHODES, Margaret (2012)
RHODES, Zandra (1983)
RHYS JONES, Griff (2001)
RICCI, Ruggiero (1983)
RICE, Tim (1976, 2004)
RICH, Buddy (1981)
RICHARD, Alison (2005)
RICHARD, Cliff (1960)
RICHARD, Wendy (1995)
RICHARDS, Dick (1965)
RICHARDSON, Ian (1983)
RICHARDSON, Sir Ralph (1953,
    1979)
RICHMOND, Robin (1977)
RIDDLE, Nelson (1961)
RIDGE, Antonia (1960)
RIDGWAY, Capt. John (1966, 1986)
RIDLEY, Arnold (1973)
RIGG, Diana (1970)
RIPPON, Angela (1982)
RITCHARD, Cyril (1953)
RITCHIE, June (1966)
RITCHIE-CALDER, Lord (1967)
RITTER, Tex (1956)
RIX, Lord [Brian] (1960, 2009)
ROBBINS, Tim (2010)
ROBENS, Lord (1965)
ROBERTSON, Alec (1957, 1972)
ROBERTSON, Denise (2012)
ROBERTSON, Fyfe (1970)
ROBERTSON JUSTICE, James
    (1955)
ROBESON, Paul (1958)
ROBEY, Edward (1973)
ROBEY, George (1951)
ROBINS, Denise (1973)
ROBINSON, Eric (1958)
ROBINSON, Gerry (1996)
ROBINSON, Jancis (1996)
ROBINSON, Robert (1975)
ROBINSON, Stanford (1969)
ROBINSON, T. R. (1963)
ROBINSON, Tony (2011)
ROBLES, Marisa (1977)
ROBSON, Sir Bobby (1986, 2004)
ROBSON, Flora (1958)
RODDICK, Anita (1988)
RODEN, Claudia (2001)
RODENBURG, Patsy (2012)
RODGERS, Clodagh (1971)

ROGERS, Ginger (1969)
ROGERS, Paul (1962)
ROGERS, Peter (1973)
ROGERS, Richard (1990)
ROLFE JOHNSON, Anthony (1992)
ROLL, Lord Eric (2001)
RONAY, Egon (1977)
ROOK, Jean (1990)
ROS, Edmundo (1958)
ROSE, Sir Alec (1969)
ROSE, Clarkson (1962)
ROSE, Sir Stuart (2009)
ROSEN, Michael (2006)
ROSENTHAL, Jack (1998)
ROSOMAN, Leonard (2002)
ROSS, Prof. A. S. C. (1970)
ROSS, Annie (1965)
ROSSITER, Leonard (1980)
ROTBLAT, Joseph (1998)
ROTHENSTEIN, Sir John (1965)
ROTHERMERE, Viscount [Vere
    Harmsworth] (1996)
ROTHSCHILD, Miriam (1989)
ROTHSCHILD, Lord [Walter]
    (1984)
ROTHWELL, Evelyn (1969)
ROUS, Sir Stanley (1966)
ROUTLEDGE, Patricia (1974, 1999)
ROUX, Albert and Michel (1986)
ROWE, Dorothy (2002)
ROWLING, J. K. (2000)
ROWSE, A. L. (1977)
ROZSA, Miklos (1984)
RUANNE, Patricia (1981)
RUBBRA, Edmund (1981)
RUBENS, Bernice (1991)
RUBINSTEIN, Artur (1971)
RUBINSTEIN, Stanley (1969)
RUNCIE, Most Rev. Robert (1989)
RUSHDIE, Salman (1988)
RUSHTON, William (1984)
RUSSELL, Anna (1962)
RUSSELL, Audrey (1957)
RUSSELL, Billy (1968)
RUSSELL, Sir Gordon (1968)
RUSSELL, Ken (1987)
RUSSELL, Sheridan (1970)
RUSSELL, Willy (1994)
RUTHERFORD, Margaret (1953)
RUTTER, John (2005)
RYAN, Elizabeth (1971)
RYDER, Lady [Sue] (1987)

SAATCHI, Maurice (1995)
SABLON, Jean (1958)
SACHS, Albie (2000)
SACHS, Leonard (1970)
SACKS, Dr Jonathan (1991)
SACKS, Oliver (1994)
SAGAN, Carl (1981)
SAINSBURY, Lord [David] (1992,
    2004)
ST JOHN-STEVAS, Norman (1975)

STEWART, Rory (2008)
STILES-ALLEN, Mme [Lilian] (1971)
STOCKS, Mary (1965)
STOKES, Doris (1985)
STOKOWSKI, Leopold (1957)
STONE, Christopher (1952, 1957)
STOPFORD, Dr Robert (1962)
STOPPARD, Tom (1985)
STOREY, David (1972)
STORR, Anthony (1993)
STOTT, Mary (1994)
STRAW, Jack (1998)
STREATFEILD, Noel (1976)
STREET, A. G. (1962)
STREETER, Fred (1957)
STREET-PORTER, Janet (2008)
STREICH, Rita (1978)
STRONG, Patience (1966)
STRONG, Dr Roy (1970)
STUART WATSON, Sylva (1971)
STYNE, Jule (1978)
SUCHET, David (2009)
SUGGS (2002)
SULSTON, Sir John (2001)
SUMMERSKILL, Lady [Edith] (1973)
SURMAN, John (1984)
SUTCLIFF, Rosemary (1983)
SUTHERLAND, Donald (2000)
SUTHERLAND, Joan (1959)
SUTHERLAND, John (2006)
SUZMAN, Janet (1978)
SUZUKI, Pat (1960)
SWAN, Donald (1958)
SWAN, Robert (2000)
SWANSON, Gloria (1981)
SWINBURNE, Nora (1953)
SWINNERTON, Frank (1943, 1974)
SWINTON, Prof. W. E. (1966)
SYAL, Meera (2003)
SYKES, Eric (1957, 1997)
SYKES, Sir Richard (1999)
SYKORA, Ken (1962)
SYMONS, Julian (1982)
SZERYNG, Henryk (1967)
SZIGETI, Joseph (1965)

TAKI (1993)
TALBOT, Godfrey (1960)
TALLENTS, Sir Stephen (1943)
TALLIS, Prof. Raymond (2007)
TANGYE, Derek (1980)
TARBUCK, Jimmy (1972, 2004)
TARRANT, Chris (2001)
TATE, Jeffrey (1989)
TAUBER, Richard (1942)
TAUSKY, Vilem (1970)
TAVENER, John (1994)
TAVISTOCK, Marchioness of [Henrietta] (1992)
TAYLOR, Dennis (1986)
TAYLOR, Lord Chief Justice [Peter] (1992)

TAYLOR BRADFORD, Barbara (2003)
TAYLOR-WOOD, Sam (2005)
TE KANAWA, Kiri (1980)
TE WIATA, Inia (1966)
TEAGARDEN, Jack (1957)
TEAR, Robert (1980)
TEBBIT, Lady [Margaret] (1995)
TEBBIT, Lord [Norman] (1992)
TENNANT, David (2009)
TENNANT, Neil (2007)
TENNSTEDT, Klaus (1991)
TERFEL, Bryn (2003)
TERRISS, Ellaline (1952)
TERTIS, Lionel (1962)
TESTINO, Mario (2005)
TETLEY, Glen (1979)
TEYTE, Dame Maggie (1951, 1968)
THALBEN-BALL, George (1959)
THATCHER, Margaret (1978)
THAW, John (1990)
THEBOM, Blanche (1957)
THELWELL, Norman (1973)
THEROUX, Paul (1976)
THESIGER, Ernest (1959)
THESIGER, Wilfred (1979)
THOMAS, Rt Hon. George (1982)
THOMAS, Graham (1975)
THOMAS, Irene (1979, 1997)
THOMAS, Kristin Scott (2003)
THOMAS, Leslie (1973)
THOMAS, Sir Miles (1964)
THOMAS, Terry (1956, 1970)
THOMAS ELLIS, Alice (1998)
THOMPSON, Daley (1980)
THOMPSON, Don (1960)
THOMPSON, E. P. (1991)
THOMPSON, Emma (2010)
THOMPSON, Eric (1975)
THOMSON, Lord, of Fleet [Roy] (1964)
THOMSON, Virgil (1961)
THORBURN, June (1959)
THORNDIKE, Sybil (1952)
THORPE, Jeremy (1967)
THROWER, Percy (1963)
THUBRON, Colin (1989)
TICKELL, Sir Crispin (1990)
TILSON THOMAS, Michael (1990)
TIPPETT, Sir Michael (1968, 1985)
TITCHMARSH, Alan (2002)
TODD, Ann (1951)
TODD, Richard (1953)
TODD, Ron (1991)
TOMALIN, Claire (2000)
TOMLINSON, David (1953)
TOMLINSON, John (1998)
TOOLEY, Sir John (1980)
TOPOL (1983)
TORCH, Sidney (1960)
TORME, Mel (1976)
TORTELIER, Paul (1964, 1984)
TOWNSEND, Gp Capt. Peter (1972)

TOWNSEND, Sue (1991)
TOYE, Wendy (1958)
TRACEY, Stan (1999)
TRAIN, Jack (1955)
TRAVERS, Ben (1975)
TRAVERS, P. L. (1977)
TREMAIN, Rose (1997)
TRETHOWAN, Sir Ian (1990)
TREVELYAN, John (1969)
TREVELYAN OMAN, Julia (1971)
TREVOR, William (1980)
TRINDER, Tommy (1951)
TROLLOPE, Joanna (1994)
TRUEMAN, Fred (1978)
TRUMPINGTON, Lady [Jean Barker] (1990)
TUBB, Carrie (1970)
TUCKER, Norman (1962)
TUCKER, Sophie (1963)
TUCKWELL, Barry (1977)
TULLOH, Bruce (1974)
TULLY, Mark (2003)
TUMIM, Judge Stephen (1993)
TURNER, Dame Eva (1942, 1956, 1982)
TURNER, Joan (1988)
TURNER, Kathleen (2000)
TURNER, Merfyn (1962)
TUSHINGHAM, Rita (1965)
TUTIN, Dorothy (1955)
TUTU, Abp Desmond (1994)
TWIGGY (1989)
TYNAN, Kenneth (1956)
UCHIDA, Mitsuko (1996)
UNWIN, Stanley (1962)
UPDIKE, John (1995)
URE, Mary (1961)
USHER, Graham (1970)
USTINOV, Peter (1951, 1956, 1977)

VADIM, Roger (1986)
VALENTE, Caterina (1971)
VALENTINE, Dickie (1958)
VAN DER POST, Sir Laurens (1959, 1996)
VAN WYCK, Wilfrid (1973)
VANEZIS, Prof. Peter (2001)
VARAH, Chad (1992)
VAUGHAN, Frankie (1958)
VAUGHAN, Sarah (1958)
VAUGHAN-THOMAS, Wynford (1952)
VAYNE, Kyra (1996)
VEGAS, Johnny (2010)
VEREY, Rosemary (1994)
VERMES, Prof. Géza (2000)
VESEY-FITZGERALD, Brian (1959)
VETTRIANO, Jack (2004)
VICKERS, Jon (1968)
VIVIENNE (1963)
VON TRAPP, Baroness Maria (1983)
VYVYAN, Jennifer (1966)
WADE, Virginia (1969)

ACKNOWLEDGEMENTS

At the conclusion of his *Desert Island Discs* encounter with Roy Plomley in January 1963, Noël Coward took his leave of the presenter with the words, 'Thank you for a remarkably painless experience.' In the same spirit, thanks are due to a number of people who have made the compilation of this book as painless as possible.

The *Desert Island Discs* team at BBC Broadcasting House were supportive on all sorts of fronts, even to the point of tracking down a rare surviving recording of Margaret Powell's laugh. Special thanks are due to Ruth Gardiner and Rebecca Stratford and to Cathy Drysdale for her close involvement with the book at all stages. Thanks are also due to Leanne Buckle, Alice Feinstein, Isabel Sargent, Sue Noakes, Corinna Jones and Emma Trevelyan.

Conversations with two former Controllers of Radio 4, Mark Damazer and Michael Green, filled in a great deal of background, and the three post-Plomley presenters – Sir Michael Parkinson, Sue Lawley and current incumbent Kirsty Young – have all been generous in their cooperation. Particular thanks go to the staff of the BBC Written Archives Centre at Caversham, especially Trish Hayes and Jess Hogg, for making the research so enjoyable: to be cut off, however temporarily, from the alarums and excursions of the world outside was a rare treat. Thanks also to Simon Rowland of the BBC Photo Library for his help with sourcing illustrations.

Thanks are due to Roy Plomley's estate for permission to use material from his books (see page xiv–xv).

At Bantam Press, thanks to publisher Sally Gaminara for unflagging support; to managing editor Katrina Whone, without whom the project would have drowned in a maelstrom of paper and who has kept the plates spinning; to the tireless Brenda Kimber and the rest of the editorial team for all manner of assistance; to Sheila Lee for researching the wondrous array of pictures; and to design manager Phil Lord.

Outside Bantam Press, the project has been extremely fortunate in securing the services of Gillian Somerscales, the world's greatest copy-editor, and Elizabeth Dobson, the world's greatest proof-reader, while at Soapbox Communications, where the book was designed and put together, it has been a pleasure to work again with my old chum John Schwartz and his colleague Rachel Bray. Thanks also to the estimable Mitchell Symons, author of *Desert Island Discs: Flotsam and Jetsam*; to Humphrey Price for editorial support; and for various sorts of assistance to Graham Sharpe, Celia Beadle, Grant Tucker, Peter Hennessy, and my sister Maureen Hammond.

Sean Magee
July 2012

INDEX

Frontispiece:

Roy Plomley, founding father of *Desert Island Discs*, 1982

Opening illustrations for each decade:

1940s: Comedian Tommy Handley with a line-up of 'modern girl secretaries' in *It's That Man Again*, February 1940

1950s: Procession to the Coronation of Her Majesty Queen Elizabeth II, 1953

1960s: Mary Quant (*right*) launching her new shoe collection, 1967

1970s: The Sex Pistols, 1977

1980s: The 1980 Olympic Games, Moscow: Steve Ovett beats Sebastian Coe in the 800 metres

1990s: New Prime Minister Tony Blair greeted in Downing Street, 2 May 1997

2000s: The London Eye, 31 December 2005

PHOTO ACKNOWLEDGEMENTS

The publishers have made every effort to trace copyright holders. Any who have been omitted are invited to get in touch.

BBC PHOTO LIBRARY
The publishers would like to thank the BBC Photo Library for supplying the images on the following pages: vi, ix, 2, 5, 23, 31, 38, 49, 50, 53, 56, 57, 60, 63, 64, 66, 69, 73, 75, 76, 80, 89, 94, 96, 101, 104, 109, 112, 116, 124, 132, 136, 140, 141, 152, 165, 178, 182, 189, 191, 193, 194, 197, 203, 207, 225, 226, 230, 234, 239, 252, 257, 262, 266, 268, 276, 280, 294, 299, 302, 303, 308, 314, 318, 328, 330, 334, 344, 349, 350, 355, 356, 358, 359, 362, 367, 374, 381, 393, 401, 403, 404, 405, 409, 411, 418, 423, 426, 428, 430, 438, 444, 445, 450, 464, 474, 475, 478, 479, 482, 489, 495, 497, 498, 500, 502.
Illustration by Victor Reingaum: *Radio Times*, 23 January 1942

OTHER IMAGES
Getty Images: ii, x (AFP), 9, 12 (Popperfoto), 17, 18, 39, 41, 47, 55, 70, 71, 81, 83, 84 (Redferns), 88 (Redferns), 90 (Popperfoto), 92 (Popperfoto), 99 (Popperfoto), 100 (Redferns), 103, 106, 111 (*Encyclopaedia Britannica*/UIG), 114, 117 (Redferns), 119, 128 (AFP), 149 (Redferns), 153 (Time & Life), 163, 169, 171, 174 (Redferns), 187, 200, 214, 227 (Time & Life), 228, 231, 235, 244, 246, 248, 249 (Michael Ochs Archives), 253, 263 (Michael Ochs Archives), 265, 267 (Hulton Archive), 282, 295 (AFP), 297, 300 (Redferns), 312 (Popperfoto), 322 (AFP), 323, 324 (Redferns), 329, 339, 346 (SSPL), 353, 354, 369 (Gallo Images), 370 (AFP), 372 (Hulton Archive), 377, 382, 398–9 (Film Magic), 419, 429 (AFP), 433 (Redferns), 436, 454 (Tim Graham), 455 (Michael Ochs Archives), 457, 459 (Film Magic), 460 (Redferns), 468, 469, 471 (Bob Thomas), 473 (Arsenal FC), 493, 501. **Huw Williams / Yada-Yada**: xii, xiii. **Alamy**: 1 (© Trinity Mirror/Mirrorpix); 7 (Amoret Tanner); 33 (© AF Archive), 36 (Pictorial Press Ltd), 123 (© Moviestore Collection Ltd/Alamy), 127 (eye35.pix), 138 (AF Archive), 147/8 (INTERFOTO), 208 (Trinity Mirror/Mirrorpix), 216 (Trinity Mirror/Mirrorpix), 224 (Victor Watts), 252 (Trinity Mirror/Mirrorpix), 282 (Trinity Mirror/Mirrorpix), 292–3 (Trinity Mirror/Mirrorpix), 296 (Geraint Lewis), 309 (Moviestore Collection Ltd), 311 (AF Archive), 387 (Niall McDiarmid), 417 (Lebrecht Music and Art Photo Library), 400 (Greg Gard), 414 (Jane Hobson), 475 (AF Archive). **Press Association Images**: 22 (AP), 27, 34 (AP), (S&G and Barratts/EMPICS Sport), 77 (AP), 78 (A), 86–7 (PA Archive), 129 (PA Archive), 143 (AP), 148 (PA Archive), 161 (S&G Barratts/ EMPICS Archive), 196 (PA Archive), 212–13 (AP), 238 (John Stillwell/PA Archive), 271 (PA Archive), 286 (PA Archive), 386 (Rebecca Naden/PA Archive), 408 (dpa-Film Warner/DPA), 412 (Barry Batchelor/PA Archive), 413 (Charles Krupa/AP), 421 (David Jones/PA Archive), 441 (PA Archive), 466 (Johnny Green/PA Archive), 484 (John Stillwell/PA Archive), 486 (PA Archive). **Corbis**: 28 (© Derek Bayes/Lebrecht Music and Arts), 45–6 (© David Boyer/National Geographic Society), 79 (© Christie's Images), 120 (© CinemaPhoto/Corbis),167 (© Dylan Martinez/Reuters), 184 (Lebrecht Music and Arts), 198 (© Jack Mitchell), 236 (© Ted Streshinksy), 340 (© Michael Brennan). **Kobal Collection**: 29 (ITV Global), 250 (RBT Stigwood Prods/Hemdale). **Topham Picturepoint/Topfoto.co.uk**: 32 (Keystone), 133 (Morris Newcombe/ArenaPAL), 135 (Mander & Mitchenson University of Bristol/ArenaPAL), 176 (Clive Barda/ArenaPAL), 277. **Ronald Grant Archive**: 59 (MGM). **NASA**: 91. **Mirrorpix**: 97, 219, 220. **Rex Features**: 131 (Reg Wilson), 156 (ITV), 215 (Chris Barham/*Daily Mail*), 223 (Peter Brooker), 240 (David Magnus), 242 (Everett Collection), 255 (Mike Floyd/Associated Newspapers), 258 (Moviestore Collection), 261 (ITV), 284 (Associated Newspapers), 290 (Chris Barham/*Dail Mail*), 306 (Hyley Madden), 319 (*Daily Mail*), 331 (Everett Collection), 345 (Emma Boam), 360 (Monty Fresco/*Daily Mail*), 364 (Jeff Morris/Associated Newspapers), 378 (Steve Back/*Daily Mail*), 439 (Peter Brooker), 452 (Susannah Ireland), 477 (Moviestore Collection), 485 (*Daily Mail*), 488 (ITV), 491. **Courtesy The Savile Club**: 154. **Bridgeman Art Library**: 152 (Geoffrey Fletcher/Private Collection), 168 (Musée d'Art Modern de la Ville de Paris); **Royal Geographical Society**: 202. **Courtesy Sir Edmund Hillary**: 206. **Lebrecht Music and Arts**: 210. **The White House**: 338. © **Stuart Holmes**: 270. **Courtesy Frances Lincoln**: 273. © **John Holmes/www.Artmasters.co.uk**: 278, **Mary Evans Picture Library**: 285 (© *Illustrated London News*), 496 (Photo Union Collection), 499 (© Illustrated London News). **akg-images**: 287. **Courtesy Sheila Ravenscroft**: 304; **Photoshot**: 327 (LFI), 366 (© Retna), 391 (© Retna). **Reproduced by kind permission of PRIVATE EYE magazine**: 321. **Sir Peter O'Sullevan**: 394. **Shutterstock**: 400. **Science Photo Library**: 465 (Gemini South GMOS/Travis Rector, University of Alaska, Anchorage/NAO/AUR/NSF). **The estate of Ronald Searle and The Sayle Literary Agency**: 437, illustration from *How to Be Topp* by Ronald Searle and Geoffrey Willans: image copyright Ronald Searle 1954. Reproduced by kind permission.

TRANSWORLD PUBLISHERS, 61–63 Uxbridge Road, London W5 5SA
A Random House Group Company, www.transworldbooks.co.uk

Published by arrangement with the BBC in 2012 by Bantam Press
an imprint of Transworld Publishers
Copyright © Sean Magee and the BBC 2012

Sean Magee and the BBC have asserted their right under the Copyright, Designs and
Patents Act 1988 to be identified as the authors of this work.

A CIP catalogue record for this book is available from the British Library.

ISBN 9780593070062

Addresses for Random House Group Ltd companies outside the UK can be found at:
www.randomhouse.co.uk
The Random House Group Ltd Reg. No. 954009

Typeset by Soapbox, www.soapbox.co.uk | Printed and bound in Germany

10 9 8 7 6 5 4 3 2 1